P9-APF-702

DEVELOPMENT, GOVERNANCE AND THE ENVIRONMENT IN SOUTH ASIA

Also by Mohammad Alauddin

THE GREEN REVOLUTION AND ECONOMIC DEVELOPMENT
The Process and its Impact on Bangladesh (*co-author*)

Development, Governance and the Environment in South Asia

A Focus on Bangladesh

Edited by

Mohammad Alauddin
Senior Lecturer in Economics
University of Queensland
Brisbane
Australia

and

Samiul Hasan
Lecturer in Geographical Sciences and Planning
University of Queensland
Brisbane
Australia

First published in Great Britain 1999 by
MACMILLAN PRESS LTD
Houndmills, Basingstoke, Hampshire RG21 6XS and London
Companies and representatives throughout the world

A catalogue record for this book is available from the British Library.

ISBN 0–333–73974–4

First published in the United States of America 1999 by
ST. MARTIN'S PRESS, INC.,
Scholarly and Reference Division,
175 Fifth Avenue, New York, N.Y. 10010

ISBN 0–312–21997–0

Library of Congress Cataloging-in-Publication Data
Development, governance and the environment in South Asia : a focus on
Bangladesh / edited by Mohammad Alauddin and Samiul Hasan.
p. cm.
Includes bibliographical references and index.
ISBN 0–312–21997–0
1. Bangladesh—Economic conditions. 2. Bangladesh—Economic
policy. 3. Bangladesh—Politics and government. 4. South Asia–
–Economic conditions—Case studies. 5. South Asia—Economic policy–
–Case studies. 6. Economic development—Environment aspects—Case
studies. 7. South Asia—Politics and government—Case studies.
I. Alauddin, Mohammad. II. Hasan, Samiul, 1954–   .
HC440.8.D467   1998
338.95492—DC21   98–30663
                                                       CIP

HC
440.8
.D467
1999

This book is printed on paper suitable for recycling and made from fully managed and
sustained forest sources.

10   9   8   7   6   5   4   3   2   1
08   07   06   05   04   03   02   01   00   99

Printed and bound in Great Britain
by Antony Rowe Ltd, Chippenham, Wiltshire

Contents

v

List of Tables

LIST OF APPENDICES

List of Figures

Preface

The question of environmental changes and degradation and its relationship to economic development now forms a key element in theoretical and empirical analyses. As a result, the past two decades have witnessed a proliferation of literature investigating the relationship between the environment and economic development. In the recent past, a third dimension, governance, has been added to the equation. International organisations such as the World Bank and other UN bodies as well as individual country and agencies emphasise the critical importance of governance and underscore the close interrelationships among the environment, economic development and governance.

This volume explores the environment-development-governance relationships in the context of South Asia. The book focuses primarily on Bangladesh in an attempt to take stock of achievements to date and to identify the challenges that lie ahead as Bangladesh positions herself for the journey into the next millennium.

At various stages in our endeavour in editing this volume we received assistance and suggestions from the following referees: Alan Duhs, Mike Fagence, Akhter Hamid, Rod Jensen, Adil Khan, Neil Karunaratne, Mano Kumarsuriyar, Bruce Mitchell, Kamal Puri, Richard Shand and Clem Tisdell. The editors and the volume have benefited from constructive criticisms and suggestions provided by the referees on earlier drafts of the contributions. We are grateful to all them. Usual *caveats* apply.

We express our profound gratitude to Professor Clem Tisdell for his support and encouragement without which the book could never have been completed. We also wish to express our gratitude to the Department of Economics, The University of Queensland for the use of facilities and the congenial atmosphere that we enjoyed while editing this volume.

The editors owe a special debt to Mr Akhter Hamid for his generous assistance at every stage of the editorial process including drawing of complex diagrams. His magnanimous help improved the overall quality of presentation and analysis. However, the usual disclaimer applies.

In relation to his contributions as an author and a joint editor Mohammad Alauddin has benefited from his participation and presentation of papers at: World Aquaculture '98 (Las Vegas) Conference, ACIAR-Thai Department of Fisheries workshop (Hatyai, Thailand 1996), and the conference celebrating twenty five years of independence of Bangladesh (Brisbane, Australia 1996). Mohammad Alauddin would further like to express his gratitude to Professors

Anthony Chisholm, Gordon Conway, Geoffrey Harcourt, W. Brian Reddaway, and Dr Richard T. Shand for their encouragement for research in this area. We wish to thank Mrs Jeannine Fowler and Mrs Robyn McDonald for typing assistance, and Mrs Alice Schwarz Brunold for desktop publishing services. Excellent research assistance by Mr Nirmal Saha is much appreciated. This book is a result of a high level of cooperation, for which the editors are extremely grateful to all the contributors.

We are grateful to Macmillan Press Ltd. especially to Mr Tim Farmiloe and Mr Sunder Katwala for accepting our manuscript and extending deadline for its completion.

Finally, we wish to thank our families for their patience, encouragement and understanding that contributed significantly toward the completion of the book.

We dedicate this book to the memory of all the martyrs who made supreme sacrifices in Bangladesh's long and protracted struggle for independence from Pakistan, and to establish a civil society based on democratic values and social justice.

MOHAMMAD ALAUDDIN
SAMIUL HASAN

Foreword

I was delighted to receive an invitation to write a brief foreword to this book. My connection with Bangladesh started in 1974 (only three years after independence I spent six months at the Bangladesh Institute for Development Studies (BIDS). This arrangement was organised by Dr Nurul Islam, who was then Deputy Chairman of the Bangladesh Planning Commission, and it was financed by the Ford Foundation. My formal position was also visiting economist at the BIDS, but it was understood that I would also give informal advice to Dr Islam on any matters on which he wanted to consult me. Both these practical problems and the research which I did at BIDS were very interesting.

The whole visit to Bangladesh proved intellectually stimulating and it led to my being appointed by a number of International Institutions (notably UNDP and ILO) to go to Bangladesh for short periods to help work on Development Plans, Food Strategy, etc. The fascinating aspects of all these jobs were that they involved **both** the consideration of general problems relevant to the development of Third World Countries **and** the application of the resultant analysis of specific questions which were important in Bangladesh. I also much appreciated the friendly relations which I formed with many people who were working on the various problems.

The book fits in admirably with the way in which I think that the economic problems of a Third World Country should be tackled. The authors have varied experience in many aspects of the field; they appreciate the importance of the political and administrative issues which inevitably arise. They **focus** on Bangladesh, but they also draw on the experience of South Asian countries.

Bangladesh has sometimes been described as 'basket case', but the lively and revealing discussions in this book are good evidence of the ways in which its inhabitants are facing up to the difficult problems which Bangladesh faces. I am cheered by the statistics in the annual *World Development Report* (published by the World Bank) which show that real progress is being achieved – albeit with international aid and assistance of various kinds. Even in the difficult field of population growth the picture is much more encouraging than many observers think. It is true that since Independence in 1971 a rapid growth in population has added to Bangladesh's problems in many ways, but this growth has occurred **despite** a substantial fall in death rates. This fall in mortality is, of course, desirable in itself, but the encouraging point is that the death rates have now reached levels from which further substantial falls are unlikely. The World Bank has foreseen a probable **stability** of the population within the next two or three decades.

W.B. Reddaway
Professor Emeritus of Political Economy
University of Cambridge

Notes on the Contributors

Akhter Ahmed is currently Lecturer in the Melbourne Institute of Business and Technology and a Visiting Research Fellow of the Development Studies Programme of the Deakin University. He holds a Ph.D degree in Economics from Deakin University, Australia. Previously he completed Honours and Master degrees in Geography from Dhaka University, Bangladesh and a Master of Economics degree from the University of New England, Australia. Prior to taking up his job in Australia in 1990, Dr. Ahmed has worked as a Senior Scientific Officer at Bangladesh Agricultural Research Council. He has several research publications in refereed journals. His research areas are applied macro and microeconomics, development economics and stabilisation policy.

Mohammad Alauddin is currently a Senior Lecturer in Economics, The University of Queensland. He graduated with Honours and Master degrees in Economics from Rajshahi University and Master and Ph.D degrees respectively from the University of Adelaide and the University of Newcastle (New South Wales). He previously taught at Rajshahi University Bangladesh and at the University of Melbourne. He was Visiting Faculty Fellow, Southwest Fisheries Science Center, National Marine Fisheries Science, La Jolla, United States, and Visiting Fellow, Research School of Pacific and Asian Studies, The Australian National University, Canberra. He has co-authored/co-edited several books including *The 'Green Revolution' and Economic Development: The Process and Its Impact in Bangladesh* (London: Macmillan 1991) and *The Environment and Economic Development in South Asia: An Overview Concentrating on Bangladesh* (London: Macmillan, 1998). He is also the (co)author of nearly fifty articles published in internationally refereed journals. His research interests include applied microeconomics, environmental economics and economics of aquaculture.

M. Yunus Ali holds a Ph.D from Wollongong and is currently a faculty member of the Department of Marketing, Monash University, Australia. He previously taught at Rajshahi University, University of Wollongong, and the University of Western Sydney, Macarthur Campus before joining his current position. His research interests include international joint ventures, international marketing and strategy, and internationalisation process. He is a member of the Academy of International Business, and Australian Institute of Management. His research has been published in the *Journal of International Business Studies,* and *Asia Pacific Journal of Management.*

Shankariah Chamala is Associate Professor in Agricultural Extension and Management at the University of Queensland. Before joining the University, he was Professor of Industrial Communication and Extension at the National Institute of Small Industry, Extension Training, Hyderabad, India. At The University of Queensland he has been teaching undergraduate and postgraduate extension courses. In 1985, he introduced a new postgraduate stream, 'Rural Development Administration and Management', in collaboration with the Graduate School of Management. He has been a visiting Professor in the Netherlands and the USA, and has been working as a consultant in South-East Asian countries. He has also conducted short specialist advanced courses for extension field managers in China, India, the Philippines, Thailand and Indonesia. He has published five books and more than 100 papers. Shankariah Chamala has developed a generic Participative Action Management (PAM) Model which is used by the Land and Water Resources Research and Development Corporation to implement five irrigation development projects. A modified PAM model has been used in designing DOOR (Do Your Own Research), a project funded by Horticultural Research and Development Corporation.

Anis Chowdhury is Associate Professor in the Department of Economics and Finance at the University of Western Sydney at Macarthur, Australia. He earned his B.Sc. (Honours) and M.Sc. degrees in Economics from Jahangirnagar University, Dhaka, Bangladesh. He has also earned M.A. and Ph.D degrees in Economics from the University of Manitoba, Canada. He has published widely and his specialisation is macroeconomic management in dynamic Asian economies. He currently edits the *Journal of Asia-Pacific Economy*

Bruce Frank has been Senior Lecturer in Agricultural Extension at The University of Queensland since 1990. He graduated Bachelor of Rural Science and subsequently did his Ph.D. He spent 21 years as an extension officer in the Queensland Department of Primary Industries. After researching constraints to technology adoption by cattlemen in North Queensland, he became interested in systemic ways of addressing complex issues confronting farmers. He is investigating alternative ways that more farmers can learn to access and use information without relying on the extension officer. He teaches agricultural extension, rural sociology, behavioural sciences and practice in extension, and communication.

M Akhter Hamid is a Decision Systems Specialist with the Queensland Department of Primary Industries. He earned his BScAg (Honours) from Bangladesh Agricultural University and MAgrSc from The University of Queensland. He is currently pursuing a joint Ph.D programme in the School of Natural and Rural Systems Management and Department of Economics at the University of Queensland. Previously he has worked as an Extension Officer with RDRS, a leading NGO in Bangladesh and Lecturer in Agricultural Extension in BAU. He has also held research positions in the New Zealand Ministry of Agriculture and Fisheries, National Institute of Water and Atmospheric Research, New Zealand, and the Department of Economics, The University of Queensland. His research interests are in primary producers' risk management and decision support systems, coastal aquaculture, agricultural/fisheries research and extension, farming systems research and development, and agricultural sustainability.

Samiul Hasan earned his Ph.D degree from the University of Waterloo, Canada and is now a lecturer in the Development Planning Programme, Department of Geographical Sciences and Planning, The University of Queensland, Australia. He also has worked in universities in Bangladesh and Canada. His present research interest is in governance and planning for development, urban environmental governance, and voluntarism. His research papers on these broad subjects have been published in refereed journals in Bangladesh, Canada, Hong Kong, India, Sweden, UK, and USA.

Akhtar Hossain is Senior Lecturer in Economics at the University of Newcastle, Australia. He earned his B.Sc. (Honours) and M.Sc. degrees in Economics from Jahangirnagar University, Dhaka, Bangladesh. He has also earned M.A. and Ph.D degrees in Economics from the University of Melbourne and La Trobe University, respectively. He has published widely on macroeconomic and monetary issues in developing countries with special reference to Bangladesh.

Moazzem Hossain obtained a master degree from the Australian National University and a Ph.D in agricultural economics from the University of Western Australia, Perth. Has worked for the Australian Bureau of Agricultural and Resource Economics (ABARE) for five years as a Senior Research Officer. He is currently working as a Senior Lecturer in Economics in the School of International Business, Griffith University, Australia.

Ahmed Shafiqul Huque is Associate Professor of Public and Social Administration at the City University of Hong Kong. He is the author of *Politics and Administration in Bangladesh* (1988) and *Paradoxes in Public Administration* (1990), co-author of *Development Through Decentralisation in Bangladesh* (1994) and *The Civil Service in Hong Kong* (1998), and co-editor of *Public Administration in the NICs* (1996) and *Social Policy in Hong Kong* (1997). Dr. Huque is the Editor-in-Chief of the semi-annual journal *Public Administration and Policy*. He has served as Vice President of the Hong Kong Public Administration Association and Associate Head of the Department of Public and Social Administration.

M. Rafiqul Islam is Senior Lecturer and Coordinator Law Masters and Ph.D research degree programme in Law at Macquire University, Sydney. He is an Economics and Law Graduate from Rajshahi University, Bangladesh. He obtained his Masters and Ph.D from Monash Law School. He had been Chairman, Department of Law at Rajshahi University and Head of Department of Law, University of Papua New Guinea. Rafiqul Islam is author of four books and over fifty articles in professional journals. He specialises in international law, constitutional law, international trade and investment and law of international organisations. He is currently engaged in research on international trade and finance law to be published by Pearson Professionals Australia Ltd.

Nilufar Jahan is currently a Senior Research Officer in the International Trade and Commodity Forecasting Section at the Australian Bureau of Agricultural and Resource Economics (ABARE) in Canberra. She graduated with Honours and Masters degrees in economics from Dhaka University, Bangladesh and Masters degree in Economics from Williams College, Massachusetts, USA and a Ph.D from The University of Queensland, Australia She has a long experience in working on food and agricultural policy of the Government of Bangladesh and Food and Agricultural Organisation (Regional Office in Bangkok). She has published in *International Journal of Social Economics*. Her research interests include environmental economics and development economics. Nilufar Jahan's research area includes applied microeconomics, women and growth, environmental accounting, international trade and development.

Shams-ur Rahman is currently lecturing at the Graduate School of Management, University of Western Australia, Australia. Before taking up the position at The University of Western Australia's Graduate School of Management, he was on the teaching and research staff of universities in Australia, Bangladesh, Thailand, and the United Kingdom. He holds an MSc in mechanical engineering from Belarus, an ME in industrial engineering & management from AIT, Bangkok, and a Ph.D in operations research from the University of Exeter, UK. He has previously published articles in journals that include *International Journal of Operations and Production Management, Opsearch, Productivity, TQM Magazine, Korean Management Science Review.* His current research interests include the theory of constraints, business process re-engineering, and service location-allocation modelling.

Richard T. Shand is the Executive Director of the Australia South Asia Research Centre in the Research School of Pacific and Asian Studies at the Australian National University. He was a previous Director of the Development Studies Centre at the same University. He has published extensively on development issues throughout Asia and the Pacific in books and international journals for over thirty years. He has specialised in South Asia and has held Visiting Professorships at the University of Colombo, the Madras School of Economics and Universiti Pertanian Malaysia. He was also a Visiting Economist in the Indian Planning Commission.

David K. Smith lectures in operational research at the University of Exeter, U.K. He studied operational research at the University of Lancaster, where he was awarded his Ph.D for studies in the modelling of water supply networks. He is the author of two books on aspects of O.R., and is author or co-author of numerous papers concerned with the theory and practice of the subject. He is particularly interested in applications in the not-for-profit sector and developing countries. Currently, David Smith is the editor of the abstracting journal *International Abstracts in Operations Research.*

Clem Tisdell is Professor of Economics at The University of Queensland, Australia. He is also an Honorary Professor of the Institute of Economic Research, People's University of China, Beijing, and has held visiting appointments at Princeton University, Stanford University and the East-West Center, United States, at the University of York, United Kingdom. He has authored, co-authored and co-edited nearly thirty books and is an author and co-author of several hundred articles in internationally acclaimed journals. Clem Tisdell has a special interest in agricultural, industrial and environmental issues of Bangladesh. He is the co-author of *The 'Green Revolution' and Economic Development: The Process and Its Impact in Bangladesh* (London: Macmillan 1991) and *The Environment and Economic Development in South Asia: An Overview Concentrating on Bangladesh* (London: Macmillan, 1998) and several dozen refereed journal articles on Bangladesh. He has visited Bangladesh and given seminars at Rajshahi University and the Bangladesh Institute of Development Studies.

Habib Zafarullah obtained Ph.D in public administration from the University of Sydney. He currently teaches at the University of New England, having previously taught at the University of Dhaka. His areas of interest include: comparative bureaucracy, development management, and Third World politics. He has authored/edited/co-edited several books on government and public administration, and his writings have appeared in journals and books published in the United States, Britain, Canada, Belgium, Australia, the Philippines, Hong Kong, Thailand, India, Pakistan and Bangladesh. He has been the editor of *Politics, Administration and Change,* a multi-disciplinary journal, since 1980.

1 Development-Governance-Environment Nexus: Views, Perspectives and Issues

Mohammad Alauddin and Samiul Hasan

1.1 INTRODUCTION

The past two decades have witnessed a proliferation of the literature investigating the relationship between the environment and economic development. It is now widely recognised that economic growth especially in LDCs, to a considerable extent, has been achieved at the expense of substantial loss of natural environments. While the question of environmental change/degradation forms a key element in theoretical and empirical analyses, of late a third dimension, governance, has been added to the equation. International organisations such as the World Bank and other UN bodies as well as individual country and agencies emphasise the critical importance of governance and underscore the close interrelationships among the environment, economic development and governance.

Economic development is closely interlinked with governance and the environment and their importance can hardly be overemphasised. While the problems of governance, the environment, low level of economic development and grinding poverty are widespread throughout the developing world, few regions have taken a more severe toll than South Asia. This region is inhabited by more than a fifth of humanity and is characterised by a shrinking supply of arable land per capita, a very high rate of population growth and a declining stock of natural resources. The absence of an incorrupt, transparent and accountable administration, and judicial independence and human rights compound the problems of overall socio-economic development.

After almost two hundred years of colonial rule the major South Asian countries gained independence from the British in 1947. The geographically contiguous Muslim majority parts of the British Indian provinces of Bengal and Assam were carved out to form the province of East Bengal and to join the geographically separated Muslim majority regions of northwestern India to form a Muslim state – Pakistan. The eastern wing of Pakistan (renamed

1

East Pakistan in 1956) seceded to emerge as a new nation state, Bangladesh, in December 1971 following a nine-month long War of Liberation with Pakistan.

Bangladesh, the third largest country (in terms of the number of population) in South Asia (that also comprises of Bhutan, India, Maldives, Nepal, Pakistan, and Sri Lanka) is more closely examined on these aspects of governance, development, and the environment interrelationships. Bangladesh's union with Pakistan embodied all the hallmarks of inter colonisation: years of neglect, regional dualism and consistent attacks on the cultural, political and economic rights of her people (Jahan 1972). Significant and widening economic disparities between the East and Western Wings of Pakistan epitomised (united) Pakistan's growth (Sobhan 1993; see also PPC 1970). Since 1971 Bangladesh has experienced significant political, social, environmental and economic changes. These changes do not seem to have been an unmixed blessing. Bangladesh has witnessed authoritarianism and confrontational politics for most of her existence and suffered political instability. However, its economic and social progress since independence has been significant. Above all its belief in its capacity to do better is firm (Shand 1996).

In the light of this background this book examines the development-governance-environment nexus focusing on the situation in Bangladesh but also considering the comparative circumstances of South Asian countries generally. Examples are drawn from other less developed countries (LDCs), as appropriate. This chapter provides an overview of issues addressed and the plan and design of this volume.

1.2   PERSPECTIVES AND VIEWS ON THE DEVELOPMENT-ENVIRONMENT-GOVERNANCE NEXUS

The primary objective of this section is to trace the historical background to the changing views and perspectives on the development-environment-governance nexus. The specific issues that are briefly discussed are:

- the neglect of environmental issues in earlier literature;

- importance of the environment in contemporary literature; and

- governance issues and their relationship to the environment and development.

Even though the concern about the environment and development is of recent origin it is long overdue. Earlier literature paid scant attention to environmental issues (for further details, see Alauddin and Tisdell 1998, especially pp.2–5). This development is reminiscent of the growth-distribution debate in the 1950s when Lewis (1955, p.9) noted that '... our problem is growth, not distribution'. About a decade and a half later, when high rates of growth in many LDCs did not translate into any significant dent on poverty, the basic tenets of this thesis came under critical examination (see for example, Haq 1976; Morawetz 1977). Similarly, environmental and ecological limits to growth begun to surface in the ruthless pursuit of growth in many countries.

The concern with environmental issues, more specifically environmentally sustainable development gained significant momentum with the publication of *Our Common Future* (WCED 1987). With important subsequent developments in both theoretical and empirical literature (see for example, Pearce 1993; Repetto et al. 1989; I. Ahmed and Doeleman 1995) the operational significance of ecologically sustainable development has assumed greater importance. This has manifested itself in two seemingly distinct but essentially interdependent developments.

First a significant shift occurred in the focus to considering the sustainability of ecosystems and environmental factors which critically impact on economic development. This is captured by World Bank (1992a) in terms of a bidirectional causal relationship between the environment and development: (i) environmental quality enhances human welfare that results from economic development; and (ii) environmental degradation can constrain future productivity growth which is a critical factor underpinning economic development (see also Woodhouse 1992).

Secondly, there was a growing realisation that the spectacular growth in many contemporary developed and developing countries may have resulted from, as well as resulted in, the cost imposed on the environment through the depletion on non-renewable natural resources and damage to the biophysical environment. This view is espoused by Repetto et al. (1989). They argue that 'a country could exhaust its mineral resources, cut down its forests, erode its soils, pollute its aquifers, and hunt its wildlife to extinction, but measured income would not be affected as these assets disappeared' (p.2). They also espouse the view that '... difference in the treatment of natural resources and other tangible assets reinforces the false dichotomy between the economy and the 'environment' that leads policy makers to ignore or destroy the latter in the name of economic development' (p.3). On the basis of this argument the foundation of the conventional systems of national accounting has been called into question and an environment-based accounting system has emerged that underscore the discrepancy between conventional GDP and NDP ('net' domestic product). The latter measure takes into account natural resource depreciation (see also Thamapillai and Uhlin 1995).

The recent addition to the equation is governance. The concept of 'governance has many ramifications in its applications to the development and politics of a country' (Sobhan 1993, p.1). The World Bank (1992b) defines governance as 'the manner in which power is exercised in the management of a country's economic and social resources for development'. The World Bank also views sound economic management and good governance to be synonymous. Furthermore, 'good governance is central to creating and sustaining an environment which fosters to sound economic policies' (World Bank 1992b, p.1).

The World Bank's views on governance concern primarily with economic management of its aid recipient countries. In recent years various donor agencies including the World Bank seem increasingly in favour of directing their programmes in the developing world towards improvement in governance. This seems to represent a somewhat narrower connotation of governance. However, governance assumes even greater significance if one takes a broader definition of economic development. In broad terms economic development may be defined as nothing less than the 'upward movement of the entire social system' or it may be interpreted as the attainment of a number 'ideals of modernisation' such as a rise in productivity, social and economic equalisation, modern knowledge, improved institutions and attitudes, and a rationally coordinated system of policy measures that can remove the host of undesirable conditions in the social system that have perpetuated a state of underdevelopment (Meier 1970, p.6; see also Todaro 1997).

However, concern with governance issues is not new. Several decades ago Lewis (1951, pp.121–8) while recognising the need for planning in backward countries also cautioned about the difficulty of executing it. Thus Lewis (p.125) noted '... planning requires a strong, competent and incorrupt administration. Now a strong, competent and incorrupt administration is just what no backward country possesses...'. Myrdal in his seminal work *Asian Drama* (Myrdal 1971a) regarded the LDCs especially those in South Asia as 'soft states' because incompetence and corruption abound and are ubiquitous. There is a widespread view that '.. if everybody is corrupt why shouldn't I be so?'. In South Asia as indeed elsewhere in the developing world 'a common method of exploiting a position of public responsibility for private gain is the threat of obstruction and delay; hence, *corruption impedes the processes of decision-making and execution on all levels. Corruption introduces an element of irrationality in all planning and plan fulfilment* by influencing the actual course of development in a way that deviates from the Plan' (Myrdal 1971b, p.237). The Lewis view as well the Myrdal view point to misgovernance or lack of governance in LDCs.

The discussion in this section so far points to a close linkage among economic development, governance and the environment. A conceptual model portraying this relationship is set out in Figure 1.1.

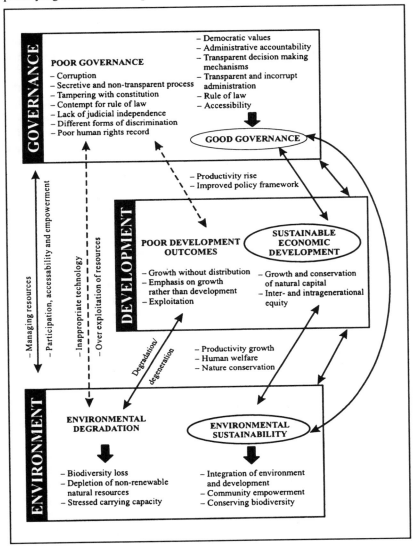

Figure 1.1   Linkages among development, governance and the environment: a conceptual model

As a prelude to a detailed discussion of issues undertaken in the subsequent section the remainder of this section is devoted to a brief overview of the state of play in the context of South Asia. Consistent with the trend elsewhere in the world, environmental issues did not feature at all let alone prominently in the development plans of the countries of South Asia (see for example Roy et al. 1992; Alauddin and Tisdell 1998; see also Dutta 1998). The issues of good governance also fared little better. The remainder of this section is devoted to a discussion of the salient features of this process.

In the context of India 'Fifty years after achieving independence, poverty, illiteracy, disease and lack of minimum social services continue to afflict hundreds of millions of our people.... Our policies and programmes must accord the highest priority to encouraging sustainable growth and productive job opportunities in all sectors.... In many cases this may call for a review and redirection of existing programmes' (GOI 1997, p.16). This also applies broadly to the rest of the region. Regarding measures for the poor and the disadvantaged, according to Krishna (1988, p.15) 'It is a significant novelty of India's political revolution that the relative balance of class forces does not operate at the stage of legislation, planning and pronouncements to prevent a progressive stance, but it effectively blocks and perverts their redistributive effects at the implementation stage'. This is reminiscent of the observation made by Myrdal almost three decades earlier. 'When policy measures have been instituted specifically aimed at ameliorating conditions for the lower strata, they have either not been implemented and enforced or have been distorted so as to favour the not-so-poor and to discriminate against the masses' (Myrdal 1971b, p.221).

Haq (1998) attributes the poor development in human capital to poor literacy resulting from poor governance in South Asia. According to Haq (1998, p.3) 'There is a real crisis of governance in South Asia. Between the great promise of South Asia and its present performance falls a dark shadow – shadow of mis-governance by its ruling elites'. While Bangladesh, according to Haq (1998) has only half the per capita income of Pakistan yet its net primary enrolment is now reaching 92 per cent, equally for boys and girls. Sri Lanka has the highest literacy rate in South Asia and one of the highest in the developing world. This is also the case with the literacy rate with some Indian states e.g. Kerala (see also S. Chakravarty 1990).

Both Bangladesh and Pakistan has been under civilian-military dictatorships for much of their existence as independent nations. Pakistan took nearly nine years to frame a constitution only to see it abrogated two years later and Pakistan put under military rule for nearly fourteen years. With a brief interruption of civilian rule for a period of five years (1972–77) Pakistan was revisited by military rule. Even when the country had been under seemingly civilian rule, palace intrigues have been fairly commonplace (M. Asghar Khan 1983). Usurping power by illegal and extraconstitutional means have been quite common in Pakistan until recently. The eventual price was the dismemberment of the eastern wing from the west when the people's verdict at the first and only general election in a quarter of century of united Pakistan was brutally suppressed and a military solution imposed by the ruling *junta*. The people of the then East Pakistan (now Bangladesh) responded by unilaterally declaring independence and waging a War of Liberation.[1]

Bangladesh started as an independent nation with parliamentary democracy and to her credit presented herself with a democratic constitution within less than a year of independence. Subsequently, however, Bangladesh experienced a few months of one party rule and almost sixteen years of military/quasi military rule until the late 1990. During that period selfish power politics and military dictatorship with the help of turncoat politicians tampered with the constitution with impunity. Since the early 1990s two free and fair parliamentary elections have been held under caretaker governments. While much remains to be done in terms of good governance there is some effort toward a constitutional resuscitation (see Chapter 9; see also Kochanek 1997).

In recent years the South Asian region has undertaken massive policy changes in regard to opening up their economies: From a predominantly regulated environment to one of a deregulated market mechanism (Shand and Alauddin 1997; Shand and Bhati 1997; Shand and Kalirajan 1997; Athukorala 1997).

1.3   CONTRIBUTIONS TO THIS VOLUME: AN INTERPRETIVE OVERVIEW

Bangladesh has become economically, socially and culturally better-off since independence from Pakistan in 1971. It has been able to provide a rising level of GDP per head (in real terms) for its population, reduce infant mortality, lower child malnutrition markedly, and increase the life expectancies of its citizens at birth. While Bangladesh remains predominantly an agricultural and rural country, major structural changes have occurred since independence resulting in rising urbanisation, a fall in the relative size of its agricultural sector and expansion of the relative size of its manufacturing and service sectors. Despite its economic progress, Bangladesh still remains a very low income country with more than half of its population in poverty. Its food production per head of population has shown a slight downward trend and its access to foreign aid is declining. Furthermore, a number of environmental problems have become apparent that may hamper Bangladesh's sustainable development. Chapter 2 outlines with comparative observations socio-economic trends for the four major South Asian countries (Bangladesh, India, Pakistan and Sri Lanka) for the last 50 years or so concentrating on Bangladesh. Clem Tisdell, argues that these four countries have made substantial socio-economic progress in terms of widely used indicators, but nevertheless still remain highly disadvantaged countries. Tisdell underscores the critical importance of political stability. It is only with a politically stable government can Bangladesh make further economic and social progress. Given that Bangladesh's population is predicted to double in the next 2–3 decades, political stability is a *sine qua non*.

Political stability brings economic growth, because the economic sector functions better in a stable environment. In the recent past in the South Asian region economic growth has been promoted through individual government's economic liberalisation policies that have been possible through some semblance of political stability. Chapter 3 analyses the comparative economic performance of the four major South Asian countries focusing on economic liberalisation in recent years. Since the opening of their economies these countries have experienced increases in foreign investment that will accelerate the pace of overall economic development. Richard Shand argues that institutional and administrative reforms are important ingredients of the reform process and emphasises the importance of good governance.

A political economy perspective is also very important in the analysis of economic growth and understanding the economic reform processes and the resultant achievements. Chapter 4 analyses the political economy of macroeconomic management in South Asia with a focus on Bangladesh. After a review of the economic performance in four major South Asian countries – Bangladesh, India, Pakistan and Sri Lanka – for the period 1970–95, the factors behind poor macroeconomic performance in Bangladesh are examined in detail within a political economy perspective. The main theme canvassed by Akhtar Hossain and Anis Chowdhury is that the growth performance of Bangladesh economy has been linked to macroeconomic and/or political stability (or lack of it) originating from a policy paradigm which can be characterised as either macroeconomic populism or macroeconomic elitism and/or opportunism.

Irrespective of its characteristics a major outcome of macroeconomic and/or political stability in Bangladesh, as mentioned earlier, has been economic liberalisation. Chapter 5 analyses the economic liberalisation policy in Bangladesh, with special emphasis on the democratically elected governments' policies since 1991. M. Yunus Ali examines the potential of the policies in achieving economic growth in the country through the involvement of the private investments. Ali analyses the economic liberalisation policies, with special emphasis on government policies on private foreign investment as a vehicle for achieving faster industrial growth. Different policy issues are reviewed in terms of their ability to attract inflow of foreign private investment. Investment inflows in different industrial sectors are also reviewed to evaluate growth potential in each. M. Yunus Ali concludes with some recommendations for achieving objectives of accelerated economic growth.

A major beneficiary of the economic reform measure has been secondary and tertiary sectors, but the primary sector also, at times, has benefited from the reform measures. Chapter 6 demonstrates the impact of structural adjustment and economic reform (liberalisation and privatisation) measures on the improvement of agricultural exports and prospects for further export. Moazzem Hossain analyses trade issues facing the primary sector in South Asian countries. Based on this analysis, the chapter proceeds to investigate the social and environmental costs of further agricultural exports, and concludes with some recommendations.

The trend of openness and globalisation have created enthusiasm for expanded trade among countries of the South Asian region. Mohammad Alauddin in Chapter 7 investigates the degree of trade complementarities and competitiveness among South Asian Nations and explores possibilities for greater intra-regional trade. The magnitude and direction of trade overall and on a bilateral basis are examined focusing on trade imbalance between India and the rest of the region. The question of transit is also examined. Alauddin argues that the region could be on the threshold of an economic take-off if intra-regional economic cooperation expands.

An economic analysis of growth and development in LDCs cannot be complete without a study of foreign aid, and its role in macroeconomic performance of the country concerned. Akhter Ahmed investigates macroeconomic impact of foreign aid employing fiscal response models for several LDCs (Chapter 8). These models, in essence, attempt to shed light on public sector fiscal behaviour in the presence of aid inflows. The underlying concern is the extent to which aid is 'fungible' – that is, whether it finances consumption expenditure and reduces taxation revenue in LDCs. Using cross-country and time series data for several Asian countries and employing econometric techniques Ahmed argues that foreign aid (defined as all foreign inflows to the official sector) is indeed fungible, albeit at different levels. Furthermore, the overall impact of aid (both loans and grants) on public sector investment, consumption, domestic borrowing and taxation varies among countries. Generally speaking, aid leads to increases in investment and consumption expenditure, but reduces taxation and domestic borrowing. Comparative analysis does, however, show that these results are highly sensitive to alternative behavioural assumptions and hence specification of models employed.

A country can achieve some economic growth through macroeconomic reform and a proper utilisation of foreign aid, but the growth or the reform measures cannot sustain without an improvement in governance or power relationship in the management of the country's economic and social resources for development. M Rafiqul Islam examines the major aspects of good governance, that include *inter alia* a populist political system, a liberal economic system, efficient and honest bureaucracy, independent judiciary, rule of law, administrative accountability, and transparency in public policy formulation and implementation, human rights and freedom of expression (Chapter 9). Islam analyses Bangladesh constitution to identify the major aspects of good governance in it, and examines why some of the aspects are absent in the constitution, while others, having been incorporated in the constitution, are not in practice in the country. He suggests that the major problem of the country has been the disregard of the regimes to the constitution, which still continues after the advent of elected government in Bangladesh since 1991. The preservation of the constitution as 'the supreme law of the Republic' is no less dauntingly uphill task today than before. Yet this is manifestly the only viable and palatable route to good governance and development in Bangladesh.

Good governance can also be seen as 'the good government of society' or 'the quality and effectiveness of society' (Chapter 10). Zafarullah adds four new elements (a participative policy process, a public integrity system, a decentralised local governmental system, and a free media) to the list of items essential for consolidating democratic governance (a robust civil society, an autonomous political society, rule of law, and efficient and responsive bureaucracy, and an economic society, Linz and Stepan 1996) in a country. He then evaluates the progress of both administrative and financial reforms in Bangladesh. While policies supporting economic liberalisation have been announced and gradually implemented, the absence of a supportive administrative environment has greatly impeded success in attracting foreign and domestic investment, developing sound government-business relations, facilitating entrepreneurism in the private sector, and improving the performance of the public sector. All the financial and administrative reforms in Bangladesh so far have been an outcome of outside pressure, mainly, of the international financial institutions, and advanced liberal democracies. Zafarullah concludes that until and unless the reform measures emanate from within the country and grow roots within the society it is highly unlikely that Bangladesh would be able to develop a democratic polity and accountable administration leading to good governance.

Six major dimensions of a good governance are: political pluralism, economic liberalism, conscientious process, transparency in governmental process, effective management, and accountability (Chapter 11). Political parties in a country can play a major role in achieving these dimensions of governance and lead the country towards development. Samiul Hasan examines the relationship among governance, politics, and development. Hasan identifies political opportunism, poly-tricking in politics, the gaps between political parties and the people, and the absence of democracy within the political parties are the root causes of poor performance of political parties in governance. This phenomenon has impacted adversely on development management and resulted in poor development outcomes that have ramifications for sustainable development.

It is true that the success in achieving the targets of development in Bangladesh has not been very impressive, but since independence, Bangladesh has struggled hard to determine appropriate strategies of development. Apparently, the process has been affected by a high degree of political instability and lack of adequate resources. Ahmed Shafiqul Huque reviews the strategies adopted by successive governments and identifies a number of dilemma that have added to the complexity of the problem. The concept of development does not appear to be clearly understood by the ruling groups in Bangladesh, and this has resulted in a number of different programmes without a comprehensive framework for development. The dilemma stemmed from a variety of sources such as ideology, finance, objectives, power relationship, and the sincerity of the governments (Chapter 12). There has been constant confusion over the choice of an ideology for guiding the process, debates on developing internal sources of finance as opposed to external assistance, ambivalence over the focus of development on people versus infrastructure, hesitation over introducing programmes that could upset the favourable balance of power for the ruling group, and the use of development for rhetorical purposes rather than substantial change. Resolution of such dilemmas is important for identifying appropriate strategies to be adopted to facilitate the process of development in Bangladesh.

Another major reason for the failure of development projects in the developing countries has been the fact that the locational decisions of these programmes are generally taken locally by government officers or by local elected leaders or by both, with little or no regards for effectiveness. Shams-ur Rahman and David K Smith briefly portray health status of people in Bangladesh and establishes its relationship to the availability of health centre facilities, and then try to analyse it in terms of locational inefficiency. One of the tools for locational analysis is quantitative location-allocation modeling, that provides a framework for investigating service accessibility problems, comparing the efficiency of previous locational decisions, and generating alternatives either to suggest more efficient service systems or to improve existing systems (Chapter 13). In the absence of any formal analysis and generation of alternatives, the final decision may be made on political or pragmatic considerations. As a result the decisions can very often be far from optimal. Location-allocation models can play a significant role in making facilities more accessible to the population in developing countries.

A remarkable growth in the delivery of development projects and programmes as well as services, in the recent past in Bangladesh, has been through the voluntary sector. Chapter 14 makes a distinction between the locally funded and initiated voluntary organisations, termed in the chapter as the fourth sector, and the externally funded and induced NGOs (the third sector) and argues that it is the former or the fourth sector that demonstrates a greater potential in achieving sustainable development parameters at local levels. The local voluntary organisations may also be an important vehicle for making improvement in governance. Samiul Hasan concludes that the fourth sector have close links with the local people, and are in advantageous position to deal with innovations in sustainable development. Unless the fourth sector is made a part of the overall development process of a country, it will lose enthusiasm and ultimately fade away. The prospect of improving the system of local governance and achieving sustainable development may thus be hampered.

Voluntary organisations apart, many government and research organisations are concerned and working on developing models in improving participatory approaches to development. The approaches like PRA (Participatory Rural Appraisal) or RRA (Rapid Rural Appraisal) are being utilised and improved by many organisations. There have been ample experiments in the recent past on research, development and extension with new participatory approaches and the development of social innovations to bring various stakeholders together from the community level to national and international levels. Shankariah Chamala summarises traditional research and extension models practised in many developing countries and provides a brief review of some of the new approaches adopted by developed and developing countries. The Dutch Agricultural Knowledge and Information System (AKIS), the US Cooperative Extension Interdependence Model, and the Australian Cooperative Research and Landcare Extension Approach are briefly summarised. Several developing countries have also initiated new approaches to attain agricultural and environmental sustainability. India has initiated Joint Forest Management (JFM) programme while Bangladesh has been trying to change the Training and Visit (T&V) system of extension with its Agricultural Support Services Project (ASSP) and Farming System Research and Extension (Chapter 15). South Asian countries could use some of the participatory philosophies and principles to bring about a paradigm shift in its approach to solving sustainable agricultural and environmental issues.

A major issue related to sustainable agriculture and environmental management is maintaining or improving the flow of income by preserving the natural resources, and meeting the basic demands of the people. Many countries in the developing world are resorting to ecotourism as an alternative means of tackling the issue. Chapter 16 deals with ecotourism in the Sundarbans of Bangladesh. The Sundarbans in the southwest deltaic coastlands of Bangladesh is the largest and one of the best mangrove forests in the world. The evergreen, pristine and resourceful Sundarbans, endowed with diverse and rare *flora* and *fauna*, is set in a picturesque of creeks, canals and rivers. It is the last remaining natural habitat of the Royal Bengal Tiger – Bangladesh's National Heritage, spotted deer and estuarine crocodiles. Being a multiple-use mangrove forest, it offers economic returns from forestry, fisheries and ecotourism sectors. The availability of a wide range of recreational activities in unspoiled vast tract of the Sundarbans has made it a leading ecotourism destination in Bangladesh for local and international tourists alike. M. Akhter Hamid and Bruce Frank examine the status of ecotourism industry in the Sundarbans under the multiple-use management system. It explores the predicaments of ecotourism industry as it relate to resource management and policy statements. It also suggests some remedies to overcome constraints the ecotourism sector faces in the Sundarbans.

Another important challenge faced by the sustainability aspect in the agriculture sector in the developing world has been the agriculture diversification programme to offset the over dependence on crop sector and resultant over exploitation of agricultural lands. This challenge has seen the growth in the aquaculture sector – especially coastal aquaculture in many developing countries. South Asian countries especially Bangladesh and India are no exception. Chapter 17 examines the spectacular growth in coastal aquaculture in many less developed countries (LDCs). In many cases aquaculture exceeds the carrying capacity of the coastal waters resulting in lower production and often complete destruction of the yield. Thus the process of coastal aquaculture stresses the fragile environment to the limit and results in significant changes in overall socio-economic milieu. Furthermore, producers are primarily price takers. Their production trends are significantly determined by international market forces and the aquaculture sector in LDCs must comply with various requirement of international buyers who in many cases seem to behave like monopsonists. Mohammad Alauddin and M Akhter Hamid investigate the process of coastal aquaculture in South Asia focusing on Bangladesh and explore environmental implications thereof. It also addresses the implications of international marketing mechanism on domestic production. Finally, it suggests value adding and product diversification as strategies of risk minimisation and reduction of market uncertainty. The major victims of environmental problems in the developing world are the poverty stricken people, especially the women. The aspect is, however, least researched. Understanding both the gender patterns and its relationship to the environment is important for the formulation of sustainable agricultural and natural resource policy. Chapter 18 argues that the poor relationship of women to the (bio-physical) environment is the result of women's position in an inconducive sociopolitical environment which needs to undergo significant changes. Recent evidence suggests that women in Bangladesh have been somewhat successful in changing/influencing the socio-political environment through group-effort. Given this and their closer affinity to nature, women are likely to emerge as better environmental managers with appropriate opportunities and incentives. Nilufar Jahan and Mohammad Alauddin examine these and argue that redressing the inequality in gender relations in economic development requires much more than directing programmes to women. The chapter underscores the critical importance of analysing gender implications at all levels of development policy, e.g. planning, implementation and evaluation.

A critical appraisal of South Asia's development during the last few decades epitomise poor development priorities: more money on defence than on education, health and the social sectors, lack of popular participation in the development process, lack of empowerment of the mass of population especially women, discrimination on the basis of ethnicity, gender and religion, environmental degradation and poor governance. In essence, development process in South Asia has not been sufficiently *humanised* and *environmentalised*. South Asia is walking a tightrope as it strives for development with a view to enhancing living standards of the masses of population embracing the linkage involving development, governance and the environment. While one should not be unduly pessimistic, there is cause for concern as the region tries to extricate itself from a low-level equilibrium growth trap. Chapter 19 places the experiences, obstacles and prospects of South Asia in a global context. Mohammad Alauddin highlights and synthesises the major themes by conceptually and empirically establishing the close and critical linkages embracing development, governance and the environment. The lessons of experience, prospects and challenges that lie ahead are discussed. Transboundary and global aspects of South Asian issues are analysed in an environment of increasing globalisation. It is argued that South Asian issues have global implications and in turn events in South Asia are influenced by events elsewhere in the world. Their mutual interdependence can hardly be overemphasised.

1.4 THE DESIGN OF THIS VOLUME

This volume explores the environment-development-governance relationship in the context of South Asia. The focus is primarily on Bangladesh. The study takes stock of achievements to-date and defines the challenges that lie ahead as Bangladesh positions herself for the journey into the next millennium. This volume draws on a subject matter which is diverse in nature. However, the centrality and focus of the topics relate to core issues of development in Bangladesh in particular and South Asia in general. Furthermore, although the volume deals with three themes many of the issues raised in respect of one are interrelated to those in other parts.

On the economic development side of the issues the focus is on broad socio-economic indicators, their trends and prospects, macroeconomic management, foreign private investment, trade, economic liberalisation, and foreign aid. These aspects are considered for in-depth investigation in Chapters 2–8.

While the essays addressing the development aspect (Chapters 2–8) touch on the other two themes, the governance theme and its linkage to the environment is taken up for a probing analysis in Chapters 9–14. More specifically Bangladesh's performance is analysed. The issues that are discussed include a critical appraisal of: constitutionalism and governance; the process of achieving democratic governance; governance, politics, and development management; the dilemmas facing Bangladesh's development strategies; locational analysis of health facilities – a major aspect of development parameters; and the role of community-based voluntary organisations in local governance and sustainable development.

Specific environmental issues especially in the context of the rural sector are taken up for in-depth investigation in Chapters 15–18. These include: New research and extension approaches to sustainable agriculture and their relevance to South Asia, ecotourism under multiple-use management of mangrove forest in the Bangladesh context; coastal aquaculture in South Asia; and the effects of changes in the environment with particular attention to gender issues.

1.5   CONCLUDING COMMENTS

Within the framework of this study the relationship embracing development, governance and the environment is examined. The central idea canvassed in the book is that both poor governance and lack of concern for the environment lead to poor development outcomes. Governance and environmental issues critically influence sustainability of development. The issues undertaken here while not exhaustive are fairly representative of those that confront South Asia especially Bangladesh. Most of the issues that arise in South Asia in connection with the development-governance-environment nexus are not unique to it. Parallels abound elsewhere in the developing world and such similarities are noted. This strengthens the overall analysis undertaken in this study.

NOTES

1 Quoting Loshak (1971, pp.98–9) Salik (1977, p.75) writes 'When the first shot had been fired, the voice of Sheikh Mujibur Rahman came faintly through on a wavelength close to that of the official Pakistan Radio. In what must have been, and sounded like, a pre-recorded message, the Sheikh proclaimed East Pakistan to be the People's Republic of Bangla Desh'. The declaration of independence by Sheikh Mujibur Rahman was first broadcast on a wavelength close to that of the official Pakistan Radio, from a TNT wireless, during the early hours on March 26, 1971. Mujib's declaration of independence read as: 'This may be my last message. From today Bangla Desh is independent. I call upon the people of Bangla Desh wherever you might be and with whatever you have to resist the army of occupation to the last. Your fight must go on until the last soldier of the Pakistan occupation army is expelled from the soil of Bangla Desh and final victory is achieved.' (GOB, 1983, p.1).

2 Socio-Economic Policy and Change in South Asia: A Review Concentrating on Bangladesh

Clem Tisdell

2.1 INTRODUCTION

Since the independence of India in 1947 and its partitioning into India and Pakistan, considerable socio-economic change has occurred in South Asia, much of it favourable. The same has happened in Bangladesh (formerly East Pakistan) since it achieved independence from Pakistan in 1971. This is not, however, to suggest that all the favourable socio-economic changes which have occurred can be attributed to political independence.

Steady socio-economic advances in South Asia have been overshadowed by much faster economic growth in recent decades in East Asia; called the East Asian economic miracle by the World Bank. This miracle, however, became a little less dazzling commencing in August 1997 with the onset of the (East) Asian economic crisis when it appeared that a substantial part of the economic hype (hyperbole) about Asia was the result of a 'bubble-effect' fed by massive international financial injections into this region. Nevertheless, despite the East Asian financial crisis of the late 1990s, many East Asian countries have in fact made solid economic progress. At the same time, however, this does not constitute a reason for ignoring the socio-economic achievements of South Asia.

In this chapter, an overview is given of the socio-economic status of the four major South Asian countries (Bangladesh, India, Pakistan and Sri Lanka) as a prelude to more detailed concentration on Bangladesh, especially its socio-economic achievements since becoming an independent nation. While all South Asian countries have undergone considerable economic liberalisation in recent years (see the next chapter), under the influence of the structural adjustment policies favoured by the IMF and the World Bank, it is unclear to what extent such policies will foster sustainable economic development, given emerging environmental problems in South Asia and difficulties of governance (Cf. Alauddin and Tisdell 1998).

17

2.2   ECONOMIC AND DEMOGRAPHIC INDICATORS FOR
       MAJOR SOUTH ASIAN COUNTRIES

The GNP per capita of the major South Asian countries is quite low by world standards as can be seen from Table 2.1. Income per head, for example in Bangladesh, is less than one-hundredth of that in high income countries. India, Pakistan and Sri Lanka recorded higher levels of income than Bangladesh and the per capita income of all of these countries increased during the decade 1985–95 with India showing the greatest average annual increase in percentage-terms.

Table 2.1   GNP per capita for major South Asian countries: Its growth
             rate and disparity with high-income economies

South Asian economies	GNP per capita 1995 (US$)	Average annual increase (%) 1985–95	Necessary multiple to equal per capita income in high-income economies
Bangladesh	240	2.1	103.9
India	340	3.2	73.3
Pakistan	460	1.2	54.2
Sri Lanka	700	2.6	35.6

Source: Based on World Bank (1997b).

With the notable exception of Pakistan and, to a lesser extent, Sri Lanka, average annual percentage increases in GNP per capita of South Asian countries have been greater in the period 1985–95 than for the whole of the period 1960–94, as can be seen by comparing figures in Table 2.2 with those in Table 2.1. Pakistan's results reflect the fact that it has maintained a high rate of population growth (the highest amongst major South Asian countries) and the rate of growth of its GDP has declined somewhat (see Table 2.3).

Table 2.2   Trends in per capita income in major South Asian countries

South Asian economies	GDP per capita (1987 US $)					Average annual rate of change (%)
	1960	1970	1980	1990	1994	1960–94
Bangladesh	146	162	142	183	196	0.9
India	206	241	262	377	407	2.0
Pakistan	135	206	251	349	373	3.0
Sri Lanka	204	252	332	440	522	2.8

Source: Based on UNDP (1997).

Table 2.3   Growth of population and production in major South Asian countries

South Asian economies	Population Average annual increase (%)			GDP Average annual increase (%)		
	1970–80	1980–90	1990–95	1970–80	1980–90	1990–95
Bangladesh	2.6	2.4	1.6	2.3	4.3	4.1
India	2.3	2.1	1.8	3.4	5.8	4.6
Pakistan	3.1	3.1	2.9	4.9	6.3	4.6
Sri Lanka	1.6	1.4	1.3	4.1	4.2	4.8

Source: Based on World Bank (1994b, 1997b).

Table 2.3 indicates that rates of population growth have tapered off significantly in Bangladesh and India but only minimally in the case of Pakistan. These growth rates imply rapid doubling of population for Pakistan as can be seen from Table 2.4. Individuals born in 1994 could expect to see doubling in the populations of Bangladesh, India and Pakistan well within their life-time. The population of the Indian sub-content is expected to increase to over 2 billion in the early part of the 21st Century if the growth rates of 1994 are sustained. Even though population growth rates may not be maintained at 1994 levels, considerable increases in population in the Indian sub-continent are to be expected in the 21st Century. Demand on natural resources and the environment in the Indian sub-continent can therefore be expected to grow considerably. The welfare of many more people than now will depend on whether or not sustainable development can be achieved, taking into account its economic, social and ecological dimensions.

Furthermore, India, Pakistan and Bangladesh will have much larger populations to govern.

Table 2.4   Estimated population with predicted population doubling dates
for major South Asian countries

South Asian economies	Estimated population (millions)			Population doubling date (at current growth rate)
	1960	1994	2000	1994
Bangladesh	51.4	116.5	128.3	2037
India	442.3	913.5	1,006.8	2036
Pakistan	50.0	132.7	156.0	2019
Sri Lanka	9.9	17.8	18.8	2065

Source: Based on UNDP (1997).

Why do the countries on the Indian subcontinent have relatively low incomes
by world standards? There is of course no easy answer to this question.
However, they are relatively resource-poor in terms of produced assets and
natural capital per capita according to the UNDP. India is considerably more
capital abundant (in terms of produced plus natural capital) than either Pakistan
or Bangladesh (see Table 2.5). However, measurement of wealth, assets and
resources is fraught with many difficulties. While countries with low
availability of capital, especially low availability of natural resource capita,
are impeded in their economic growth, such constraints need not condemn
them to perpetual poverty as, for example, the historical experience of Japan
indicates.

Table 2.5   State of wealth in major South Asian countries 1990

South Asian economies	Bottom-up ranking	Estimated per capita wealth (US$'000)	Sectoral share of wealth (%)		
			Human resources	Produced assets	Natural capital
Bangladesh	12	3.1	79	14	7
India	20	4.3	64	25	11
Pakistan	33	6.8	81	13	6
Sri Lanka	42	9.4	77	17	6

Source: Based on UNDP (1996a, p. 9).

2.3   SOME SOCIAL WELFARE/DEVELOPMENT INDICATORS FOR SOUTH ASIA

It is widely recognised that income or GDP per capita is an inadequate indicator of human welfare. Many new indicators of social welfare and of development have been suggested such as the Human Development Index (HDI) which has featured in reports of UNDP. HDI has a maximum value of unity (UNDP 1994) and consists of a linear weighting of life expectancy, adult literacy and mean years of schooling, and GDP per capita. In practice, these variables tend to be positively correlated.

As can be seen from Table 2.6, Bangladesh, India and Pakistan have very low HDI-values even though these values have increased slightly in recent years. Sri Lanka has a higher HDI-value but overall its HDI-value declined during the 1990s. Indicators for the socio-economic status of women rank Bangladesh, India and Pakistan low in global comparisons (Cf. Roy and Tisdell 1996).

Access to safe water in all the four South Asian countries mentioned above increased significantly in the 1990s compared to the 1980s but access is still far from complete. The same is true of sanitation, except for Sri Lanka where sanitation coverage remained stationary. Nevertheless, life expectancy rates have risen at birth and infant mortality rates have fallen dramatically as can be seen from Table 2.7. Whether or not the structural adjustment policies adopted by South Asian countries will significantly increase inequality or access of their population to health services remains to be seen.

Table 2.6   Trends in Human Development Index (HDI) ranking of major South Asian countries

South Asian economies	1990 (1987)*			1993 (1990)*			1997 (1994)*		
	HDI value	HDI rank	No.of countries below this rank	HDI value	HDI rank	No.of countries below this rank	HDI value	HDI rank	No.of countries below this rank
Bangladesh	0.318	108	22	0.189	147	26	0.368	144	31
India	0.439	94	36	0.309	134	39	0.446	138	37
Pakistan	0.423	95	35	0.311	132	41	0.445	139	36
Sri Lanka	0.789	48	82	0.663	86	87	0.711	91	84

Note: * Years in parentheses refer to the reference years.

Table 2.7   Some selected health indicators in major South Asian countries

South Asian economies	Infant mortality rate (per 1,000 live births)		Prevalence of malnutrition (% under 5)	Total fertility rate		Life expectancy birth (years)
	1980	1995	1989–95	1980	1995	1995
Bangladesh	132	79	84	6.1	3.5	58
India	116	68	63	5.0	3.2	62
Pakistan	124	90	40	7.0	5.2	60
Sri Lanka	34	16	38	3.5	2.3	72

Source: Based on World Bank (1997b).

2.4   STRUCTURAL CHANGE IN SOUTH ASIA

Economic growth and development is normally accompanied by economic structural change. The relative size of the agriculture sector declines, the size of the manufacturing/industry sector expands, at least initially, and the service sector grows in relative terms so that eventually it becomes the dominant sector. This process is also accompanied by growing urbanisation. All of these processes affect the structure of society.

Transformations of the above type have been occurring in South Asian countries since their independence. The distribution of GDP by sectors for selected years 1970–1995 are shown for example in Table 2.8. Table 2.9 provides information on the distribution of the labour force by sector for the major South Asian economies for selected years between 1960 and 1992. It is clear that agriculture still retains a high proportion of labour of these economies, approximately half or more of their labour force. However, the sectoral contribution of agriculture to GDP per employee is much lower than in services and lower than in industry.

Partly due to income differentials and the changing structures of South Asian countries, a drift to urban areas has been apparent in the last half of the 20th Century. This is illustrated by Table 2.10. Increasing urbanisation is predicted. Nevertheless, the predominate proportion of the populations of South Asia still live in rural areas and are expected to do so for some time to come. Although South Asia contains a number of mega-cities, by developed-country comparisons, South Asia still remains very rural. It will therefore remain important for these countries to conserve the natural resource base of their rural industries (Cf. Alauddin and Tisdell 1998).

Table 2.8   Structure of production in major South Asian countries

South Asian economies	Distribution of GDP (%)											
	Agriculture			Industry			Manufacturing			Services		
	1970	1980	1995	1970	1980	1995	1970	1980	1995	1970	1980	1995
Bangladesh	55	50	31	9	16	18	6	11	10	37	34	52
India	45	38	29	22	26	29	15	18	19	33	36	41
Pakistan	37	30	26	22	25	24	16	16	17	41	46	50
Sri Lanka	28	28	23	24	30	25	17	18	16	48	43	52

Source: Based on World Bank (1995b; 1997b).

Table 2.9   Labour force distribution in major South Asian countries

South Asian economies	Percentage of labour force in								
	Agriculture			Industry			Services		
	1960	1985–88	1990–92	1960	1985–88	1990–92	1960	1985–88	1990–92
Bangladesh	86	56.5	59	5	9.8	13	9	33.7	28
India	74	62.6	62	11	10.8	11	15	26.6	27
Pakistan	61	41.3	47	18	10.2	20	21	48.5	33
Sri Lanka	57	42.6	49	13	11.7	21	30	45.7	30

Source: Based on UNDP (1990; 1995; 1996b).

Table 2.10 Urbanisation in major South Asian countries

South Asian economies	Urban population as % of total				Average annual change in urban population (%)	
	1960	1980	1995	2000	1960–94	1994–2000
Bangladesh	5	11	18	21	6.3	5.4
India	18	23	27	29	3.4	3.0
Pakistan	22	28	35	38	4.3	4.6
Sri Lanka	18	22	22	24	2.4	2.7

Source: Based on UNDP (1997) and World Bank (1997b).

2.5   EXTERNAL DEPENDENCE

South Asian countries receive considerable official aid. In 1994 India was the major recipient in terms of absolute quantity of aid (see Table 2.11) but Bangladesh and Sri Lanka received most aid per capita. It is rather surprising that Sri Lanka should receive so much aid considering that its GDP per capita is the highest of the four countries listed in Table 2.11.

Table 2.11 International economic relations in major South Asian countries

South Asian economies	Total net official development assistance received 1995			Export-import ratio (exports as % of imports) 1994	Exports (as % of GDP) 1994
	US $ million	As % of 1994 GNP	Per capita (US $)		
Bangladesh	1,269	4.8	11	67	12
India	1,738	0.6	2	80	12
Pakistan	805	1.5	6	66	16
Sri Lanka	553	48.0	31	72	35

Source: UNDP (1997).

All of the countries concerned ran substantial trade deficits in 1994 but, except for Sri Lanka their relative dependence on exports as a percentage of GDP was low. In the early 1990s, they (Sri Lanka excepted) were much less globalised than many other countries, especially East Asian countries including China (Cf. Tisdell 1993). With their adoption of structural adjustment policies, the trade dependence of these South Asian countries is likely to increase.

Let us now consider the socio-economic experiences of one of these countries, Bangladesh in some detail. Bangladesh, by most indicators, is the most disadvantaged of all the major South Asian countries. Nevertheless, we should not overlook its achievements.

While all the major South Asian countries have had major socio-economic achievements in the last 50 years or so, all are plagued by problems of governance which can sap their further progress or even undermine gains achieved to date.

2.6   AN INTRODUCTION TO SOCIO-ECONOMIC TRENDS IN BANGLADESH

Bangladesh has made considerable economic progress since gaining its independence from Pakistan in December 1971. Furthermore, many of its social welfare indicators show improvement. For example, expected length of life at birth has increased and the relative occurrence of poverty in Bangladesh has fallen. There is little doubt that Bangladesh has become economically, socially and culturally better off since becoming an independent state.

This is not, however, to say that it has entered the Garden of Eden or the equivalent. It is still a very poor country by world standards. According to the World Bank (1997), it was in 1995 the twelfth lowest income country in the world with an estimated GNP per capita of US$220 per head, that is a little over $4.00 per head per week. Furthermore, social welfare or human development indicators show that is a very disadvantaged country by international comparison. The human development index (HDI) of the United Nations Development Programme (UNDP) places Bangladesh in the bottom half of countries exhibiting a low level of human development. However, its global position is higher in terms of this index than if purely decided on the basis of its estimated GNP per head.

A major contributor to Bangladesh's economic growth has been the 'Green Revolution' (Alauddin and Tisdell 1991). The 'Green Revolution' has provided a basis for significant structural change in its economy since independence. However, the productivity gains from the 'Green Revolution' era seem to be faltering and environmental changes are occurring which could threaten the sustainability of Bangladesh's development. Furthermore, internal political instability has become a serious problem with adverse impacts on Bangladesh's economy. In addition, foreign aid for Bangladesh is in a state of decline not only because high-income countries are reducing the levels of their foreign aid generally, but they have also been redirecting it within Asia. Australia has done this, for example.

2.7   TRENDS IN BROAD ECONOMIC AND DEMOGRAPHIC INDICATORS

Bangladesh experienced a decline in its GNP per capita in the period 1965–1980, the major portion of which is included in its pre-independence period. The exact causes are not entirely clear but its dependent status on West Pakistan seems to have been a contributing factor. Its dependent status resulted in cultural conflict and political disruption and eventually armed rebellion and then independence. Furthermore, indigenous entrepreneurship in Bangladesh had little chance to develop when it was a region of Pakistan and major efforts were required after its independence to foster local industrial and entrepreneurial leadership.

Since 1980, the growth rate of Bangladesh's GNP per head has been positive. In the period 1980–85, Bangladesh's GNP per head grew at around 4 per cent per annum, but fell in the period 1987–92 to around 3 per cent (World Bank 1994b). In fact, in the period 1980–95, the average annual growth rate of GNP per head in Bangladesh was 2.1 per cent (World Bank 1995b, p. 162). The overall situation appears to be that since 1980 GNP per head in Bangladesh at first increased relatively rapidly, but this growth rate while still positive has tapered off.

There are various reasons for these trends. The rapid spread of the 'Green Revolution' in the earlier part of the 1980s resulted in significant rises in agricultural productivity which boosted the operation of Bangladesh's economy and assisted the development of its manufacturing sector, even though this was a relatively small sector. By the early 1990s, 'Green Revolution' technologies had already been adopted on most land environmentally suitable for their use. The scope for further significant economic growth of Bangladesh through the spread of these technologies was for all practical purposes exhausted. Furthermore, rice yields in some cases were beginning to decline due to soil degradation caused by this technology. The high intensity of cropping of such technologies results in nutrient-mining of the soil, a breakdown in its structure, and the loss of organic material from the soil. While yields can be maintained at high levels for a time, by using artificial fertilisers (and Bangladesh has substantially raised its use of these), rates of application often have to be raised continually to maintain yields. In consequence, acidification of the soil and loss of valuable soil *flora* and *fauna* occurs. Mineral deficiencies in the soil or the availability of minerals to plants can also arise. Consequently, it becomes more and more difficult to maintain crop yields and falling economic returns come onto the horizon.

'Green Revolution' technologies are high-external-agricultural-input systems. Biophysically they are not self-sustaining and as they continue to be used, their external-input requirements tend to rise. In the longer-term, they may not be sustainable biophysically or economically, not at least without major modifications.

While the initial bonus provided by the 'Green Revolution' has increased overall economic welfare in Bangladesh, doubts about its sustainability characteristics are worrying. This is especially so since Bangladesh has not been able to use its 'Green Revolution 'bonus to transform itself into a modern industrial economy, for example, in the way that Japan did. That is not to say that the 'Green Revolution' failed to support urbanisation and industrialisation in Bangladesh. It has. However, there are few signs that the bonus has been adequate and able to be used to place Bangladesh firmly on the path of becoming a modern industrial economy, no longer highly dependent on agriculture for its economic well-being.

It is quite amazing how much GDP per capita in Bangladesh has increased since the mid-1980s. Some estimates suggest that it has doubled (World Bank 1994b). It is possible, however, that official measures of this type overstate the real increase. This is because GDP measures the value of marketed or exchanged goods only. Commodities used for subsistence purposes, but not exchanged, are *not* as a rule, included in it. However, with economic growth and the spread of markets, they increasingly become subject to market exchange. Their inclusion then in estimates of GDP tends to give an inflated impression of increases in economic welfare as measured by rises in GDP.

There is also another cause for concern. Although GNP per head has grown in Bangladesh and agricultural production has expanded considerably, food production per capita in Bangladesh declined between 1973 and 1993. Furthermore, supplies of high protein food (e.g., pulses, fish and poultry) and fresh fruits and vegetables have fallen on a per capita basis. Thus doubts have been raised about the trend in the level of nutrition being supplied by the changing Bangladeshi diet in its post-1980 period of economic growth (Alauddin and Tisdell 1991). Nevertheless, vital statistics suggest that living conditions have improved. For example, in 1975 total life expectancy at birth was 45 years (World Bank 1994b). In 1995, 20 years later, it was 56 years (World Bank 1995b). This is a very significant improvement. The infant mortality rate has also fallen greatly, in fact, by more than one-third since 1975 (World Bank 1994b).

There has been a tendency to draw parallels between Malthus's theory of population growth and economic development and the situation of Bangladesh. However, since its independence, Bangladesh's birth rate has fallen considerably, and its death rate has fallen dramatically. In 1970, births per 1,000 of its population were 48 and in 1995, 35. Deaths per thousand of its population were 21 in 1970 and 11 in 1995 (World Bank 1995b). The overall result has been a fall in the average annual growth rate of its population from 2.8 per cent in the period 1970–80 to 2.1 per cent in the period 1980–1995. This is still a high rate of population growth by world standards. However, for those who see population growth as a serious impediment to improvement in the economic welfare of Bangladesh the change is in the appropriate direction.

The signs are that Bangladesh is in the early stages of demographic transition. The chances of this transition actually being completed, however, are going to depend upon its ability to sustain a rising level of per capita increase. Unfortunately there can be no guarantee that it will be able to do so. The bonus of the 'Green Revolution' gave Bangladesh a chance to escape from its low-level equilibrium development trap (Leibenstein 1957). However, it is possible that this injection has not proven adequate in itself to jolt Bangladesh permanently out of its low-level equilibrium trap. The 'Green Revolution' does not appear to have been able to bring about sufficient structural change in Bangladesh's economy for one to be confident that a process of sustainable development has begun, even though considerable restructuring of Bangladesh's economy has occurred.

2.8 STRUCTURAL CHANGE IN THE BANGLADESH ECONOMY

The major portion of Bangladesh's labour force is still employed in agriculture but the percentage of the total labour force so employed has dropped significantly. It was estimated to be 84 per cent in 1965 but was 59 per cent in 1990–92. In the same time frame, the percentage employed in industry rose from 5 per cent to 13 per cent of the labour force and that employed in services was up from 11 per cent to 28 per cent (UNDP 1995). If the distribution of GDP is used as an indicator of industrial structure, it turns out that the service side is now Bangladesh's major sector with agriculture in second place, followed by industry and manufacturing.

It is clear that a strong industrial sector has yet to emerge in Bangladesh. While I do not support the Marxian view that the service sector is unproductive, it is a worry that the service sector of such a poor country has become relatively so large (see also Lewis 1966). Service industries cannot provide staples and, if the economy is heavily tilted in their direction, provide no leeway if a failure in physical production should occur. Whereas China had an unbalanced economy before its reforms in the sense of not having a large enough tertiary sector (Cf. Tisdell 1993), one wonders whether Bangladesh's relatively large tertiary sector is an economic liability. It may of course be symptomatic of lack of other economic opportunities.

It was mentioned earlier that the type of Bangladesh's agricultural development may not be sustainable. In addition, it should be observed that Bangladesh is suffering from a variety of environmental problems and growing shortages of natural resources and continuing population increase. These are making increasingly difficult to sustain its growth momentum.

Bangladesh is fortunate to have considerable reserves of natural gas. This is a bonus for it since it is otherwise extremely short of fuel and energy resources. This energy shortage is affecting household economies and small industries in many parts of Bangladesh, especially in its western sectors. Women spend much time collecting firewood and fuel. Brickworks find it difficult to obtain fuel. This has resulted in serious loss of tree cover. Supplies of natural gas can significantly overcome this problem, but there have been long delays in supply of this to regions such as the above. However, natural gas is an important source of fuel supply for parts of the eastern region of the the country. Natural gas provides a means for Bangladesh to expand its manufacturing industry and to help conserve its living natural resources, such as tree cover. Bangladesh has not yet been able to use this to its full advantage.

2.9   BANGLADESH'S INTERNATIONAL ECONOMIC RELATIONS

Bangladesh is a relatively small country in terms of its area and the size of GDP. From an economic point of view, it could be expected to reap considerable economic benefits by being a part of a wider market or trading bloc. While structural reforms have been undertaken in an attempt to globalise its economy to a greater extent than hitherto, the impact of these adjustments have yet to be fully seen. However, Bangladesh has not yet been able to become a part of any effective international trading bloc. Even though it is a member of SAARC (South Asian Association for Regional Development), so far this organisation does not appear to have been very effective. It has also been confronted by some difficult conditions in relation to its international trade. For example, the value of its jute exports has declined substantially due to technological change. The demand for jute is much reduced because of competition from man-made fibres and the greater use of bulk carriage of grains.

Furthermore, Bangladesh has suffered a serious decline in official development assistance (ODA). Its ODA peaked at US$2,047 million in 1990 and by 1993 was down to US$ 1,386 millions. This is both a reflection of the falling sum being made available for development assistance by high income countries and a redirection of available funds. In Asia, China has received an increasing share of aid and so has Vietnam. Globally, aid to former communist countries has also increased. Bangladesh has therefore lost out in relative terms. Australian aid to Bangladesh followed a similar pattern, with Australia also redirecting its aid in Asia towards countries such as China, Laos and Vietnam that is more towards East Asia (AIDAB 1994). Nevertheless, Bangladesh is allocated by far the greater share of Australia's overseas development assistance to South Asia.

Bangladesh has a very large trade deficit and is highly dependent on aid to assist it with its balance of payment problems. However, its balance of trade situation improved in the period 1980–95 compared to 1970–80. In the latter period its exports grew at an annual average rate of 9.8 per cent and its imports by 4.8 per cent.

Australian readers may be interested to know that Bangladesh is a comparatively minor trading partner of Australia but Australia's balance of trade with Bangladesh is positive, very much in Australia's favour. In 1994–95, Australia's exports to Bangladesh amounted to $91m. and Australia imported $21m. worth of products from Bangladesh (McLennan 1996). Trade between the two countries is relatively stationary. In relation to its merchandise exports, Bangladesh is heavily dependent on exports of textile fibres, textiles and clothing. Its exports of other manufactures are negligible.

2.10   CONCLUDING COMMENTS

Bangladesh has made considerable socio-economic progress since becoming an independent nation. Given the extremely disadvantaged status of the country economically, the extent of the progress which it has made is truly remarkable. Compared to the pre-independence situation, GNP per capita in Bangladesh appears to have doubled approximately (World Bank 1994b, p. 26) and its level of grain imports has fallen substantially. Furthermore, the extent of poverty in the country has shown a significant downward trend. For example, the World Bank (1994b, p. 26) reports that using a high income poverty line 79 per cent of Bangladesh's population was in poverty in the period 1980–85 but that this had fallen to 49 per cent in the period 1987–92. For a lower level of the poverty line, 54 per cent of Bangladesh's population were in poverty in 1980–85 but this fell to 29 per cent in 1987–92. Despite difficulties in specifying poverty lines, the trend in the incidence of poverty is very favourable. Nevertheless, the incidence of absolute poverty in Bangladesh still remains high and at least around one in three of its population is in poverty.

Today it seems that Bangladesh also is facing a testing future. The growth-inducing impact of the 'Green Revolution' has been virtually exhausted. While the 'Green Revolution' has supported significant structural change in Bangladesh's economic pattern, such as some growth in manufacturing and greater urbanisation, it is not clear that the use of the 'Green Revolution' bonus has been adequate to foster non-agricultural industries sufficiently to provide for Bangladesh's future economic support. As pointed out, the growth of a relatively large service sector in Bangladesh may become an area of future economic problems. Bangladesh's future economic needs are likely to be considerable. While its rate of population growth has moderated, it is still very high. Given current predictions, Bangladesh's national output must increase by at least 2 per cent per year to continue to provide for its population at the current standard of living. A larger rate of increase is required for improvement.

Bangladesh's road is also being made increasingly difficult by the fact that foreign aid is now less readily available than in the past and in recent years Bangladesh has suffered considerable cuts in the foreign aid available to it. Furthermore, the international trading environment has become more difficult. This creates heightened competition for Bangladesh in exporting manufactured goods. Additionally, the political instability in Bangladesh has had adverse economic consequences. However, this instability itself may be partly a consequence of hardening economic circumstances. It is now more important than ever for Bangladesh once again to have national unity in order to consolidate its socio-economic advance of the last 25 years and to meet the challenges of a difficult economic future. Whether policies for increased free trade and various structural adjustment policies will be adequate to meet Bangladesh's economic challenges remains to be seen. The present study argues that they need to be supported by other measures. However, they are bound to fail if internal political stability cannot be maintained.

Political instability is a continuing problem for all the major South Asian countries, and it threatens peace, order and good government in this region. All major countries have made substantial socio-economic progress in the last 50 years or so, as signalled by several widely used indicators. Nevertheless, it is not only Bangladesh which has problems with political governance. Pakistan has a government dominated by the military, Sri Lanka is debilitated by political conflict resulting in terrorism and repression, and India has been struggling with a series of short-lived coalition governments and faces insurgency in some of its states. This is not to suggest that India, the world's most populous democracy, is about to collapse. In fact, democracy seems to be firmly entrenched in India which is clearly the dominant nation in South Asia.

3 South Asia in Reform Mode: Experiences, Obstacles and Prospects

Richard T. Shand

3.1 INTRODUCTION

Most South Asian countries are only in the initial phase of implementation of comprehensive programmes of economic reform and liberalisation. Attempts at reform in these countries commenced in the 1970s and 1980s but were piecemeal and had little impact, except in India in the 1980s when the average growth rate rose above 5 per cent. Sri Lanka is the exception in the group, commencing its programme of liberalisation as early as 1977.

The decade of the 1990s marks a turning point for all countries in South Asia when political parties of every ideological persuasion committed themselves irreversibly to the path of economic liberalisation, and through the democratic process. The focus is now on how these latecomers can perform as they seek the benefits of economic liberalisation both domestically through increased reliance on the private sector, and internationally through greater dependence on foreign trade and investment.

The economies of South Asia offer great potential for development but pose some of the most difficult challenges. In size they range globally from India as one of the largest economies to Bhutan and the Maldives, amongst the smallest, and Nepal, amongst the poorest and most externally dependent. In population terms, they include Pakistan amongst the fastest growing, and Bangladesh amongst the most crowded. They include Sri Lanka with a relatively long history of economic liberalisation but with the most serious long-term governance problems.

Economic liberalisation is typically judged in terms of the achievements of growth and stability in an environment of increasing economic openness. Macroeconomic stability and structural change are seen as necessary conditions for achievement of high and sustained growth, while institutional reforms and good governance are seen as crucial enabling factors for a successful reform process. This chapter first analyses the recent achievements of the five major South Asian countries during the 1990s in terms of major indicators of economic growth and stability, external trade and investment. It then considers the influence of existing institutional structures and governance and the new directions for these as enabling factors to advance the process of economic liberalisation.

3.2   ECONOMIC PERFORMANCE IN THE 1990S[1]

3.2.1   Economic growth

In the aftermath of a crisis in 1991, India has performed the most impressively of all countries in South Asia. From 1992, when the impact of the crisis was felt most strongly with a GDP growth rate of only 0.2 per cent, recovery was not only rapid, but reached unprecedented heights of over 7 per cent for three years from 1995 to 1997. While this momentum slipped in 1998 to a projected 5.5 per cent, growth of 7 per cent is now widely accepted as a base rate, which could be lifted again, once the momentum of reforms is regained.

Pakistan outshone its neighbours in growth performance prior to the 90s, with GDP growth averaging 5.2 per cent in the 1970s and 6.2 per cent in the 1980s. In the 1990s, the growth rate has fluctuated widely, from 1.9 per cent to 7.8 per cent, but the average was a disappointing 4 per cent from 1993 to 1997, reflecting poor performance during the reform programme in the 1990s (Shand and Bhati 1997).

Bangladesh's weakness has been its low growth path. Real GDP growth from 1991 to 1996 averaged 4.3 per cent per annum which is barely an improvement over the average of 4.8 per cent in the 1980s. The '4 per cent syndrome' has persisted for almost 15 years regardless of political regimes. In recent years, however, there are more promising signs. From 1996 to 1998, growth has consistently topped 5 per cent, averaging 5.6 per cent.

Sri Lanka's growth performance improved substantially following the implementation of a programme of economic liberalisation from 1977. GDP growth rate rose from an annual average of 4 per cent in 1960–76 to 5 per cent during 1977–95. There were variations in the latter period, including a slump in the 1980s due to the ethnic conflict and other factors that reduced the growth rate to a low of around 2 per cent in the second half of the 1980s. But a major recovery took place in the early 1990s, coinciding with the second wave of reforms and some return to political stability, reaching 6.9 per cent in 1993. Growth has fluctuated since, but the average growth rate of 5.6 per cent in the first half of the 1990s suggests a positive impact of the second wave of economic reforms.

Nepal has had a poor growth record in the 1990s, with a six-year average of 3.6 per cent per annum ranging between 3.1 per cent and 4.2 per cent. A gradually increasing trend over this period may reflect some impact of liberalisation policies introduced from 1991, but Nepal has been subjected to a number of exogenous shocks including drought, which make it difficult to discern real trends during this early period.

3.2.2   External trade orientation

At the commencement of the 1990s, the most striking general feature of the external trade performance of South Asia as a whole was the initially low ratio of exports to GDP. This reflected the effects of the mostly closed economic policies, particularly in India which became marginalised in world trade and recorded a ratio of only 6 per cent in 1991. There was a gradual expansion in these ratios through the 1990s. In the space of six years India increased its ratio to more than 10 per cent. Pakistan was marginally more open to international trade in 1991 with a ratio of 13 per cent but failed to improve on this until 1997 when it increased to 15.5 per cent. Exports of cotton manufactures increased at the expense of raw cotton exports, but Pakistan failed to diversify its exports over this period.

Bangladesh commenced with a low export ratio of 7 per cent in 1991 and showed some improvement to 13 per cent in 1996 as a result of successful efforts to increase and diversify its external trade with ready-made clothing, frozen shrimps and fish replacing traditional jute and jute goods in importance. Landlocked Nepal recorded a poor performance, with a ratio increasing from only 6 to 8 per cent, mainly due to rising exports of carpets. The important exception to this pattern was Sri Lanka. With its relatively long history of economic liberalisation and external trade orientation from 1977, it had already achieved a relatively high ratio of exports to GDP of 29 per cent in 1991 and increased this further to 36 per cent in 1995.

India's ratio of total trade to GDP was roughly double that of its export ratio throughout the 1990s, indicating similar growth trends in exports and imports. All other countries showed total trade ratios more than double those for exports indicating that imports have expanded more rapidly than exports. Sri Lanka was outstanding with ratios rising from 68 per cent in 1991 to 82 per cent in 1995. In recent years, Sri Lanka's import pattern has been dominated by intermediate and capital goods linked to its rapidly expanding export trade in textiles and garments so its expansion in imports and exports have been closely interrelated (Athukorala 1997). To a lesser extent this has also been true for Bangladesh where a rapid expansion of ready-made garments exports was paralleled by an expansion of imports of raw cotton and fibres (Shand and Alauddin 1997). For all countries, the early years of opening up of their economies with trade liberalisation have shown marked expansion in both exports and imports.

3.2.3   Foreign direct investment

Apart from Sri Lanka, countries of South Asia only began to offer the incentives needed to attract foreign direct investment (FDI) in the 1990s. India relaxed restrictions on FDI and portfolio investment in 1993, and a substantial inflow commenced in 1994 reaching an estimated $3.5 billion in 1997. Early inflows were dominated by short term capital from non-resident Indians (NRIs) and from foreign institutional investors (FIIs). FDI only caught up with FII flows in 1996.

Net foreign direct investment in Pakistan was negligible in the 1980s. It has attracted limited FDI in the 1990s, in a range from $200 million in 1991 to $400 million in 1995, averaging around $310 million annually. There was a sharp increase in 1996 associated with a single investment in a power plant, but it fell to $684 million in 1997 (SBP 1997). Inflow of portfolio investment in the 1990s was initially low at $84 million in 1992. It rose to around $270 million in 1992 and 1993 and more steeply to $1.3 billion in 1995 associated with the privatisation of the Pakistan Telecommunications Corporation but fell to $378 million in 1997.

Bangladesh has recently been attracting small and variable volumes of FDI in the 1990s ranging from $41.5 million in 1992 to $407.5 million in 1994, falling to $104 million in 1995. The variations were due to investments in a large fertiliser plant. FDI was negligible in 1996 and 1997 owing to political disturbances in 1996. In Nepal, new incentives have succeeded in attracting small inflows in recent years. From 1992 to 1995, authorised FDI in joint ventures and collaborations totalled $784 million of which actuals were $624 million.

In Sri Lanka, there was a surge of FDI from 1989, accompanied by a substantial but variable inflow of portfolio investment in the 1990s. The second wave of reforms set the stage for the surge, aided by new internationalisation moves by manufacturers in Japan and the newly industrialised economies (NIEs) in East Asia (especially Korea) in response to their massive exchange rate appreciation and domestic wage increases. Annual inflows increased from around $50 million in 1990 to $187 million in 1993. The inflow fell away following the change in government in 1994. The total number of projects contracted by the Board of Investment (BOI) declined from 327 in 1993 to 270 in 1994, and only 139 projects in 1995. The foreign component of total estimated investment in contracted projects has declined dramatically from over 77 per cent during 1989–92 to less than 45 per cent during 1993–95. A comparison of the Sri Lankan experience with that of other countries in Asia, such as Malaysia, Thailand, Indonesia, Vietnam, and even India, suggests that the significant decline in FDI in Sri Lanka was predominantly an isolated 'home-made' phenomenon and not part of a regional pattern (Athukorala and Shand 1997).

3.2.4   Fiscal deficits

All South Asian countries exhibited substantial fiscal imbalances in the 1990s. India experienced problems through excessive expenditure in the late 1980s, resulting in a high fiscal deficit of 8.1 per cent of GDP in 1991. Contractionary fiscal measures have progressively reduced the level, though with fluctuations, to 5.8 per cent in 1996, but this was still well above the official target of 4.5 per cent. In keeping with its emphasis on control of macroeconomic balances, Bangladesh reduced its deficit from a high of 7.2 per cent of GDP in 1991 to around 6 per cent in 1994. It rose a little to 6.8 per cent in 1995, but was reduced again to 5.1 per cent in 1997 and 5.2 per cent (provisionally) in 1998. Nepal recorded a high 11 per cent deficit to GDP in 1991. It has had some success in reducing it but it was still high at 7.7 per cent of GDP in 1996. Pakistan showed a similar picture with the deficit at 6.2 per cent of GDP in 1997, while Sri Lanka's deficit remained high throughout the 1990s, ranging from 11.6 per cent in 1991 to 8.4 per cent in 1995 and was a high 8.9 per cent in 1996.

3.2.5   Inflation

India experienced an initially high inflation phase in the 1990s, with the CPI rising to 13.5 per cent in 1992, as reform policies became operational. This was reduced to 7.5 per cent in 1994, but climbed to 10 per cent in the following two years. It fell slightly to 9.4 per cent in 1997.

Heavy borrowing by the Pakistan government for budgetary support, large fiscal deficits, successive devaluations and poor agricultural crops contributed to worsening double digit inflation in the 1990s. It rose from 10 per cent in 1991, eased from 13 per cent in 1995 to 11 per cent in 1996 but rose again to almost 12 per cent in 1997.

In Sri Lanka, the first wave of reforms was accompanied by high levels of inflation during the 1980s generated by massive public investments and high overseas worker remittances. CPI inflation reached a peak of 21.4 per cent in 1990 but declined over the following five years, and 1995 registered a second year of single digit inflation. The improvement was due to the contractionary budgetary and monetary policies under the stabilisation and structural adjustment policy package implemented in 1989, which reduced public sector infrastructure investment, lowered import duties and raised domestic food production. However, inflation intensified in 1996 reaching 15.5 per cent due to deficit financing for defence purposes, cuts in food subsidies, an increase in petroleum prices and a drought causing shortages of power and consumer goods. High inflation is expected to continue.

Bangladesh has been exceptionally successful in controlling inflation in the 1990s. The CPI fell from an average of 10 per cent in the 1980s to below 2 per cent in 1993 and 1994, but rose to 5 per cent in 1995. It fell again to 3.9 per cent in 1997. In Nepal, the inflation rate averaged 10.4 per cent in the latter half of the 1980s. A trade and transit dispute with India pushed it to 11.5 per cent in 1990. Then a devaluation in 1991, price rises of public sector goods, rising food prices from drought and India's high inflation rate combined to lift it to 21 per cent in 1992. It was reduced to single digit levels thereafter, at 9 per cent in 1993 and 1994 and 8 per cent in 1995 and 1996.

3.2.6   Current account balance

India was consistently closest to current account balance during the 1990s although the decade did not begin that way. In 1991, there was a large deficit of 3.2 per cent at the height of the country's balance of payments problems. This was quickly reduced to only 0.4 per cent in 1992, rising a little to 1.5 per cent in 1993. It has since risen only as high as 1.7 per cent in 1996. India was the only South Asian country to record a substantial improvement in its current account balance through the 1990s.

Pakistan's current account deficit in the 1990s fluctuated widely in the 1990s. From a peak of over 6 per cent in FY93, it was held below 4 per cent in 1994 and 1995 but blew out in the next two years to 6 per cent or more, mainly due to high import growth in the absence of exchange rate adjustments.

Bangladesh commenced the 1990s with a substantial deficit of 4.2 per cent in FY91, but through its stabilisation policies and with external assistance, this was reduced to only 1.7 per cent in 1994. It rose again to 5.5 per cent in the 1996 but has since moderated again to 3.5 per cent in FY97. Deficits were recorded in Nepal commencing with a peak of 8.2 per cent in 1991, followed by some improvement to 4.2 per cent in 1994 and deterioration to 9.9 per cent in 1996. Sri Lanka has also shown high deficits through the 1990s. At best, it was 3.8 per cent in 1993 and at worst was 6.5 per cent in 1994 and 6.4 per cent in 1996.

3.2.7   Foreign exchange reserves

External assets measured in import months of foreign exchange reserves varied greatly across countries and over time during the 1990s. In 1991, India's position was highly vulnerable at the time of its balance of payments crisis, with average reserves of only 2.5 months, and at one point with only 6 weeks of imports equivalent. Subsequently, with the government's stabilisation programme, there was a swift recovery and India's reserves rose steadily to 9.5 import months in 1995, slipping somewhat to 6.3 months in 1996.

Pakistan's foreign exchange reserve position has been highly precarious and has typically been measured in terms of import weeks. During the 1990s, Pakistan has either been in, or has verged on, crisis in its foreign exchange reserves. From 1991 to 1994 inclusive, average annual reserves have been at or less than one month. This improved in the following two years to just below three months, but again this does not reflect the amplitude of fluctuations within years. Within 1996 for example, foreign reserves fell to $567 million and the ensuing balance of payments crisis was a major factor in the dismissal of the Benazir Bhutto government.

Bangladesh also had low reserves in 1991 with 3.3 months of imports, but built these up progressively to reach a comfortable 8 months in 1994 with a slight reduction to 7.1 months in 1996. With its consistently large trade and current account deficits and lack of substantial foreign direct investment, Nepal has depended heavily upon foreign aid donors and international development agencies to provide a cushion of reserves, varying from six to eight months of imports.

Sri Lanka's foreign reserves fell to a relatively low level of 4.4 months of imports in 1991, but stabilisation policies improved this position steadily in subsequent years to a high of 6.5 months of imports in 1993 and 1994, falling slightly to 5.7 months in 1996.

3.2.8   External debt

High levels of external debt are features of external accounts in South Asia. India's external debt of $92.2 billion in 1996 placed it as the fourth largest debtor among developing countries. While this is relatively high and its management remains a policy priority, total external debt as a proportion of GDP has been reduced rapidly from a peak of 41 per cent in 1992 to 26 per cent in 1997.

For Bangladesh, it has risen from 52 per cent to 57 per cent in the 1990s; it is over 50 per cent for Nepal. In Sri Lanka, it was over 70 per cent from 1991 until 1996 when it fell slightly. In Pakistan, total external debt amounted to $29.6 billion in FY1997 making it a highly indebted developing country. The external debt to GDP ratio of 47.9 per cent of GDP in 1997 is heavy, having risen from 39 per cent in 1991. With domestic debt at 43 per cent of GDP in 1997, total debt in that year was 90 per cent of GDP. Escalation of Pakistan's debt has followed from a lack of control over the fiscal deficit. With government expenditure exceeding revenue, bank borrowing is increasingly financing the deficit. With limits on domestic borrowings, there is greater resort to external borrowings which in turn has placed mounting pressure on the current account.

3.2.9   Debt-service ratio

In India, the debt-service ratio rose to almost 30 per cent in the early 1990s. The growth of external borrowing declined in the 1990s, initially due to lack of access to funds during India's fiscal crisis but later to conscious policy of reducing the country's debt. Concessional and commercial debt-creating flows were replaced by non-debt-creating foreign investment flows. This policy has brought down the debt-service ratio from 31 per cent in 1992 to 26 per cent in 1996.

High and sustained levels of foreign economic assistance (and migrant remittances) have assisted Bangladesh and have provided stability to its balance of payments. However, this assistance has substantially increased external debt and debt-service liabilities. The latter placed pressure on foreign exchange reserves and the debt-service ratio rose to 25 per cent of export earnings in 1991. Merchandise exports expanded throughout the 1990s along with workers remittances from abroad, which eased pressures on foreign exchange reserves, and the debt-service ratio declined to only 12 per cent in 1995.

With an increasing burden of external debt during the 1990s, Pakistan has experienced a rapidly rising debt-service ratio. It is currently the highest amongst South Asian countries, increasing from 38 per cent of export earnings in 1990 to 62 per cent in 1997. The ratio of debt-service payments to foreign exchange earnings was also a substantial 38 per cent in 1997.

In Sri Lanka, there was a heavy reliance on foreign financing following the reforms in 1977 as a result of the implementation of a number of massive public sector investments. The debt-servicing ratio, however, remained low as a large majority of this foreign assistance consisted of grants and long term loans. More recently, reliance on foreign commercial borrowing has increased as concessionary finance dried up and as a result, the debt-service ratio rose to 25 per cent at the end of the 1980s. However, the debt-service ratio improves substantially in the 1990s, declining to a low of 13.3 per cent in 1994, though with a upward movement to 15 per cent in 1996.

Nepal has also been greatly assisted by high levels of foreign economic assistance which has supported the balance of payments. The debt-service ratio rose in the early 1990s to 16 per cent but dropped in 1996 to only 11 per cent.

3.3   IN REVIEW

This review of performances shows that, of the five South Asian countries, to date only India has been able to commence the desired transition sequence from crisis to stabilisation and through structural reforms to accelerated growth. But while the three recent years of growth exceeding 7 per cent is unprecedented in India, the subsequent fall in growth to 5.5 per cent in 1997 is indicative of continuing shortcomings in the reform process. Political instability of short-lived coalition governments has introduced discontinuities in the implementation of reforms as new governments have cobbled together policy programmes acceptable to diverse interests. There has been a lack of progress in key areas of the reform process such as infrastructure, agriculture and small-scale industry. There has been a continuing difficulty in achieving targets in some macroeconomic policies, particularly in reducing fiscal deficit to an acceptable level, and in tax reform (Chelliah 1996).

Weaknesses in the sequence have been more pronounced in the performances of other countries. Pakistan has yet to achieve its initial goals of stabilisation. It remains in or near macroeconomic crisis with minimal foreign exchange reserves, substantial inflation, severe internal and external debt levels, inability to attract substantial and sustained foreign direct investment, heavy dependence on the Bretton Woods institutions for short and medium term bail-outs, and on its Aid Consortium for development assistance.

Bangladesh has achieved considerable success with economic stabilisation, with low inflation and control of its fiscal and current account deficits and has made progress in developing new export-oriented industries. But it is still caught in a low growth trap with low levels of savings and investment, weak agricultural growth, lack of substantial foreign direct investment, and heavy dependence on external assistance from its Aid Consortium for its development programme.

Sri Lanka shows a mixed record over its 20 years of economic liberalisation. It has notched up an impressive record of liberalisation through reforms in external trade, foreign investment, exchange control, privatisation and labour markets, but its performance remains severely handicapped by an inability to achieve political and social unity and stability. Its current macroeconomic problems can largely be attributed to the ongoing war in the Northeast. It has attracted substantial foreign direct investment for its size, but at levels far below its potential owing to its high risk status. Least impressive to date has been Nepal, whose record after a promising start to economic reform in 1991, has been constrained by discontinuity in liberalisation policies caused by frequent changes in government. Its location and remoteness provide much of its potential but are factors that are also responsible for high costs of development and trade in the liberalisation process.

3.4   INSTITUTIONAL CONSTRAINTS

Economic liberalisation in South Asia involves radical change in the policies, institutions and functioning of the economies. Above all, it involves a paradigm shift in development strategy from government control to a market regime, i.e. a shift from centralised State planning of the direction of economic activity towards a free and competitive market-oriented strategy dominated by private sector activities and supported by a transparent legal and regulatory framework. This shift is a story of redefinition of the role of government and its agencies *vis-a-vis* the market in the encouragement of economic activity and the reshaping of government and its institutions to best serve the country in this new environment.

The extent of autarchy and state control of economic activity prior to the shift determines how radical the change must be. While South Asian countries stopped short of adopting the command economy strategy of the former USSR and always retained markets, they all embraced a closed economy strategy with heavy protection and intervention by the state in almost all areas of economic activity. In Sri Lanka, political power alternated between two parties with widely different approaches to planning (Fernando 1997). The United National Party (UNP) preferred market and private sector-led growth. The Sri Lankan Freedom Party (SLFP) coalition favoured state ownership. But by the mid-1970s, the role of the state was dominant, the private sector was marginalised, and the country had one of the most controlled and regulated economies outside the communist block (Athukorala and Shand 1997). In this, Sri Lanka went far beyond India where producers and consumers still had freedom of choice and market institutions were firmly entrenched, although there too state control over resource allocation permeated throughout the economy via a maze of regulatory systems of licenses and permits.

The inward-looking development strategy of protectionism and domestic control and regulation became highly institutionalised in these economies with a plethora of official rules and regulations through which decisions were disseminated and implemented. It is abundantly clear from evidence that these institutions are not only unsuited to the new directions of economic liberalisation but their continued existence presents serious obstacles to reform in the 1990s.

In the early 1990s, reforms have been concentrated in areas with urgent problems associated with economic stabilisation such as inflation, the fiscal regime, current account balances and foreign exchange reserves, and longer term structural adjustments in trade and industry, and in the banking and financial sector. While these have brought results, further and deeper reforms are clearly needed. Some of these are in real sectors, such as agriculture and manufacturing, and in the labour market, but just as importantly, some are in the institutions that have been the support mechanisms for the control regimes. These latter reforms are fundamental to the achievement of accelerated growth, in minimising the previously high costs of government and maximising the effects of the revised facilitatory and supportive roles of government.

This chapter identifies three major areas of institutional reforms considered to be most crucial in the ongoing reform process within the paradigm shift in South Asia: public sector enterprises, banking and finance and infrastructure.

3.5 MAJOR AREAS OF INSTITUTIONAL REFORMS

3.5.1 Public sector enterprise (PSE) reform

Nationalisation of industries in South Asia in the 1960s and 1970s led to the spread of public sector involvement far beyond the core activities or commanding heights of the economy as originally envisaged, into the production of goods and services normally undertaken by private enterprise.

In India, there were around 1,000 Central and State PSEs that accounted for 17 per cent of GDP and 23 per cent of employment in the organised sector. PSEs were in manufacturing, construction and services and monopolised the key industries of power, oil, steel and fertilisers. In Pakistan, the public sector accounted for only 6–7 per cent of manufacturing value added in the 1980s, but it dominated the utilities (railways and civil aviation), and the financial and energy sectors. In the early 1990s, there were around 200 PSEs. In Bangladesh, the government appropriated all abandoned foreign property and larger locally-owned manufacturing enterprises, and in 1973 controlled some 800 public manufacturing enterprises (PMEs) with a share of 92 per cent of total manufacturing output. They monopolised utility and infrastructure sectors such as power, gas, water, railways and telecommunication, banking and insurance and in large-scale manufacturing they contributed about 23 per cent of value added. In Sri Lanka, nationalisation took place from the late 1950s to the mid-1970s. By 1977 there were state owned enterprises (SOEs) in real sectors. The public sector contributed nearly 34 per cent of GNP, over one-third of investment, 40 per cent of employment in the formal sector, and ranged over manufacturing, mining, trade, services and plantation agriculture (Kelegama 1998). In Nepal, the development strategy of the 1980s gave high priority to public enterprises (PEs) in production and socio-economic policies (World Bank 1994a). Some 68 were established over two decades in manufacturing, trading, services, social and financial sectors and public utilities.

Public sector enterprises were expected to generate surpluses on an increasing scale, but throughout South Asia they failed to meet expectations. Overall performances were usually bolstered by monopoly profits from a few large and highly profitable enterprises, particularly public sector oil companies, but with their exclusion, net profits were generally marginal or negative. The widespread economic failure of PSEs contributed to high levels of internal debt, and remain a major contributor to the fiscal deficits in South Asia.

In some instances, PSEs were established in sectors where they had no comparative advantage. In others, the financial, technological and managerial demands of these enterprises exceeded the capacities of the public sector. Frequently, intervention at the political level meant that these undertakings became an extension of government power and patronage, with interference in recruitment, product pricing, investment and other areas of management. Results were also constrained by multiple and sometimes contradictory objectives, 'soft budgets', monopoly power in the market, lack of managerial skills, and pressures for overstaffing. Many also had to carry the burden of substantial subsidies.

In India, most PSEs suffered from chronic inefficiencies and became a substantial drain on Central and State budgets. More than 40 per cent of Central PSEs incurred cash losses in 1989–90. Total investment in Central PSEs earned a net profit of only 2.8 per cent on capital in 1995 and about one half made losses which had to be covered by loans from government banks (Jalan 1996). Public enterprise losses also became a major source of implicit subsidy at state level. Uneconomic pricing led to huge financial losses in key public enterprises such as the state electricity boards (SEBs) and road transport corporations and these have been rising over time (Rao 1998). In FY1996, the SEBs together made a commercial loss of 13.5 per cent on total net fixed assets (Rao et al. 1998). These losses in turn led to fiscal deterioration in the States, restricting investments in critical sectors such as power, education and health and leading to rising public indebtedness. Major reasons for PSE inefficiency have been multiple objectives, cost plus pricing, price and distribution controls, protection from competition, and the 'soft budget' constraint which propped up sick units with budgetary assistance and credit from the captive banking sector (World Bank 1991a).

In Pakistan, PSEs were typically inefficient and their losses placed excessive claims on the budget at the expense of funds otherwise available for public investment and the private sector. Limited data indicate the performance of the public sector in Bangladesh has declined over the last decade (Sobhan ed. 1996). In 1991, 1700 sick industrial units were registered with the Ministry of Industry, but little is known about their health since then. In Sri Lanka, SOEs were established without economic analysis and proved inefficient and financially non-viable. Some enjoyed monopoly profits but overall they were a drain on fiscal resources (Athukorala and Rajapatirana 1998). In Nepal, the performance of PEs was handicapped by interventionist control policies of government leading to poor financial management, over-staffing, wage pressures and operational inefficiencies. Financial losses grew sharply in the late 1980s and early 1990s.

In the light of performance, governments in South Asia recognised the critical need for inclusion of PSEs in programmes of structural reform.

The reform strategy followed by India has consisted of:

- a reduction in the number of reserved industries from 18 to 7

- restructuring or closure of all loss-making PSEs

- full or partial divestment of selected PSEs, to improve performance and public accountability by broadening the basis of management and ownership

- phasing out of budget support for non-infrastructure PSEs

- encouragement of PSEs to raise new equity from the private sector rather than from government

- subjecting public monopolies to competition from new private enterprises in most sectors

- making the institutional relationship between government and commercial enterprises more contractual

- elimination of privileges granted to PSEs

- amendments to the Sick Industries Act (SICA) to enable sick PSEs to be referred to the Board for Industrial and Financial Reconstruction for closure or rehabilitation

- establishment of a National Renewal Fund as a social safety net to provide compensation and transitional support for displaced employees

India has not yet accepted privatisation as a policy measure for rectifying the mounting problems of PSEs owing to opposition from vested interests such as organised labour. Critics consider the existing reform measures to be inadequate compared to the potential benefits from privatisation (Jalan 1996).

In India, progress with public enterprise reforms has been slow with the primary focus on disinvestment and industrial sickness. Disinvestment itself has been slow. The Rangarajan Committee on Disinvestment in its recent report (1996) mapped out a strategy and is currently considering 40 major PSEs for equity restructuring. On industrial sickness, 188 references had been made to the end of 1996, 99 per cent of which were small-scale units. In March 1995, there were 271,200 sick industrial units that involved 13.3 per cent of total bank advances to industry (GOI 1997). The recently elected BJP government has announced its intention of speeding up the process of disinvestment.

The Pakistan government actively pursued privatisation as a central theme in the reform package of 1991 as a result of the poor performance of PSEs, scarcity of financial resources, and pressure from international funding agencies (Kardar 1998). The privatisation process has made considerable progress in the face a number of constraints: unclear objectives, lack of policy clarity, lack of and poor access to information, lack of transparency, and most important, the limited absorptive capacity of domestic capital markets.

Sales of PSEs have taken place across a range of the strongest performing industrial, financial and infrastructure assets yielding substantial proceeds. Until 1995, 91 medium and large industrial enterprises of a planned 121 had been privatised and two of four nationalised commercial banks (NCBs). The next more difficult phase will include the larger manufacturing units, the largest NCB, all development finance institutions (DFIs) and privatisation of power and energy. Steps are also being taken to establish effective regulatory authorities to engender competitive pressures to improve efficiency and quality. Committees are also reviewing the performance of major PSEs and formulating remedial measures to improve their financial situation in preparation for future privatisation. There are problems in sustaining the privatisation process as those remaining include loss-makers and some that are subject to relatively complicated regulatory frameworks. Nevertheless, the current government is pressing ahead with further privatisation plans.

Bangladesh realised early that it could not sustain a large public enterprise sector. Privatisation commenced as early as in 1973, continued in the 1980s but slowed in the 1990s (Bakht 1997). Despite the divestitures in the 1970s and 1980s, 225 non-financial SOEs, 4 large commercial banks, 3 insurance corporations and 3 DFIs remained in 1994. SOEs then accounted for over 25 per cent of total fixed capital formation and 6 per cent of GDP. In 1996, SOEs in manufacturing still accounted for 12.5 per cent of value added in large and medium enterprises and 8.2 per cent of total manufacturing value added. There were 134 manufacturing SOEs, all with large accumulated losses and concentrated mostly in the jute sector (Bhattacharya 1996). The gross FY93 losses of all SOEs amounted to 27 per cent of the Annual Development Programme, 45 per cent of all external project aid and 2 per cent of GDP. SOE losses have been largely financed by lending from the NCBs which have weakened the financial system and eroded portfolio quality and interest rate margins.

The slow pace of disinvestment in Bangladesh was largely due to the decision of government to privatise enterprises with large and unsustainable debts to reduce the drain on the budget. Private buyers were reluctant to take on such enterprises, and their transfer to the private sector usually led either to liquidation or default on loans. The efficiency of disinvested units was low as purchasers also had to retain the workforce without retrenchment for a year on existing terms and conditions. Most of the divested units were small and had a depleted asset base and heavy liabilities. The Ministry of Industries recently found that 57 per cent of the disinvested enterprises were either closed or liquidated and that the performances of those in production were no better than their public sector counterparts (M. Rahman and Bakht 1997). The fate of over 700 units disinvested over the last two decades is not known.

In Sri Lanka, moves towards privatisation commenced in 1984 but an active programme was implemented only from 1989 (Kelegama 1998). In the first phase from 1989 to 1995, more than 60 SOEs were privatised, chosen for their commercial functions, their profitability, their size in relation to domestic capital market constraints and their political neutrality. A second privatisation phase commenced from 1995, after a change in government. A new emphasis is being given to transparency and selling price. Some 20 have been privatised in this latest phase by the Public Enterprise Commission

(PERC) established in 1995. Importantly, management of state-owned plantations was brought under long-term contracts with private sector companies in 1995 and *de facto* privatisation has proceeded since then (Athukorala and Rajapatirana 1998).

In Nepal, attempts at privatisation of PEs in the late 1980s were unsuccessful owing to inadequate commitment, opposition from organised labour and concern over foreign ownership. These constraints diminished in the early 1990s and privatisation has been directed to include all PEs except those covering utilities and social services and to improve the operational efficiency of those to remain in the public sector. The government has also encouraged private investment in those areas previously the preserve of PEs.

3.5.2   Banking and financial sector reforms

The banking systems were a primary focus of government efforts to increase resource mobilisation and to allocate capital under the control regimes in South Asia. Nationalisation of commercial banks and other financial institutions was undertaken to achieve more effectively the broad aims of growth and equitable coverage and access to credit within these economies. The public ownership and control of financial systems also enabled governments to allocate resources to priority sectors. Bank credit was extended to agriculture and small-scale industry, and development finance institutions were expanded to cater for the medium and long-term finance requirements of industry.

The positive outcomes of these policies were an expansion of the geographical spread of banking, growth in transactions volume in relation to GDP and growth in deposit accounts which provided the banking system with an increasing volume of financial resources and a functional spread of services. But these outcomes were achieved at the expense of profitability. In India for example, gross profits the average return on assets in the second half of the late 1980s was about 0.15 per cent (Joshi and Little 1996). The banking and financial system in Pakistan still has a high rate of loan defaults. In June 1997, ratios of default to total loan portfolios were 23 per cent for development finance institutions, 21 per cent for domestic banks and 4 per cent for foreign banks. In Bangladesh in 1991, around 25 per cent of loan portfolios of banks were non-performing, excluding large scale non-performing jute debts and unclassified agricultural loans (World Bank 1993b). There has been rapid growth of the region's financial sectors but institutional weaknesses in the NCBs and development finance institutions (DFIs) have endangered their viability and capacity for credit delivery and frequently have required recapitalisation.

A range of factors adversely affected income and expenditures of the banking systems and accounted for a decline in profitability, including:

- social objectives for nationalised banks set by government, the pursuit of which depressed income and potential profitability

- the system of directed investment comprising minimum statutory requirements that were set aside in the form of liquidity ratios (SLRs) and variable cash reserve ratios (CRRs). In India, these requirements amounted to over half of total resources mobilised by the banking system in 1990 (Narasimham 1991). Interest rates paid by government on these funds were well below market rates

- the system of credit directed to priority areas at concessional interest rates which succeeded at the cost of growing loan overdues, declining recovery rates and frequent loan waivers, and

- loans at concessional interest rates involving heavy subsidies, provided especially to public sector enterprises (PSEs) whose losses were covered by loans from NCBs.

- political and administrative interference in credit decision-making, associated with:

  (i)   populism in loan allocations and waivers that affected a large proportion of loans to agriculture and small-scale industry. This influence also extended to the medium and large-scale sectors particularly through loans directed to non-viable (sick) industrial units. In 1990, 7 per cent of bank lending in India was to large and medium-sized sick industrial units

  (ii)   patronage, including the granting of loans and their rescheduling at the expense of bank discipline and credibility of policy-makers. In Bangladesh, this led to a perception of a 'default culture' (Sobhan ed. 1996; Ahmad et al. 1997)

  (iii)   lack of autonomy of the central bank

Expenditures were boosted by:

- high costs of loan administration in extending branch banking to industries and locations with over-manning, declining quality of manpower and outdated operational technologies

- support of non-viable ('sick') industrial units within the public sector
- weak regulation and supervision

Governments have given high priority to measures for this sector in programmes of structural reform and economic liberalisation in the 1990s. The major objectives of reforms in the banking system and capital markets have been to:

- de-regulate entry of domestic and foreign private sector banks and liberalise branch licensing to encourage competition and allow more freedom for branch expansion to match market needs, increase competition among banks and to increase allocational efficiency of the system (Sarkar and Agrawal 1997)

- de-regulate interest rates and introduce a liberal interest rate policy

- free the banking system from external interference and impose financial discipline

- privatise banks and DFIs

- reform the NCBs with recapitalisation, improvement of their operating systems, non-performing loan portfolios and their loan recovery system and development of strategic approaches for their future development

- strengthen laws and procedures for pursuing defaulters

- enhance the autonomy of central banks and their ability to engage in prudential regulation and supervision and insulate state-owned banks from political interference

- improve the legal environment for loan recovery and enforce financial contracts

- reform banking legislation and regulation and unify the banking court system

The impact of these reforms to date has been limited and much of the reform agenda remains to be implemented. In India, the deposits and advances of public sector banks have lagged behind those of the private sector banks, as have the accumulation of non-performing assets and overall profitability.

Significant improvements in the policy of priority sector lending have occurred with reductions in interest rate subsidies and a greater emphasis on lending along commercial lines, but overall, public sector banks have not yet adequately improved efficiency and profitability. NCBs have lost some market share to private sector banks, but their oligopolistic dominance has continued because of their advantages over private sector banks through their extensive branch networks. In 1996, Indian public sector banks still controlled over 80 per cent market share in both deposits and advances markets. Competition from the private sector banks has been insufficient to raise the efficiency of public sector banks, there are no requirements for public sector banks to perform well, and the government still bails non-performing banks.

In Pakistan, the State Bank (central bank) has been granted autonomy and was given full authority in 1997 to conduct the monetary policy of the country and to oversee the entire financial sector including its restructuring (SBP 1997). There has been an expansion of the number of domestic and foreign commercial banks and their branch numbers. Privatisation of NCBs has proceeded but slowly and was still incomplete in 1997. The Nawaz Sharif government views the ongoing weaknesses of the financial system as a major factor in the slowdown of real growth in the economy, in the decline in domestic savings and in the continuation of macroeconomic imbalances. It has identified further comprehensive reform of the banking system as a key priority (Aziz 1997).

Since Financial Sector Reform Program (FSRP) was introduced in 1990, the performance of NCBs in Bangladesh has had a mixed record. The loan portfolio expanded, but loan recoveries have not shown a major improvement (Hassan 1997). There were high proportions of debt defaults and overdue loans in the public and private sectors in 1995.

The Bangladesh government now allows banks to fix their lending rates except for priority areas of agriculture, export and cottage industries where subsidised loans are given by government (A. Hossain and Rashid 1997). Furthermore, the GOB has reduced floor rates on savings and time deposits. Despite this, the weighted average of interest rates has not fallen much and the spread between advances and deposits has increased, with benefits going to the banks and not to the customers. The large spread between advances and deposits shows weak competition in the banking sector. To date there has been little progress in privatisation of nationalised banks, partly due to their unsound financial condition and partly to opposition from vested interests (A. Hossain and Rashid 1997).

The loan recovery situation of NCBs in Bangladesh has a mixed record. The loan portfolio expanded to 1994 under the Financial Sector Reform

Programme (FSRP) introduced in 1990, but loan recoveries have not shown a major improvement (Hassan 1997). There were high proportions of debt defaults and overdue loans in the public and private sectors in 1995 (Ghafur 1996).

The issue of autonomy of the Bangladesh Bank (central bank) from the Ministry of Finance still needs to be addressed as the Bank is currently still seen as an extension of the Ministry of Finance. The authority of the Bank needs to be defined under law, otherwise the exercise of its authority and its oversight functions will remain difficult.

3.5.3   Infrastructure reforms

Until recently infrastructural development in South Asia, was recognised as an essential contributor to economic growth but was not highlighted, at least partly because infrastructure investment and the provision of its services were considered to be properly a preserve of the public sector. Infrastructure services were seen as monopolistic; the investments were large, involving heavy initial outlays, gestation periods and externalities, which obstructed recovery of capital and operational costs from user charges, and therefore these services should be provided only by public sector enterprises and/or by government departments.

In practice, under increasing pressure of demand, the performance and quality of most infrastructure services became inadequate over time. There was a massive shortfall in the expansion of capacity in almost all sectors as investments remained below planning targets. Heavy and worsening public sector losses were incurred and had become an increasing burden to governments by the 1990s. A combination of changes for public infrastructure services at minimal levels and little private sector participation resulted in growing supply-demand gaps, low levels of efficiency, declining rates of cost recovery and negligible returns on investments (World Bank 1993c).

In the 1990s, the provision of adequate infrastructure facilities has been given an enhanced priority and a new dimension in South Asia. To a large degree this has followed from the growing pressure on governments to deliver higher growth rates both to satisfy rising community expectations and to match the record of other developing economies in Asia. This has coincided with a new approach of commercialisation of infrastructure sectors through privatisation and deregulation to improve efficiency and service quality.

An Indian Expert Group (1996) identified five factors driving enhanced commercialisation:

- greatly expanded capital requirements arising from these higher growth rates which require governments to seek new sources of finance in an environment of fiscal stringency in the region

- growing awareness of the importance of efficiency in such investments and past experience with public sector performance that have necessitated reassessment of the ability of public sector entities to deliver infrastructure services on a commercial basis

- changes in technology in infrastructure that are reducing the lumpiness of investment, permitting charges for marginal use of infrastructure services and enabling the unbundling of services vertically and competition horizontally. In this, telecommunications, with cellular and wireless telephones, is a lead industry

- the increasing emphasis on globalisation of trade in South Asia places additional pressure on countries to provide infrastructure services cost-effectively to enable firms to compete on international markets

- the new dynamism and integration of world capital markets which has expanded the scope for raising large scale funding of infrastructure investment on a commercial basis by the private sector as well as by governments

This new direction has important implications not only for the attraction of a greater inflow of foreign savings but also of domestic savings through an expanding domestic capital market. There is an increasing need not only for equity but more importantly for long-term debt instruments and contractual savings such as insurance, provident and pension funds. Thus there is a need for legislative and institutional reforms in this area, particularly in the debt market, to open up new sources of domestic finance to satisfy the growing demand for infrastructure investment. There is also an associated need for specialised financial intermediaries to assist in mobilising the resources needed with long term maturities.

Infrastructure projects are complex and relatively risky and require a clear understanding of the relevant legal, regulatory and institutional arrangements, particularly as these projects involve non- or limited-recourse financing. Regulation becomes a means of allocating risk among the principals and as the Infrastructure Report (1996) points out: 'Hence it is necessary to have an articulate regulatory framework, which is radically different from the existing legal framework in terms of transparency, clarity of obligations, duties and responsibilities between the participants in the infrastructure projects.'

It is also necessary to simplify the existing legal structure within a single statute and establish an autonomous regulatory body for each sector. There is a massive challenge for South Asian governments to raise the level of infrastructure investment to meet this burgeoning demand, to ensure the quality and efficiency of service provision and to incorporate privatisation and commercialisation through institutional change.

In India's Eighth Five Year Plan (1992–97, IPC 1992), the public sector dominated infrastructure development with a supplementary role for the private sector, but public sector performance fell far short of all targets owing to lack of resources. The Plan contained the first articulation of a strategy for infrastructure development where a possible role for the private sector was recognised, but at that time public sector was still seen as the natural supplier (Ahluwalia 1998).

In India, the pace of macroeconomic development is critically dependent upon the growth of the energy sector and power supplies. The Eighth Plan period was characterised by persistent power shortages. Despite a commitment of resources to new generation capacity, the public sector was unable to provide adequate finance to meet the rapidly growing demand. This was largely due to the financial sickness of the State Electricity Boards (SEBs), almost all of which were making losses (Parikh et al. 1997). These losses were principally due to subsidised sales to agriculture and domestic consumers, but also to high losses in transmission and distribution. These problems were created and compounded by the political control exerted over the SEBs, evident in social subsidies, overstaffing, inefficiencies and lack of accountability.

Government has begun to tackle the problem of investment shortfalls by opening up the power sector to foreign and domestic investment with a range of incentives. Eight fast-track Independent Power Producers (IPPs) with GOI counter guarantees that will sell power to SEBs for distribution spearhead this initiative.

Restoration of financial viability of SEBs is of similar priority and the first steps were taken by introducing reforms and restructuring in the state of Orissa in 1996, and more recently in Haryana, Rajasthan, Andhra Pradesh and Gujarat. In Orissa, the State Electricity Board has been disbanded and corporatised and its functions unbundled. An autonomous State Power Regulatory Commission was established with jurisdiction over issues relating to tariffs, licensing and standards of performance of bodies entrusted with power generation and distribution, and the first moves have also been made towards privatisation of electricity distribution.

In 1996, the GOI initiated moves to finalise a National Energy Policy. Under a Common Minimum National Action Plan for Power, each State will set up a State Electricity Regulatory Commissions (SERC) to determine tariffs, and the Union Government will set up a Central Electricity Regulatory Commission (CERC) to fix bulk tariffs for all Central generating and transmission utilities. The Central Electricity Authority would be reviewed by the Central Government. The States will move to provide maximum autonomy to the SEBs, modernise their operational practices and management, encourage co-generation/captive power plants, and shift towards a gradual programme of private sector participation in electricity distribution. An Ordinance for setting up the Electricity Regulatory Commissions was issued in 1998 (GOI 1998).

The opening up of the telecommunications sector in India began early in the 1990s with deregulation of the equipment manufacturing industry and granting entry of foreign equity in 1991. A policy of privatisation of mobile telecom, permitting foreign equity, was introduced first with cellular mobile services and radio-paging services in 1992 and in other value added services later. The public sector monopoly on basic telephone services ended in 1995. The policy for private investment was contained in the National Telecommunication Policy of 1994. Progress in this sector has been favourably judged in terms of growth of telephone connections, telecom prices and reduction of overstaffing in the Department of Telecommunications, but there has been criticism that the spread, quality and price of services have not measured up to international performance standards (Shah 1997). In 1997, the Telecom Regulatory Authority commenced operations in 1997 to provide a level playing field in the sector for service providers and to protect customer interests.

In civil aviation, new policy encourages private investment including foreign equity (but not foreign airline) participation in domestic airlines. Modernisation of air traffic services and facilities, upgradation of airport services and expansion of the number of international airports have been recent initiatives in India.

Railways, roads and ports have long suffered from inadequate investment levels to meet expanding demands, but the resource gap has widened in the 1990s as the demand pressures have heightened. With inadequate investment in railway freight capacity, the pressure has increasingly fallen on road transport, but the national road network reflects prolonged neglect (Ramanathan 1997). In the absence of increased public investment, maintenance has suffered. Private investment is difficult to attract owing to factors such as resistance to tolls and land acquisition problems.

Ports currently represent a major handicap to accelerated growth and global competitiveness. Major weaknesses include inadequate capacity, obsolete technology, restrictive labour practices and low productivity, and outdated customs clearance procedures leading to long delays in clearances and costs well in excess of those in other Asian ports. High turnaround times, berthing delays and inadequate investment are major causes of poor performance (Ahluwalia 1998). In 1997, a policy for private investment was announced in which major ports will still remain in the public sector but individual activities are to be privatised. This year marked the first major investment, in Jawarharlal Nehru Port in Mumbai, and the first commissioning of a private port.

Overall, there has been inadequate expansion of capacity in all infrastructure sectors in India other than telecommunications in the 1990s. Public investment has been short of targets and private investment stalled by problems, as in power, or has contributed too late for results. Economic growth could accelerate by taking up unused capacity in the system, but this has limited prospects and is no substitute for the creation of new capacity.

The broad strategy is for public and private investment to expand as joint contributors, though prospects for expanded public investment are not encouraging owing to the level of fiscal deficit and other competing demands. Also, serious organisational weaknesses in government agencies (SEBs, Port Trusts and PWDs for road construction) have led to poor utilisation of existing capacity and use of resources for expanding capacity. It is generally agreed that a turnaround is needed in performance during the Ninth Plan (1998–2002) in infrastructure if reform objectives are to be achieved.

In Pakistan, the combination of heavy losses from public utilities and an inability of the public sector to provide adequate infrastructure for the growing economy has led the government to turn rapidly to privatisation or to private sector partners in the 1990s. The 1994 power sector policy leaves thermal power plants to the private sector. In 1997, the Privatisation Commission extended its areas of activity to include airports, roads, oil and gas and public utilities. Foreign investors are now permitted to buy disinvested public sector assets.

The government is still dominant in public utilities and financial services but is in the process of further substantial disinvestment. In particular, there are moves towards restructuring of the seven largest remaining public sector enterprises in railways, telecommunications, electricity, gas supply and oil and gas development which together are the main source of financial losses in the public sector.

New policy was recently announced for private sector participation in the railways (transport of fuel oil to private thermal generation plants), and roads and highways (BOT basis), hydroelectricity, and a range of activities in oil and gas. In the financial sector, the aim is to privatise all NCBs and non-bank DFIs. Reforms to the capital market are to include measures to develop the secondary market for debt instruments with non-residents able to trade freely in corporate debt instruments (SBP 1997).

In expediting both public and private sector efforts to meet basic infrastructure requirements, the government is also developing regulatory frameworks for energy, telecommunications, water/sanitation and other infrastructure. In a new role for government, it has established a series of regulatory authorities for autonomous and transparent regulation of public enterprises, privatised entities and established new private concerns. It aims to level the playing field and remove barriers to entry in attracting private investment while protecting consumers.

The areas of infrastructure reform pursued in Bangladesh to date have been railways, power, water and telecommunications. Only rail and road are still reserved for the public sector. Heavy losses on the railways led to implementation of a Recovery Programme which focused on reduction of deficit through adjustment of tariffs, removal of open-ended subsidies, labour rationalisation with staff reductions, organisational reforms and adoption of a rational investment programme. The aim is to transform the railways into an autonomous, market-responsive organisation accountable to the users. Similarly the commercial performance of the power sector utilities has been poor with heavy losses.

In Sri Lanka, infrastructure investment was confined to the state until recently, but owing to fiscal problems and a reduction in capital expenditures, state investment in infrastructure declined and from 1993, the government decided to attract the private sector. But it took the new government until after 1994 to develop this approach in a range of projects proposed for privatisation (Kelegama 1997). In transportation, new roads have been identified for construction on a BOT basis as possible toll roads. The development of a port has been recommended on a BOT basis, and in railways, there are two network extensions and two electrification proposals for which procedures for privatisation are in prospect. In telecommunications, the government has made plans to improve market access and promote competition by opening up wireless-based telephone services to private operators in addition to the cellular services already permitted in competition with the government-owned Sri Lanka Telecommunication, and by establishing local telephone companies and cooperatives. Consideration is also being given to deregulation of the government-owned utility. In electricity, the government is exploring the possibility of identifying potential suppliers from the private sector on a BOO/BOT basis. Plans for privatisation in other areas such as water supply and solid waste are at an early stage of exploration.

3.6   GOVERNANCE

Governance is taken here as encompassing the form of political regime, the processes by which authority is exercised in managing a country's economic and social resources, and the institutional capacity of the government to design and implement (World Bank 1994a), or more simply as the politico-administrative factors that impinge on policy (Dunham and Kelegama 1998). The form of political regime that has planned and delivered development in post-Independence South Asia has varied across countries from autarchy to democracy, but in absolute terms, no political regime has achieved its targets nor has its performance matched those of countries in Northeast and Southeast Asia over the same period. Performance has been ultimately determined by the other components of governance: the ways in which authority has been exercised, and the institutional capacity of governments, although the record indicates better results under democratic governance. It is significant in this regard that all countries have become committed to democratic governance in the 1990s.

Across the region, economic governance in all countries was exercised through control regimes with government policy assigned a central role in economic decision-making supported by a vast public service and a proliferation of public sector institutions.

One broad criticism of this strategy of economic governance is that the exercise of authority has been excessive and unworkable. Jalan (1996) has argued that command planning in India could not work effectively as the economy was too heavily influenced by the private sector. The basic assumptions, which led to the State being given the role as arbiter in economic decision-making were wrong, as producers and consumers had freedom of choice in making economic decisions. The existing legal and judicial framework effectively blocked the power of the State to enforce economic decisions, and limitations in administrative resources and capability became increasingly important constraints to development.

Another criticism is that this strategy could not meet its objectives owing to the distortionary effects of interventionist policies on resource allocation. Bhagwati and Srinivasan (1993) pointed out that India already had a functioning financial sector and the extensive licensing system imposed upon it by government overrode its allocative role, just as the protection given to firms and labour removed the market's role as an efficient allocator of labour. In Bhagwati's view (Bhagwati 1994), inward-looking trade and foreign investment policies, and the extensive bureaucratic controls over production, investment and trade, together diminished the private sector's efficiency in

India. Inefficiency in a vast public sector, which intruded into almost all areas of economic activity, diminished its contribution to the economy and constrained the returns from investment.

Many common weaknesses have been identified in the process of resource management by governments in the region. Amongst these, lack of political accountability has been prominent. It has led to the sheltering of inefficiency in public sector enterprises and heavy subsidisation of services, which have weakened the state with fiscal deficits, diminished capital available for investment, and has sapped the viability of public financial institutions with heavy debts. Populist programmes addressing short term issues have taken precedence over longer term programmes and have weakened macroeconomic performance and the sustained commitment to implementation of reforms. Public policies have lacked responsiveness, consistency, predictability and credibility. Government has been too large, overcentralised and wasteful of resources.

Lack of political accountability has been hand-in-hand with lack of bureaucratic accountability. Performance of agencies has been undermined by inadequate financial controls and scrutiny by legislators. Processes have been unresponsive, prone to delays, subject to discretionary decisions, and swayed by side-payments, the soft budget constraint and by officials who acted according to their vested interests and privileges.

Development assistance has played a highly significant role in development strategy in South Asia, but poor governance has seriously reduced its impact, particularly in the poorer countries. Poor performance in the administration of development assistance has been evident in:

- lags in utilisation and reporting of expenditures

- lack of modern monitoring mechanisms

- lack of reliable measures to estimate expenditures and to control quality of expenditures, and

- lack of effective oversight leading to delays in project completion and failures to monitor completed projects.

The Indian Draft Ninth Five Year Plan (IPC 1998) subjects the past planning process to critical retrospective analysis to explain the shortfalls in past Plan performance to identify the weaknesses in the formulation and implementation of Plan programmes and in the delivery system. Major inadequacies in design and implementation were found to stem from:

- time and cost overruns in public sector, which have been widespread and substantial in infrastructure and investment projects
- weaknesses in administrative, planning and delivery mechanisms which have limited the benefits in the social sectors to the beneficiaries
- unrealistic or overly optimistic assumptions of technical and non-technical parameters that impeded progress in implementation

The performance of development programmes and social sectoral projects have been affected by inadequate resource allocation, faulty design, weaknesses in implementation and institutional bottlenecks.

In Pakistan, past weaknesses which have constrained effective implementation of economic policy included:

- a lack of decision-making in policy which weakened macroeconomic policy
- populist programmes that deepened the three major economic problems of an unsustainable fiscal deficit, critical external imbalances and large non-performing loan portfolios in the banking sector
- impediments at lower levels of the bureaucracy from corruption, over-staffing and red-tape delays

Weak governance has been a major constraint on effective implementation of economic reform in Bangladesh. The change from presidential to parliamentary rule in 1991 greatly improved political governance but parliamentary control over the executive is still inadequate owing to the lack of mutual trust between government and opposition parties. Ahmad (1998) observes that 'A true democratic order is yet to be established in this country.......democratic values have not yet taken root in the body politic of the country to guide the approaches of government and opposition parties to the articulation and operationalisation of their respective responsibilities and working relationship'. Q. K. Ahmad (1998) stresses the need for people's participation, especially the poor, for true democratisation of society, but comments that, currently, little has been achieved towards the goal of participatory democratic governance and economic management.

Political accountability has been weak due to a dominant executive, weak legislature, slow development of political parties, lack of independence of the judiciary and a weak electoral system (M. M. Khan and A. K. M. Ahmad 1997).

Government was seen as preoccupied with process, too highly centralised, overly bureaucratic, too discretionary, unaccountable, unresponsive and wasteful. Weaknesses have been most apparent in areas of public administration, linkage of the judiciary with the executive, in law and in the operation of the banking system The low growth trap in Bangladesh has been attributed to government inability to plan and manage key reforms, weak implementation capacity and inefficiencies of public institutions (World Bank 1993b). It has been attributed to the poor performance of aid utilisation (World Bank 1990), evident in low project aid disbursement ratios. The number of projects has exceeded availability of local resources and aid-funded financial projects have been under-funded.

The role of government in economic governance in a market economy is still being reviewed. The World Bank (1997b, p.1) now argues: 'The message of experience...is...that the state is central to economic and social development, not as a direct provider of growth but as a partner, catalyst and facilitator'.

More specifically, the government's role, redefined under economic liberalisation, is frequently seen in terms of intervention to provide basic needs, promote market efficiency and to facilitate rapid and sustained market-driven growth. It should provide an appropriate legal framework for enforcing contracts as a basis for the working of an efficient market. Institutional structures should help to minimise transaction costs with well defined and enforced property rights, contracts and guarantees, limited liability and bankruptcy laws. The State should act as guarantor of these rights and institutions, providing a tight legal framework for contractual enforcement Labour laws should be reformed to enable adjustments and deployments in response to market and technical signals (Bardhan undated).

In domestic and international trade and investment, new regulations are needed to safeguard against anti-competitive behaviour such as anti-dumping procedures and market-disruption problems. Instruments, which restrict entry of foreign direct investment, need adaptation to encourage flows within freer limits (Bhagwati 1994).

Legal and institutional reforms should be directed at reducing transaction costs and gaining productivity from economies of scale and improved technology, thus improving market efficiency and growth. Legislative reform is required to modernise outdated legislative frameworks, e.g. for regulation of companies, enforcement of contracts, reduction of transaction costs. Regulatory reform is needed to establish independent regulatory and quasi-judicial bodies to ensure competition, efficiency and growth in the market and responsible corporate behaviour. The legal and judicial system needs to be strengthened for timely resolution of disputes and to provide credible rule of law. Streamlined regulations, laws, and processes between government, private sector and the public should enhance the level and nature of accountability and responsiveness of public agencies to the citizenry. India's new thinking on the role of government sees intervention as necessary 'to promote competition, by enacting appropriate legislation on monopoly and other restrictive practices and to provide the institutional mechanism for adjudicating and enforcing such discipline' (IPC 1998). This envisages the updating of the legislative framework for company regulation. Judicial processes need to be simplified to enable enforcement of commercial contracts and responsible corporate behaviour and to reduce transaction costs of legal cases. Independent regulatory and quasi-judicial bodies are needed to encourage competitiveness and transparency in corporate behaviour.

Pakistan adopted a medium term programme in 1996 (World Bank 1997a) which aims for better governance over the short and long term through:

- further deregulation and reduction of scope for discretion in routine decision-making

- strengthening the judicial system

- transparent, competitive public sector procurement processes

- greater accountability of the public sector through beneficiary participation and monitoring

- depoliticising of the civil service and levels of remuneration to create performance incentives to counter corruption

- decentralisation to forge a link between revenue raising and expenditure decisions and results on the ground

- creating an enabling environment for the development of NGOs and community based organisations

Dunham and Kelegama (1998) argue that good governance in Sri Lanka should be sought through:

- a clear separation between the public and the private without diversion of public resources for private gain

- establishment of a predictable framework of law and government behaviour conducive to development, without arbitrariness in the application of rules and laws

- rules, regulations, licensing arrangements which facilitate the functioning of markets and discourage rent-seeking
- priorities consistent with development, leading to efficient allocation of resources
- broad and transparent decision-making

In Sri Lanka, the process of withdrawal of government involvement that began after 1977 in favour of market forces and the private sector continues in the forms of privatisation and deregulation. The key roles for the state (Wanasinghe 1994) include regulatory oversight of:

- consumer protection in product standards
- healthcare and education
- monopolies in supply of goods and services
- labour markets
- financial institutions through the central bank
- environment

As in other countries of South Asia, these are new to the administrative system and make new demands on the bureaucracy (ADB 1995b). For these tasks, there is a need for a reduction in the size of the public service and in its orientation, and in relation to the private sector, kinds of skills and ways of service delivery. In this connection, Wanasinghe (1994) identified a number of key recommendations from the Report of the 1986 Administrative Reforms Committee which needed to be addressed:

- redefinition and rationalisation of the functions of government, organisation reviews and cadre management
- creation of a senior policy management group in the public service
- strengthening and reorganisation of training and career development
- systems improvements and strengthening of financial management
- objectivity in personal management process and productivity and efficiency of human resources
- effective management of those enterprises which would remain in the public sector

In Nepal, the combination of the emergence of a democratically elected government in the early 1990s and the shift to economic liberalisation elsewhere in the region has underlined the need for restructuring and strengthening of the main institutions responsible for economic and development management. To this end, the capacities of the Ministry of Finance, line Ministries and the National Planning Commission are to be strengthened. A monitoring unit is envisaged for the Ministry of Finance to follow fiscal performance, and financial implementation of the core economic programme. The National Planning Commission is to screen, monitor and evaluate projects, and review and track the public investment portfolio. Institutional management of development projects is to be enhanced by raising the quality of the public investment programme, strengthening financial reporting and budgetary control and with closer monitoring of projects. Longer-term reforms to public administration will follow redefinition of the roles of the public sector, and the central and local level agencies (World Bank 1994b). An Administrative Reform Commission was established to formulate a reform programme. Its 1993 report recommended reducing the size of the civil service, increasing the role of the NGOs, and user groups and streamlining the civil service to make it more effective in fewer functions. It addressed systemic issues: the organisational structure of institutions and the incentive structure for employees. The need for decentralisation of management and decision-making was recognised in addition to budgetary reforms. Together, these measures would greatly enhance the public accountability of government agency performance.

3.7   CONCLUDING COMMENTS

The foregoing analysis has provided insights into ways in which institutional aspects of public sector enterprises, banking and financial infrastructure sectors, and governance, have constrained recent development performances.

The progressive removal of barriers to trade and private sector investment and emphasis on market-driven development has highlighted further legacies of government intervention under previous control regimes that require reform. The most prominent and common consequence of these has been limited supply of investment capital, both public and private, and in large and small economies alike. The most urgent need is for a faster and larger inflow of direct foreign investment throughout the region, even in India where its expansion has been rapid since 1992.

The need for reforms in these areas is well understood, and the process of reforms has already commenced, but in the main it has not been effective. Democratic government, installed throughout South Asia in the 1990s or earlier, holds the promise of better governance. But policy uncertainties, arising from frequent change of governments, together with a continuing lack of transparency of economic governance continue to deter foreign investment, particularly in the more difficult and risky area of infrastructure. There is scope for increasing the efficiency of use of development aid which is still an important source of support for the poorer countries, but the developed world is becoming aid-weary which is likely to reduce the significance of this option, other than on humanitarian grounds.

In the domestic economies, problems associated with continuing dominance of government in banking and large proportions of non-performing assets which cloud the viability of banking sectors are obstructing the expansion of the domestic capital markets. Budget finance and bank funds continue to be tied up with public sector enterprises as progress in privatisation and disinvestment of private sector enterprises has been uneven and generally slow. Infrastructure sectors are still starved of funds which again underlines the growing need for foreign funding of such projects.

The analysis demonstrates that the strongest reform challenge ahead of South Asia still remains as the creation of a stable political and market-oriented environment to attract an adequate supply of private investment for rapid growth of private sector and public investment to support this objective. This analysis of the 1990s indicates that considerable but uneven progress towards that goal has been made but that without pressing home reforms, legacies of past policies will continue to obstruct further progress and moderate performances.

NOTES

1 This section draws heavily on material in Shand (1998).

4 The Political Economy of Macroeconomic Management: The Case of Bangladesh

Akhtar Hossain and Anis Chowdhury

4.1 INTRODUCTION

South Asia remains a slow growing region in Asia and has largely been left out of Asian economic dynamism (Rana 1997). Since the early 1970s the debate on economic development in this region has been whether industrial, trade, and investment policies which have created an elaborate control system has stifled economic growth. India has been the focus of this debate. Bhagwati (1993), Dubey (1994) and others have strongly argued that India's slow economic growth since independence has been the result of its flawed development strategy. Hughes (1994) points out that, despite the introduction of various poverty-reducing direct measures, it is slow economic growth that has failed India in its efforts to reduce massive poverty. Like India, Bangladesh, Pakistan and Sri Lanka also adopted public sector-led dirigistic development strategy to promote economic growth and have been unsuccessful in reducing poverty substantially (A. Hossain and Rashid 1996).

Some changes are afoot. Like other developing countries, South Asian countries faced major macroeconomic problems in the 1970s, which induced them to introduce various stabilisation and structural adjustment policies. Although these have somewhat improved macroeconomic performance, they have not been enough to raise the standards of living of the ordinary people. Along with macroeconomic policy discipline, these countries need deep structural reforms to achieve rapid economic growth. But they are constrained to do so for lack of reform-oriented political leadership and for resistance from various organised interest groups.

This chapter focuses on the political economy of macroeconomic management in South Asia concentrating on Bangladesh. After reviewing the economic performance in four major South Asian countries – Bangladesh,

India, Pakistan and Sri Lanka – for the period 1970–95, the factors behind poor macroeconomic performance in Bangladesh are examined in detail. It is argued that the growth performance of the Bangladesh economy has been linked to macroeconomic and/or political stability or lack of it originating from a policy paradigm which can be characterised as either macroeconomic populism (Dornbusch and Edwards 1991) or macroeconomic elitism/opportunism.

4.2   SOUTH ASIA'S ECONOMIC PERFORMANCE, 1970–95

The 1970s were a period of economic turbulence for both developed and developing countries. South Asian countries were not an exception. They had political problems as well. After 24 years of political partnership, Bangladesh and Pakistan broke up in 1971. This rupture affected the economic performance of both countries. The Indian economy also suffered from its war against Pakistan in 1971. The sharp rise in OPEC oil price in 1973–74 was an additional shock to South Asian economies. It created serious inflation and balance of payments problems. The Bangladesh economy was particularly hit by the oil shock as it came at a time when the country was yet to recover from the destruction of the War of Liberation. Severe droughts and floods caused further havoc to the economy. The situation reached a climax in 1974 when the country experienced a famine and then plunged into a deep political crisis following a series of military coups in 1975. The second half of the decade was relatively stable, both economically and politically.

The 1980s were a period of structural adjustment for South Asian economies. Persistent low economic growth, high inflation, large trade deficits, and rising external debt have induced South Asian countries to undertake structural adjustment measures designed by the IMF and the World Bank and are based on the neoclassical paradigm that market forces are superior to state planning and/or intervention for resource allocation and output distribution.

The structural adjustment measures undertaken by South Asian countries are:

- fiscal discipline – small budget deficits, spending controls, removal of subsidies, and broadening of taxes

- monetary discipline – low rate of money supply growth and a restricted access of the government to credits from the banking system

- price reform – the removal of controls over interest rates, exchange rates, wages, and output prices

- trade reform – the removal of controls over imports, exports, and capital flows, and the encouragement of foreign private investment, export promotion

- the privatisation of government-owned financial institutions and industrial enterprises

The goal of these policy and reform measures has been to create an economic environment which promotes saving, investment, and economic growth (A. Hossain and Rashid 1996).

Table 4.1 reports indicators of macroeconomic performance for four major South Asian countries. It can be seen that although policy reforms have brought macroeconomic stability in a relative sense, they have not raised the real performance of the economy in a significant way. Rana (1997, pp.15,18) suggests that 'Reforms have led to macroeconomic stability in all the countries with the sole exception of perhaps Pakistan. The data suggest that the reform programmes have yet to lead to a sustained improvement in the real sector of the South Asian countries'.

It is possible to identity a number of factors behind the slow response of South Asian economies to policy reforms.

- all policy reforms have been partial and macroeconomic in nature; deep and microeconomic structural reforms are yet to be undertaken

- economic reforms have not been associated with administrative, legal, and political reforms needed for the efficient operation of a market economy

- infrastructural bottlenecks have reduced the supply response of policy reforms

Table 4.1   South Asia: Main macroeconomic indicators, 1971–95

Period	Bangladesh	India	Pakistan	Sri Lanka
Growth rate of real GDP (%)				
1971–75	5.1[a]	3.0	3.6	3.0
1976–80	5.2	3.6	6.0	5.5
1981–85	3.8	5.4	6.0	1.0
1986–90	4.1	6.1	6.0	3.4
1991–93	4.0	3.7	6.8	5.4
1994	5.1	5.1	4.0	5.7
1995e	5.7	6.1	4.6	6.0
Gross Domestic Saving (% of GDP)				
1971–80	2.2	20.5	10.1	13.8
1981–90	2.6	20.3	10.3	13.3
1991	4.1	23.1	13.2	13.7
1992	5.8	20.0	17.3	16.4
1993	6.5	20.2	13.2	17.7
1994	7.1	22.1	16.2	13.6
1995	7.8	23.3	14.4	14.9
Gross Domestic Investment (% of GDP)				
1971–80	7.3	20.8	16.4	19.4
1981–90	11.4	23.9	18.7	24.8
1991	11.5	23.6	19.0	22.6
1992	12.3	22.0	20.1	23.9
1993	13.6	20.4	20.7	25.3
1994	14.8	22.5	20.1	24.7
1995	15.5	23.5	18.3	26.3
Budget deficits (% of GDP)				
1971–75	−8.4[a]	−3.6	−6.8	−6.1
1976–80	−6.8	−5.0	−8.0	11.1
1981–85	−6.8	−6.8	−6.1	−10.7
1986–90	−6.7	−8.3	−7.7	−9.6
1991	−5.2	−5.8	−6.3	−9.5
1992	−4.9	−4.8	−7.4	−7.1
1993	−5.4	−7.4	−8.0	−8.1
1994	−5.6	−6.7	−5.8	10.1

Period	Bangladesh	India	Pakistan	Sri Lanka
Growth rate of the narrow money supply (%)				
1971–75	38.0[b]	12.8	13.2	9.0
1976–80	18.1	17.4	21.1	22.9
1981–85	21.0	15.0	13.7	15.7
1986–90	8.1	16.0	15.2	16.2
1991–93	13.3	15.6	16.2	13.9
1994	24.3	27.4	15.1	18.7
1995	16.7	11.1	12.8	6.7
Inflation rate (%)				
1971–75	33.2	12.2	16.1	7.5
1976–80	8.1	4.2	8.7	10.3
1981–85	11.9	9.4	7.2	12.2
1986–90	9.6	8.4	6.8	12.6
1991–93	8.6	10.7	8.5	11.8
1994	1.8	11.0	12.5	8.4
1995	5.8	10.2	12.3	7.7
Current account deficits (% of GDP)				
1971–75	–2.6[a]	–0.9	–5.9	–2.1
1976–80	–5.0	–0.3	–4.9	–4.5
1981–85	–4.1	–1.7	–2.8	–4.7
1985–90	–3.0	–2.9	–3.1	–5.3
1991	–0.7	–3.5	–3.3	–6.6
1992	0.8	–1.1	–3.8	–4.6
1993	0.8	0.2	–5.7	–3.6
1994	–2.0	–0.6	–3.0	–5.9
1995e	–1.0	–0.4	–3.4	–5.5

Notes: a = 1973–1975; b = 1972–1975; e = ADB staff estimate.

Sources: IMF (various years), IFS Yearbook; World Bank (various years), World Development Report; ADB, Asian Development Outlook (various years).

4.3   BANGLADESH'S MACROECONOMIC PERFORMANCE, 1972–96

Table 4.2 summarises the key macroeconomic indicators of Bangladesh roughly by political regime since 1972. It is evident that in so far as economic growth is concerned, there exists little difference among the four regimes of Sheikh Mujibur Rahman (1972–75), Ziaur Rahman (1976–81), Hussain Mohammad Ershad (1982–90) and Khaleda Zia (1991–96). Although inflation was brought down from 40 per cent to less than 10 per cent per annum since the mid–1970s, the gain was not translated into high economic growth. The real GDP growth rate has remained roughly at about 4 per cent per annum since the mid 1970s. As a result, the per-capita real GNP, which fell by –0.4 per cent per annum during 1973–75, grew by only about 2 per cent per-annum since then (A. Hossain 1996). Gross domestic saving remained at a low level, and the investment rate was far less than what was required to break the 'vicious circle of poverty' and the 'low-level equilibrium trap' (Srinivasan 1988). The failure to raise the domestic saving rate meant a continued dependence on foreign aid for investment and economic growth. Besides the obvious external debt servicing difficulties and the loss of policy autonomy (Taslim 1994), the large-scale capital inflows in the form of aid and loans (and overseas workers' remittances) have caused an appreciation of the real exchange rate and through it, the decline of industries which produce tradeable – 'the Dutch disease syndrome' (A. Hossain 1997a).

4.3.1   Inflation and the balance-of-payments crisis, 1972–75

Bangladesh had a bad start on the economic front after independence. It experienced high inflation and a balance-of-payments crisis during 1972–75. The economy grew at a rate of about 2 per cent per annum during this period. This was also primarily due to the catching up factor as the economy was recovering the loss suffered during the War of Liberation.

The annual average inflation rate of about 40 per cent during 1972–75 was the highest since the 1943 Bengal famine. Such an inflation rate hurt the low income earners in both the rural and urban areas. Lifschultz (1974) identified three schools of thought which offered explanations of inflation in Bangladesh during 1972–74 – the 'smuggler school', the 'hoarder school', and the 'money printing school'. The government blessed the first two explanations of inflation because they were politically convenient. However, a prominent member of the Planning Commission during the Mujib period, Rehman Sobhan (1993, p.22) attributed inflation to 'liberal money creation' in the post-Independence period. Monetary accommodation was at least

Table 4.2   Bangladesh: Main macroeconomic indicators, 1972–96

Fiscal Year	Growth rate of of real GDP (%)	Gross domestic saving (% of GDP)	Gross domestic investment (% of (GDP)	Trade deficits (% of GDP)	Current account deficits (% of GDP)	Foreign debt servicing (% of foreign exchange earnings)	Inflation rate (%)
1973	–0.3	–1.9	3.0	–5.8	–1.4	n.a	49.0
1974	9.6	0.7	7.1	–5.0	–3.6	4.2	54.8
1975	–4.1	1.0	6.3	–4.6	–2.5	14.4	21.9
1973–75	**1.7**	**0.1**	**5.5**	**–5.1**	**–2.5**	**9.3**	**41.9**
1976	5.7	–3.0	9.9	–11.2	–9.2	11.7	2.3
1977	2.7	6.0	11.1	–3.5	–1.1	9.1	4.8
1978	7.1	1.7	11.8	–8.0	–4.5	9.2	5.3
1979	4.8	1.6	11.3	–7.7	–2.9	9.9	14.7
1980	0.8	2.3	15.3	–11.2	–5.9	8.8	13.8
1981	4.3	3.4	16.2	–10.6	–4.9	6.3	16.2
1976–81	**4.1**	**2.0**	**12.6**	**–8.7**	**–4.8**	**9.2**	**9.5**
1982	1.2	0.5	15.5	–12.5	–6.9	7.1	12.5
1983	4.9	0.6	13.4	–10.5	–2.1	8.9	9.4
1984	5.4	1.3	12.3	–9.1	–1.9	7.6	10.5
1985	3.0	2.3	12.9	–9.0	–4.2	10.2	10.7
1986	4.3	3.2	12.5	–7.8	–3.2	11.2	11.0
1987	4.2	3.5	12.9	–7.7	–2.6	11.3	9.5
1988	2.9	3.0	12.4	–7.9	–1.7	12.6	9.3
1989	2.5	2.6	12.9	–8.6	–3.5	11.7	10.0
1990	6.6	2.7	12.8	–8.4	–3.6	10.9	8.1
1982–90	**3.9**	**2.2**	**13.1**	**–9.0**	**–3.3**	**10.2**	**10.1**
1991	3.4	4.1	11.5	–6.2	–0.6	11.0	7.2
1992	4.2	5.8	12.1	–5.1	0.9	9.8	5.1
1993	4.5	7.00	14.3	–5.9	0.2	9.5	1.3
1994	4.2	7.5	15.4	–4.8	1.1	10.4	1.8
1995	4.4	7.7	16.6	–6.1	–0.5	8.5	5.2
1996	4.7	7.8	17.0	–7.2	–3.0	8.3	5.0
1991–96	4.2	6.7	14.5	–5.9	–0.3	9.6	4.3

Note: n.a =not available.

Sources: Author's computations/compilations based on BBS (1993), GOB (1996), BB (various issues); and A. Hossain (1996c).

responsible for exacerbating inflation 'caused' by both domestic and external supply shocks (for example, droughts, floods, and the sharp rise in OPEC oil prices, A. Hossain 1996c). With the winding up of international aid in 1973, the economy began to show signs of distress. Along with high inflation rates, on the external front the overvalued exchange rate of the domestic currency taka, the smuggling of raw jute, rice, and other essential goods to India, and the oil price shock increased trade deficits and gradually dwindled foreign exchange reserves (A. Hossain 1995). By 1974 the balance of payments problem mounted to a crisis point. The government did not have foreign exchange reserves to finance even basic food and raw materials imports. The macroeconomic problems reached a climax when the country was struck by a devastating famine which led to a colossal loss of human lives (Alamgir 1980).

4.3.2   Macroeconomic stabilisation, 1975–90

On 15 August 1975 the Mujib presidency came to a sudden and shocking end. After a series of military coups and counter coups, on 7 November 1975 Ziaur Rahman became the de facto leader of a military-civilian government. The initial task of the Zia Government was to bring economic and political stability in the country. The political consolidation of Zia government was associated with a distinct change in the direction of development strategy reminiscent of the development strategy followed by the Ayub regime of the 1960s. The hall-mark of this policy regime was selective import substituting industrialisation and export drive and state patronage of business by selling public enterprises to a select group.

The macroeconomic performance of the Zia regime is summarised below:

- About 5 per cent annual growth in GDP and a significant reduction in the inflation rate from over 40 per cent to less than 10 per cent per annum

- Increase in domestic savings rate to 2.2 per cent of GDP and the investment rate to 10.5 per cent of GDP. However, as both government revenues and spending increased, there was only a marginal reduction in budget deficits

- Increase in trade deficits from 6 per cent to nearly 10 per cent of GNP because of a sharp increase in imports following the removal of some import controls

- A significant increase in external debt outstanding and consequential increase in the level of debt servicing liabilities expressed as a percentage of export earnings. However, debt servicing liabilities expressed as a percentage of total foreign exchange earnings were stable

Nine months after the abrupt end of the Zia regime, General Ershad seized power in a bloodless coup in March 1982. In terms of economic and political philosophies like the Zia regime, the Ershad regime was a lineal descendant of the Ayub regime.

Although the Zia regime brought some stability to both economic and political fronts, the economy remained weak and suffered from structural weaknesses. The Ershad Government introduced IMF-World Bank structural adjustment programmes in 1982/83. Since then Bangladesh has practically remained under structural adjustment programmes of one form or the other (A. Hossain 1996b). The economy grew at a rate of about 4 per cent per annum during the Ershad period. However, the inflation rate remained at around 10 per cent per annum and trade deficits increased to the level of around 10 per cent of GDP. So the Ershad regime brought neither durable stability nor sustained economic growth.

4.3.3 The economy in transition to a high growth path since 1991

Since the seizure of state power by Ershad in 1982, Bangladesh's politics was dominated by the people's struggle to resist his authoritarian and illegitimate rule. Success came in 1990 when his Government was overthrown by an urban-based middle-class uprising. Democracy was restored in 1991 when a relatively fair parliamentary election brought the Bangladesh Nationalist Party (BNP), under Begum Khaleda Zia, to power. Her Government (1991–96) presided over a period of macroeconomic stability despite an endemic political instability. The size of trade deficit declined from 9 per cent of GDP during 1981–90 to 6 per cent of GDP during 1991–96. The current account balance position improved from a deficit of 3.3 per cent of GDP to a deficit of 0.3 per cent of GDP during 1991–96. This improvement in both trade balance and current account position was a major achievement as it was associated with a deceleration of inflation from 10 per cent per annum during 1982–90 to 4 per cent per annum during 1991–96.

A consensus view is emerging that the Bangladesh economy is in transition to a high growth path (Quibria 1997). Any transition of the Bangladesh economy to a high growth path in the range of 5.5 to 7 per cent is dependent on its undertaking broader and deeper structural reforms. However, this chapter argues that political stability is a crucial requirement for high economic growth. There is a close connection among political instability, macroeconomic instability and low economic growth.

4.4   THE POLITICAL ECONOMY OF MACROECONOMIC INSTABILITY AND ECONOMIC GROWTH

The experience of high performing East and South East Asian economies shows that a stable macroeconomic environment is a necessary precondition for sustained economic growth . It is essentially a public good which a government must provide at an early stage of development. Low and stable inflation and positive real interest rates are the basic macroeconomic foundations for economic growth. A stable macroeconomic policy environment is also important for gaining high returns from social investment programmes (Quibria and Srinivasan 1994).

Bangladesh's average annual real GDP growth rates and inflation rates during 1973–95 show that the pattern is consistent with what has been observed elsewhere. If the figures for the first two years after independence are disregarded as they are outliers, the overall relationship between inflation and economic growth appears negative. One channel through which inflation affects economic growth is current account deficits. By adversely affecting international competitiveness, high and variable inflation exacerbates the external constraint on economic growth.

A. Hossain (1996c) examined the relationship between inflation and money supply more formally within an error correction model for Bangladesh. One main finding is that the wholesale price index, real output and the broad money supply form a cointegral relationship. Such a relationship appears robust as the error correction term is found significant in an error correction model of inflation. It appears that the excessive money supply growth is the result of large budget deficits of weak governments driven by either populist sentiment or legitimacy crisis of the regime requiring patronage. The government depended heavily on the banking system for financing budget deficits during the early 1970s. The mode of deficit financing has changed somewhat since then. Data compiled by Ghafur and O.H. Chowdhury (1988) show that the bulk of budget deficits in Bangladesh during 1973–84 was financed from foreign sources such as aid and that the domestic resource gap (overall budget deficit less foreign aid) is met by borrowing from the banking system. Domestic bank credit to the private sector was the single most important source of the money supply during the 1980s. The rapid expansion of bank credit to the private sector reflects the industrial policy shift toward increasing liberalisation and privatisation of the economy. Credit to the public sector is also an important source of monetary expansion. The government keeps the financial transactions of the public sector enterprises outside the budgetary accounts. As a result, while the size of government budget deficit appears low, the public sector deficits have remained high, causing an expansion of the money supply.

There are three broad overlapping explanations (hypotheses) for deficit financing in developing countries. The first, found in the literature on hyperinflation, maintains that deficit financing through money creation is a deliberate act to create inflation as a devise for 'forced savings' (A. Hossain and A. Chowdhury 1996). The second view, prominent among the structuralists, is that 'the authorities have imperfect control of the fiscal apparatus and that under these conditions, money creation is the only source of finance" (Dornbusch and Fischer 1981, p.330). Tanzi (1982) identifies five 'structural causes' of fiscal deficits in developing countries. They are: the price-inelastic tax system, the public sector enterprise performance, increased expenditure for political exigencies or administrative weaknesses, temporary export boom, and worsening of the external terms of trade. The third and emerging view is the political economy explanation, such as macroeconomic populism and macroeconomic opportunism. The former refers to a situation where a populist government undertakes ambitious programmes and gives priority to distributive objectives, whereas the latter arises when a non-democratic regime attempts to maintain and legitimise its rule by buying allegiance through state patronage. They are reflections of the weakness of the state where the government either caves in to the demands of narrow interest groups or courts interest groups for its survival. In both cases, the government underestimates the risk of deficit financing, inflation, external constraint, and the reaction of economic agents to aggressive non-market policies.

4.5   THE WEAKNESS OF THE STATE OF BANGLADESH

There is a close link between the nature of the state and the orientation of macroeconomic policies. Macroeconomic populism or macroeconomic opportunism arises when the state is weak and ravaged by rent-seeking groups. The weakness of the state, in turn, is the result of the nature of the political party/regime in power. A stylised flow chart of the weak state and macroeconomic crisis under both democratic and military governments is shown in Figure 4.1. Here a brief review of this nexus is explained in the context of Bangladesh.

**Petty-Bourgeoisie/ Socialist Political Party Government
and the Weak State**
↓↓
Redistributional/Populist Politics
↓↓
Expansionary Macroeconomic Policies, and Expansion of the Public
Sector, With Redistributional Objectives
↓↓
Soft Budget, Rent-Seeking, Budget Deficits, Money Creation
↓↓
Inflation, Trade Deficits Low Economic Growth, Foreign Debt, etc.
↓↓
MACROECONOMIC CRISIS

Military/Civil-Military Government and/or the Weak State
↓↓
Legitimization and Constituency Building
↓↓
Lobbying, Patronizing, Vote Buying
↓↓
Expansionary Macroeconomic Policies, and Reduction of the Public
Sector, with Patronizing Objectives
↓↓
Soft Budget, Rent Seeking, Budget Deficits, Money Creation
↓↓
Inflation, Trade Deficits Low Economic Growth, Foreign Debt, etc.
↓↓
MACROECONOMIC CRISIS

Figure 4.1   The weak state and macroeconomic crisis

The present state of Bangladesh is weak and not capable of maintaining what
Bardhan (1993, p.46) calls 'the discipline of the market against the inevitable
lobbies of group predation' in distributive politics. The Awami League is a
petty-*bourgeoisie* party. Since the autonomy movement in the late 1960s, it
adopted an inclusive strategy and attempted to satisfy all interest groups.
After Independence, the imposed nationalisation of industries, banks and
insurance companies, state trading, and central planning for economic

development provided an opportune vehicle for this political objective. The result was the creation of a patronage system, where the interest groups, including politicians and bureaucrats, got an easy access to state resources and then enriched themselves.

The Zia Government began dismantling the nationalised sector and reduced the role of central planning, a process accelerated during the Ershad Government. While this was a move in the right direction, the process was, in effect, used for the realignment of interest groups. Denationalisation was a means of drafting economically and politically powerful allies by transferring nationalised units to them. A new class of 'dubious' entrepreneurs was created and then the state rewarded them with various kinds of financial incentives. This *nouveau riche* class was the core bureaucratic-oligarchic political power base of both Zia and Ershad (Maniruzzaman 1992).

Three important organisational branches of government that affect macroeconomic policy configurations are the bureaucracy, the central bank and the parliament. A strong and elite bureaucracy often prevent governments from adopting expansionary populist policies by exposing their economic costs (World Bank 1993). Bangladesh does not have such a bureaucracy. To begin with, it lost a significant number of experienced top bureaucrats who opted for Pakistan. Then on the ground of collaboration with the Pakistani regime, the Awami League government purged the bureaucracy which weakened it further (M. Ahmad 1987). The final nail in the coffin was the politicisation of the bureaucracy. Thus the creation of a strong administrative capacity, one of the founding blocks of a 'good state' (Dornbusch 1993), was compromised during the early years after independence. Although a competitive selection process, albeit not rigorous, was put into effect at a later stage, the subsequent pseudo-civil regimes of Zia and Ershad contaminated the bureaucracy by implanting military officers at the top civil administrative positions as a means of excreting controls over an important government organ. They also used the bureaucracy as a refuse for retired (forced or otherwise) military officers either to silence the dissent or to buy support (Maniruzzaman 1992).

There is some evidence that a strong and independent central bank with a mandate for lower inflation can act as a constraint on government's deficit making propensity (Alesina and Summers 1993). The Bangladesh Bank has never been strong; it is just as another department of the Ministry of Finance. The Bank also does not have a mandate in achieving any clear-cut objective. The Ministry of Finance in its 1995 review (GOB 1995) summarised four objectives of monetary policy:

- growth of the economy
- stability of the external and internal value of the national currency
- reasonable price stability
- creation of productive capacity in the long run

When an organisation is given multiple and often conflicting objectives, there will obviously be trade-offs. It, however, does not say how this trade-off is weighed. When one takes into account of how the Board of Directors is constituted and the compliance requirement of government directives under the Bangladesh Bank Order 1972, there is little doubt that short-run political objectives always dominate. The multiplicity of conflicting objectives also allows the authority to pursue its own aim and hide its failure in one respect against the achievement in another. In other words, this is a recipe for avoiding accountability and incompetence.

In mature democracies, governments remain accountable to the parliament and the budgetary process goes through strict scrutiny. Unfortunately, this institution is also weak in Bangladesh. To begin with, the Awami League government had absolute domination of the parliament and did not tolerate any form of political opposition (Maniruzzaman 1980). It rigged the first parliamentary election of 1973 to prevent any opposition members from being elected when its victory and absolute majority was almost guaranteed. The subsequent parliaments were rubber-stamps and lacked political legitimacy. Thus the budgetary process remained at the whim of the ruling party which used government coffers to buy political supports.

The experience of successful economies of East and South East Asia shows that the pursuance of export-oriented, rather than inward-looking, industrialisation policies can act as an external constraint on the mismanagement of the economy. The external constraint is reinforced when there is a well developed financial sector which is generally averse to inflation. Unfortunately, none of these were (are) present in Bangladesh. While it followed an inward-looking industrialisation policies, the result was financial repression that retarded the development of a well functioning financial sector (A. Hossain and Rashid 1997). Thus, Bangladesh lacked both internal and external constraints that induce government to undertake responsible macroeconomic policies. In such a situation, government failures simply compound market failures which the government is supposed to mitigate through intervention.

4.6   CONCLUDING OBSERVATIONS

In the presence of imperfect political climate and market imperfections, there is a need for building institutions that would minimise both market and government failures. The main sources of market failures include monopoly imperfections, externalities, public goods, imperfect/asymmetric information, and transaction costs. In addition, it is often held that the market system does not typically produce a 'fair' distribution of income, implying a biased distribution of income in favour of the rich. One can identify at least four sources of government failures:

- lack of administrative capacity

- overzealous government rules and regulations

- inefficient political cycles

- rent-seeking behaviour

Most developing countries (including Bangladesh) are not endowed with a large pool of skilled administrators or bureaucrats. In addition, the lack of sufficient training can lead to a limited capacity to interpret and enforce rules and regulations. The situation in Bangladesh was made worse by successive regimes' attempt to corrupt and politicise the bureaucracy. Therefore, the institutional change must start with administrative reform as the creation of a strong administrative capacity is one of the founding blocks of a good state. It is paramount that a meritocratic civil bureaucracy recruited through a highly competitive examination is ensured. This must be boosted with the provision of a high quality training programme to enhance the administrative capacity. Administrative rules must be simplified and objectives of such rules be made clear to reduce the scope for corruption. Also the government departments must have clear demarcation of functions and should not have both social and economic objectives, which are often conflicting. This will enhance accountability and transparency. Any administrative reform must be supplemented by the legal system reform. Once the property rights are clearly defined and enforced by an independent judiciary, the area where government interventions are genuinely required becomes limited. The government should intervene only when there is a clearly defined market failure and concentrate in areas where it has a clear advantage, such as the maintenance of law and order, the enforcement of property rights, and the provision of infrastructure. Where government interventions are necessary, market based instruments (price) should be given priority over quantitative restrictions as a general principle.

The political process in Bangladesh is not accountable. Hence, political reforms are necessary to develop an accountable and responsive political system that creates an economically-aware and technically trained political/ bureaucratic elite for the management of the economy. Although a development-minded, authoritarian political regime may have certain advantages over democracy in promoting economic growth during the early stages of development, it can breed social and political instability in an underdeveloped society. What is important for development is the relative autonomy or insulation of the state against the ravages of both rent-seeking groups and pork-barrel politics by decision-makers: Authoritarianism is neither necessary nor sufficient for such insulation of the state (Bardhan 1988). A competitive democratic political system under well-defined rules and norms can accommodate the political aspirations of the people. However, it may remain exposed to rent seeking and pork-barrel politics unless the role of the private sector vis-a-vis public sector is sufficiently increased in economic activity. If the economy is adequately deregulated and opened up, the scope of patronage by both politicians and bureaucrats in a market-driven economic system will be limited. Politics may then become a relatively less attractive profession in economic sense and the state may be insulated from rent-seeking groups if price distortions are eliminated.

Any political reform should attempt to prevent the emergence of a coalition government or a situation where minority parties hold the balance of power. A coalition government is often found to delay adjustments as it is difficult to achieve agreement among partners on how to stabilise. Therefore, the institution of proportionality may not be conducive to swift fiscal reform when they are needed (Alesina 1992). If a situation does arise where minor parties hold the balance of power there is a danger of 'war of attrition' as each party waits for the other to concede. This happens as the cost of delay to each party is a private information. This sort of situation can be avoided in two ways. First, the cost of delay must be made explicit. Here lies the importance of an economically literate elite bureaucracy. Second, devise some institutional mechanism whereby the gainers compensate the losers.

Next turn to the crucial issue of macroeconomic performance of the government in the presence of inefficient political cycles which arise from either vote-maximising behaviour of politicians or legitimacy crisis of the regime. An independent central bank with a clear mandate for price stability enhances macroeconomic performance. Therefore, the Bangladesh Bank Order 1972 should be amended to give it a mandate to control inflation only rather than a host of conflicting objectives. This is in line with what has been proposed above in order to enhance accountability and transparency of government departments.

Therefore, the credibility of government's fiscal and monetary policy lies ultimately in the accountability and transparency of the budgetary process. Here lies the importance of an independent fiscal board (IFB). The IFB must have sufficient power to review government expenditure programmes and all new initiatives must be cleared by it. The idea of IFB is akin to an independent judiciary. Just as an independent judicial system monitors political interference with institutions for greater political efficiency, an IFB will ensure that the budgetary process is transparent and not influenced by political considerations. The transparency of the budgetary process will enhance efficiency in macroeconomic management. IFB is a superior arrangement than a 'fiscal constitution' restricting the government to a balanced budget. Such a constitutionally binding arrangement could be unnecessarily debilitating. IFB should work closely with an independent central bank in order to avoid any co-ordination problem between fiscal and monetary policies.

In a country where politicians have little respect for either constitution or institutions, and is prone to *coup-d'eta*, what guarantee is there that the arrangements suggested above would prevail? Here lies the importance of trade and financial liberalisation. The persuance of export-oriented, rather than inward-looking, industrialisation policies can act as an external constraint on the mismanagement of the economy. Large and persistent budget deficits can fuel the expectations of accelerating inflation and create balance of payments and exchange rate crises that lead to an eventual sharp devaluation of domestic currency. The fear of large depreciations of currency may cause massive capital flight, exacerbating the exchange rate crises. Most military dictators try to avoid exchange rate crisis and capital flights as they deepen their legitimacy crisis. Incidentally, macroeconomic stability and economic growth are powerful weapons that legitimise the dictatorial regimes. Trade liberalisation must be supplemented by financial sector development. A well developed financial sector will act as an internal constraint on inflationary financing.

In sum, institutional change, administrative, legal and constitutional reforms along with liberalisation of the economy are essential ingredients for a sustained improvement in macroeconomic performance. The changes suggested here are compatible with a democratic political system.

5 Economic Liberalisation and Growth in Bangladesh: The Role of Foreign Private Investment

M. Yunus Ali

5.1 INTRODUCTION

Bangladesh, a relatively younger member of the world community of independent nations, is the third largest country in South Asia in terms of area, population, and total GNP (next to India and Pakistan). The *near-homogenous* community of 120 million people is a potentially attractive market for many consumer products. But the country suffers from an image problem in the foreign business community that affect its programmes of economic development. Poverty and natural disaster is the only stereotypical image of Bangladesh that the world community seems to be aware of. The foreign media still find much interest in the news items of 'human and ecological disasters' in Bangladesh (Wright 1994). However, the country has achieved some positive economic results in recent years and progressing steadily towards its goal of economic growth. Some achievements[1] include *inter alia*: increase in real GDP growth (5.7 per cent in 1997 compared to 5.3 per cent in 1996 and an average of 4.3 per cent during 1992–95 and 4.1 per cent during 1985–90), export growth (on an average of 21.6 per cent during 1992–96), gross capital formation (16.9 per cent in 1996 compared to an average of 13 per cent during 1991–95 and 12.7 per cent during 1985–90) and a low inflation rate (2.7 per cent in 1996 compared to 4.5 per cent during 1990–95, and 9.8 per cent during 1985–90).

The gradual economic liberalisation that started in the early 1980s is taking shape under democratically elected governments since 1991. This chapter will analyse the liberalisation programmes since the 1980s and their impact on attracting foreign investment in Bangladesh and on economic growth. Different policy issues are reviewed in terms of their ability to attract inflow of foreign private investment. Investment inflows in different industrial sectors are also reviewed to evaluate growth potential in each. The chapter concludes with some recommendations for achieving objectives of accelerated economic growth.

5.2   BACKGROUND TO RESTRICTIVE ECONOMIC POLICY IN BANGLADESH

The restrictive economic policies of Bangladesh has historical links to colonial British rules in India up to 1947 as well as similar economic policies of Pakistan between 1947 and 1971. Both India and Pakistan adopted restrictive economic policies after independence from the British rule in 1947. Imports were restricted through licensing and foreign exchange control mechanisms. Import substituting industrial policy protected local industries through high tariffs. Foreign direct investments were reacted with suspicion and the question of whole foreign ownership of industrial assets was considered to be economic imperialism of the mighty western Multinational Corporations (Vernon 1971). Technology licensing and joint ownership with local firms were most preferred forms of foreign investments in the sub-continent. This restrictive foreign ownership policy, however, was a clear deterrent for major Transnational Corporations (TNCs) who seek internalisation of markets through uninterrupted investment in foreign markets (Dunning 1988; Williamson 1975). This policy especially discouraged major TNCs from investing in high R&D and marketing oriented manufacturing sectors as part of their corporate policy of protecting technology and know-how from possible dilution due to sharing of ownership and control with local firms. This affected adequate industrial growth and created some private investment-shy sectors, especially in heavy industries. This was the case especially in this agro-based region of Bangladesh which suffered from lack of local capital and industrial entrepreneurs.

In the 1960s, the Pakistan government established state-owned development corporations in the industrial and financial sectors for direct collaboration with private entrepreneurs. These corporations provided long-term industrial finance to private entrepreneurs and were responsible for establishing large capital intensive projects for future divestment to private entrepreneurs. This created a significant stake of the state-owned corporations in the country's overall industrial and financial sectors. In the then East Pakistan, the entire financial and manufacturing sectors were dominated by state-owned enterprises and private investments by West Pakistani entrepreneurs. Pakistan government created this region a 'captive market' for West Pakistani private entrepreneurs and discriminated against foreign private investment. Only 22 foreign companies had some direct investment in pre-independent Bangladesh (see Table 5.1) and total foreign investment constituted only one percent of fixed industrial assets (Reza et al. 1987).

5.3   PRIVATE SECTOR DURING THE EARLY YEARS OF BANGLADESH

At the time of independence from Pakistan in 1971, Bangladesh inherited a large public sector and also increased that base through the take-over of abandoned businesses previously owned by [West] Pakistani owners. The government also nationalised major industries, banks and insurance (except foreign) companies.

The socialist oriented industrial policy of 1973 assigned a very minor role for the private sector in the industrial activities. A ceiling of Tk 2.5 millions was fixed for initial investment which could be increased up to Tk. 3.5 millions for reinvestment of profits. However, the initial pessimism of the government policy makers about the role of private sector started to falter. The revised industrial policy of 1974 started to encourage private sector by enhancing the ceiling to Tk 30 millions, and encouraging both local and foreign private investors to set up industries in joint collaboration with public sector corporations in certain industries. It also offered incentives to private investments including tax holiday and concessional tariffs on imports of machineries and parts. However, these incentives did not encourage many private investors due mainly to lack of investors' confidence and growing economic volatility. Investment in trading businesses was more lucrative than investment in industrial ventures.

Although no foreign company was nationalised and the industrial policy of 1974 explicitly declared a moratorium on any expropriation or nationalisation of foreign interest, the socialist oriented economic policy of the government acted as a deterrent for potential foreign investors to reach the shore of Bangladesh. The next two years was a period of extreme political and economic turmoil. The brutal killing of President Sheikh Mujibur Rahman and other ministers of his cabinet followed by a series of military *coups* and counter *coups* gave birth to military regimes of one form or another for the next 15 years. The country lost the opportunity of setting up a long term economic direction and effective rules for better economic management (see also Chapter 4).

Table 5. 1   Foreign investment outside export processing zones

Financial Year	Number of projects registered	Foreign capital involvement (in million Taka)
Pre 1971	22	203.51
1972–1976	0	0
1977	4	9.73
1978	0	0
1979	3	88.99
1980	10	61.67
1981	3	6.00
1982	7	206.33
1983	14	521.06
1984	7	122.13
1985	5	145.91
1986	8	90.82
1987	17	1829.03
1988	17	1845.32
1989	11	1210.77
1990	34	2122.80
1991(end June)	12	137.88
1991–92	24	433.99
1992–93	28	1369.32
1993–94	100	27519.30
1994–95	145	12501.76
1995–96	127	47276.45
1996–97	138	26044.40
Total	736	123747.17

Sources: Compiled by the author from the list of Foreign Private Investment and updated information supplied by the Board of Investment, Prime Minister's Secretariat, People's Republic of Bangladesh, Dhaka, Bangladesh.

5.4   FOREIGN PRIVATE INVESTMENT DURING 1976–90

The military regime of General Ziaur Rahman introduced certain changes in the industrial policy in 1976. These included an increase in private investment ceiling up to Tk. 100 million, opening up of several sectors for private investment and deletion of the assurance of a moratorium on nationalisation which was considered to be a deterrent for private investment. In addition, the programme of privitisation was adopted to reduce the size of public sector and increase confidence of private sector participation. But these changes did not encourage inflow of much foreign private investment into the country. Only four joint venture projects were registered in 1977 with three more in 1979 (see Table 5.1). Total foreign capital in those seven projects was around Tk.100 million. Complete foreign ownership still remained restricted.

Some significant changes were introduced in 1980 with the enactment of two pieces of legislation. These changes opened up the country for foreign private investment. The Foreign Private Investment (Promotion and Protection) Act 1980 provided for the protection and equitable treatment to foreign investment, indemnification of any losses of foreign investment, protection from unilateral change of any terms of sanctioned conditions, and more importantly, guarantee against expropriation or nationalisation of foreign private investment without compensation, and repatriation of invested capital and profits. This encouraged a few foreign investors in 1980 when 10 small foreign investment projects were registered with a total foreign capital of Tk. 61.67 million. But the tempo levelled off in the following year due to another political turbulence after the assassination of President Ziaur Rahman in 1981 and military take-over by General Hussain Mohammad Ershad in 1982.

The second Act of the parliament passed in 1980 paved the way for foreign investment in special economic zones to promote export oriented industrialisation and employment creation. The Bangladesh Export Processing Zones Authority Act 1980 created an Authority to establish special economic zones known as Export Processing Zones (EPZs) in two port cities and in Dhaka to facilitate value-added export operations. The Act provided for the exemption of a zone from the operation of all or any of the provisions of certain enactments including income tax, foreign exchange control, customs and excise, employment and industrial relations. Foreign investments in complete foreign ownership or joint venture were encouraged in export oriented projects. The first EPZ in Chittagong (CEPZ) started operation in 1983 but its utilisation level remained below the expectation level for several years. Total investment figure in the CEPZ did not reach even the 50 million mark until 1990–91 and most of the growth occurred since the democratic government came to power in 1991 (see Table 5.2).

Ershad continued with the policy of economic liberalisation. The industrial policy of 1986 opened up of some more sectors for private investment and emphasised the expedition of privatisation of nationalised and taken-over industrial enterprises. Board of Investment (BOI) was established in 1989 as a one-stop shop for registration and providing support services to foreign and local investors. Several important changes were made in the revised industrial policy in 1990 to encourage investment. These included allowing 100 per cent foreign ownership in industrial enterprise outside EPZ areas, abolishing the need for prior BOI approval for minority foreign owned joint venture projects with total investment not exceeding Tk. 100 millions, and withdrawal of the provision for compulsory public issue in joint venture projects with total paid-up capital not exceeding Tk 50 million.

Despite these positive moves, only a few foreign investment projects were attracted during this period (see Table 5.1) and only 72 foreign firms were operating at the end of 1990. The most plausible explanation for this low response could be the lack of investors' confidence due to lack political stability in the country and investors' perceived gap between government's promises and actual delivery of those promised incentives[2]. This was the longest serving regime in the political history of Bangladesh but the period was politically the most turbulent one as well. Both major political parties (the Awami League and the BNP) resisted stabilisation of this regime throughout the period and finally forced its end through a mass upsurge in 1990 reminiscent of the overthrow of the Ayub regime in 1969.

5.5   LIBERALISATION POLICIES OF THE DEMOCRATICALLY
       ELECTED GOVERNMENTS

Democratically elected government led by the BNP came to power in 1991 and adopted several economic liberalisation policies. A comprehensive reform package was introduced. The package included tax reform (introduction of Value Added Tax) liberalisation of tariff protection, and liberalisation of industrial sector. The Industrial Policy of 1991 emphasised the role of private sector to accelerate the rate of industrialisation and promised to 'remove obstacles' and 'simplify complex procedures' of private investments. The policy emphasised that 'the government will play a catalytic role rather than a regulatory one' (GOB 1991a). To this end government abolished the need for prior permission for setting up industries with entrepreneurs' own fund (including non-repatriable foreign exchange) or with funds from private banks or financing institutions. The development financing institutions and

Table 5.2 Investment, employment and exports by project in export processing zones, 1983–84 to 1997–98

Financial Year	Investment		Number	Employment		Amount (million & investment US$)	Export ratio**	Export		
	Amount (million US$)	Cumulated total investment		Cumulated total employment	Investment dollars per employee*			Export dollars per employee***	Total (million US$)	EPZ Export as % of total export
1983–84	0.87	0.87	624	624	1394.23	0.16	.18	256	822.00	0.20
1984–85	1.60	2.47	1156	1780	1384.08	4.45	1.80	2500	934.44	0.48
1985–86	3.60	6.07	732	2512	4918.03	7.59	1.25	3022	819.20	0.93
1986–87	6.63	12.70	728	3240	9107.14	15.27	1.20	4713	1073.77	1.42
1987–88	1.79	14.49	198	3438	9040.40	13.93	.96	4052	1231.12	1.13
1988–89	2.72	17.21	769	4207	3537.06	16.08	.93	3822	1285.92	1.25
1989–90	8.58	25.79	2794	7001	3070.87	34.21	1.33	4886	1523.70	2.25
1990–91	22.05	47.84	2363	9364	9331.36	47.99	1.00	5125	1717.55	2.79
1991–92	23.66	71.50	5250	14614	4506.67	76.99	1.08	5268	1993.09	3.86
1992–93	22.05	93.55	3114	17728	7080.92	127.05	1.36	7167	2382.89	5.33
1993–94	37.40	130.95	8608	26336	4344.80	145.6	1.11	5529	2934.00	4.96
1994–95	35.93	166.88	6141	32477	5850.84	228.26	1.37	7028	3733.00	6.11
1995–96	32.59	199.47	10706	43183	3044.09	337.02	1.69	7804	3917.00	8.60
1996–97	53.90	253.37	12773	55956	4219.84	462.76	1.83	8270	4256.00	10.64

Notes: Investment, Employment and Export figures up to 1993–94 period are for Chittagong Export Processing Zone only.

* Investment dollars per employee = Total investment of the year ÷ number of employment created.

** Export/Investment ratio = amount of export from EPZs ÷ cumulated investment up to the year

*** Export dollars per employee = amount of export from EPZs ÷ cumulated number of employment up to the year.

Sources:

a. Investment, Employment and Export figures from Bangladesh Export Processing Zone Authority, Dhaka, Bangladesh.

b. Total Export figures from World Bank (1995a, p.188) and EIU (1997, p.5). Other analytic statistics are computed by the author.

nationalised commercial banks were initially given power to sanction industries worth up to Tk. 300 million and without limit since 1992.

The new policy provided tax incentives (including tax holidays of up to 12 years, non-discriminatory duties and taxes for private and public sector and accelerated depreciation of up to 100) protection for private investors from the impact of fluctuation of exchange rate on foreign currency loans, and special incentives to encourage foreign currency investments by non-resident Bangladeshis. Export-oriented industrialisation was re-emphasised by providing new incentives (such as simplifying duty drawback scheme, local tax exemption, cash incentives and venture capital facilities for export oriented firms in crash-thrust sectors) and continuing other incentives such as concessional duty on imported machineries, special bonded warehouse facilities for imported materials, liberal loans, and export credit guarantee schemes.

Government attached special importance to encouraging foreign investments. Major liberalisation provisions of this new direction in policy include:

- no limit on foreign equity participation (i.e. up to 100 per cent)

- no obligation for joint venture or wholly-owned foreign companies to sell shares through public issue irrespective of the amount of paid-up capital

- allowing foreign investors to obtain working capital loans equivalent to their foreign equity amount

- allowing foreign investors to buy shares through stock exchanges

- provision for rules to protect intellectual property rights such as patents, designs and trade-marks and copyrights

- tax exemption on royalties, technical know-how and technical assistance, interest on foreign loans, and capital gains from transfer of shares.

These policy directions and other macroeconomic reforms have led to greater foreign capital inflows. The number of private foreign investment project approved by BOI and the amount of foreign capital inflow increased dramatically, especially during 1993–94 to 1995–96 (see Table 5.1). The investment inflows in EPZs also increased significantly during this period (see Table 5.2). The average investment inflows in EPZs during the 1991–92 to 1995–96 period exceeded US$30 million per annum compared to US$5.98 million per annum during the 1983–84 to 1990–91 period.

Investment growth in EPZs also significantly contributed to the boost in employment and export during this period (see Table 5.2). Volume of employment surged from a cumulated total of 9364 person years during the 1983–84 to 1990–91 period (an average of 1170 per annum) to a cumulated total of 43183 person years by the end of the 1991–92 to 1995–96 period. Export grew from around US$48 million in 1990–91 to US$337 million in 1995–96.

A further analysis of the investment, employment and export statistics of EPZs revealed some interesting results. Further insights on these statistics are provided in Table 5.2 and briefly discussed in this section. First, the investment dollars per individual employment in the EPZs were reasonably low (on an average of US$5060 with a range between US$1384 and US$9331) indicating labour intensity of the EPZ projects. Labour intensity of the projects even increased since the democratically elected BNP government came to power. The average investment per employee was reduced to slightly less than US$4500 during the 1991–92 to 1995–96 period from around US$5100 during the 1983–84 to 1990–91 period. Second, labour productivity in terms of export per employee also jumped from US$4017 per annum during the 1984–85 to 1990–91 period to over US$6560 per annum during the 1991–92 to 1995–96 period. Ratio of export to investment also increased significantly from an average of 1.08 during the first eight years to an average of 1.36 during the 1991–92 to 1995–96 period[3].

An analysis of export from EPZs as a proportion of total export of Bangladesh over the years also revealed an interesting trend of growth. Export from EPZs as a proportion of total export grew from less than half a percentage point in 1984–85 to up to 2.79 percent by the 1990–91 financial year; but it reached 6.11 percent of total export by the end of the next five years period. These performances show some signs of positive outcomes of the export-led industrial growth strategy. Moreover, the reform programme was able to bring macroeconomic stability which can be fruitfully exploited for faster economic growth (World Bank 1995a).

The general election of 1996 brought the Awami League to power. The new government reiterated the importance of private sector in the country's industrialisation. Industrial policy reforms of the government included:

- further liberalisation of industrial policy

- approval of policy parameters and incentives for private power generation

- enactment of laws allowing private sector to establish Export Processing Zones where industrial units will enjoy facilities similar to those in Government EPZs

- lifting 'lock-in' rule for portfolio private investors to encourage inflow of foreign funds
- steps taken for full convertibility of the local currency in 1998
- creation of Law and Administrative Reform Commissions to up-date existing laws and modernise administrative system
- enhancement of other incentives and simplifying procedural matters (BOI 1997a)

Increasing investors' interest in the investments in EPZs in recent years has encouraged the government to expand the Dhaka EPZ and establish third EPZ at Gazipur (near Dhaka) and enact law allowing establishment of EPZs at the private sector. South Korean investors are leading foreign investors at Chittagong and Dhaka EPZs and more investors are showing greater interest in them. South Korean entrepreneurs led by a leading investor at Chittagong and Dhaka EPZs have also applied for establishing wholly-owned foreign private EPZ at Chittagong (BOI 1997c). So far foreign investment projects approved by BOI and investment inflows at EPZs are maintaining trend of the last five years. Foreign investment project approval by the BOI during the 1996–97 financial year slightly increased. Although foreign capital involvement in these projects was less than the previous year, it maintained the average growth of capital inflows during the 1991–92 to1995–96 period. Growth in the EPZ sector was more encouraging than the previous years (see Table 5.2). Both capital inflow and employment surged to a record high in 1996–97 financial year (US$53.9 million and 12773 respectively). Export from EPZs also reached a record of 10.64 per cent of total exports. Recently, more than a dozen of international petroleum companies negotiated agreement for oil and gas exploration in Bangladesh. These continuing growth statistics certainly indicate signs of growing investors' confidence on the country's continuing liberalisation of the economy and macroeconomic reforms.

5.5.1   Growth performance since 1991

A World Bank Report on Bangladesh suggests that the country's macroeconomic stability provides an unprecedented window of opportunity for the government to accelerate reforms aimed at reaching a high GDP growth path of 6 to 7 percent per annum over the medium term (World Bank 1995b, p.33). The report suggested an accelerated reforms scenario to achieve high growth and a slow reforms scenario that may lead the country to a stagnant investment and GDP growth path. Table 5.3 compares Bangladesh's performance with the accelerated reforms scenario. The performance records on GDP growth rate and gross fixed investment are far below the expected levels for an accelerated growth scenario. Especially its performance on gross fixed investment (on an average 13 per cent of GDP) is alarmingly low and clearly in line with the low reforms scenario.

Bangladesh performed rather well on three external indicators (exports, imports, and current account balance). Export growth throughout the period clearly indicates its achievement in pursuing the export oriented industrialisation target. A significant part of the export growth can be attributed to investment and export growths in EPZs, and successful implementation of the on-going programmes of increasing investment in government and private sector EPZs can push the export growth further up. Import growth also exceeded World Bank's expectations for an accelerated reforms scenario. Current account over the years shows much better than expected level of performance and much of the credit could be attributed to the growth of foreign remittance from non-resident Bangladeshis. National savings for the fiscal year 1996–97 (14.2 per cent compared to 11.9 per cent in 1995–96) is a good sign for the country with low savings record. A significant source of this growth can also be attributed to the growth of remittance from non-resident Bangladeshis. This picture indicates that much need to be done to increase domestic savings to finance the accelerated economic growth agenda. Furthermore, proper channelisation of remittances from non-resident Bangladeshis to industrial capital formation is important for sustainable economic growth.

5.5.2   Miles to go to attain expected economic growth

This mixed performance record raises questions on the whole reforms programme as well as the political developments in Bangladesh. The role of political institutions in economic stability and growth cannot be ignored (A. Hossain 1997a). Highly impressive incentive package for foreign and local private investment could be meaningless for the investors unless political stability and stability of reforms agenda are established. Consensus among major political parties on some reform agenda and procedures of delivering them is an important precondition for economic stability and growth. A. Hossain (1997a) explained how arch rivalry between two major political parties use the strategy of confrontational politics for political gains. This strategy has severely affected the much needed political stability to transform the economic stability into economic growth.[4]

Another irony of the political institutions in Bangladesh is their inability to insulate the State from rent-seeking groups. Privatisation of the state-owned

Table 5.3   Bangladesh economic performance, 1992–93 to 1997–98

Economic	Fiscal Year ending June				
Indicators	1993	1994	1995	1996	1997	1998
GDP Growth Rate (%):						
World Bank Expectation**	4.5	4.8	5.2	5.7	6.3	6.7
Current Performance***	4.5	4.2	4.4	5.3	5.7a	5.4b
Gross Fixed Investment						
(% of GDP):						
World Bank Expectation	12.7	13.8	15.4	17.0	18.1	18.7
Current Performance	NA	NA	21.3	12.8	13.1a	12.3b
Exports/GDP (%):						
World Bank Expectation	9.6	10.3	11.0	11.6	12.1	12.5
Current Performance	10.6	11.5	12.9	12.6	12.9a	13.6b
Imports/GDP (%):						
World Bank Expectation	–16.6	–16.7	–17.7	–18.9	–19.8	–20.6
Current Performance	–15.3	–17.0	–20.1	–21.1	–22.3a	–23.6b
Current Account Balance:						
World Bank Expecation	–2.20	–1.80	–2.50	–3.10	–3.80	–4.30
Current Performance	0.36	0.20	–0.82	–0.96	–1.09a	–1.16b
National Savings:						
World Bank Expectation	10.5	12.0	12.9	13.9	14.3	14.4
Current Performance	NA	NA	NA	11.9c	14.2c	NA

Notes: **   World Bank estimate for Accelerated Reform Scenario
                    (World Bank 1995).
             ***   Actual figures unless otherwise indicated.
             a   estimate of Bangladesh officials and EIU;
             b   estimate of EIU;
             c   World Bank update, *News From Bangladesh*
                    (Internet Edition), Dhaka, 15 August 1997.

Source: Compiled by the author from World Bank (1995b) and
             EIU (1997).

industrial enterprises are in the agenda of most political parties but their commitment to that agenda was questioned in some forums (World Bank 1995a). Transparency of the privatisation programme is important to reach the target and increase public and investor confidence.

Performance of the money and capital markets is another area of concern for the investors. Banking sector of the country is ranked highly on restrictions, lack of innovativeness and inefficiency (World Bank 1995a). The default culture of a section of the country's industrial borrowers has created a serious problem in the money and capital markets. Undue political interference in financial institutions' lending policies and decisions, and government's inability to insulate the state-owned financial institutions from the rent-seeking privileged groups are partly responsible for this default loan culture[5]. The present government's declared policy of not supporting any default borrowers is certainly a big step to curve default culture[6]. The Banks' lending and loan collection practices need immediate attention to increase depositors' and investors' confidence. Government's reform agenda for the banking sector need immediate attention because of the turmoils in the money and capital markets of Southeast Asia.

Bangladesh needs immediate reforms in the Administrative Services areas to deliver the government's reforms in other sectors. Rigid bureaucracy, red tape and lack of transparency in government procedural requirements are some of the reasons for administrative inefficiencies in Bangladesh. The term 'simplification of complex procedures' used repeatedly in most industrial policies in recent years has rarely been practised. The procedural documents must be transparent, clearer and made public for potential users so that users can understand what they can expect from whom in the bureaucratic ladder. The current government's agenda on reforms of administrative services should provide for accountability of the service providers in every step.

Cheap labour is the major resource-base for the country's competitive edge. Labour productivity in Bangladesh is one of the lowest in the World. However, the labour sector has the reputation of quick trainability. Technical training and trade courses to feed the export-oriented industrial sectors can generate a pool of readily employable labour force and increase labour productivity. Other South and Southeast Asian countries are also competing for entry into the global market with similar or better resource base. For example, of late India has liberalised its economy but her huge local market potential, good literacy base coupled with other factors such as entrepreneurship attracted a significant boost in foreign capital inflows. Capital inflow galloped from less than two hundeded million US dollars to a billion dollar in US$155 million in 1991 to US$950 million in 1994 and and to two billion US dollars in 1996 (Shand and Kalirajan 1997, pp.28–9). To compete with a large competitor on the same footing, Bangladesh needs a well organised human development programme.

5.6   CONCLUDING OBSERVATIONS

This chapter highlights some of the recent developments in the foreign investment climate in Bangladesh. It clearly shows the sigh of economic stability under the economic liberalisation agenda of the democratically elected governments since 1991. The state of stability remained unchanged in terms of some macroeconomic indicators indicating a growth potential slower than desired to get out of the 'vicious cycle of economic, social and political stagnation'. Some other reform agenda need to be implemented immediately to transform the stability to growth. A strong political leadership with correct economic policy direction is important to attain that objective. Stable government policies for the private sector, transforming the current interventionist governmental role to a supportive one, and the freeing of the public sector corporations' policy-making from political interference can create a more attractive investment climate in Bangladesh.

The government of Sheikh Hasina has emphasised the regional economic cooperation through bilateral and multilateral arrangements for faster economic growth. Normalisation of relation with other South Asian countries through peaceful settlement of disputes and removal of impediments to peaceful coexistence in the region, strengthening regional cooperation, and the formation of sub-regional economic groups are some of the positive steps of the government. However, some form of consensus among major political parties is an important precondition to benefit from these initiatives. The recently concluded trilateral business summit of the prime ministers and business leaders of Bangladesh, India and Pakistan can provide an opportunity to carry forward the agenda of expanding trade, investment and business ties within the region for mutual benefits. This author's own research on a cross-section of international joint ventures in Bangladesh revealed that some joint ventures from neighbouring South Asian countries fared relatively well compared to other groups (M. Yunus Ali 1995; Sim and M. Yunus Ali 1997). Cooperative business ventures between firms from within the region can benefit from the advantages of cultural similarity and psychic proximity over similar joint ventures with firms from outside the region (Ali and Sim 1996). However, a positive political environment is necessary to encourage intra-regional investment and business ties for mutual benefits. Political leaders of the country should learn from the increasing trend of economic regionalisation in Southeast Asia, Europe, America, and in the Pacific region so that much needed economic cooperation within the region takes a real shape. All major political parties in Bangladesh recognise the role of foreign private investments for faster economic growth, and anti-foreign investment sentiment is not in the political agenda of any political party. This is certainly an important positive point in the assessment of political risks in Bangladesh. But the country's political environment has been suffering from another syndrome which is scanned negatively by the global business community. Opposition bashing tactics of the political parties affects the much needed responsible politics in the country. Many productive days have been lost due to this political reason since the democratically elected government came to power in 1991. This could easily be avoided through responsible political thinking of the leaders in the best interest of the country.

ACKNOWLEDGEMENTS

The author would like to thank an anonymous reviewer and a joint editor, Dr. Mohammad Alauddin for helpful comments on earlier drafts of this chapter. He is also grateful to Mr. Abul Kalam Azad (Trade Consul, Bangladesh High Commission, Canberra) Mr. A.Z.M. Azizur Rahman, (BEPZA, Dhaka) and Mr. S.H.M. Zahirul Haque, (BOI, Dhaka) for their assistance in supplying up-to-date information on foreign investment in Bangladesh. The usual *caveats* apply.

NOTES

1 Figures for 1996 and 1997 from EIU Country Report, *Bangladesh,* 3rd Quarter 1997; and those for 1985 to 1995 from A. Hossain (1997a, p.6).

2 For example, during personal interviews with this author, several expatriate senior management personnel of international joint venture projects in Bangladesh expressed their dissatisfaction with government bureaucracy on delivering the legal entitlement of the promised facilities. One senior manager complained 'Bangladesh government promise more to encourage investors but deliver a little when the investor is already in'.

3   The analysis of the ratio of export to investment is only for exploratory purpose. Time lag between the start of a project (the actual inflow of capital) and commercial production (actual export) must be taken into consideration for such an analysis. The actual time lag of the EPZ projects in Bangladesh was not available for rigorous analysis of that extent. Taken that time lag into consideration, actual ratio should be higher than those reported here.

4   Comments of former British Prime Minister John Major, the US and South Korean envoys clearly warned against the growing political instability and its effect on the business environment in Bangladesh.

5   Based on this author's interviews with senior executives of some major financial institutions in Bangladesh during 1991–92.

6   See Prime Minister Sheikh Hasina's comments during the meeting with the Executive Committee of Dhaka Metropolitan Chamber of Commerce and Industry, *The Daily Ittefaq* (Internet Edition) 8 January 1998, pp.7–8.

6 South Asia's Agricultural Commodity Exports: What Prospects?

Moazzem Hossain

6.1 INTRODUCTION

The successful conclusion of the GATT Uruguay Round and the subsequent implementation of the agreements under the World Trade Organisation (WTO) have opened up access to new markets for agricultural commodities in both more developed and developing countries. South Asia, one of the major growers of agricultural commodity, and a major growth region in the present world, has bright prospects in exporting agricultural products. The trade prospect in South Asia is to be influenced by the region's attempts in stabilisation, and reforming the economic policies as well as by changes in the external environment and internal policy adjustments to those changes. The principal external factors that need to be watched closely are: economic growth, inflation and interest rates in industrial countries, world commodity prices, international capital flows and world trade.

This chapter investigates the world trade factor in the context of South Asia. It, however, concentrates only on the four major countries in the region: Bangladesh, India, Pakistan and Sri Lanka. The specific objectives of this investigation are to:

- examine the prospects these South Asian nations have for expanding their current trade in agricultural commodities; and

- identify the potential areas of exports in terms of products and markets particularly for Bangladesh.

In the recent past, major trade models within the World Bank, GATT, OECD and other international organisations have estimated the gains and losses from the Uruguay Round for developed nations. Some models are based on individual country and others are structured in more aggregated terms with regional data. The purpose here is not to evaluate these models or review their quantitative results. The objective is to make a qualitative assessment of the Round and to assess how the Round's outcome will impact on South Asia's future trade.

6.2   URUGUAY ROUND AND TRADE ISSUES

Like all other participants, South Asia is likely to experience gains and losses from the Uruguay Round agreements. It is difficult to quantify at this stage the exact value of gains and losses. However, it is possible to identify the areas and industries where gains are likely to be achieved and where losses are likely to occur. Let us, first, look at the areas of gains. In the four South Asian nations under study, the gains are not expected to be similar. This is due mainly to the qualitative differences in the nature of liberalisation introduced in these countries. It is expected that as Sri Lanka undertook significant measures of economic reform over the last two decades, it will gain substantially more than the other three countries. The gains for the remaining three nations will be modest due to their inability to bring substantial structural reforms in their economies.

Regarding the agreements of the Uruguay Round the major concern in this region is about trade in agriculture, textiles and clothing. In agriculture, particularly in the region's food grain importing countries, the cost of food imports is likely to be higher and create adverse impacts. It is, however, important to note that the South Asian nations currently import lesser volume of food grains compared to their imports in the 1960s and 1970s. Effectively, all the countries under study currently enjoy self-sufficiency in food grain production except Sri Lanka and Bangladesh. Bangladesh, however, in recent years has been successful in cutting the shortfalls and is likely to become self-sufficient in the near future.

Due to the elimination of the multifibre arrangement (MFA) in textiles and clothing, it is likely that all developing countries will suffer from reduced rents in post-2005 era (Pigato et al. 1997). South Asia, however, will be in a better position than other developing nations with respect to expanding exports, to the restricted developed markets. World Bank (1995a, p.37) argues that 'by liberalizing their own trade, passing price changes through their producers, and pursuing flexible economic policies at home, developing countries will be able to exploit the market access advantages offered by the industrial countries and reap the benefits of the induced investment'. The GATT Secretariat expects that several sectors of South Asian trade will receive a comparative advantage over others in receiving a boost from the outcome of the Uruguay Round. It has been estimated that after 10 years the clothing trade will be up by 60 per cent more than it would without the Round. Similarly, textile will be up by 34 per cent and agricultural, forestry, marine, processed food and beverage products by 19 to 20 per cent more (World Bank 1995a). South Asia's loss from the outcome of the Round can be expected in two major areas: (1) erosion of trade preference in the post-Uruguay Round era and (2) high cost of food imports. All South Asian nations enjoyed preferential trade with almost all OECD nations on a bilateral basis. This preference will erode under the Uruguay Round agreements. South Asian nations enjoyed preferential trading with EU and North American countries, particularly in the areas of textiles and clothing. These facilities will not be available to these nations in the post-Uruguay Round period. It is, however, argued by Lall (1994) that the effects of Uruguay Round tariff changes on Asia's least developed countries (13 nations including four countries under present study) will be minimum. Lall (1994) estimated the impact of the Round agreements on the exports of Asia's least developed countries in three markets: US, EU and Japan. The estimates showed that only 2.37 per cent of the total exports by Asian least developed countries to these markets will be affected. In monetary terms, this loss will be only $38.43 million. These figures, however, suggest that the erosion of preferential trading is not a major issue for South Asia's least developed countries including the countries considered in the present study.

In the pre-Round era the industrial countries have been intervening in agricultural markets heavily in terms of import protection and export subsidies that contributed to low prices of agricultural commodities, especially food products. However, through the Round agreements such an intervention by the industrial countries will disappear and as a result the world food prices are likely to increase. The increased food prices in the world market will add to the import bills of the food importing nations. The South Asian nations, as explained earlier, will be affected least because South Asia currently imports a smaller quantity of foodgrains.

It is, however, argued that since the actual agricultural liberalisation achieved by the Round is relatively limited, price changes ranging from 1 to 4 per cent are expected for major food groups. Table 6.1 shows the changes in agricultural prices in the post-Uruguay Round. It is seen from Table 6.1 that the price of only wheat and coarse grains will be affected to a large extent. The South Asian nations are not big importers of wheat and will face only a little impact of this price change.

Table 6.1   Annual percentage changes in agricultural prices due to
agricultural liberalisation to 2002

Commodity	Changes in Prices
Beef, Veal and Mutton	0.6
Coarse Grains	2.3
Cocoa	–0.7
Coffee	–1.5
Cotton	–1.2
Dairy	1.2
Rice	–0.9
Sugar	1.8
Tea	–1.4
Vegetable Oils	–0.3
Wheat	3.8
Wool	–0.9
Other Agriculture	0.8
Other Food Products	–1.4
Other Meats	–0.6

Source: World Bank (1995a) Cited in Goldin and Ven der
Mensbrugghe (1995).

6.3   COMPOSITION OF SOUTH ASIAN TRADE

The composition of South Asian trade have changed substantially over the
last two decades. The existing composition of South Asian trade can be
presented in two forms: commodity trade and trading with services.

6.3.1   Commodity trade

In the recent years, all countries under study have undergone changes in their
commodity trade.

Bangladesh's imports in the recent years comprise more manufactured
goods, machinery and transport equipment compared to traditional food items.
Prominent manufactured items are: textile yarns, cement, iron and other metals,
rubber products, paper and paper boards and metal manufactures. Bangladesh
is also at present less dependent on traditional exports such as jute, leather
and tea. The 'non-traditional' garment industry overtook jute as a major export
earner and in recent times comprises more than 60 per cent of the total exports.

There has been considerable success in developing a sufficient export trade in frozen and other processed fish products of which shrimps are the dominant export item under this category.

A major feature of India's trade in the recent years has been the radical change in its composition. Jute and tea were the major export items in the 1960s but at present the major exports include engineering goods, cut diamonds, chemicals, leather goods, fish products and garments. On the import side, the process of import substitutions of food grains and of finished manufactures have led to a sharp fall in the proportion of imports of consumer goods with a rise in the share of raw materials and intermediate goods led by petroleum and uncut diamonds. The demand for imported fertilisers, paper, steel and non-ferrous metals has been rising in recent years.

Pakistan's trade with outside world has been diverse in the recent years, however, the country has seven major export items that dominate the export trade: raw cotton, rice, cotton cloth, cotton yarn, garments, leather and carpets. These products contribute to 60 per cent or more of total exports. Pakistan's largest imports are petroleum and petroleum products. More recently, however, manufactured goods have become a major import item.

In Sri Lanka, agricultural exports still remain at least a third of total exports. Three major traditional exports dominate the sector. These are: tea, rubber and coconut. But in the last decade garments overtook tea to become the country's leading export item. Imports have been concentrated in basic foodstuffs such as rice, sugar and wheat.

6.3.2 Trade with services

It appears that in South Asia the market and volume of trade are widening. At the same time more and more products are becoming internationally tradable. Many services considered non-tradable only a few years ago are now being actively traded. A significant shift has been noticed in the service sector where both trade and foreign direct investment (FDI) have been growing very fast. The reasons for such growth are:

- Rapid expansion of telecommunications and information technology

- Inclusion of more products into the competition, and contesting with the industrial countries, have created new opportunities for long distance service exports

- Efficiency and competitiveness in trade with services in the region

- Region's recent adoption of liberal trade and investment regime (World Bank 1995a)

Services comprise a wide range of economic activities and could be divided into two distinct groups: knowledge-based services and information-technology-based services. Knowledge-based services are professional and technical services, banking and insurance, modern health care and education, financial products and skill transfer in chemical processes. Information technology-based services are computing facilities and software services. In the recent years, India has secured the leading role in South Asian region in exporting these services outside the region. Within the region, the demand for these services has been growing steadily. For example, computer reservation systems for airlines have contributed many-fold increase in air travel in the region. Further, India is catering to a huge health and education services to the neighbouring countries.

South Asia is a labour-abundant region. Thus its growth in service trade has been centred on remittances from skilled and unskilled labour force working overseas. All four countries considered in this study have substantial workforce temporarily working in the Middle East and South East Asian countries. Table 6.2 shows the growth achieved in remittances in the last two decades in these four countries.

Table 6.2   Private unrequited net transfers (1971–94)

| Country | Private Transfers (US$ million) | | |
	1971	1981	1994
Bangladesh	–	900*	1,115
India	209	2,867	4,979
Pakistan	–	–	1,446
Sri Lanka	–	–	698

Note: * 1992 figure.

Source: IMF, *Balance of Payments Yearbook* (several years).

6.4   AGRICULTURAL COMMODITY TRADE

Almost all developing countries have introduced modern technology in agricultural production during the last quarter of a century. There are two main reasons for this to:

- attain food self-sufficiency to feed a growing population

- increase the supply of raw materials for the newly established industrial sector

The countries in South Asia, Indonesia and the Philippines are commonly identified as the cases for the former; and South Korea, Taiwan, Thailand and Malaysia are regarded as the cases for the latter.

Agricultural technology, however, is classified into two categories: mechanical technology and biological (or biological-chemical) technology. The mechanical technology, in general, involves lumpy machinery capital that has labour-saving effect. In contrast, the biological technology depends on divisible inputs such as seeds and fertiliser, and usually are geared to increase output per unit of land (Hayami and Ruttan 1985).

These technologies revolutionised agriculture in the 1970s and 1980s and resulted in Green Revolution. Numerous studies so far have explained the impact of 'Green Revolution' in South Asian countries. The intention here is not to survey such a vast volume of literature. It has been, however, claimed in the literature that the additional production of food grains, wheat and rice, are the prime success sectors of the Green Revolution. In the next section a brief account of this success story is provided for the countries under study.

Cropping contributes more than 80 per cent of value-added in agriculture in South Asia. The cropping sub-sector's progress, particularly, rice and wheat account for more than three quarters of value-adding in cropping. Therefore, the increases in food grain production are the major source of agricultural growth in the four countries under study. Table 6.3 presents the growth in production of cereals and rice between 1985 and 1994. The figures suggest that in Bangladesh cereal and rice production grew more than 14 per cent over this ten year period. In India, the production growth of these crops was more than 15 per cent and in Pakistan it was 13.5 per cent for cereals and 7 per cent for rice. The Sri Lankan growth, however, remained relatively poor over this period.

Table 6.3   Cereals and rice production, 1985–94 (5 year averages), 000 tonnes

| Country | Cereals | | Rice | |
	1985–89	1990–94	1985–89	1990–94
Bangladesh	25,008	28,354 (13.5)	23,777	27,225 (14.5)
India	174,006	201,056 (15.5)	97,723	113,402 (16.0)
Pakistan	19,456	22,092 (13.5)	4,820	5,171 (07.0)
Sri Lanka	2,429	2,522 (03.8)	2,383	2,483 (04.0)

Note:	Figures in the parentheses are growth from last period in per cent.
Source:	ADB (1996).

Table 6.4 shows the productivity performance in rice in four countries over the same ten year period. Out of these countries, Bangladesh has achieved the highest growth in productivity in rice, while India achieved the second highest growth rate. These growths in productivity are mainly the effects of seed-fertiliser-irrigation technology introduced in these countries during the last quarter of a century. Pakistan and Sri Lanka's growth were negligible, nevertheless, Sri Lankan achievement in absolute terms has been highest in the region.

Table 6.4   Yield of rice (kilogrammes per hectare), 1985–94

| Country | Rice | | |
	1985	1994	
Bangladesh	2,196	2,796	(27)
India	2,329	2,834	(22)
Pakistan	2,350	2,500	(6)
Sri Lanka	3,071	3,130	(2)

Note:	Figures in the parentheses are percentage changes over the 1985 levels.
Source:	ABD (1995a).

Overall agricultural growth in four countries in value-added terms is presented in Table 6.5. In aggregate, the initial three years' growth in the 1990s has been good in Bangladesh and Pakistan. India's and Sri Lanka's growths during this time, however, were almost half of that of Bangladesh and Pakistan. These trends reversed in the 1993–95 period, when India and Sri Lanka registered good growths, while Bangladesh and Pakistan grew by less than one per cent. Therefore, it is meaningless to generalise agriculture's growth and performance in the South Asian nations. Each of these countries have their own peculiarities in agriculture. The most important factors among them are the natural calamities and the amount of destruction they inflict to this sector every year. Particularly, in Bangladesh and India flood and drought are the common problems.

Table 6.5   Annual growth rate of value-added in agriculture (%), 1965–95

Country	1965–80	1980–86	1990–92	1993–95
Bangladesh	1.5	2.7	4.6	0.2
India	2.8	1.9	2.5	2.9
Pakistan	3.3	3.3	5.8	0.8
Sri Lanka	2.7	3.9	2.9	3.5

Source: ADB (1996); Chaudhry (1991).

6.5   AGRICULTURAL TRANSFORMATION: FOOD DEFICITS

It is claimed in the literature that, in the South Asian region food shortages were unheard of until World War II (Chaudhry 1991). It was only during the great famine of Bengal in 1943 that a food shortage was recorded. Even at the time of independence in 1947, there was hardly any country in the region with a significant food deficit (cited in Chaudhry 1991). The deficit started to emerge only in the 1950s and early 1960s due to rapid growth in population and stagnating agricultural and cereal production. Due to shortages in food grain production the countries in South Asia spent a large amount of foreign exchange on food imports and also became dependent on the food aid programmes mainly from the US (through PL 480, for example). It is in the wake of these events that achieving food self-sufficiency became a prime objective in South Asia in the late 1960s and early 1970s. The problem is South Asia's planning departments regard the term 'self-sufficiency' as the overall fulfillment of food grain requirements from domestic production. It has nothing to do with the fulfillment of adequate food requirements at household level. The agenda of achieving self-sufficiency in food at the national level has been intensely pursued by adopting new technology in agriculture. As a result net cereal imports began to taper off as early as in 1967–68 in India, Pakistan (Bangladesh then the eastern wing of Pakistan) and Sri Lanka. It is apparent from Table 6.6 that Pakistan became self-sufficient in 1975 and India reached self-sufficiency in 1988. Bangladesh and Sri Lanka still import rice and wheat but the quantity has been declining in the recent years. Bangladesh's deficit has been unpredictable because of its losses of cereal production due to flood or drought. In some flood free good years the country reaches close to self-sufficiency, for example in the years 1992–93 and 1996–97. The last two years' bumper harvest (1995–97) has brought the country close to a self-sufficiency level, once again.

Table 6.6   Average value of net imports of wheat and rice per year (US$ million current price), 1965–95

Country	1965/70	70/75	75/80	80/85	85/88	92/93	93/94	94/95
Bangladesh	–	129	240	236	257	5	168	476
India	488	475	513	140	–82	–11	–325	–344
Pakistan	105	–10	–142	–279	–65	–323	–235	–146
Sri Lanka	69	63	98	105	106	75	60	16

Source: SAARC (1992); GOI (1996); GOB (1996).

In sum, the above analysis provides some clear indications that the region has achieved to a large extent the goal of food self-sufficiency. To achieve this goal, all countries have been following a uniform policy instrument, providing adequate seed-fertiliser-irrigation technology to the farmers including the small farmers. It is unlikely that in the near future any future government in the region will shift from such a policy until the population growth rate is neutralised with agriculture's rate of growth.

6.6 PRODUCTION OF EXPORT CROPS AND
ALLIED PRODUCTS

The record in production of export crops has been much less impressive than that of food crops in all the countries in the region except India. Much of the export crop sector in the region has an indifferent performance over 1980 and 1994. Bangladesh's jute, jute products and tea exports have declined over the last decade. However, frozen fish and shrimp export have grown strongly. In nominal terms, the export growth of agricultural and allied product has remained stagnant since the 1990 (Sobhan 1996).

India has a strong export growth for all products. The most important among them are spices, oil cake and fish and fish preparation. The total export growth in nominal terms has been more than six folds between 1980–81 and 1993–94. The export of spices has increased by 52 folds, oil cake export has increased by almost 19 folds and fish and fish preparation export has increased by more than 11 folds (TATA 1996; SAARC 1992).

Since 1992, Pakistan has a dismal performance in the export of its cash crops and allied products. There has been a huge decline in export earnings in all three areas. On an average the decline was almost 57 per cent between 1992 and 1994. The export of raw cotton in nominal terms has declined by more than 450 per cent, rice has declined by 102 per cent and cotton yarn by 12 per cent (SAARC 1992).

Sri Lankan exports of agricultural and allied products have grown at a moderate pace between 1990 and 1994. The overall growth of export values in nominal terms has been five per cent per year (SAARC 1992). The export values of all three major crops have grown: tea has grown by 5 per cent, rubber has grown by 16 per cent and coconut has grown by 38 per cent between 1990 and 1994.

The four countries under study registered inconsistent performances in regard to agricultural export earnings over the last 15 years. While Bangladesh and India appear to have made some progress, Pakistan and Sri Lanka have lagged behind. In recent years (1990–94), all these nations have been experiencing depreciation in their currencies against the US dollar. Due to this reason, it is not easy to identify the areas of export progress in real terms since the export values are reported in nominal terms and with local currencies. Apparently, India has a bright export progress in the areas of oil cakes, cashew kernels and fish and fish preparations. Pakistan has in cotton yarn. Nothing is promising from Sri Lanka except the conventional export product, tea. Bangladesh's prospects, however, are addressed in greater detail in the next section.

6.7   PROSPECTS FOR BANGLADESH'S AGRICULTURAL
          EXPORTS

The illustrations in the preceding section show that out of these four countries in the region, Bangladesh and India have achieved substantial growth in exporting selected agricultural products over the last 15 years. This section examines Bangladesh's prospects with agricultural exports. It appears, Bangladesh's agricultural exports grew, mainly, in frozen fish and shrimps sector between 1981 and 1994. This sector's growth has doubled in the decade of 1980. However, the growth rate in the 1990s was moderate (only 28 per cent). It appears, therefore, that the prospects of agricultural exports from Bangladesh are limited to one sector.

The producing areas of shrimp in Bangladesh are mainly scattered in the southern districts with a facility of coastal access. Shrimp cultivation has replaced cultivation of transplanted rice in this region. Currently four methods of shrimp cultivation are in use: extensive method, improved extensive method, semi-intensive method and intensive method (Alauddin and Hamid 1996). The common practice of shrimp cultivation is with the extensive method that covers almost 90 per cent of the farms. This practice involves traditional form of cultivation with low cost of production and low yield per hectare, but with an immense damage to the environment.

The major destinations of Bangladesh's shrimp have been the EU countries and the US. Since the early 1990s, the EU suspended shrimp imports from Bangladesh due mainly to their concerns about the quality. In the recent months, the EU has agreed to open its market to Bangladesh on condition that the country meets some EU guidelines on quality assurances.

To improve market prospects, it is necessary for Bangladesh to undertake a detailed study on the production methods and strategies, and formulate marketing plans to address environmental concerns, as well as the concerns from its trading partners on quality. The strategies for upgrading production efficiency should also be considered to gain competitiveness without government's support measures (Palawija News 1997). Within the context of competitiveness the following measures should be considered when formulating the policies to improve market prospects of shrimps from Bangladesh:

- Aspects of quality control and standardisation of the product are the major area of concern. Quality defects in the past have been harmful to both the image and marketability of shrimps. This problem needs to be addressed, once for all.

- Bangladesh has to switch from the traditional production method to modern technology based method. This will bring efficiency in production and contribute minimum damage to the environment.

- A transformation of the production technology is essential to cut the cost of production, as well as to meet the specific requirements of the market.

- The presentation of the product in recent times has become, in effect, as important as the quality of the product itself. It is essential to develop brand names that will be able to certify product quality automatically.

In fact, in the present trend of globalisation and the course of implementing the Uruguay Round's agreements, both the developed and developing countries have been striving for gaining a competitive edge. Bangladesh is not an exception. Bangladesh has to follow closely the policy guidelines mentioned above not only for the shrimp sector but also to gain a permanent foothold on developing agricultural exports with other products and also to diversify exports with new products.

7 Trade Among South Asian Nations: Experiences and Prospects

Mohammad Alauddin

7.1 INTRODUCTION

The decade of the 1980s has been characterised by a distinct shift in the evolution of development policy. Even though often portrayed as a technical set of policies, structural adjustment represents a process of institutional reforms. It refers to a 'set of policies propelled by the World Bank and the IMF. The explicit aims of opening up the Third World countries to world market competition are to: (1) promote their exports and (2) restrain domestic expenditure. Such policies seek to create a better climate for investment and to enhance economic growth' (Messkoub 1992, p.198). These stand in sharp contrast to the macroeconomic policy agenda of the two preceding decades. These policy initiatives also represent a radical shift from the management of the macroeconomy *per se* to that of both the macro – and microeconomy. In many less developing countries, structural adjustment policies permeate all aspects of their economies, the precise extent depending critically on the extent of reliance on the concessional assistance (S. H. Rahman 1992; Shand and Alauddin 1997). More recently further changes have occurred in international economic relations. The successful conclusion of the Uruguay Round of the GATT and the establishment of the World trade Organisation (WTO) have opened up new opportunities for exploiting comparative advantage that many LDCs including those in South Asia enjoy. The opportunities resulting from a liberalised world trade environment, however, have exposed structural limitations of many LDCs and underlined the critical importance of appropriate policy reforms (see also Chapter 3).

The trend of openness and globalisation seems to have created enthusiasm for expanded trade among countries of the South Asian region. This chapter investigates the degree of bilateral trade among the countries of South Asia. The magnitude and direction of trade overall are examined. Trade imbalance between India on the one hand, and the other countries of the region on the other, is examined in detail with a special emphasis on the growing bilateral

117

trade imbalance between Bangladesh and India. Progress in expanding trade within the region has been slow (Hossain et al. 1997). It is argued that the region could be on the threshold of an economic take-off if economic cooperation expands in terms of greater volume of intra-regional trade.

7.2   STRUCTURE, COMPOSITION AND DIRECTION OF TRADE

Table 7.1 sets out information on the broad structure and composition of trade for Bangladesh, India, Pakistan and Sri Lanka. The exports and imports of these countries consist of a large number of goods both from the primary sectors and the manufacturing categories. The broad commodity compositions of imports and exports of these countries appear to be similar. On the whole, however, India's foreign trade is more broadly based than that of her neighbours.

The broad picture stemming from Table 7.1, however, does not capture the dynamics of composition of trade in South Asia. The changing structure and composition in South Asia's foreign trade are identfied and analysied in the remainder of this section.

7.2.1   The export trade

Bangladesh's exports grew at annual rates of 5.6 per cent, 5.2 per cent and 16.2 per cent respectively during the 1981–86, 1987–91 and 1991–94 periods. The structure and composition of Bangladesh's exports have undergone significant transformation over the years. Manufactured goods account for nearly 90 per cent of Bangladesh's export trade in the mid-1990s compared to less than 60 per cent in early 1970s. Ready-made garments have been the most dominant source of this change replacing jute-based exports which until recently completely dominated Bangladesh's export trade (Shand and Alauddin 1997; Alauddin 1997). Even though the share of primary exports have declined there has been a significant growth of processed primary goods through the exports of frozen fish and shrimps and leather products especially footwear. In the primary goods category shrimp has replaced raw jute as the most dominant item of exports with little diversification in evidence. In the manufactured goods category ready-made garments have replaced jute goods as the single most important group of exports. 'The changing composition of Bangladesh's exports could be interpreted more as a process of two groups of items (shrimp and ready-made garments) replacing two others (raw jute and jute manufactures) respectively rather than heralding a process of real export diversification' (Alauddin 1997, p.105).

Table 7.1   Structure of foreign trade of South Asia

Country	Exports	Imports
Bangladesh	Food and live animals; tea; crude materials; textile fibres; jute and jute goods; leather and goods; textile yearn; chemical fertilisers; ready-made garments; crustaceans; frozen fish and products; mollies; vegetables and fruits; petroleum products.	Food and live animals; cereals; transport equipment; machinery; textile fibres and yearns; metal products; medicine and pharmaceutical products; crude fertilisers; food items; petroleum and petroleum products; manufactured products; clothing and accessories; beverages and tobacco.
India	Food and live animals; fruits, vegetables and spices; tobacco and beverages; textile fibres; ferrous and nonferrous metals and products; minerals; pharmaceutical products; basic manufactures; transport equipment; textiles, footwear and clothing; instruments; watches and clocks; electrical and non-electrical machinery; jute yarn and fabrics.	Food and live animals; cereals and preparations; fruits and vegetables; animal feeding staff; beverages and tobacco; textile fabrics and yarn; crude fertilisers; minerals; petroleum and products; chemical and pharmaceutical products; chemical fertilisers; ferrous and non-ferrous metals; electrical and non-electrical machinery; metal and non-metal products; timber and products; raw cotton and products; basic manufactures; watches and clocks; transport equipment.
Pakistan	Food and live animals; cereals and preparations; fruits and vegetables; beverages, tobacco and products; animal feeding stuff; chemicals; petroleum products; textile yarn; machinery transport equipment; textiles materials and manufactures; cotton and cotton yarn; leather and products; textiles, footwear and clothing.	Food and live animals; cereals and preparations; fruits and vegetables; animal feeding staff; beverages and tobacco; textile fabrics and yarn; crude fertilisers; minerals; petroleum and products; edible oils; chemical and pharmaceutical products; chemical fertilisers; ferrous and non-ferrous metals; electrical and non-electrical machinery; metal and non-metal products; timber and products; raw cotton and products; basic manufactures; watches and clocks; transport equipment; medical and pharmaceutical products; medical and scientific instruments; fuel lubricants and related items.

Table 7.1   Structure of foreign trade of South Asia (continued)

Country	Exports	Imports
Sri Lanka	Natural rubber; beverages; coconut and products; spices; food and live animals; crude materials; fish and preparations; textiles and garments; manufactures; textiles fibres and yarn.	Food and live animals; cereals and preparations; fruits and vegetables; animal feeding staff; beverages and tobacco; textile fabrics and yarn; crude fertilisers; minerals; petroleum and products; chemical and pharmaceutical products; chemical fertilisers; ferrous and non-ferrous metals; electrical and non-electrical machinery; metal and non-metal products; timber and products; raw cotton and products; basic manufactures; watches and clocks; transport equipment

Sources: Based on information contained in Athukorala (1997); Shand and Alauddin (1997); Shand and Bhati (1997); Shand (1997); Shand and Kalirajan (1997).

As can been seen from Table 7.2 major destinations of Bangladesh's exports comprise a handful of countries in the European Union and North America. In a dynamic context the destinations of Bangladesh's exports are becoming increasingly concentrated. For instance, as set out in Table 7.3, developed countries consisting primarily of those in the European Community and the United States, account for more than 85 per cent of destinations of Bangladesh's exports. This contrasts with less than 50 per cent of their relative importance until the mid-1980s. This dynamic pattern is consistent with the increasingly greater relative importance of ready-made garments and shrimp related items of exports as their markets primarily lie in the developed countries of Western Europe and North America. The period over two decades since the mid-1970s has witnessed a significant crowding out of the developing countries of Africa, Asia, Middle-East and Europe as markets for Bangladesh's exports. As Hossain et al. (1997, p.167) rightly argue that 'such a degree of market concentration, is to a great extent explained by the high degree of export commodity concentration and the non-diversification of Bangladesh's export-base'.[1]

Significant changes have taken place in the composition of India's exports since the mid-1980s. Over the decade to 1996, the share of manufactures rose to 77 per cent from 58 per cent in 1986 while that of agricultural products declined to 19 per cent from 28 per cent. 'Labour intensive goods including gems and jewellery (a strong growth area), ready made garments and to a lesser extent the more traditional categories of leather products and handicrafts' (Shand and Kalirajan 1997, p.32). In recent years a uniform incentive structure, comprising of favourable exchange rate, and income tax exemption for export earnings acts as a catalyst for export promotion with high domestic value added content. This incentive structure is expected to further enhance agro-processed and labour-intensive and light engineering products in which India has a distinct competitive advantage (Shand and Kalirajan 1997).

Over the years relative importance of the destinations of India's exports have also undergone changes. On the whole, however, the Indian export market is much more diverse than that of Bangladesh. Indian exports to Western Europe have increased markedly while those to Eastern Europe OPEC countries have declined. Amongst the Southeast and East Asian countries, Hong Kong, Singapore and Thailand feature prominently as India's export destinations. In a dynamic context the relative importance of developed countries of Western Europe, North America and the Far East remain much the same over a period of two decades. The relative importance of Middle-East countries as well as that of the developing countries of Europe have declined considerably. These declines, however, have been compensated for by emerging markets in developing countries of Asia, Africa and elsewhere. This is clearly evident from the information set out in Table 7.3.

Pakistan's export market is seemingly diversified (Table 7.2). However, as portrayed in Table 7.3, the relative share of developed countries as destinations for Pakistan's exports is growing in importance from less than 40 per cent until 1980 to around 60 per cent in recent years. The relative shares of developing countries in Asia and Africa have remained fairly stable while those for the developing countries of the Middle-East and Europe have less than halved over the two decades to 1996. Pakistan's merchandise exports revolve around raw cotton and cotton manufactures which alone account for more than two thirds of Pakistan's exports. There has been a significant shift of export base within the cotton complex. For example, Pakistan's exports comprised 13 per cent of raw cotton and 56 per cent of cotton manufactures during the 1991-95 period compared to 35 per cent and 31 per cent respectively during the 1986–90 period. The increase in the relative share is indicative of the growth in value adding to raw cotton (Shand and Bhati 1997, p.29). Even though Pakistan accounts for only 0.2 per cent of world exports its share in world exports in textiles and clothing is over two per cent, and in leather and leather goods is 2 per cent. However, Pakistan is a significant player in carpets, carpeting and rugs accounting for 15 per cent of world export trade. Seemingly the share of primary exports have declined steadily from 92 per cent in 1970 to 25 per cent in 1994. This decline however masks the continued importance of tea and other agricultural products. In terms of net foreign exchange earnings agriculture is much more important than indicated by the value of exports. The most important export item–textiles and garments are fairly import-intensive in nature. Sri Lanka's export market is much less diversified than the list of countries provided in Table 7.2. The market for Sri Lanka's export is shrinking in relative importance in every region of the world except for the developed countries of Western Europe and North America. Even though a very small economy it has a significant market share in export of tea in that it accounts for more than 20 per cent of world trade in that commodity.

7.2.2   The import trade

The structure and composition of Bangladesh's import trade have changed considerably over the years especially since the early 1980s. Major categories of import include agricultural, crude petroleum and petroleum products, fertilisers, cement, raw cotton and fibres and capital goods. As Shand and Alauddin (1997, pp.27–8) argue the pattern indicates that the share of consumer goods has more than doubled from 18 per cent in 1981 to 38 per cent in 1993 while that of capital goods reduced to less than 40 per cent of the 1981 level. This is due to only a moderate growth in GDP and weak investment levels epitomising the '4 per cent syndrome'. This is also caused by and reflected in the a disproportionate share of the services sector in the Bangladesh's GDP (see Chapter 2 and Chapter 19). Bangladesh's import sources are fairly diverse as can be seen from Table 7.3. Developed countries as a source of Bangladesh's imports have registered a steady decline in relative importance from 56 per cent in 1975 to 27 per cent in 1996. The relative importance of developing countries of Asia has increased five-fold over two decades to 1996. The important Bangladesh's import sources in this group of countries include *inter alia* India, China, Thailand, Hong Kong, Singapore and South Korea. The combined relative share of developing countries of Africa, Middle-East, Eastern Europe and other countries of the developing world has declined from mid-thirties in the late 1970s to less than 20 per cent in recent years.

As can been seen from Table 7.2 major sources of India's imports originate in the developed countries of the European Union and North America. Their relative importance has hovered about the 50 per cent level over the two

Table 7.2   Major trading partners of South Asian economies

Country	Major destination of exports	Major sources of imports
Bangladesh	United States, United Kingdom, Germany, Belgium-Luxemberg, France, Italy; Netherlands.	India, China, Hong Kong, South Korea, Japan, Pakistan, Thailand Australia, Singapore; Thailand.
India	Bangladesh, Hong Kong, Singapore, Sri Lanka, Thailand, United States, Japan, Germany, United Kingdom, China, Belgium-Luxemberg, France, Italy, Netherlands, Russia, Saudi Arabia, United Arab Emirates.	Japan, Germany, United Kingdom, China, Belgium-Luxemberg, France, Italy, Netherlands, Russia, Saudi Arabia, United Arab Emirates.
Pakistan	Bangladesh, Hong Kong, South Korea, Singapore, United States, Australia, Japan, Germany, United Kingdom, China, Belgium-Luxemberg, France, Saudi Arabia, United Arab Emirates.	South Korea, Singapore, United States, Australia, Japan, Germany, United Kingdom, China, France, Saudi Arabia, United Arab Emirates.
Sri Lanka	South Korea, Hong Kong, Singapore, Thailand, United States, Australia, Japan, Germany, United Kingdom, China, Belgium-Luxemberg, France, Italy, Netherlands, Russia, Saudi Arabia, United Arab Emirates.	South Korea, Hong Kong, Singapore, Thailand, United States, Australia, Japan, Germany, United Kingdom, China, Belgium-Luxemberg, France, Italy, Netherlands, Russia, India, Saudi Arabia, United Arab Emirates.

Source: Based on information contained in Athukorala (1997); Shand and Alauddin (1997); Shand and Bhati (1997); Shand (1997); Shand and Kalirajan (1997); IMF (various issues).

decades to 1996. The developing countries of Asia and Africa as India's import sources have been growing in importance at the expense of those in Eastern Europe or the Middle-East. As of 1996, capital goods (28 per cent) petroleum and related products (21 per cent) and miscellaneous items (27 per cent) constitute bulk of India's imports (Shand and Kalirajan 1997, p.33). Consumer goods account for only 3 per cent of total imports. Thus India's imports are primarily geared to building investment capabilities and intermediate inputs to domestically produce consumer goods. Pakistan's import sources are fairly diversified (Table 7.2). However, as portrayed in Table 7.3, the relative share of developed countries as sources of Pakistan's imports has remained relatively stable around the 50 per cent level. With considerable fluctuations the Middle-East remains a significant source of Pakistan's imports. The developing countries of Asia and Africa are growing in importance as import sources. As of 1995, Japan, USA, Malaysia, Germany, UK, Saudi Arabia and Kuwait are important import sources of Pakistan. The majority of Pakistan's imports are consumer goods and raw materials for consumer goods. Their share seems to have changed little between 1987 and 1995 (from 56 per cent to 60 per cent). The share of capital goods fell from 44 per cent in 1987 to 40 per cent in 1995 (Shand and Bhati 1997, pp.29–30).

As set out in Table 7.3 majority of Sri Lanka's imports have their origins in the developed world and the developing countries of Asia. The growing importance of the developing countries of Asia as suppliers of goods to Sri Lanka is clearly evident. The relative importance of the developed countries of the European Union, North America and East Asia has declined from around 45 per cent in the mid-1970s to below 40 per cent in the mid-1990s. The other regions of the world e.g. the Middle-East, Eastern Europe have been steadily declining in importance as origins of Sri Lanka's imports. The composition of Sri Lanka's imports have changed over the years. Investment goods and intermediate goods taken together account for nearly three-fourths of Sri Lanka's imports in the mid-1990s compared to about 70 per cent in the early 1970s. Food imports have declined somewhat as have imports of consumer goods (Athukorala 1997, pp.19–20).

7.3   BANGLADESH'S TRADE RELATIONSHIP WITH
       SOUTH ASIA AND THE REST OF THE WORLD

Against the background of the preceding discussion this section undertakes an in-depth analysis of the intensity of Bangladesh's trade relationships with her South Asian neighbours and the rest of the world. Table 7.4 sets out information which suggest a progressive increase in Bangladesh's reliance on South Asia as a source of import. The relative importance of South Asia in Bangladesh's import trade has more than doubled over a period of two decades since the mid-1970s. The most dramatic increase has been India's share in Bangladesh's imports. India accounts for more than 90 per cent of Bangladesh's imports from South Asia. As can be seen from Table 7.4 an insignificant percentage of Bangladesh's exports find their destination to South Asian neighbours. The combined share of Bangladesh's exports to India, Pakistan and Sri Lanka is progressively declining. In recent years the three countries taken together account for only around 2 per cent of the total value of Bangladesh's exports. *On the whole, Bangladesh's import from India excepted, most of Bangladesh's foreign trade is destined for or originate from outside the South Asian region* (see also Hossain et al. 1997)

       In order to obtain a comprehensive view of the trade relationship between Bangladesh *vis-a-vis* her South Asian neighbours as well as her trading partners in the rest of the world, trade-intensity indices are calculated. Intensity of trade was first used by Brown (1948) and later on developed and popularised by Kojima (1964) to study the pattern of international trade among advanced countries. Intensity of trade index than concentrates attention of variations in bilateral levels which results from differential resistances, by abstracting from the effects of the size of the exporting and importing countries (Drysdale and Garnaut 1982, pp.67–8). Following Kojima (1964, p.19) two measures of trade intensities are defined as:

Import intensity index $m_{ij} = \dfrac{M_{ij}}{M_i} \div \dfrac{X_j}{X_w - X_i}$

Export intensity index $x_{ij} = \dfrac{X_{ij}}{X_i} \div \dfrac{M_j}{M_w - M_i}$

where

M_{ij} = value of import of country i from country j
X_{ij} = value of export of country i to country j
M_i = value of total import of country i
X_i = value of total export of country i
M_j = value of total import of country j
X_j = value of total export of country j
M_w = value of total world import
X_w = value of total world export

According to Kojima (1964, p.19) $M_j/(M_w - M_j)$ represents country j's relative purchasing power (or demand) of world imports. Thus *the import (export) intensity of trade of country i with country j is defined as the ratio of share of country j in the total imports (exports) of country i to the share of country j in the total world exports (imports) net of country i's share* (Kalirajan 1983, p.275). A trade intensity index of equal to, greater than or less than unity implies that country j is equally represented, over represented or less than represented respectively in country i's imports (exports). Table 7.5 provides Bangladesh's export and import intensity indices over the 1975–96 period *vis-a-vis* her trading partners in South Asia and elsewhere in the world.

The export intensity indices suggest considerable fluctuations over time for most trading partners as well as across countries. In some years India is over-represented while in some others the reverse is the case. Until very recently both Singapore and Pakistan seem to be over-represented while Sri Lanka seems to be consistently over represented. South Korea, Japan, Thailand and Hong Kong are consistently under-represented. Germany, UK, Netherlands, Italy, Belgium and France after having been under-represented during the initial years of the time series are consistently over-represented in later years. After fluctuatiing between over- and under-representations during first decade of the time series, USA is consistently over represented during the second half of the period. Australia after having been primarily over-represented until the later 1980s is under-represented in the 1990s. Similar is the case with China.

The import intensity indices suggest fluctuations to a lesser degree over time. Throughout the period India, Pakistan, Singapore, Sri Lanka, are consistently over-represented. Countries such as South Korea, Thailand, Japan, China, Australia and Hong Kong are, for majority of the years especially during the latter half of the series, consistently over-represented. Germany, Netherlands, Italy, Belgium and France are consistently under-represented throughout the time series. For most years USA and UK are under-represented.

7.4   BANGLADESH'S BILATERAL TRADE WITH INDIA

In the light of the preceding discussion it is clear that Bangladesh's bilateral trade balance with India is heavily tilted in favour of India. As can be seen from Table 7.4 a significant percentage of Bangladesh's imports originates from India with India's share accelerating in recent years. As of 1996 India accounted for more than 16 per cent of Bangladesh's total imports. This, according to A. Hossain and Rashid (1998) represents nearly 40 per cent of Bangladesh's global trade deficit for the relevant year. On the other hand, only a very insignificant percentage of Bangladesh's exports finds market in India. Only in three years (1990, 1991 and 1993) in the decade to 1996 have Bangladesh's exports to India accounted for more than one per cent of her global exports.

Table 7.6 sets out some important indicators of Indo-Bangladesh bilateral trade. The lopsidedness of trade in India's favour is clearly evident from the ratio of Bangladesh's imports from and exports to India. Bangladesh's exports as a percentage of India's total imports is next to nothing. On the other hand, Bangladesh's imports as a percentage of India's total exports have increased steadily assuming greater significance. Bangladesh enjoys positive trade balance with her major trading partners of Western Europe and North America but in deficit with the countries of the developing world.

The emergence of India as an increasingly important source of Bangladesh's imports has several dimensions. A considerable percentage of imports originating from India are inputs for export oriented industries (I. Hossain et al. 1997, p.178). These in turn result in positive trade balance with some of Bangladesh's trading partners in the developed world especially the USA.

Bangladesh's official trade does not, however reflect the trues state of the Indo-Bangladesh bilateral trade. The findings of a recent study reported by I. Hossain et al. (1997, p.178) suggest that the unofficial exports account for nearly 90 per cent of legal trade. If this is taken into account Indian exports to

Bangladesh could account for nearly a quarter of Bangladesh's' total imports (A. Hossain and Rashid 1998).

The composition and direction of illegal trade between Bangladesh and India according to a joint NCAER-BIDS survey conducted in 1994 (reported in World Bank 1996)[2] suggest that: (1) livestock, poultry, fish and related products, and other agricultural products constituted about 52 per cent while processed food and tobacco, textiles, and other consumer goods constituted about 43 per cent of Bangladesh's illegal imports from India, and (2) copper, brass and other metals and fish constituted about 91 per cent of illegal exports from Bangladesh to India (A. Hossain and Rashid 1998; see also Chaudhari 1995).

The large and growing bilateral trade deficits have become a matter of concern given the traditional sensitivities in Indo-Bangladesh relations. A. Hossain and Rashid (1998) attribute this widening gap to the two major factors: (1) a sharp appreciation in the value of Bangladesh taka against Indian rupee; and (2) non-tariff barriers. A. Hossain and Rashid (1998) further argue that Bangladesh and India are not structurally different.

In contrast, I. Hossain et al. (1997, p.192–3), while acknowledging the role of overvalued bilateral exchange rate of Bangladesh taka *vis-a-vis* the Indian rupee, cautioned that 'it would, however, be naive to assume that an appreciated taka lies at the root of Bangladesh's trade imbalance with India'. I. Hossain et al. (1997, p.193) identified several factors: (1) much larger size, diversity and technological maturity of the Indian economy compared to Bangladesh; (2) the geographical proximity of India along with the familiarity of Bangladesh's importers to India's production capacities with globally competitive edge both in terms of price and quality in Bangladesh's market. Furthermore, I. Hossain et al. (1997) rightly point out that Bangladesh's import liberalisation has reinforced an increasingly porous border and has made Bangladesh virtually an open market for India. India's ability to export in a globalised market is significantly enhanced by the fact that India's economy is much more diversified than that of Bangladesh both in terms of export commodity diversification as well as market destinations. These factors, despite India being at a somewhat similar level as Bangladesh in the economic development ladder measured by broad indicators, largely explain Indian penetration in Bangladesh's market. This contrasts with the view espoused by A. Hossain and Rashid (1998).

A very similar development has occurred in respect of Bangladesh's bilateral trade with China. The information contained in Table 7.7 clearly indicates a growing trade imbalance. The percentage of Bangladesh's exports destined for China has fluctuated considerably over the years but recently has been reduced to around 0.5 per cent. On the other hand, the percentage of Bangladesh's imports originating from China has been assuming greater significance especially in the 1990s. As of 1996 China's share in Bangladesh's total imports is more than 10 per cent. Bangladesh's import-export ratio *vis-a-vis* China has been increasing over the years and in 1996 stands at 36. Bangladesh's exports to China as a percentage of China's total imports have been falling steadily and has been reduced to around one hundredth of one per cent in the 1990s. In contrast, Bangladesh's imports from China as a percentage of China's total exports have been rising at a steady pace. As of 1996 it stands at nearly one half of one per cent.

In the development ladder China and India are not significantly different. But for the Indo-Bangladesh cross-border illegal trade the patterns of market access to Bangladesh's market by India and China are not significantly different. These similarities notwithstanding '... persistent and growing deficit with India demands attention because of its political as distinct from economic implications. Such implications appear to suggest a need for diplomatic attention since the market mechanism remains imperfect due to the asymmetry both in the economic structures as well as policy regimes of the two countries' (Sobhan 1997, p.12; see also Shand and Kalirajan 1997).[3]

7.5   CONCLUDING COMMENTS

Despite a global trend toward openness nations within the South Asian regions have not engaged in expanding trade relations. According to I. Hossain et al. (1997, p.194) trade among the members of the South Asian Association for Regional Cooperation (SAARC) countries in recent years stand at 3.7 per cent of their global trade which is less than the 5 per cent level of the 1980s. Furthermore, some of the countries in SAARC group compete intensely with each other for a share of the global market for some of their products. Bangladesh and India compete in the EU and North American markets for jute and jute goods while all the major countries are competitors in the ready-made garments export trade. As I. Hossain et al. (1997) and Shand and Bhati (1997) rightly point out the competition among most of the SAARC countries for textiles and apparels especially in the US market is likely to become more intense with the phasing out of the multi fibre agreement (MFA).

Except for India a limited number of goods epitomises export trade in South Asia.[4] By far the Indian export trade is much more diversified. In terms of destination fewer countries dominate in case of both Bangladesh and Sri Lanka. The import trade of all the major South Asian countries is much more diversified.

One important facet of the intra-regional trade in South Asia is the growing penetration of the Bangladesh market by Indian goods. Bangladesh is also becoming an increasingly export destination for China. In case of India the issue is compounded by illegal trade across the border on the one hand and politically sensitive relation between the two neighbours on the other . It might be added that the Indo-Pakistan cross-border illegal trade is estimated to be about US$500 million dollars (I. Hossain et al. 1997, p.194). However, the growing Indo-Bangladesh bilateral trade imbalance should not be viewed in isolation from the Bangladesh's global trade. A significant part of the Indian imports into Bangladesh provide inputs to export-oriented industries.

Slow expansion of intra-regional trade is largely the result of the sluggish pace of removal of para, non-tariff barriers and across the board reduction of tariffs. The signing and subsequent ratification South Asian Preferential Trading Agreement (SAPTA) is a step in the right direction. The issue of transit remains an important unresolved matter. Greater cooperation within South Asia in the area of transport may according to one estimate may result in the expansion of intra-regional trade by nearly US$2 billion (I. Hossain et al. 1997, p.195). Nepal can significantly benefit from the transit facilities by India in terms of her export competitiveness. In the broader issue of trade expansion can hardly be meaningful if the question of transport and transit facilities is left out of the agenda. Trade, transit and transport issues need not only be resolved on a bilateral basis but requires regional level resolution. These are likley catalysts for increased trade and greater regional integration. The findings of a gravity model suggest that other regional blocs such as EU, ASEAN, NAFTA have made significantly positive contribution to export growth. It seems logical that SAPTA 'can be a potential stimulant to enhancing intra-regional trade ' within South Asia (I. Hossain et al. 1997, p.198).

NOTES

1 The Gini-Hirschman indices for Bangladesh' exports in terms of both its commodity composition as well as for market destination show a trend toward increasing degree of concentration over time. For example, the value of the index for net exports increased from 0.324 in 1991–92 to 0.386 in 1995–96. The concentration index for exports to all countries increased 0.12 to 0.32 between 1979–80 and 1994–95. The value of the for exports to 15 major trading partners of Bangladesh increased from 0.04 to 0.25 over the same period (Hossain et al. 1997, pp.166–7).

2 The survey using common questionnaire and methodology was conducted simultaneously at the Indian and Bangladesh borders.

3 The political imperative can hardly be ignored when the ideological orientation of some of Bangladesh's major political parties hinge on friendly relations with China and anti-Indianism (A. Hossain 1996, p.177).

4 Bangladesh relies primarily on low wages as the source of price competitive edge and much less on productivity in case of its most important export good, ready-made garments. Exports from Bangladesh have only one unique salable proposition with low price based on low wages rather than higher productivity (DCCI nd; Hussain 1993).

Table 7.3   Changing destinations and sources of South Asia's exports and imports, 1975–96

Year	Percentage of exports to						Percentage of imports originating from					
	Developed countries	Developing countries of				Others	Developed countries	Developing countries of				Others
		Africa	Asia	Middle-East	Europe			Africa	Asia	Middle-East	Europe	
Bangladesh												
1975	40.8	14.3	5.3	17.0	16.2	6.4	56.6	0.1	10.3	8.0	7.8	17.2
1980	36.0	11.2	26.0	13.2	10.4	3.2	48.1	0.1	15.8	10.0	5.1	20.9
1985	47.8	11.6	14.6	15.3	9.9	1.0	44.0	0.2	24.0	10.7	4.6	16.5
1990	71.4	3.3	10.1	9.3	4.9	1.0	42.9	0.2	34.0	5.1	2.5	15.3
1991	75.8	1.8	10.5	4.4	5.8	1.7	36.5	0.1	33.5	5.6	1.9	22.4
1992	78.8	1.6	9.7	2.3	5.3	2.3	33.2	0.3	39.3	6.2	1.6	19.4
1993	78.7	1.9	10.5	3.0	3.4	2.5	35.5	0.1	40.7	4.1	1.5	18.1
1994	80.3	1.9	10.3	1.8	3.9	1.8	31.8	0.3	44.2	3.3	2.6	17.8
1995	82.8	1.8	9.0	2.2	3.2	1.0	30.9	0.3	52.1	3.6	1.8	11.3
1996	85.4	1.6	7.2	2.0	3.1	0.7	27.2	0.4	54.0	2.6	1.6	14.2
India												
1975	45.8	4.0	8.9	21.4	19.3	0.6	61.0	1.9	2.2	21.7	12.0	1.2
1980	57.6	3.3	10.6	14.9	12.6	1.0	48.5	2.3	9.3	23.0	11.6	5.3
1985	56.8	2.8	9.9	9.5	20.6	0.4	53.7	1.7	11.5	18.6	11.0	3.5
1990	55.6	1.8	12.1	7.1	18.4	5.0	56.9	2.8	11.2	18.3	8.0	2.8
1991	57.7	2.6	15.4	9.7	11.3	3.3	52.1	4.7	9.2	17.2	4.3	12.5
1992	62.3	3.3	17.2	10.7	2.2	4.3	54.2	6.1	11.6	22.9	3.0	2.2
1993	59.3	3.0	21.3	11.7	1.5	3.2	56.5	5.8	10.4	24.8	1.0	1.5
1994	58.4	3.3	20.4	10.2	4.5	3.2	50.4	4.9	14.2	24.2	3.2	3.1
1995	54.7	4.4	21.9	8.9	4.9	5.2	48.3	4.6	13.9	21.4	4.4	7.4
1996	55.1	4.5	24.4	8.5	2.8	4.7	51.3	4.2	18.9	15.9	3.6	6.1

Table 7.3 continued

Year	Percentage of exports to						Percentage of imports originating from					
	Developed countries	Developing countries of					Developed countries	Developing countries of				
		Africa	Asia	Middle-East	Europe	Others		Africa	Asia	Middle-East	Europe	Others
Pakistan												
1975	35.6	5.9	24.4	22.8	8.4	2.9	59.5	0.9	12.4	20.4	4.8	2.0
1980	36.4	5.9	24.9	25.4	5.6	1.8	50.1	0.9	13.7	30.5	3.8	1.0
1985	49.5	5.7	18.5	18.1	7.2	1.0	54.8	2.0	14.5	25.1	2.6	1.0
1990	60.8	4.0	20.9	8.7	5.3	0.3	55.2	2.5	19.3	19.1	3.0	0.9
1991	56.0	4.2	22.7	12.2	4.3	0.7	58.4	1.9	18.7	14.9	4.0	2.1
1992	55.0	3.9	25.0	13.2	2.2	.07	58.2	1.7	19.8	15.6	3.1	1.6
1993	58.7	3.4	19.7	12.9	3.3	2.0	55.1	2.1	21.7	17.7	1.8	1.6
1994	60.7	4.2	21.1	10.8	1.7	1.5	50.2	2.1	22.8	20.9	3.0	1.0
1995	56.1	3.7	23.10	11.6	3.4	2.1	49.5	2.4	23.5	19.6	3.4	1.6
1996	57.1	4.0	23.4	10.6	2.7	2.2	49.3	2.7	20.8	22.6	2.6	1.7
Sri Lanka												
1975	34.4	4.2	23.9	16.7	5.5	15.3	45.4	0.6	31.7	17.0	3.7	1.6
1980	39.6	2.5	15.2	22.1	12.2	8.4	45.3	4.2	19.9	24.0	1.9	4.7
1985	50.8	1.7	11.3	22.9	5.1	8.2	46.0	2.0	23.5	21.7	2.1	4.7
1990	61.5	1.2	9.6	17.7	3.9	6.1	40.2	4.4	40.4	11.5	2.2	1.3
1991	65.5	0.7	10.8	16.0	1.5	5.5	36.8	3.0	47.9	8.0	2.2	2.1
1992	76.5	0.9	7.3	9.8	1.6	3.9	36.8	2.2	51.8	5.5	2.2	1.5
1993	75.4	0.6	7.8	8.7	2.8	4.7	34.9	1.4	48.8	4.8	2.0	8.1
1994	75.1	1.0	9.4	8.8	2.1	3.6	40.9	1.3	48.4	5.4	1.6	2.4
1995	75.5	0.9	9.2	7.1	4.1	3.2	37.4	1.1	49.9	7.3	1.3	3.0
1996	73.5	0.8	8.6	7.4	5.9	3.8	37.5	1.3	49.8	8.3	1.5	1.6

Sources: IMF (various issues).

Table 7.4 Bangladesh's trade with her trading partners in South Asia and the rest of the world, 1975–96.

A: Export trade

Year		Total exports of (million US dollars)			Bangladesh's exports to (million US dollars)			% of Bangladesh's exports to				
	Bangladesh	India	Pakistan	Sri Lanka	India	Pakistan	Sri Lanka	India	Pakistan	Sri Lanka	South Asia	Rest of World
1975	327	4364	1051	556	5	0	3	1.62	0.00	0.89	2.51	97.49
1976	400	5020	1162	569	7	11	0	1.78	2.68	0.15	4.60	95.40
1977	474	6025	1174	725	0	32	8	0.13	6.65	1.58	8.35	91.65
1978	513	6627	1490	874	2	48	6	0.45	9.36	1.11	10.92	89.08
1979	656	7014	2056	978	12	37	2	1.84	5.70	0.30	7.85	92.15
1980	790	7911	2618	1039	8	55	5	1.01	7.00	0.61	8.62	91.38
1981	791	7844	2881	1020	20	42	3	2.55	5.35	0.34	8.24	91.76
1982	768	9753	2402	996	20	42	0	2.64	5.48	0.07	8.19	91.81
1983	931	9831	3075	1054	7	51	0	0.74	5.52	0.05	6.32	93.68
1984	999	10638	2559	1436	28	63	0	2.83	6.34	0.03	9.20	90.80
1985	889	10211	2738	1265	30	42	0	3.33	4.67	0.02	8.02	91.98
1986	1077	10516	3383	1163	8	36	0	0.71	3.30	0.06	4.07	95.93
1987	1796	12430	4168	1363	11	28	0	0.61	1.55	0.01	2.18	97.82
1988	1291	13325	4509	1461	9	33	18	0.67	2.59	1.39	4.65	95.35
1989	1305	15846	4660	1540	11	23	7	0.82	1.79	0.50	3.11	96.89
1990	1672	17813	5587	1895	22	23	8	1.32	1.38	0.48	3.17	96.83
1991	1687	17872	6494	1987	23	39	6	1.36	2.31	0.36	4.03	95.97
1992	2037	18498	7269	2488	4	30	11	0.20	1.47	0.54	2.21	97.79
1993	2277	20258	6701	2859	13	26	9	0.57	1.14	0.40	2.11	97.89
1994	2650	24195	7332	3210	24	19	4	0.91	0.72	0.15	1.77	98.23
1995	3129	30537	7991	3810	36	3	11	1.15	0.08	0.35	1.59	98.41
1996	3350	34407	9299	4097	20	4	2	0.60	0.10	0.06	0.76	99.24

Table 7.4 continued

B: Import trade

Year	Total imports of (million US dollars)				Bangladesh's imports from (million US dollars)			% of Bangladesh's imports from				
	Bangladesh	India	Pakistan	Sri Lanka	India	Pakistan	Sri Lanka	India	Pakistan	Sri Lanka	South Asia	Rest of World
1975	1320	6198	2219	745	82	22	6	6.23	1.63	0.43	8.29	91.71
1976	940	5102	2133	549	63	9	1	6.67	0.96	0.15	7.78	92.22
1977	1125	6664	2452	656	49	12	2	4.35	1.04	0.14	5.53	94.47
1978	1502	7820	3285	964	43	22	4	2.86	1.43	0.23	4.53	95.47
1979	1928	9042	4061	1449	40	22	4	2.07	1.14	0.21	3.43	96.57
1980	2611	13456	5350	2035	56	35	5	2.13	1.34	0.18	3.65	96.35
1981	2651	15169	5410	1938	64	47	2	2.41	1.75	0.08	4.24	95.76
1982	2418	15904	5460	1773	43	26	0	1.79	1.05	0.01	2.86	97.14
1983	2291	15900	5326	1795	38	17	5	1.65	0.75	0.21	2.62	97.38
1984	2693	17687	5852	1846	60	19	4	2.23	0.69	0.15	3.07	96.93
1985	2526	17769	5889	1832	65	18	5	2.57	0.70	0.19	3.46	96.54
1986	2550	18996	5367	1829	57	26	8	2.24	1.03	0.30	3.57	96.43
1987	2730	20683	5819	2124	74	37	5	2.73	1.37	0.18	4.27	95.73
1988	3034	19149	6588	2279	90	63	8	2.97	2.06	0.25	5.28	94.72
1989	3618	20535	7107	2087	121	26	14	3.34	0.72	0.40	4.45	95.55
1990	3656	23990	7383	2636	170	70	8	4.65	1.91	0.22	6.78	93.22
1991	3421	19509	8431	3061	189	57	5	5.52	1.67	0.15	7.34	92.66
1992	3731	23227	9375	3473	284	88	6	7.61	2.36	0.16	10.13	89.87
1993	4015	21482	9492	4005	380	90	7	9.46	2.24	0.17	11.88	88.12
1994	4584	25981	8884	4767	467	110	7	10.19	2.40	0.15	12.74	87.26
1995	6496	34456	11460	4767	994	138	11	15.30	2.12	0.17	17.60	82.40
1996	7074	40090	12150	5028	1138	87	11	16.09	1.23	0.16	17.47	82.53

Sources: Based on data from IMF (various issues).

Table 7.5   Intensity of Bangladesh's trade with its trading partners in South Asia and the rest of the world, 1975–96.

A: Export intensity indices

Year	India	Hong Kong	South Korea	Paki-stan	Singa-pore	Sri Lanka	Thai-land	USA	AUS	Japan	Germany	UK	China	Belgium	France	Italy	Nether-lands
1975	2.15	0.07	0.00	0.00	2.04	9.81	0.00	1.27	1.61	0.27	0.14	0.87	0.00	0.67	0.17	0.40	0.43
1976	3.24	0.50	0.00	11.68	3.44	2.54	3.06	1.13	2.03	0.37	0.20	1.48	2.69	0.87	0.34	0.41	0.44
1977	0.20	0.17	0.04	29.04	1.81	25.85	0.98	0.95	1.97	0.51	0.20	1.41	5.47	0.82	0.29	0.89	0.42
1978	0.71	0.29	0.02	35.48	1.39	14.36	0.36	1.03	1.85	0.73	0.16	0.89	5.99	0.63	0.15	1.02	0.37
1979	3.20	0.34	0.42	22.03	2.06	3.30	0.30	0.94	2.42	0.87	0.23	1.30	3.26	0.73	0.14	1.45	0.40
1980	1.46	1.81	1.14	25.30	6.07	5.77	0.98	0.70	2.64	0.53	0.19	0.84	3.87	0.88	0.15	0.73	0.38
1981	3.22	1.25	0.15	18.93	5.92	3.37	2.16	0.71	1.83	0.46	0.15	0.83	2.36	0.54	0.09	0.63	0.55
1982	2.98	0.42	0.03	17.98	7.29	0.66	0.96	0.72	2.12	0.81	0.22	0.89	3.17	0.82	0.15	0.65	0.47
1983	0.81	0.34	0.42	17.98	0.99	0.52	0.78	0.72	1.57	0.79	0.14	0.79	1.63	1.12	0.12	0.75	0.43
1984	2.97	0.36	0.01	20.07	2.28	0.30	0.84	0.70	1.48	0.84	0.20	1.20	0.71	1.82	0.20	1.41	0.41
1985	3.54	0.71	0.14	14.96	2.23	0.23	1.15	1.06	1.18	1.17	0.26	0.99	0.63	1.68	0.09	0.82	0.46
1986	0.78	0.49	0.08	12.67	1.54	0.63	0.42	1.04	0.93	1.07	0.25	0.74	1.10	1.03	0.08	0.87	0.42
1987	0.72	0.45	0.04	6.46	1.59	0.13	0.16	1.02	0.93	0.55	0.24	0.49	0.80	0.51	0.11	0.88	0.27
1988	0.98	0.41	0.06	10.88	1.35	16.86	0.69	1.57	1.86	0.85	0.56	0.86	0.84	0.95	0.29	1.96	0.55
1989	1.20	0.46	0.03	7.57	3.01	7.16	0.14	1.73	1.47	0.61	0.48	0.88	1.34	0.80	0.34	1.33	0.49
1990	1.92	0.41	0.03	6.53	1.62	6.37	0.13	2.07	1.46	0.58	0.65	1.12	0.97	0.93	0.55	0.20	0.65
1991	2.53	0.51	0.05	9.94	1.07	4.21	0.45	1.89	1.01	0.48	0.96	1.46	0.71	1.28	0.84	1.32	0.99
1992	0.33	0.63	0.09	6.09	1.03	6.03	0.66	2.53	0.81	0.43	0.78	1.30	0.37	1.06	0.85	1.40	1.01
1993	1.00	0.73	0.08	4.54	0.90	3.72	0.54	2.11	0.46	0.40	1.14	1.58	0.10	1.27	1.05	1.35	1.10
1994	1.50	0.85	0.10	3.47	0.52	1.36	0.12	2.09	0.47	0.41	1.00	1.82	0.17	1.33	1.09	1.45	1.25
1995	1.71	0.99	0.08	0.37	0.30	3.79	0.12	2.13	0.39	0.50	1.09	1.98	0.22	1.38	1.13	1.08	1.30
1996	0.80	0.77	0.06	0.46	0.21	0.64	0.28	2.11	0.40	0.53	1.23	2.16	0.23	1.71	1.35	0.12	1.62

Table 7.5 continued

B: Import intensity indices

Year	India	Hong Kong	South Korea	Paki-stan	Singa-pore	Sri Lanka	Thai-land	USA	AUS	Japan	Germany	UK	China	Belgium	France	Italy	Nether-lands
1975	11.49	0.56	0.01	12.48	1.40	6.25	0.08	1.93	2.61	0.78	0.48	0.60	0.27	0.06	0.12	0.06	0.37
1976	12.18	0.19	0.10	7.55	2.88	2.40	0.13	1.33	3.08	0.91	0.25	1.12	1.40	0.17	0.28	0.03	0.47
1977	7.53	0.53	0.84	9.25	1.07	2.05	3.86	1.12	1.69	1.14	0.37	0.79	2.52	0.14	0.29	0.05	0.38
1978	5.20	0.29	1.09	11.56	3.30	3.21	3.25	1.07	0.95	1.63	0.34	1.02	4.10	0.07	0.17	0.04	0.82
1979	4.50	0.27	1.11	8.45	3.50	3.31	2.03	0.92	2.44	2.02	0.38	1.46	4.45	0.20	0.13	0.06	0.45
1980	5.03	0.36	1.23	9.54	3.38	3.24	1.64	1.17	1.63	1.62	0.38	0.96	4.18	0.07	0.13	0.05	0.66
1981	5.64	0.53	1.14	11.15	2.07	1.35	3.87	0.46	2.94	1.32	0.46	0.77	3.94	0.09	0.29	0.03	0.74
1982	3.15	0.26	0.49	7.54	1.73	0.21	1.54	0.70	1.45	1.57	0.35	0.59	3.52	0.15	0.30	0.04	0.85
1983	2.83	0.57	0.85	4.11	5.46	3.42	1.62	1.00	0.57	0.84	0.43	0.85	1.94	0.15	0.28	0.06	0.65
1984	3.75	0.99	0.93	4.83	7.17	1.90	8.55	0.78	3.24	1.02	0.32	0.80	2.91	0.08	0.29	0.05	0.98
1985	4.56	1.21	1.50	4.63	6.60	2.72	7.41	0.86	1.19	1.26	0.35	0.62	2.17	0.06	0.17	0.07	0.95
1986	4.24	1.04	1.32	6.06	6.38	5.10	2.29	0.76	0.97	1.17	0.36	0.66	1.84	0.08	0.34	0.06	0.54
1987	5.16	1.55	1.37	7.71	4.91	3.16	6.93	0.65	1.56	1.42	0.24	0.57	1.79	0.09	0.19	0.09	0.59
1988	5.99	1.70	1.38	12.30	3.57	4.68	1.49	0.50	1.38	1.60	0.09	0.73	1.81	0.13	0.14	0.10	0.87
1989	6.13	1.46	1.40	4.49	3.88	7.52	3.81	0.63	1.72	1.34	0.25	0.48	2.04	0.11	0.12	0.10	0.82
1990	8.84	1.89	2.22	11.60	7.14	3.91	1.44	0.44	1.43	1.55	0.28	0.59	1.83	0.09	0.22	0.10	1.01
1991	10.81	2.07	2.43	8.98	5.04	2.57	0.67	0.43	1.81	1.00	0.32	0.55	2.09	0.10	0.17	0.15	0.61
1992	15.43	2.44	2.81	12.16	3.51	2.42	0.99	0.58	1.47	0.87	0.28	0.70	2.53	0.11	0.13	0.12	0.45
1993	17.36	2.19	3.16	12.43	2.29	2.27	1.07	0.35	1.22	1.28	0.30	0.64	2.06	0.12	0.15	0.19	0.76
1994	17.87	2.15	3.19	13.89	2.10	2.02	1.19	0.39	1.68	1.23	0.20	0.55	2.29	0.11	0.19	0.15	0.41
1995	25.38	1.89	2.59	13.47	2.61	2.25	1.05	0.53	1.13	1.05	0.42	0.57	3.15	0.09	0.16	0.18	0.29
1996	24.60	1.80	2.39	6.96	2.48	2.00	1.07	0.27	1.79	1.09	0.27	0.47	3.56	0.11	0.41	0.23	0.26

Sources: Based on data from IMF (various issues).

Table 7.6   Bangladesh's bilateral trade with India, 1975–96

Year	Bangladesh's import-export ratio *vis-a-vis* India	Bangladesh's exports to India as a percentage of India's total imports	Bangladesh's imports from India as a percentage of India's total exports
1975	15.51	0.09	1.88
1976	8.83	0.14	1.25
1977	81.50	0.00	0.81
1978	18.70	0.03	0.65
1979	3.31	0.13	0.57
1980	6.95	0.06	0.70
1981	3.17	0.13	0.82
1982	2.13	0.13	0.44
1983	5.49	0.04	0.39
1984	2.12	0.16	0.56
1985	2.19	0.17	0.64
1986	7.43	0.04	0.54
1987	6.76	0.05	0.60
1878	10.34	0.05	0.68
1989	11.28	0.05	0.76
1990	7.73	0.09	0.95
1991	8.22	0.12	1.06
1992	71.00	0.02	1.54
1993	29.23	0.06	1.88
1994	19.46	0.09	1.93
1995	27.61	0.10	3.26
1996	56.90	0.05	3.31

Source: Based on data from IMF (various issues).

Table 7.7   Bangladesh's bilateral trade with China, 1975–96

Year	Bangladesh's exports to China as % of her total exports	Bangladesh's imports from China as % of her total imports	Bangladesh's import-export ratio *vis-a-vis* China	Bangladesh's exports to China as % of China's total imports	Bangladesh's imports from China as % of China's total exports
1975	0.00	0.20	0.00	0.00	0.04
1976	1.50	0.93	1.45	0.12	0.14
1977	3.23	1.64	1.21	0.24	0.27
1978	4.76	2.96	1.82	0.25	0.51
1979	2.96	3.52	3.49	0.14	0.56
1980	3.94	3.82	3.21	0.16	0.58
1981	2.39	4.28	6.00	0.10	0.57
1982	3.35	4.47	4.21	0.14	0.49
1983	2.00	2.55	3.14	0.09	0.26
1984	0.99	4.04	11.00	0.04	0.44
1985	1.42	3.28	6.57	0.03	0.30
1986	2.31	2.90	2.97	0.06	0.24
1987	1.43	3.01	3.19	0.06	0.21
1878	1.67	3.20	4.50	0.04	0.20
1989	2.64	3.71	3.90	0.06	0.25
1990	1.50	3.39	4.96	0.05	0.20
1991	1.24	4.30	7.00	0.03	0.20
1992	0.79	5.76	13.44	0.02	0.25
1993	0.26	5.08	34.00	0.00	0.22
1994	0.45	6.52	24.92	0.01	0.25
1995	0.58	9.25	33.39	0.01	0.40
1996	0.60	10.23	36.20	0.01	0.48

Sources: Based on data from IMF (various issues).

8 Aid and Fiscal Behaviour in Developing Asia

Akhter Ahmed

8.1 INTRODUCTION

Many lofty expectations surrounded the role and impact of development aid in the early days of its provision. According to the protagonists of aid many developing countries could not grow at sufficiently rapid, eventually self-sustaining, rates required to modernise their economies. Of course, there were many early critics, who saw aid as a way of keeping poor countries poor and dependent upon their much richer, western counterparts. This group was as adamant of the negative effects of aid as the proponents of its positive effects. Applied research on the macroeconomic impact of aid has contributed little to this debate, to the extent that the relevant literature fails to settle the issue either way. The present study argues that the exiting literature's theoretical underpinnings are at best vague and at worst non-existent, data sets are too aggregate and statistical methods too primitive. Yet even more serious is that the literature (with one important exception of Heller 1975) has all too often ignored the precise process or channels through which aid affects such macroeconomic variables such as income and growth.

The basic premise of this study is that since almost all foreign aid goes initially to the public sector, understanding this sector's response to aid is a pre-requisite to understanding its wider macroeconomic impact. Thus, while stopping short of the wider macroeconomic impact of aid, this study builds on a very recent development in the literature by empirically modelling the public sector response to the inflow of foreign aid. The basic objective is to analyse the impact of aid on public sector behaviour of aid recipient countries, by determining the effect of aid on public investment, recurrent expenditures, domestic taxation and borrowing using pooled cross-section data for Bangladesh, India, Pakistan and the Philippines for the 1965–92 period.

This study follows the seminal work of Heller (1975) and its subsequent applications of Heller's fiscal response model. It modifies and extends this pre-existing research through the following theoretical and empirical contributions:

- a utility function more consistent with maximising public sector behaviour

- an estimation procedure which takes into account recent development in time series econometrics

- a model catering for financing of investment as well as recurrent expenditures by domestic borrowing

- the use of time series as opposed to pooled cross-section data

It proceeds first of all with a brief review of the fiscal response literature. This is followed by a discussion of the model. Estimation procedures are then discussed. Finally, the empirical results are analysed and concluding observations made.

8.2   FISCAL RESPONSE LITERATURE: A BRIEF REVIEW

Fiscal response implies deciding between various sources of revenues and areas of expenditures. A number of previous studies including Griffin and Enos (1970), Areskoug (1973), Weisskopf (1972a; 1972b), and Chenery and Eckstein (1970) found a negative relationship between aid and savings and that there was substantial leakage out of aid to consumption purposes or aid is fungible.

The *fungibility* concept has more closely been examined by researchers like Heller (1975), Mosley (1986), McGuire (1987), Khilji and Zampelli (1991), Gang and H. Khan (1991), H. A. Khan and Hoshino (1992), and Pack and Pack (1990). Instead of using the aid-savings model assumed by Griffin (1970), these researchers used fiscal response models which analyse the effect of aid on different budgetary variables of the recipient countries.

Heller (1975) developed a public sector behaviour model in the form of a utility function to investigate the effect of foreign aid on intermediate policy variables such as public investment, government consumption and taxes. Heller used time series data for eleven African nations. Employing pooled time series-cross section model he used government investment, government civil and socio-economic consumptions, domestic taxation, and domestic borrowing as explanatory variables. Distinctions were made between alternative types of foreign capital inflows (such as grants and concessional loans) and between alternative sources of aid (such as bilateral vs. multilateral and private vs. public). Heller employed two budget constraints:

- the first shows that investment is financed by entire borrowing, part of taxes, and part of different categories of aid

- the second constraint assumes that recurrent government expenditures are financed by part of taxes and remaining part of aid

Heller found that the increment in total spending is about 30–60 percent of the value of aid inflow. Official grants was found to have a disproportionate leakage into consumption *vis-a-vis* private grants. Loans appear to have the most positive effect on investment compared to other expenditure categories. Heller also found that aid reduces domestic taxation efforts in those countries. Since then, the model has been adopted by Mosley and Hudson (1984), Gang and H. Khan (1991) and H. A. Khan and Hoshino (1992). The most important economic variables considered by the above studies, were government investment, revenue (taxation), and current government consumption (developmental and non-developmental expenditures). All the studies recognised the possibilities that aid may reduce revenue earning efforts (taxation) and that aid may be substituted between government investment and current consumption.

The present study uses Heller's framework as the base model. But a straightforward application of the Heller's model is hazardous because of the following problems: specification of the utility function, domestic borrowing, target variables, constraints, and treatment of income (for further details see Ahmed 1996). Heller, Gang and H. Khan, and H. A. Khan and Hoshino have used linear terms in their loss function. The objective here is to achieve the unconstrained maximum value of U as zero when targets are achieved. Binh and McGillivray (1993) have shown that given the above specification of the model it is not possible to obtain a result. To overcome this problem, Binh and McGillivray (1993, p.175) suggested use of a quadratic loss function without the linear terms. Heller, Gang and H. Khan, and H. A. Khan and Hoshino assumed that domestic borrowing is only used for financing investment expenditure. The model assumes that domestic borrowing funds are not only used for financing government investment but a portion of this is used to finance government recurrent expenditures. Another criticism for the fiscal response models in general is that these models do not capture income feed-back effects due to increase in aid. This study incorporates expected income feedback effects into the tax target equation. Further details on these are provided in Section 8.3.1.

8.3   A NEW FISCAL RESPONSE MODEL

Assumptions underlying fiscal behaviour of the recipient country are:

- in addition to financing public investment, borrowing is also assumed to be used for financing different public sector expenditures
- the assumption that target level borrowing is zero will be relaxed
- a quadratic utility function as opposed to linear-quadratic form that is, utility function without linear terms
- target specification

Based on the above assumptions and discussion we may write the public sector utility function of any less developed country in period t as follows:

$$U = F[I_g, (Y - T), G_d, G_{nd}, B] \tag{1}$$

where

I_g =   government capital investment expenditure including human development expenses, gross capital formation such as total infrastructural development, highways, roads, bridges, hospitals and educational buildings plus net loans to other sectors of the economy

$(Y\text{-}T)$ =   the private sector's disposable income

G_d =   public sector recurrent developmental expenditures which includes current expenses on health, transport, agriculture and transfer of resources to the local bodies

G_{nd} =   government expenditure for non-developmental purposes but essential for maintaining peace and stability of the country. This include expenditures on civil administration, maintaining police and armed forces, foreign liaison, public debt servicing, etc.

B =   all domestic public borrowing from all sources.

It is assumed that T and B are endogenous. This model assumes that the recipient governments recurrent expenditures (G_d and G_{nd}) are financed by borrowing (B). Disbursed grants (A_1) and disbursed other inflows or loans (A_2) will continue to be assumed as endogenous to the model. Based on these assumptions the utility function can be written as follows :

$$U = \alpha_0 - \frac{\alpha_1}{2}(I_g - I_g^*)^2 - \frac{\alpha_2}{2}(T - T^*)^2 - \frac{\alpha_3}{3}(G_d - G_d^*)^2$$

$$- \frac{\alpha_4}{2}(G_{nd} - G_{nd}^*)^2 - \frac{\alpha_5}{2}(B - B^*)^2 \tag{2}$$

$$T + B + A_1 + A_2 = I_g + G_d + G_{nd} \tag{3}$$

In contrast to the Heller model the present study assumes that G_d and G_{nd} are also partly financed by B. Thus, the final set of constraints take the following form:

$$I_g = \rho_{1,1}T + \rho_{2,1}A_1 + \rho_{3,1}A_2 + \rho_{4,1}B \tag{4}$$

$$(G_d + G_{nd}) = \rho_{1,2}T + \rho_{2,2}A_1 + \rho_{3,2}A_2 + \rho_{4,2}B \tag{5}$$

First order conditions for the utility function (2) are derived using the set of associated constraints (4 and 5) and applying the Lagrange multiplier. The structural equations are derived as follows:

$$\alpha_0 - \frac{\alpha_1}{2}(I_g - I_g^*)^2 - \frac{\alpha^2}{2}(T - T^*)^2 - \frac{\alpha_3}{2}(G_d - G_d^*)^2 - \frac{\alpha_4}{2}(G_{nd} - G)$$

$$- \frac{\alpha_5}{2}(B - B^*)^2 + \lambda_1 I_g - \lambda_1\rho_{1,1}T - \lambda_1\rho_{2,1}A_1 - \lambda_1\rho_{3,1}A_2 - \lambda_1\rho_{4,1}B$$

$$+ \lambda_2(G_d + G_{nd}) - \lambda_2\rho_{1,2}T - \lambda_2\rho_{2,2}A_1 - \lambda_2\rho_{3,2}A_2 - \lambda_2\rho_{4,2}B = 0 \tag{6}$$

$$G_{nd} = \beta_1\rho_{1,2}T + \beta_1\rho_{2,2}A_1 + \beta_1\rho_{3,2}A_2 + \beta_1\rho_{4,2}B - \beta_1G_d^* + \beta_2G_{nd}^* \tag{7}$$

$$G_d = \beta_1G_d^* - \beta_2G_{nd}^* + (1 - \beta_1)(\rho_{1,2}T + \rho_{2,2}A_1 + \rho_{3,2}A_2 + \rho_{4,2}B) \tag{8}$$

$$T = \beta_3T^* - \beta_4B - \beta_5A_1 - \beta_6A_2 + \rho_{1,2}\beta_7G_{nd} \tag{9}$$

$$I_G = \beta_8I_g^* + \beta_9(\rho_{1,1}T + \rho_{2,1}A_1 + \rho_{3,1}A_2) + \beta_{10}(G_d - G_d^*) \tag{10}$$

$$B = \rho_{4,1}\beta_{11}I_g^* + \rho_{4,2}\beta_{12}G_{nd} + \beta_{13}G_d^* - \beta_{14}T - \beta_{15}A_1 - \beta_{16}A_2 \tag{11}$$

Equations (10) and (11) for I_g and B respectively assume that the target level borrowing is equal to zero ($B^* = 0$). The structural equations for I_g and B assuming target level borrowing (B^*) are:

$$I_g = \delta_1 I_g^* + \delta_2 (\rho_{1,1} T + \rho_{2,1} A_1 + \rho_{3,1} A_2 - \rho_{4,1} B^*) - \delta_3 (G_d - G_d^*) \tag{12}$$

$$B = \gamma_1 B^* + \rho_{4,2} \gamma_2 (G_{nd} + G_d^*) - \gamma_3 T + \rho_{4,1} \gamma_4 I_g^* - \gamma_5 A_1 - \gamma_6 A_2 \tag{13}$$

While specifying the target level variables previous studies such as Heller (1975) and Gang and H. Khan (1991) have ignored the possibilities of expected income feed-back effects of foreign aid on the level of taxation McGillivray and Papadopoulos (1992). Note that similar explanations for the target level borrowing (B^*) is also valid. For example level of taxation rises with the increase in income. It is possible that an increase in foreign aid will positively affect the level of income. As a consequence the level of taxation will also be affected. This scenario can be captured by treating tax target as a function (among others) of expected income. Expected income (Y^e) is dependent on previous period's income (Yt_{-1}) and previous period's all foreign capital inflows (A_{t-1}). The target tax equation:

$$T^* = \gamma_1 Y^e + \gamma_2 M^e$$

where

$$Y^e = \gamma_3 Y_{t-1} + \gamma_4 A^e$$

with A^e is all expected foreign aid commitments defined as:

$$A^e = \gamma_5 A_{t-1};$$

and

$$M^e = \gamma_6 M_{t-1},$$

where M represents imports. Imports are added since income generated as customs and excise duties due to imports alters the level of taxation. Substituting the value of A^e (iii) into (ii) gives

$$Y^e = \gamma_3 Y_{t-1} + \gamma_4 (\gamma_5 A_{t-1})$$

Again substituting (v) and (iv) in (i)gives

$$T^* = \gamma_1 \gamma_3 Y_{t-1} + \gamma_1 \gamma_4 \gamma_5 A_{t-1} + \gamma_2 \gamma_6 M_{t-1},$$

or

$$T^* = \alpha_6 Y_{t-1} + \alpha_7 A_{t-1} + \alpha_8 M_{t-1}$$

where:

$$\alpha_6 = \gamma_1 \gamma_3 \; ; \; \alpha_7 = \gamma_1 \gamma_4 \gamma_5; \; \alpha_8 = \gamma_2 \gamma_6.$$

The remaining target equations are assumed to be determined by the following relationships:

$$I_g^* = \alpha_9 Y_{t-1} + \alpha_{10} I_{p_{t-1}} + \alpha_{11} \Delta N + \alpha_{12} F_{t-1} + \alpha_{13} I_{g_{t-1}};$$

$$G_d^* = \alpha_{14} G_{d_{t-1}} + \alpha_{15} Y_{t-1} + \alpha_{16} E_{t-1};$$

$$G_{nd}^* = \alpha_{17} Y_{t-1} + \alpha_{18} G_{nd_{t-1}};$$

$$B^* = B_{t-1} + T_{t-1} + A_{1t-1} + A_{2t-1}$$

where

Y_t	=	the current year GDP
ΔN	=	change in size of population
I_p	=	private sector investment
F	=	foreign exchange reserve
ED	=	school enrolment up to year twelve
M	=	value of total real imports

The target level of public sector investment I_g^* is derived from a target rate of growth of the economy, the perceived role of public sector in achieving that growth, the relative productivity of public sector investment, and the absorption capacity of the public sector. Due to non-availability of comparable annual investment targets in the country development plans, I_g^* are defined as dependent positively on the previous period's income (y_{t-1}). Both Heller (1975) and Gang and H. Khan (1991) assumed that current period government investment I_g^* is dependent on the current period private investment (I_{pt}). This assumption does not relate to the reality since it is not possible to obtain an accurate statistics of the Ipt at the beginning of that period. It is more plausible to explain I_g^* in terms of I_{pt-1}. Hence this study uses the latter variable as one of the explanatory variables which is expected to have a negative impact on I_g^* (although sometimes these two variables can be positively related when similar kinds of technologies are used in both the sectors). In contrast to Heller and Gang and H. Khan the present study includes three more explanatory variables (such as ΔN, F_{t-1}, and I_{gt-1}). It is expected that an increase in population size and an increase in the level of foreign exchange reserve will have positive impact on the level of I_g^*. Also it is expected that previous period's actual government investment (I_{gt-1}) will have a significant impact on the level of target investment in the current period. Both the Heller and Gang and Khan studies ignored the possibilities of such correlation.

Several instruments are used to determine target level government developmental or socio-economic expenditure (G_d^*). It is always the case that educational expenditure constitute a substantial fraction of government's developmental expenditure. Hence previous year's school enrolments up to year twelve (ED_{t-1}) is used to measure the level of this activity. The level of G_d^* is also assumed to be directly dependent upon previous year's actual G_d and income.

In the case of target non-developmental or civil consumption expenditure G_{nd}^* it is assumed that the variable is linearly related to its value in the previous period. This assumption reflects the fundamental continuity of this service. The present study assumes that government non-developmental expenditure is also dependent on expected income of the current period (Y_t^e) which is determined using similar techniques as discussed previously.

In the target borrowing equation (18) it is assumed that the target borrowing in the current period (B_t^*) will depend on the actual level of borrowing in the previous period (B_{t-1}). It assumed that higher the level of B_{t-1} lower will be the target borrowing in the current period. Also higher the level of taxation and foreign inflows in the previous period it is expected that lower will be the level of borrowing in the current period. While specifying the target tax equation (14) it was assumed that the target tax in the current period is positively related to the level of expected income (Y^e) in the current period. In the case of target borrowing it is postulated that the variable is inversely related to Y^e. This is because higher the level of expected income lower will be the need to borrow money for financing different expenditures.

8.4   DATA AND ESTIMATION PROCEDURE

Since the data (details of data sources are provided in the appendix) are in the form of time-series, it calls for testing for the presence of unit root and consequently cointegration. To test for unit root the Augmented Dickey-Fuller (ADF) procedure has been adopted and for cointegration the procedure developed by Engle and Granger (1987) has been used. The former test shows that in every data series there is presence of unit root, I(1). The subsequent test for cointegration reveals that the individual data series, despite being individually non-stationary, are cointegrated. Therefore, there exists a long-run relationship between the data series. Hence, to estimate the target equations first difference using the Error Correction Mechanism (ECM) has been used. The structural equations are a set of simultaneous equations. Therefore, an application of the least squares techniques is likely to yield biased and inconsistent estimates. The three-stage least squares (3SLS) method of estimation. As opposed to the single equation techniques, the 3SLS considers the structure of the model with all the restrictions that this structure imposes on the values of the parameters. If any model has a simultaneous equation system then it is almost certain that the random variable of any equation ui will be correlated with the random variable of the other equations. While the OLS ignore this fact, the 3SLS recognises this during the process of computation.

Estimation of the target variables calls for some additional work. In the ideal situation one would know the values of the targets. But a close investigation of the published data sources (both national and international) reveals that there is no mention of targets. The only values which are available, apart from the actual ones, are forecasts of different economic variables. But these forecasts are not targets. Forecasts are made based on targets. Since targets are not readily available we are left with no other choice but to estimate the targets. Estimation of targets can be done in either of two ways:

■ to approximate targets by regressing the explanatory variables on a series of instrumental variables and obtain the target values by subtracting computed error terms from computed values of the dependent variable (see Gang and H. Khan 1991), or

■ define the targets as linear combinations of the instrumental variables, then plug the whole target equation into the utility function and obtain the targets (see Heller 1975).

The present study employs the first method due to some limitations of the second. These are discussed in detail in A. Ahmed (1996) and are not repeated here.

8.5   EMPIRICAL RESULTS

The model is estimated twice:

- it is assumed that the desired borrowing level is zero (**Model 1**)
- the desired borrowing is assumed to be not equal to zero (**Model 2**)

8.5.1   Interpretation: Results of estimates using Model 1

This model (equations 7–11) assumes that domestic borrowing is not only used for financing government investment but a portion of which is used to finance recurrent expenditures. The desired level of borrowing is assumed to be zero. The results are set out in Table 8.1. This model is similar to the one used by McGillivray and Papadopoulos (1992) in the case of Greece data. It can be seen from Table 8.1 that the estimates of ρ_1 across the countries are significantly different from zero at 0.05 level. This indicates that when the policy makers are allowed to use borrowing funds for financing recurrent expenditures they do not take much of the tax revenue away from investment expenditures. The estimations of ρ_1 for India indicating that 49 percent of taxation and domestic recurrent revenue have remained in recurrent budget with the balance being allocated to investment. This result is some what similar to the McGillivary and Papadopoulos (1992) who found the value of ρ_1 to be 0.77. From this result it can be concluded that a significant level of public savings has been achieved. In the case of ρ_2 it is found that only in the case of Bangladesh the estimate is significantly different from zero, the absolute value of which is 0.48.

This estimate is consistent with *a priori* expectation since it is expected that the recipient governments would try to use aid funds more for the investment purpose although there is some evidence of fungibility. The estimate of ρ_3 is found to be significant in the case of India and The Philippines and the absolute values are found to be more than one. For example, in the case of India the estimated value of ρ_3 is 1.56 indicating that not only one extra rupee of non-grant foreign inflow remains in the recurrent budget but also pulls funds away from investment expenditure, thus confirming the *Please effect*. In the case of India and The Philippines ρ_2 is found to be insignificant confirming that foreign aid grant do not have any statistically significant effect on the government recurrent expenditures.

With regard to ρ_4 (parameter associated with the domestic borrowing) it can be seen from Table 8.1 that only in the case of India and Pakistan are the estimated values significantly different from zero. For India given the value of 0.99 it can be concluded in contrast to previous studies, that 99 percent of the domestic borrowing is used to finance recurrent expenditures while only one percent goes to the investment expenditure. Almost similar explanation can be given for The Philippines. None of the previous studies such as Heller (1975), Gang and H. Khan (1991) and H. A. Khan and Hoshino (1992) did keep the provision of using the domestic borrowing funds for recurrent expenditures in their constraint equations. This made their constraint equation very much restrictive.

Now turn to the estimates of the structural equation parameters (βs). It can be seen from Table 8.1 that the estimated value of β_1 across the countries are significantly different from zero and are less than one. Given the value of β_1 for Bangladesh (0.95) it may be said that 95 percent of each additional taka allocated to the recurrent budget has been used to finance non-developmental consumption while the rest is used for developmental consumption. Similar explanation can be given for the estimated value of the coefficient for the remaining countries. Link between targeted and actual expenditures and the tax revenue is shown by the estimated values of β_3 and β_7. Assume that G^*_{nd} is higher than G_{nd} so that targeted non-development expenditure exceeds the actual. With $\rho_1 > 0$ and $\beta_7 < 0$ would imply that in this case the tax burden is reduced. In the case of Bangladesh and India this assumption holds true, whereas for the Philippines and Pakistan the opposite is true. β_3 close to one implies that higher targeted tax will actually increase tax burden. The estimate of β_{13} reveals that only in the case of Pakistan and Bangladesh the targeted developmental expenditure has positive impact on the level of borrowing. Estimate of β_{14} reveals that only in Pakistan the actual level of tax and domestic borrowing are inversely related.

8.5.2   Interpretation: Results of estimates using Model 2

Model 2 assumes that the domestic borrowing is used for investment expenditure as well as for government recurrent expenditures. But the desired level of borrowing (B^*) is assumed to be zero. In this model the last assumption is relaxed, that is, the desired domestic borrowing is assumed to be a positive number. Table 8.2 sets out the results for Model 2. It should be noted here that the definition of ρ_1 to β_{16} remains exactly the same as of model B. Due to the non-zero assumption of targeted borrowing, the equations for I_g and B have changed and hence the above two equations are estimated twice.

A cross table comparison between Tables 8.1 and 8.2 reveals that in general across the countries the estimated values of most of the parameters (with some exceptions) have not changed significantly due to the non-zero assumption of the targeted borrowing. For example, in both the models the estimates of ρ_1 across the countries are more or less similar to each other with the exception of Pakistan. This implies that allocation of the tax revenue among competing usage is not influenced by the fact that the participating governments are having a positive target level of borrowing. But a significant difference can be observed with regard to the estimates of ρ_2 in both the tables in the case of India and The Philippines. In the case of India the estimate is statistically insignificant in Table 8.1, where as in the later case the estimated value is –6.92 and significant. This suggests a strong pro-investment bias of foreign grants (*fly-paper effect*). When there exist a positive targeted borrowing the policy makers may have relied on the borrowing funds to finance recurrent expenditures. In the case of the Philippines quite a reverse trend has been found (ρ_2 = 2.54). With regard to foreign loans the estimated coefficient is found to be more or less similar in both the models across the countries. The estimated value of ρ_4, the coefficient for borrowing is found to be different only in the case of Philippines (from a negative and insignificant value in Table 8.1 to a positive (0.67) and significant value in Table 8.2). This implies that 67 percent of any additional domestic borrowing is used to finance recurrent expenditures while the rest is used to finance the investment expenditure.

Insignificant estimate of ρ_4 in the case of Bangladesh suggest that all the additional domestic borrowing money is used to finance the investment expenditure. Since the estimates of βs are somewhat similar across the tables we shall not discuss them here, rather attention will be given to interpret the estimated coefficients of the equations for I_g and B of Table 8.2 when $B^* \neq 0$ (equations 12 and 13). Recall that the above two equations are estimated twice in model 2 because of the different assumptions adopted for desired borrowing level. β_8, β_9 and β_{10} (equation 10) represents estimated coefficients of the I_g equation when $B^* = 0$, while δ_1, δ_2 and δ_3 are the coefficients of investment equation when $B^* \neq 0$ (equation 12). Similarly β_{11} to β_{16} are the coefficients of the borrowing equation when $B^* = 0$ (equation 11) and γ_1 to γ_6 are the coefficients in the borrowing equation when $B^* \neq 0$ (equation 13). First consider the equations for investment (10 and 12). It can be seen from the Table that coefficients for targeted investment across the countries are basically same with or without the zero or non-zero assumptions for borrowing. Similar is the case with β_9 and δ_2. A significant difference can be noticed in the case of Pakistan with respect to the estimate of β_{10} and δ_3 while the estimated value of the former is 2.37 and the latter is -2.0 and both are significant. The estimated value of β_{10} implies that when the targeted borrowing is assumed to be zero, if $G_d > G^*_d$ then an increase in G_d will also increase I_g and vice-versa. Opposite explanation is true for δ_3 when the targeted borrowing is assumed to be zero.

Consider now the estimates of the equations for borrowing (11 and 13). It can be seen from the Table 8.2 that the estimates of β_{11}, γ_1, β_{12} and γ_2 are insignificant for Bangladesh and India although major differences can be noticed with regard to the estimates of the above two parameters for Pakistan and The Philippines. In the case of Pakistan β_{11} is found to be insignificant but γ_1 is significant with absolute value of 0.06. This implies that when the desired borrowing is non-zero an increase in targeted investment will positively affect the actual level of borrowing. This result is in conformity with the set objectives of the policy makers who want to use the borrowed funds to increase investment. Assumption of zero targeted borrowing seems to have faulted the estimate of β_{11}. In the case of the Philippines the estimate of β_{11} is equal to 2.05. The restrictive assumption of desired borrowing again seems to have over estimated the value.

Estimates of β_{12} and γ_2 are also interesting. In the case of Bangladesh and Pakistan the estimates did not change at all which are insignificant for Bangladesh and significant for Pakistan. The results indicate that actual non-developmental expenditure has no impact on the level of actual borrowing in the former country while the effects did not change in the latter case even after altering the definition of the desired borrowing. Estimates of β_{13} is to be matched with the estimate of γ_3. It can be seen that in all the countries but Philippines estimates of the above two parameters did not change significantly although in India the absolute value of the coefficient for targeted developmental expenditure G_d^* has decreased from 699.27 to 0.99. Again it seems in this case the assumption of zero desired borrowing leads to overestimation of the parameter. In the case of the Philippines due to the assumption that desired borrowing is zero, turned the estimated value of β_{13} from -0.58 and significant to 0.49 and significant. While the negative value implies that G_d^* and B are inversely related the positive value implies just the opposite.

In general it can be concluded that the non-zero assumption of desired borrowing has improved the quality of the estimated coefficients in the sense that more economic information can be gathered from the estimates.

8.6   CONCLUDING OBSERVATIONS

All the countries under study both individually and collectively, received huge amount external resources in the form of the grants and the loans. External assistance is seen as necessary for getting the country's struggling economy out of a rut within a reasonably short period.

Employing a new fiscal response model the present study investigates the impact of aid on the budgetary variables of the recipient countries.

The estimated constraint equation parameters for the model suggest that, both domestic financing and foreign capital inflows are fungible at various levels among which the other inflow variable (mainly loans) is the least fungible. One of the important aspects of the results is that most of the assumptions concerning the sign and magnitude of the utility function and constraint equation parameters hold true. They reveal a fair degree of interdependence of the recurrent and capital budgets. It is also found that the signs of the structural equation parameters are consistent with some behavioural assumptions. For example, an increase in tax revenue has a positive effect on various expenditure categories and vice versa.

Empirical results suggest that foreign capital inflows affect both the revenue and expenditure side of recipient government budgets. With an increase in foreign aid, government consumption has increased although some public investment is also financed out of aid money. This study examines the effects of aid on fiscal response behaviour of the recipient countries. It is seen that a considerable amount of such foreign aid inflows is being used for consumption purposes. Apparently, it indicates the failure on part of these countries to use the aid money for desired purposes.

While it is most desirable that total aid money is used for its intended purposes, one point ought to be considered is that as long as the aid money is diverted from its desired uses to other development expenditure categories (such as health, transport, etc.) this should not necessarily be treated as a total waste. This is because an increase in expenditure in these sectors may still ultimately positively affect the rate of economic growth. On the other hand, if aid money is channelled to other government non-developmental categories (such as civil administration, police or military), then one could draw a conclusion that aid money is wasted. In this study it is found that quite a significant portion of aid money is diverted to the first category of expenditures.

The policy implications of this study's findings are relatively straightforward:

■ Firstly, since aid has in fact proved to be fungible, donors should mainly provide it in that category which is least fungible

■ Secondly, both donors and recipients ought implement controls which limit the extent of fungibility. From a donors perspective, this may dictate the tying of all aid to very specific projects or expenditure categories

The present study has not explored the relationship between public and private investments. Attention needs to be given on the effect of aid on the real exchange rate and the growth of money supply. Further research is warranted.

Table 8.1   Estimated Results of Model 1 for all Countries.
n = 27. Non-Linear 3SLS Estimates of Structural Parameters

Parameters	Bangladesh	India	Philippines	Pakistan
ρ_1	0.57 (1.37)	0.49 (4.47)	0.94 (5.42)	1.0 (9.23)
ρ_2	0.48 (1.78)	0.35 (0.09)	1.24 (0.78)	-0.77 (-0.83)
ρ_3	0.46 (0.83)	1.56 (3.68)	2.68 (1.86)	-0.10 (-0.89)
ρ_4	0.001 (0.0001)	0.99 (4.53)	-0.87 (-1.15)	0.69 (4.63)
β_1	0.95 (4.83)	0.33 (2.71)	0.80 (5.79)	0.96 (17.89)
β_2	0.94 (5.64)	0.74 (6.45)	0.19 (1.34)	0.02 (0.48)
β_3	1.04 (1.65)	0.10 (0.37)	0.71 (3.31)	0.52 (2.97)
β_4	1.78 (0.18)	-1.83 (-1.98)	0.47 (0.93)	0.12 (0.78)

Table 8. 1 continued

Parameters	Bangladesh	India	Philippines	Pakistan
β_5	0.95 (2.63)	−13.04 (−1.71)	1.97 (2.19)	−1.27 (−1.60)
β_6	0.91 (2.07)	−4.10 (−1.52)	−0.05 (−0.05)	−0.08 (−0.85)
β_7	0.73 (0.73)	−0.89 (−0.67)	0.86 (2.25)	0.67 (3.27)
β_8	0.99 (3.02)	0.37 (0.98)	1.01 (16.83)	0.91 (14.36)
β_9	0.98 (4.29)	0.74 (2.13)	0.03 (0.13)	0.08 (1.11)
β_{10}	0.83 (0.82)	0.68 (1.35)	0.19 (0.30)	1.37 (1.31)
β_{11}	0.25 (0.0001)	−0.45 (−0.17)	0.68 (0.86)	1.98 (4.10)
β_{13}	0.94 (4.14)	5.44 (0.57)	−0.55 −1.60)	1.45 (3.35)
β_{14}	0.88 (0.94)	4.21 (0.56)	−0.49 (−1.68)	1.38 (4.40
β_{15}	0.96 (3.21)	−12.37 (−0.29)	−1.04 (−0.88)	−0.98 (−0.776)
β_{16}	0.96 (2.11)	−5.54 −0.42)	−1.74 (−1.87)	−0.14 (−0.89)

Assumptions: (i) Fraction of the domestic borrowing is diverted to investment.
(ii) Target level borrowing $(B^*) = 0$.

Notes: Figures in the parentheses are asymptotic t-values 2. ρi's are the constraint equation parameters. ρ_1 is tax parameter, ρ_2, ρ_3 and ρ_4 are grant, loan and borrowing parameters respectively. 3. Critical *t*-values are: 1.703 (.05 level) and 1.314 (.10 level).

Table 8.2   Estimations of model 2 for all countries (n = 27) non-linear
3SLS estimates of structural parameters

Parameters	Bangladesh	India	Philippines	Pakistan
ρ_1	0.60 (1.71)	0.71 (24.75)	0.63 (12.8)	0.73 (6.62)
ρ_2	0.48 (1.90)	6.92 (−2.66)	2.54 (3.81)	0.98 (0.86)
ρ_3	0.47 (1.03)	1.45 (3.76)	1.59 (2.63)	−0.02 (−0.22)
ρ_4	0.06 (0.01)	0.71 (67.5)	0.67 (4.51)	0.99 (14.73)
β_1	0.96 (5.55)	0.83 (80.12)	0.78 (12.67)	0.71 (16.16)
β_2	0.94 (7.21)	0.16 (17.29)	0.22 (3.48)	0.30 (7.65)
β_3	0.99 (2.49)	0.27 (3.14)	0.78 (8.35)	0.51 (3.96)
β_4	1.05 (0.15)	1.49 (11.28)	1.09 (7.13)	0.38 (2.34)
β_5	0.94 (3.22)	−13.17 (−2.55)	2.63 (4.18)	0.28 (0.25)
β_6	0.91 (2.29)	5.93 (6.65)	−0.55 (−0.89)	0.02 (0.25)
β_7	0.81 (1.12)	3.94 (11.43)	1.42 (4.47)	1.40 (6.09)
β_8	1.00 (3.86)	2.01 (1.33)	1.01 (19.19)	0.97 (10.50)
β_9	0.98 (5.67)	0.005 (3.19)	−0.02 (−0.43)	0.08 (1.12)
β_{10}	0.91 (1.66)	−113.25 (−21.77)	0.23 (0.47)	2.37 (1.93)
β_{11}	0.49 (0.21)	151.66 (0.52)	2.05 (1.96)	−123.7 (−0.02)
β_{12}	7.00 (0.01)	−2590 (−1.29)	1.44 (3.31)	0.79 (9.20)

Table 8.2 continued

Parameters	Bangladesh	India	Philippines	Pakistan
β_{13}	0.96	699.2	−0.58	0.93
	(2.50)	(0.003)	(4.39)	(3.82)
β_{14}	0.96	0.22	0.74	0.57
	(2.50)	(0.003)	(4.39)	(3.82)
β_{15}	0.95	185.12	1.00	1.05
	(3.68)	(0.20)	(1.58)	(1.15)
β_{16}	0.95	−20.29	0.62	−0.01
	(2.62)	(−0.65)	(1.13)	(−0.13)
δ_1	1.01	2.02	1.01	0.95
	(2.39)	(1.33)	(20.6)	(11.42)
δ_2	0.97	−0.002	−0.03	0.09
	(3.89)	(−2.18)	(−0.65)	(1.24)
δ_3	0.95	−113.8	−0.18	−2.00
	(1.00)	(−21.77)	(−0.37)	(−1.78)
γ_1	0.48	−0.006	0.54	0.06
	(1.00)	(−0.5)	(2.09)	(1.99)
γ_2	6.51	1.93	0.62	0.82
	(0.01)	(28.3)	(1.70)	(9.55)
γ_3	0.90	0.99	0.49	0.55
	(2.21)	(14.44)	(2.51)	(3.83)
γ_4	0.50	0.06	1.88	−197.3
	(0.19)	(0.42)	(1.96)	(−0.002)
γ_5	0.96	−9.57	0.85	0.99
	(4.03)	(−2.57)	(1.65)	(1.05)
γ_6	0.96	2.01	−0.56	−0.01
	(2.71)	(3.77)	(−0.86)	(−0.18)

Assumptions: (i) Some fraction of the domestic borrowing is diverted to investment. (ii) Target level borrowing $(B^*) \neq 0$.

Notes: Figures in the parentheses are asymptotic t-values 2. ρ_is are the constraint equation parameters. ρ_1 is tax parameter, ρ_2, ρ_3 and ρ_4 are grant, loan and borrowing parameters respectively. 3. Critical t-values are: 1.703 (.05 level) and .314 (.10 level).

APPENDIX 8.1   NOTES ON DATA SOURCES

Data for all the four selected countries were collected for the years from 1965 onward. The details are set out in the appendix. Data for domestic borrowing for all countries is measured as the difference between total income (such as total domestic revenue plus foreign capital inflows) and total expenditures (such as government investment plus recurrent expenditures).

For Bangladesh, data for all the variables from 1973 to 1992 were collected from various editions of the *Statistical Year Book* (1976, 1979, 1985, 1989, and 1993) published by the Bangladesh Bureau of Statistics. Data from 1965 to 1972 were collected from the *Pakistan Economic Survey* 1973. Data for India were collected from various issues of the *Economic Survey of India* (1969, 1972, 1977, 1987 and 1993) published by the Government of India. Data for Pakistan were obtained from various issues of the *Pakistan Economic Survey* (1976, 1980 and 1993) published by the Statistics Division of the Ministry of Planning. Data for The Philippines were collected from *The Philippines Statistical Year Book* (1976, 1983, 1987 and 1989) published by the National Statistical Coordination Board and the *Statistical Bulletin* (1982 and 1990), published by the Central Bank of The Philippines. Data from 1990 to 1992 were obtained from the *Government Financial Statistics Year Book* (1993) published by the World Bank. All the data except the population growth rate (N) and education (ED) have been converted into constant prices using a country specific GDP deflator as a price index and taking 1987 as the base year. All the data series except N and ED have been converted into US million dollars using yearly exchange rates for each country.

9 Constitutionalism and Governance in Bangladesh

M. Rafiqul Islam

9.1 INTRODUCTION

The quest of the *Bangalees* for political emancipation through constitutional rule and democracy culminated into a war of national liberation in 1971 out of which Bangladesh was born. Notwithstanding this history and the advent of constitutional order with features of good governance in 1972, the working of its political process has been drifting from crisis to crisis. Successive uses of the constitution as a political tool with impunity have diluted the integrity of, and intensified widespread concern and suspicion about the future of constitutional governance in Bangladesh.

The Constitution has received a number of amendments (GOB 1991b) to insulate selfish power politics and unlawful acts. These amendments have eroded certain crucial aspects of good governance and caused an extraordinary crisis in the constitutional history of Bangladesh. A sustainable order of constitutionalism, good governance and democratic process warrants a minimum standard of responsible political behaviour and culture of respect for the constitutional rule of law. The political process of Bangladesh has failed to protect and enhance this standard and culture both by what it has done and by what it has failed to do. Almost three decades after Bangladesh's independence, few matters have assumed greater significance than the issue of resuscitation of constitutional governance. Attempts have now been intensified to bring back the original constitution along with its major aspects of good governance. This study grapples with this issue by highlighting and commenting upon major amendments and their effects on the development of a good government propelled by a constitutional order.

9.2 THE LEGACY OF PAKISTAN

The constitutional crises in Bangladesh intuitively echo the practice of power-sponsored vandalism to constitution in Pakistan during 1947–71. The erosion of constitutional rule in the first decade and the advent of all-powerful authoritarian rule in the second decade marked the beginning of the end of united Pakistan. The Jinnah-Liaquat era ignored the overriding importance of enacting a constitution and holding elections. Without a constitution, Pakistan was governed, in its first seven years, virtually by the Governor-General backed by an active alliance of the civilian and military bureaucracies. Upon independence in 1947, Jinnah, unlike Nehru, opted not for the Westminster system and Prime Ministership, but for the Viceregal system and Governor-Generalship with the Government of India Act 1935 as the interim constitution. Jinnah found no contradiction in adopting a system of government and the 1935 Act that he regarded in pre-partition days as autocratic and reactionary. The end in view was to personify and monopolise the political power process not to be dictated by constitutionalism (M. Ahmed 1970).

Ghulam Muhammad, a civil servant, became the Governor-General after the Jinnah-Liaquat era, and refused to act as a constitutional head. He arbitrarily dismissed the Nazimuddin cabinet in 1953 when the cabinet had the majority support in the Constituent Assembly. He personally appointed Mohammed Ali (then a diplomat), as the Prime Minister, all other ministers and distributed their portfolios. He also summarily sacked the United Front Ministry of East Bengal in 1954, the first ever elected provincial government with an absolute majority. He finally dissolved the First Constituent Assembly in 1954 and established a pliable Second Constituent Assembly in 1956. Ghulam Muhammad thus replaced the political and constitutional process, democratic institutions and politicians by a full bureaucratic rule.

The first Constitution enacted in 1956 introduced the parity of representation from both East and West Pakistan. This artificially denied the numerical majority of East Pakistan and paved the way for the installation of a minority-rule in Pakistan. However, this Constitution that took long nine years to enact survived a little over two years. It was abolished by the proclamation of martial law in 1958, installing the military dictatorship of Ayub (Gledhill 1959).

Ayub's centralised administration was dominated by high ranking civil and military officials. He promised to restore democracy and constitution. He thought that parliamentary democracy was unsuitable for Pakistan, invented one of his own – basic democracy, a blended synthesis of autocratic elements in the British Viceregal system controlled by an autocratic civil-military axis. Ayub enacted his Constitution in 1962, introducing a constitutional dictatorship that collapsed in 1968–69. Another General, Yahya took over as a gift from departing Ayub[1] and became the *de faco* ruler of Pakistan with the introduction of martial law.

Yahya disclaimed any political interest, promised democratic election, a constitutional rule and promulgated the Legal Framework Order to these ends. The results of the election held in 1970 gave the Awami League headed by Sheikh Mujib an absolute majority in the National and East Pakistan Assemblies. Yahya did not respect this ballot and did not call upon Mujib to form a government. Instead he postponed the opening session of the National Assembly *sine die*, dismissed his civilian cabinet and took over full control through the army. He commenced political talks with Mujib in Dhaka which ended abruptly. He left Dhaka unnoticed, ordered the army to fully restore the authority of his government, imposed strict martial law provisions, banned all political activities, outlawed the Awami League and arrested Mujib. He thus launched a machinery of repression and reign of terror in East Pakistan which responded by proclaiming and gaining independence in 1971. Hence, commencing with the greatest hope for a democratic and constitutional rule, the Yahya era ended with the disintegration of Pakistan and the independence of Bangladesh (Feldman 1975).

East Pakistan as an integral part of Pakistan during 1947–71 witnessed the collapse of democratic forces and constitutional ideals. The working of constitutionalism had successively been sabotaged by vested and ambitious interests of a military oligarchic rule. Such a rule institutionalised bureaucratic participation in government, politicised the army and introduced the practice of running the government without politicians, political institutions and process, and a constitution. This process of non-participation, powerlessness and alienation of politicians and the ruling elites' mistrust of democracy paralysed the growth of constitutionalism in Pakistan. The politico-constitutional crises of Bangladesh especially since 1975 may partially be attributable to this historic legacy. A circumspect dissection of these crises exposes their close resemblance to those of Pakistan.

9.3   THE CONSTITUTION OF BANGLADESH

Bangladesh was physically liberated on 16 December 1971. The Bangladesh Government immediately set up a Constituent Assembly, composed of the members of the National and East Pakistan Assemblies elected in 1970, to draft a constitution for Bangladesh. The Constituent Assembly held its first session on 10 April 1972 and passed the Constitution on 4 November 1972. The Constitution was authenticated by the Speaker on 14 December 1972 and came into force on 16 December 1972. Until this date, Bangladesh was governed under the Provisional Constitution of Bangladesh.

The Constitution drawn out and implemented in 1972 contained nearly every aspect of a good government. It introduced a parliamentary form of government with the President as the constitutional head. It provided a responsible executive, a non-sovereign legislature and an independent judiciary with appropriate separation of powers and checks and balances between them. It embodied the principle of ministerial responsibility, both individual and collective, to Parliament and ultimately to the people, the source of 'All Powers in the Republic' (Art. 7.1). Being the solemn expression of the will of the people, the Constitution was proclaimed as 'the supreme law of the Republic' (Art. 7.2). Introducing a populist political system and a liberal economic system, the Constitution sought to ensure transparency in public policy formulation and implementation with administrative accountability and bureaucratic efficiency. The recognition of human rights, fundamental freedom and rule of law for all without any distinction whatsoever with provisions for appropriate judicial scrutiny and enforcement (Arts. 44 and 102) was the central driving force for a good and responsible government. Without dwelling on a strength-weakness analysis, it may be asserted that, on balance, this Constitution was by far the best one could reasonably hope for in a Westminster model. Unfortunately many of these constitutional features of good governance have been dissipated and rendered unworkable by subsequent amendments.

9.4   CONSTITUTIONAL AMENDMENTS

The 1972 Constitution has undergone profound transformation through multiple amendments involving wide-ranging matters and engendering widespread controversies. A number of past political impasses with far reaching impacts on constitutionalism and good governance in Bangladesh may be attributable to some of these amendments. The remainder of this section is devoted to a critical appraisal of these amendments and possible implications thereof.

9.4.1   The fourth amendment: From parliamentary to presidential

The Second Amendment of the Mujib Government on 22 September 1973 created special powers for the government to arrest and detain without trial, and established the procedures for the proclamation of an emergency with provisions for the suspension of fundamental rights. President Muhammadullah proclaimed emergency and the Emergency Powers Ordinance No. XXVII of 1974 on 28 December 1974 concentrating all powers in the Prime Minister. The practical utility of special powers during crisis situations may not be gainsaid. But its limitless scope is likely to render the power susceptible to abusive uses for political ends. The *Bangalees* have been the principal target and victims of dogmatic adherence to emergency powers by the Pakistani rulers whenever they were in political troubles in East Pakistan. Mujib and his Awami League were strong critics and opponents of unlimited emergency powers. In Bangladesh, governments are not free from the accusation that they have frequently resorted to this absolute special powers in a bid to suppress their political opponents. But this special powers provisions remain intact even today despite various governments' promise for their annulment.

The present Awami League government promised to repeal special powers but is yet to do so. It is now trying to establish a human rights commission in Bangladesh.[2] In an era when governments all over the world are the main perpetrators of human rights violations, it is difficult to appreciate the effectiveness of such a commission in presence of the special powers. The proposed commission is expected to provide justice to the people by protecting their human rights and dignity. Whereas the special powers are the arbitrary powers of the Government which may be used to transgress human rights with impunity. In reality, human rights and the special powers are not complementary but mutually exclusive and obstructive and as such cannot co-exist harmoniously. The special powers clearly interrupt the delicate checks and balance between the executive and the judiciary and as such militate against the operation of a good and responsible government.

Equipped with these comprehensive powers, the Mujib Government passed its Fourth Amendment on 25 January 1975 adopting a presidential form of government with an all-powerful President to be elected directly by the people. The competence of Parliament was reduced. The Supreme Court lost its jurisdiction over the enforcement of fundamental rights. Judges of all courts would be appointed by, responsible to, and could hold office during the pleasure of, the President. This direct control compromised the independence of the judiciary. This amendment made provisions for the establishment of a one-party state under the National Party (Part VIA). Pursuant to this amendment, Mujib became the President and arrogated all powers to himself, and launched the *Bangladesh Krishak Sramik Awami League (BAKSAL)* on 7 June 1975 (Ziring 1992).

The monopolisation of executive, legislative and judicial powers in the President interrupted appropriate checks and balances and diluted the separation of powers between the three organs – a fundamental corner stone of the 1972 Constitution. Mujib criticised similar concentration of all powers in the Presidents of Pakistan as dictatorial, reactionary and not conducive to the growth of democratic institutions. His one-party system was a coercive attempt to eliminate formalised political opposition - an intolerant democratic process. The Mujib Government found no contradiction in enacting this amendment – an act somewhat parallel to what Jinnah did by introducing the Indian Act, 1935 as the interim constitution of Pakistan in 1947. The Fourth Amendment contemptuously betrayed the pre-independence political values, shared aspirations and lifelong commitment of the *Bangalees*, as well as Mujib and his party to a multiparty parliamentary democracy. The Mujib Government accomplished these radical changes without referring them to the people.

However, the one-party system was abandoned by a Presidential Proclamation on 8 November 1975. After 16 years of presidential rule, parliamentary rule has been restored through a referendum on 15 September 1991. Nonetheless this amendment generated far reaching consequences on the political process and constitutional governance in Bangladesh. The Mujib Government conceived it as an answer to political challenges and outstanding problems. Instead, it became counterproductive with ample signs of political weakness of the regime. Its disregard for constitutional constraints on unconstitutional or extra-legal political power play precipitated some depreciation in the constitutional order with a corresponding increase in the strength of those desirous of creating and exploiting disorder.

9.4.2   The fifth amendment and the Indemnity Ordinance 1975

Mujib was assassinated along with 21 family members and relatives in a military coup on 15 August 1975 by some army officers who captured the governmental power and installed Khandakar Moshtaque Ahmed (Moshtaque) as the President with the proclamation of martial law. The identity of the assassins was known through their self-admission in public statements.[3]

Notwithstanding these successive and voluntary confessions, Moshtaque promulgated 'The Indemnity Ordinance, 1975' on 26 September 1975 purportedly indemnifying the self-confessed perpetrators of these murders and prohibiting any legal or other proceedings against them. Overseas diplomatic appointments were accorded to them presumably as rewards for murders. Immediately after becoming the President on 21 April 1977, Major General Ziaur Rahman (Zia) validated the Indemnity Ordinance, 1975 through a proclamation on 23 April 1977 and subsequently appended to the Constitution as a new Article 3A under the Fourth Schedule through the Fifth Amendment on 6 April 1979. The Ordinance of Moshtaque and the Proclamation of Zia were explicitly insulated from judicial or public scrutiny by inserting the clause that these 'have been validly made ... and shall not be called in question in or before any court or Tribunal on any ground whatsoever'. This is how the Indemnity Ordinance, 1975 *supposedly* became an integral part of the Constitution. This Ordinance was of wider significance. It went far beyond the constitutional law and encroached onto other areas of law and justice. This Ordinance exonerated those involved in the murders from facing the criminal justice system of Bangladesh. They were thus regarded as above the law of Bangladesh in violation of Article 27 of the Constitution. It also artificially prevented the aggrieved relatives of the victims from resorting to available legal remedies and natural justice. This defied Articles 31 (right to protection of law) and 32 (protection of right to life) of the Constitution. It coercively caused the relatives of the victims to suffer grave injustices without any right to redress. A head of state can waive or reduce the punishment of an offender after encountering trial according to the ordinary law of the land. So is the situation in Bangladesh (Art. 57 of the Constitution). The president can neither decriminalise any recognised criminal act or exempt its perpetrators from the full force of law. Nor can the president supersede, take away or abridge the right of the relatives of the victims to justice guaranteed in the legal system. In other words, the president cannot create a right for the self-confessed murderers which does not exist in law and cannot usurp the legal rights of the relatives of the victims beyond the authorisation of law. The Indemnity Ordinance just did that. It was intended not to try and punish the offenders, but to ensure their security and immunity from the court of law. As such, it was a fundamental negation to any civilised legal norms and the administration of natural justice.

The invalidity of the Ordinance was quite apparent when it was tested in terms of the Constitution of Bangladesh which remained in force at the time of its proclamation. When Moshtaque took over the Presidency, the 1972 Constitution was not suspended or abrogated by the coup leaders or by their President. Article 48 required the President to be directly elected. In the absence of a regular President, the Vice-President or the Speaker would act as the acting president under Article 55. In the absence of all of them, Parliament would appoint the acting president. Following the killing of President Mujib, both the Vice-President and the Speaker were present in Dhaka. But the normal constitutional successors were not allowed to take over. Moshtaque was neither the Vice-President, or the Speaker. Nor was he appointed by the Parliament. The Presidency of Moshtaque was therefore unconstitutional and was not competent to promulgate the Indemnity Ordinance, 1975. Since the Ordinance was ordained and sanctioned by an incompetent authority, it lacked a decisive attribute of legitimacy which in effect rendered it invalid.

The Indemnity Ordinance, 1975 was promulgated under Article 93 of the Constitution. This Article imposes definite restrictions on the ordinance-making power of the President. The President must secure the parliamentary approval of any ordinance within 30 days after it was presented before the first meeting of Parliament after the promulgation. The Indemnity Ordinance, 1975 was never laid independently before Parliament for approval. Article 93 also prevents the President from making any ordinance with provisions (a) 'which could not lawfully be made under this Constitution by Act of Parliament' and (b) 'for altering or repealing any provision of this Constitution'. The Indemnity Ordinance, 1975 was necessary, as repeatedly asserted in the Ordinance itself, for 'the historical change and the Proclamation of Martial Law on the morning of the 15 August 1975'. Nowhere was it claimed that it was essential and justified in the interest of the people and the state. Both violent and/or unconstitutional access to power and the proclamation of martial law have unconditionally been outlawed in the Constitution. The subject-matter of the Indemnity Ordinance was inconsistent with, indeed repugnant to, the Constitution. Parliament, whose powers are limited by Article 7 of the Constitution, was not empowered to validate these unlawful acts. Since the subject-matter of the Indemnity Ordinance was unlawful, it could not validly be subsumed under the Constitution of Bangladesh.

The Indemnity Ordinance, 1975 was proclaimed, preserved and validated in repudiation of existing legal and constitutional principles. It was an ill-conceived, ill-thoughtout and sinister act of a desperate President installed by, and subservient to, those responsible for the killings. The Zia regime convicted and sentenced Moshtaque to 5 years imprisonment for corruption and abuse of official powers on 24 February 1977. Yet the regime made no hesitation to annex the Ordinance as an integral part of the Constitution through its Fifth Amendment. It is only the present Awami League government and the Seventh Parliament (elected June 1996) that have repealed the Ordinance and criminal proceedings have been drawn against the killers of Mujib.

9.4.3   The fifth and seventh amendments and the martial law regimes

Following the coup of 7 November 1975, Zia gained real power and control over the Government of Sayem, the then Chief Justice of the Supreme Court, who took over the Presidency from Moshtaque on 6 November 1975. Sayem postponed the proposed parliamentary election indefinitely on 21 November 1976 and appointed Zia as the Chief Martial Law Administrator on 29 November 1976. Finally, Zia became the President on 21 April 1977 as the nominee of the outgoing President.[4] The Presidency of Zia derived its authority from this act of nomination which calls for comments. This method of changing the Presidency from one hand to another on a personal choice basis happened once before when Ayub stepped down by handing over the Presidency of Pakistan to Yahya through a letter of 24 March 1969. Neither the 1962 Constitution of Pakistan, then was in force, nor the Bangladesh Constitution contains any provision authorising such an act. Rather both Constitutions embody explicit provisions and procedures of appointing the Acting President should the position fall vacant. Such appointments were unconstitutional and illegal (Islam 1987a).

The Bangladesh Constitution is unequivocal on this point that Sayem lacked the competence to select his successor. Unlike his real estate property, he did not own the Presidency so that he could nominate its subsequent beneficiary. Both the acts of nomination by Sayem and acceptance by Zia were *ultra vires* under the constitutional law of Bangladesh. The proclamation of Moshtaque on 20 August 1975, which enabled Sayem to nominate Zia as the President, itself was invalid as observed before. The legitimacy of Zia's assumption of the Presidency could not be derived from an illegitimate source. It was precisely because of political corruption and abuse of power such as this, *inter alia*, the Sayem-Zia Government arrested, convicted and imprisoned Moshtaque on 24 February 1977. Yet they found no contradiction in resorting to a proclamation of Moshtaque in nominating for, and accepting, the Presidency of Bangladesh.

Notwithstanding this precarious legitimacy of his Presidency, Zia, both as the Chief Martial Law Administrator and the President, made numerous amendments to the Constitution through martial law and Presidential orders, proclamations and ordinances till he won the Presidential election on 3 June 1978. His newly formed political party – The Bangladesh Nationalist Party – also won the Parliamentary election held on 18 February 1979. All constitutional amendments made by the martial law authorities from 15 August 1975 to 9 April 1979 were placed in a single Bill and passed by this Parliament on 9 April 1979 as the Fifth Amendment Act. A new clause 3A was inserted in Schedule 4 of the Constitution. Thus Parliament put a stamp of constitutionality on all martial law regimes since the assassination of Mujib, their orders, actions, regulations and amendments as if they were duly made by competent authorities. It was expressly mentioned in the Fifth Amendment that its contents and subject-matters would not be called in question in any court or tribunal on any ground whatsoever.

Following the footstep of Zia, Ershad ratified and confirmed his martial law proclamation and four and a half years of martial law rule through the Seventh Amendment on 10 November 1986. Ershad's Parliament also added another new clause 3B in the Fourth Schedule of the Constitution. This Amendment too regarded all martial law acts as 'validly made and shall not be called in question in or before any court, tribunal or authority on any ground whatsoever'.

Both the Fifth and Seventh amendments purported to afford a legal and constitutional coverage to the martial law regimes. It was only when their respective Parliament agreed to confer parliamentary sanction on their regimes that both Zia and Ershad withdrew their martial law on the eve of the amendments. The obvious fundamental questions are: why were the validation of martial law regimes necessary? Were they invalid so that they required validation at the time of their termination? If they were valid in the first place, there was no need for their subsequent validation. If inherently invalid in the first place, how could they be made retrospectively valid at a later date? Was Parliament competent to validate those that were otherwise invalid?

The Constitution of Bangladesh contains no provision for the proclamation and/or validation of martial law on any ground or under any circumstances. The change of government must take place pursuant to the Constitution which provides an adequate procedure in Part IV. The omission to include a provision for the proclamation of martial law or its subsequent validation is not incidental but intentional, based on the historic experience of Pakistan where the implementation of a democratic government and constitutional order was frequently frustrated by army takeovers (Sobhan 1993).

The lack of a constitutional authorisation does not necessarily imply that unconstitutional access to power is always unlawful. Any unconstitutional access to power is an act of revolution which occurs in defiance of, indeed through the abrogation of, the existing constitution. There are ample examples and judicial recognition of the validity of such revolutionary access to power. The revolutionary access to power through the annulment of the 1956 Constitution of Pakistan by Ayub in 1958 was held valid by the Supreme Court of Pakistan in *State v Dosso*, PLD 1958, SC 33. Such a validation is based on a legal principle called the Kelsenian doctrine of validity. According to this doctrine, the legitimacy of revolutionary access to power emanates directly from the very success of the act (revolution), not from any pre-existing or subsequently enacted constitution. The revolution itself becomes a law-making fact whose legality springs from its success. Constitutionality or lack of it is immaterial for the purpose of its legitimacy. There is no need and room for its validation by acts of Parliament. Nor can it be appended to any pre-existing constitution which has been disposed of by the successful revolution.[5]

Had there been any measures of legitimacy of unconstitutional access to power by Zia and Ershad, it would have been emanated from the Kelsenian doctrine of validity, not from the Constitution. Their access to power was not an act of revolution through the abrogation of the Constitution, which remained in force. And as such they could not validly assume power beyond the constitutional authorisation. Their access to power was comparable with that of Yahya in 1969 – all three cases fall short of complying with the requirements of the Kelsenian doctrine and therefore illegal (Islam 1987b). In *Asma Jilani v The Government of Punjab* PLD 1972 SC 139, the Supreme Court of Pakistan relied on the Kelsenian doctrine to determine the validity of the Yahya regime. The Court held that the military rule imposed on Pakistan by Yahya and his subsequent acts were illegal. This implied that Yahya committed an act of treason under the 1962 Constitution of Pakistan which remained in force at the time of Yahya's access to power.

Both Zia and Ershad were well aware of the fact that their access to power were unconstitutional and not covered by the Kelsenian doctrine. They surmised that all of their actions could have been nullified and declared illegal in a court of law with appropriate legal consequences. They could face prosecution by a future constitutional government, probably much along the line of the trial of two former Presidents of South Korea.[6] In fact, Ershad repeatedly asserted that he would lift martial law if Parliament would protect him from possible sedition charges.[7] Presumably this awareness led them to seek and receive parliamentary sanction. In a bid to avert the Asma Jilani situation, they ironically sought impunity under the same Constitution that they arrogantly defied at the time of accession to power. They unduly derived their authority from martial law regimes which they themselves created parallel with, and repugnant to, the existing constitutional regime. Now it is legally hollow and self-defeating to argue that they could derive their authority to gain access to power from the former and justify it under the latter when the latter outlaws the former. By artificially insulating them from the scope of ordinary law and the jurisdiction of court, Parliament made them more equal than others and above the law – a vindication not only unavailable in, but also a clear violation of, the Constitution.

There was another political factor behind this Parliamentary approval of martial law regimes. The President enjoyed disproportionate power with respect to Parliament including an unlimited authority to dissolve Parliament at any time through public notification (Art. 72). This power hanging over Parliament compromised its independence significantly. By resorting to this political weapon, the President was in a position to compel captive Parliament to support unilateral and arbitrary acts of the President. This had exactly happened in both cases. Pliable Parliaments and their members had no other alternative but to accept and validate the martial law regimes of their presidents which in turn ensured their own continuity (Islam 1987c). Both Fifth and Seventh Amendments have been classified as indemnity provisions and appended to the Fourth Schedule under Article 150 of the Constitution. Article 150 deals with certain transitional and temporary matters having the force of law. These matters are categorically and exclusively mentioned in the Fourth Schedule in response to a special, indeed an extraordinary situation of the past. The starting point of Bangladesh as an independent state commenced with its unilateral declaration of independence on 26 March 1971 (Islam 1983). The Constituent Assembly took about a year to draft the Constitution that came into effect on 16 December 1972. During this period between 26 March 1971 and 16 December 1972 the Bangladesh Government had to make laws, orders and performed a whole range of governmental functions in the absence of any constitution. These interim measures of the pre-constitutional period were regularised retrospectively by inserting an indemnity clause 3 in the Fourth Schedule. This was indispensable in maintaining the continuity of Bangladesh and its Government since 26 March 1971 and to avoid any legal vacuum. There was no constitution of Bangladesh during this period to follow. The establishment of Bangladesh and its government had no relation with the pre-existing constitution of Pakistan. Consequently the issue of unconstitutionality of those acts did not arise.

The indemnity provision expressly says that it is applicable only 'in the period between the 26 day of March, 1971 and the commencement of this Constitution'. Combined reading of Article 150 and clause 3 of the Fourth Schedule reveals that the validation of any unconstitutional act in the post-constitutional period under the indemnity provision is unsubsumable. No such act subsequent to the commencement of the Constitution can come within the purview of the indemnity clause. Hence the unconstitutional act of proclamation of martial law in the post-constitutional period could not validly be indemnified under, and appended to, the Fourth Schedule. But both Zia and Ershad through their parliaments just did this – an act of legalising by ballot something which was achieved illegally by bullet. Undeterred by their profound lack of legal and constitutional validity, both Fifth and Seventh amendments have been made an integral part of the Constitution of Bangladesh.

9.4.4   The eighth amendment: State religion

Secularism was one of the fundamental principles of state policy under Article 8 of the 1972 Constitution. Upon swearing in as the President on 21 April 1977, Zia issued the Proclamation (Amendment) Order 1977 on the next day amending some important provisions of the Constitution. He dropped 'secularism' and inserted 'Absolute trust and faith in the Almighty Allah'. This amendment fell short of expressly endorsing 'the religion of Islam' as one of the fundamental state policies. The Parliament of the Ershad era formally accorded 'Islam' the status of state religion through the Eighth Amendment on 9 June 1988 and inserted a new Article 2A to this effect.

This constitutional status of Islam has seemingly placed the minority communities –the Hindus, Christians and Buddhists in a subservient position with the majority Muslims in respect of religious rights. Its spillover effects on some fundamental rights under the Constitution is discernible. Article 27 ensures the equality of all citizens before, and equal protection under, law. Articles 28(1) and 29(2) outlaw any discrimination of the citizens on the ground of religion or any other attributes. Article 28 (2) confers equal rights on women with men in spheres of state and public life. Article 29(1) guarantees equal opportunity for all citizens. These Articles are not merely declaratory but contain substantive legal force to be enforced by the Supreme Court under Articles 44 and 102. The contents of these Articles have been taken from the west-oriented secular and non-communal approach perhaps reflected in the 1948 Universal Declaration of the Human Rights and other UN sponsored human rights instruments. As such, the meaning and scope of these fundamental rights may be difficult to subsume within the value system of any given religion.

The existence of Article 2A in the Constitution is likely to influence the interpretation of many provisions, turning them into sources of false hope and rising frustration. It has the potential of enacting laws biased in favour of or against the one community or the other. It is fraught with the risk of violating human rights and fundamental freedoms of about 16 million non-Muslim Bangladeshis under a number of international human rights instruments of which Bangladesh is a party.[8]

In a cost-benefit analysis, the constitutionalisation of Islam has divided an otherwise undivided homogenous and monolithic state. It is an artificial source of unnecessary controversies. It sustains a sense of insecurity and alienation on the part of the minority communities. It has brought no special benefit to the Muslims either. Their status remains unchanged. Nor is there any extra privileges for them. It has not added any special dimension to the practice of Islam in Bangladesh. This is merely because the recognition of Islam as the state religion is superficial and confined only in Article 2A. It does not prescribe and implement Islamic values, teachings, ideals and institutions in other provisions of the Constitution. It is engineered and introduced with a narrow political end in view which in effect creates a host of inconsistencies in the fundamental law of Bangladesh. Politically, this is a provocative act which is likely to serve as a constant source of suspicion and fierce communal controversies.

The unqualified endorsement of secularism in the 1972 Constitution was not superimposed by outside powers. It was there not as a matter of coincidence but of historic design deeply rooted in the struggle for Bangladesh that grew in stages and over time into a formidable one. Many *Bangalees* sacrificed their lives for some cherished value oriented goals that they were passionately desirous of implementing in Bangladesh. These solemnly expressed sacred will of the people found expression in the 1972 Constitution. With the vivid memory of communal riots during the partition of India in 1947 and the abusive practice of Islam for selfish political and economic purposes in Pakistan, the *Bangalees* drifted to secularism as an alternative ideological means. This commitment to non-communalism reflected beyond doubt in all pre-Bangladesh movements and the 1970 election results. Participation in the 1971 liberation war was indiscriminate – the Muslims, Hindus, Christians and Buddhists sought and fought for Bangladesh with lofty ideals that we all including our future generation would live in a true non-communal environment.

This is, however, not to assert that a state religion is something illegal in constitutional law. At present there are about 46 states which have accorded constitutional status to religion in one form or another (Alam 1991). The validity of these cases may easily be derived from their historical, social and political developments that preceded the framing of their constitutions. The validity of constitutional status of religion in Pakistan for example is based on the two-nation theory of Jinnah that shaped the Pakistan movement. The Afghan *mujahidins* fought an ideological war against the former Soviet backed communist regime of Kabul. The driving force behind the adoption of state religion in Pakistan and Afghanistan is somewhat parallel to what necessitated the adoption of secularism as a fundamental state policy in Bangladesh. If the Parliament of Pakistan now refuses to endorse the constitutional status of religion it would be tantamount to asserting that the two-nation theory, the very basis of Pakistan, was wrong. The deletion of secularism from, and the introduction of state religion in, the Constitution is yet another blatant insult to basic ideals out of which Bangladesh was born.

Both major oppositions of the time, the Awami League and the BNP, opposed this Amendment.9 The BNP Government in its full five years term in office (1991–96) did nothing about the issue of state religion – an alien element in the basic structure of the Constitution. The present Hasina Government is completely silent on the issue. As noted before, secularism was embodied in Article 8 of the Constitution in response to an overwhelming popular mandate. Both Zia and Ershad removed it with no popular mandate. Notwithstanding the requirement of a referendum under Article 142 of the Constitution for any amendment of Article 8, no such referendum was ever held on the issue. Instead Zia complied with the requirement of referendum by illegally abolishing it. The content of Article 8 under the 1972 Constitution has a powerful sentimental attachment to the historic genesis of Bangladesh. It is inextricably connected with the soil of Bangladesh and the blood of its people. It cannot be removed by disguised military dictators' order or by acts of their pliable Parliament without referring to the people. Until the religion-based constitutional order is endorsed by the people, any claim for its legitimacy is not only sectarian but also hollow and self-defeating.

9.4.5 The thirteenth amendment: A non-political caretaker government

The Sixth Parliament has enacted the Thirteenth Amendment on 26 March 1996 with provisions for holding all future general elections under a non-political caretaker government. It has also conferred certain additional but real powers on the Presidency. This Amendment purports to serve the cause of free and fair election by combating vote rigging, proxy votes, election fraud and corruption which were rampant during 1975–90. The idea of free and fair elections under a neutral caretaker government received its greatest momentum from fraudulent elections during the Ershad era. Following the overthrow of Ershad by popular movement, the first two such elections were held on 27 February 1991 and 12 June 1996 which were widely regarded as free and fair.

The Thirteenth Amendment has inserted a new Article 55A on the application of Chapter II and a new Chapter IIA consists of a new Article 58(A–D) in Part IV of the Constitution. These new provisions deal with the formation of a non-political caretaker government to govern the country and conduct the general elections during the interim period extending up to the date on which the new Prime Minister is sworn in after the general elections and the creation of a new Parliament. The idea is intuitively appealing and exemplary for many Third World countries striving to restore public confidence in their election results. But the Thirteenth Amendment has made the President in charge of the caretaker government with the sole power to appoint and remove the chief adviser (equivalent to the prime minister) of the caretaker government. Both the chief adviser and the ten advisers have been made collectively responsible to the president. Articles 61 and 62 of the constitution have made the president as the ceremonial commander in chief of the defence forces – a power to be exercised on the advice of the Prime Minister pursuant to the practice of the Westminster system of government. The Thirteenth amendment has amended Article 61 affording the President to gain absolute control over the defence forces during the tenure of the caretaker government. These are the common features of a presidential, not parliamentary form of government.

The Thirteenth amendment have conferred some real and absolute powers on the President who is not entitled to all these powers under the Constitution. In exercising these powers, the President is beyond the reach of the caretaker government and being not directly elected, not accountable to the people either. The Thirteenth amendment thus transforms the figurehead President to an all-powerful president, effectively introducing an interim Presidential form of government during the tenure of the caretaker government. It has created two separate but potentially conflicting sources of governmental power: the President and the caretaker government. These are affirmatively inconsistent with, and repugnant to, the basic structure of the Constitution. It is not necessary that the means of holding free and fair elections under a caretaker government be contrary to the Constitution. The means could well be based on a foundation of strict respect for the basic constitutional spirit and framework. The Thirteenth Amendment has sought to achieve a desired end through unconstitutional means.

The Thirteenth Amendment may work well if the President is also non-political. But constitutionally a party in power is entitled to nominate and appoint a President of its own political persuasion in a bid to achieve political advantage through its loyal President. This had precisely happened on 18–20 May 1996, just three weeks prior to the general elections under the caretaker government, when the President removed the Army Chief and two other senior military commanders unilaterally and arbitrarily without any consultation with or advice of the caretaker government. This power of the President over armed forces undermined the ability of the caretaker government in maintaining law and order at the time of elections. It has a wider ramification in Bangladesh where bullets, not ballots, have often been the preferred mode of changing government. The Thirteenth Amendment is therefore far from being non-political and about a neutral caretaker government. It has introduced a non-party caretaker government subservient to an all-powerful President who may well be a political choice (Islam 1996).

9.5   THE SUPREMACY OF THE CONSTITUTION

The obvious question is: Why is not the Bangladesh Parliament, being the appropriate law-making body, competent to amend the Constitution? The answer is simple. The supreme law of Bangladesh, the Constitution, confers only limited law-making competence on Parliament. Unlike the British Parliament which is not created by a written Constitution, the Bangladesh Parliament is created by, and operative under, a written Constitution. Parliament does not possess any intrinsic law-making power which actually comes from the Constitution. This power therefore, however extensively one may construe, must be understood and exercised within, not beyond, the Constitution. Once Parliament and its acts defy and surpass the Constitution, they both suffer from legitimacy crisis. The Bangladesh Constitution imposes a cardinal restriction on the law-making power of Parliament. Article 7 prevents Parliament from making any law or/and amendment which is inconsistent with, or repugnant to, the Constitution. A failure to comply would render such acts of Parliament invalid to the extent of inconsistency or repugnancy.

The Bangladesh constitution does not contemplate any unconstitutional access to power and the promulgation of martial law. Parliament, whose power to legislate is subject to the constitutionality of its legislation, cannot transform these unconstitutional acts constitutional. The amendments validating these unconstitutional acts are clearly inconsistent with, indeed repugnant to, the Constitution and as such they are invalid pursuant to Article 7. In these amendments, the Constitution has been made subservient to the will of Parliament through a legislative power unavailable in, rather overtly forbidden by, the Constitution.

In a written constitutional regime, the judiciary is the guardian of the Constitution. The Supreme Court of Bangladesh has the power and jurisdiction to determine the constitutionality of a given act of Parliament. This is designed to maintain adequate checks and balances between the government organs in order to avoid abusive exercise of their separate powers. Both the Fifth and the Seventh Amendments contain saving clauses precluding any judicial or public scrutiny of their constitutionality. It is difficult to appreciate how a non-sovereign Parliament can operate beyond the constitutional arrangement of checks and balances to remain immune from the jurisdiction of the judiciary. By virtue of the preclusion clauses, Parliament has elevated itself to a status over and above the Constitution and acted as a judge in its own cause – a striking negation in any legal system, *albeit* the Constitution of Bangladesh.

The Supreme Court of Bangladesh is empowered to assess the constitutionality of these amendments and the power of Parliament to undertake them. The Court has exercised this judicial review power in *Anwar Hossain Chowdhury and Others v Bangladesh* vol. IX (A), BLD(SPI)I, 1989. The Court held that the amendment to Article 100 creating six permanent branches of the High Court Division altered the basic structure of the judiciary under the original Constitution. That the amending power of Parliament is not original but deviate from the Constitution. As such Parliament lacked the competence to amend the basic structure of the Constitution and held the amendment to Article 100 as unconstitutional.[10] Viewed from these perspectives, most of the amendments referred to would not survive any judicial scrutiny in terms of Article 7.

9.6   CONCLUDING COMMENTS

The constitutional history of Bangladesh since its inception reveals that some major amendments have been accomplished by incumbent governments not in response to genuine needs for modifications but to perpetuate their position in power. This process has consistently tampered with the dignity and integrity of the Constitution, rendering it a helpless victim of corruptionist power politics. The changes brought about by the Fourth Amendment have almost dissipated. The Constitution now provides for a parliamentary form of government with a multiparty political system. The judiciary is yet to be given its full independent status as enshrined in the 1972 Constitution. Both Zia and Ershad formed new political parties with many leading 'turncoat' politicians and rubber stamp parliaments as handy tools for running a military dictatorship with a democratic outfit, often accused of widespread government sponsored vote rigging in the election process. The cumulative effect of all these has stultified the development of a good and responsible government and a political process which ensures orderly change in government and yields political leaderships and institutions.

It may be naive to suggest that there could be no situation where the army takeover of government may be appealing and in order as a last resort to redress mass sufferings in the hands of corrupt and dishonest politicians in power. In so doing, the military authority may resort to other means for validity. But the military authorities in Bangladesh have taken shelter under the existing Constitution which provides them no protection whatsoever. In a bid to accommodate their actions, they have tailored the Constitution to afford a semblance of constitutionality to their rule. They have treated the Constitution with utmost abhorrence and genuflected to it only to conceal their illegal acts and deceive the people. In this process, the Constitution has suffered in their hands frequent undue and mischievous interference and violations, stripping it of its true essence and coherence. It is now a self-contradictory document. Moreover, repeated experience of military rule ought to discourage ambitious and politicised army generals to believe that they should assume the role of the custodian of the national interests and can serve better in government. They must now stop thinking that they can safely play and *tamper* with the Constitution.

Politicians must not think that they enjoy a monopoly over governmental power and extract maximum possible benefits while in power. This seems to be, by and large, the prevailing pattern. A minimum standard of consistent political behaviour and order is expected of politicians. They must show their habitual obedience and responsibility to the people and national interests. They must exercise their powers pursuant to the Constitution. This culture of compliance is a pre-requisite for a stable political order for good governance with democratic institutions as its propeller. Given the dysfunction of political order in Bangladesh, a code of conduct for politicians may prove to be rewarding. Such an instrument may serve as an internal safety-valve affording protection to all justifiable exercise of rights and powers, whilst preventing their denial and abuses. Should politicians fail to engineer and sustain a stable political order and institutions for good governance within the constitutional ambit, unconstitutional access to power, however undesirable, may be difficult to avert.

The Bangladesh Constitution is a sacred and authenticated norm setter for law-making to sustain an orderly society. It is not a convenient magic tool for overcoming legal and political barriers. The Bangladesh Parliament too is not a touchstone so that anything it touches becomes inviolable law. Its amendments referred to are well within the purview of Article 7 and the judicial review power of the Supreme Court which may be called upon to clean up the constitutional mess and restore the basic structure of the original Constitution. Such an act will make the Constitution a meaningful, coherent and integrated document – a precondition to facilitate the rehabilitation of good governance based on the constitutional rule of law and order. The retroactive judicial scrutiny of these amendments is likely to generate a deterrent effect prospectively on those anxious of exploiting the Constitution as a political ploy to camouflage their illegal acts to be perpetrated to serve sectarian or vested interests.

Ever since its independence, Bangladesh has witnessed the disintegration of its political process dominated by political and military personalities who have hamstrung the worth and dignity of constitutionalism and good governance. The preservation of the Constitution as 'the supreme law of the

Republic' is no less dauntingly uphill task today than before. Yet this is manifestly the only viable and palatable route to a dignified political existence for Bangladesh.

NOTES

1   Ayub handed over power to Yahya, the Commander-in-Chief of the army through a letter of 24 March 1969. On 25 March 1969 almost all newspapers in Pakistan published this letter.

2   The author's informal discussions with the Minister for Law, Justice and Parliamentary Affairs (Abdul Matin Khasru) in Sydney on 22 October 1997.

3   These army officers negotiated their departure from Bangladesh to Bangkok on 3 November 1975 where they held a press conference and acknowledged the responsibility for murders including the killings of four national leaders while under detention in the Dhaka Central Jail prior to their departure – an admission they reiterated in *London Sunday Times* of 30 May 1976 and in a TV interview in London on 2 August 1976.

4   According to the first presidential proclamation of Moshtaque on 20 August 1975 which enabled the President to nominate his successor when he resigned before the expiry of his term.

5   The decision of the High Court of Uganda in *Uganda v Commissioners of Prisons* [1966] EA514; the Rhodesian High Court in *Madzimbamuto v Lardner-Burke*, GD/CIV/23/66, and the Privy Council.

6   One receiving death penalty and the other life imprisonment for their unconstitutional imposition of martial law and excessive use of force.

7   *Asiaweek*, 27 July 1986, p 23; the interview of Ershad with the BSS newsagency was reported in *Time*, no. 37, 15 Sept. 1986, p.25.

8   In the main these include: the 1948 Universal Declaration of Human Rights, the 1965 International Convention on the Elimination of Racial Discrimination, the 1966 International Covenants on Human Rights, and the 1979 UN Women Rights Convention.

9   The Awami League leader Sheikh Hasina vowed to cancel the amendment when returned to power, whilst the BNP leader Begum Khaleda Zia said that the amendment would divide the nation and hence unacceptable, *Dhaka Courier*, **4**(44), 10 June 1988, pp 9–10.

10 The Bangladesh Parliament amended Article 100 to create six permanent branches of the High Court Division of the Supreme Court to be seated in six districts in addition to one in the capital city Dhaka. It is noteworthy that this amendment was a party of the Eighth Amendment, other part being the state religion.

10 Consolidating Democratic Governance: One Step Forward, Two Steps Back

Habib Zafarullah

10.1 INTRODUCTION

During the past one and half decades, the world has witnessed the dramatic and, at times, rapid transformation of authoritarian polities. Military withdrawal from politics and the transition to democracy has been the most common event in many Third World countries. Indeed, this 'third' wave[1] of democratisation in Eastern Europe, Asia, Africa and Latin America has been 'one of the most spectacular and important political changes in human history' (Huntington 1997, p.4) because of its impact not only in establishing or remodelling the formal institutions of the state but also for introducing new forms of political interactions, linkages and transactions in democratic governance.

One of the countries to be splashed by the democratisation wave was Bangladesh. Almost nine years of military/quasi-military rule was finally ended by a mass upsurge in 1990. The anti-authoritarian movement that began soon after the military takeover but took a little while to gain pace was spearheaded by the two main opposition parties, the Bangladesh Nationalist Party (BNP) and the Awami League (AL); it was gradually supported by the civil society, the bureaucracy, as well as the military. The process of democratisation began with general elections in 1991 under a non-party caretaker administration (NCA). This was followed by the transfer of power to an elected government, significant political reforms, attempts at revitalising political institutions, some policy shifts, administrative rearrangements at the political level, routine electoral practices (e.g., by-elections), and the completion of almost the full term of the incumbent government. The credibility of the electoral process was enhanced when the major opposition party won another free and fair parliamentary election and took over the reins of power in 1996.

To any casual outside observer all this would appear to be indicative of the remarkable success of the democratisation process in the country. However, a dispassionate analysis of events surrounding the institutionalisation, consolidation and operations of democracy and the behaviour and performance of politicians and parties would represent a rather shadowy portrayal of democratisation pointing to a depressing prospect for democracy in the country. Similarly, a kind of nonchalance has typified the efforts of the two governments since 1991 in adopting and operationalising the principal tenets of democratic governance; their dereliction of the fundamental issues of good governance or, at best, half measures in public sector reform complicated the process of making the executive government responsible, transparent and accountable and the administration responsive, efficient and effective. Economic liberalisation has almost stagnated or, if favourably viewed, moved at a snail's pace.

What has gone wrong? What factors are inhibiting the consolidation of democracy – the development of a truly democratic operating system and the establishment and institutionalisation of sound governance in Bangladesh? To what extent have the conditions of democratic consolidation been met or have remained unattended? How are the different component parts of the polity shaping up to support democracy? These are some of the questions, this chapter will strive to explore.

10.2   THE IMPERATIVES OF DEMOCRATIC CONSOLIDATION

The transition to democracy begins with the displacement of an authoritarian regime and the gradual dismantling of non-democratic institutions (Robinson 1996, p.70). The first phase in the transition is the holding of multi-party elections either supervised by the outgoing authoritarian regime itself or by an ephemeral independent non-partisan administration (Shan and Linz ed. 1995 ed., pp.5–8). These elections, widely participated and genuinely contested, must be free and fair to provide legitimacy for the new democratic government (Lowenthal and Dominguez 1996, p.50). Such legitimacy is crucial for political and economic reforms initiated by it to have any positive effect on the polity and economy. A pluralist political culture favouring an impartial administration of the rules of the political game and the creation of an equilibrium in social and economic competition among a host of competing elements may take time to develop in the aftermath of authoritarian rule (Smith 1996, p.172). Nonetheless, a sound electoral system designed to provide all competing parties an equal chance of winning political power is fundamental in fostering and supporting pluralism in the political system.

The first election in a post-authoritarian polity is the necessary first step towards the transition to democratic rule but it does not, by any means, sig-nify the attainment of complete democracy. A system of regular elections premised on acceptable regulations and free from malpractices would ensure legitimacy to the winning party or coalitions assuming power from another and give it/them the mandate to govern and execute policies for a specified term. Acceptance in good grace of electoral defeat by parties, either in government or in opposition, will be a great boost to democratic consolidation. But even with regular elections in place which are spontaneously contested, a democracy will only be partially consolidated unless other more critical conditions are met. As Diamond (1997, p.33) points out, '[democratic] consolidation is the process of achieving broad and deep legitimation...[which] must be more than a commitment to democracy in the abstract; it must also involve a shared normative and behavioral commitment to the specific rules and practices of the country's constitutional system'.

Thus the construction of new forms of political institutions must be accompanied by a change in the political behaviour of politicians, parties and the people. To a large extent, the consolidation of democracy depends on political crafting, an important role played by the political leadership (representing both the government and the opposition) who have the determination and the talent to accomplish democratisation (Huntington 1996, p.4). While those in power have greater responsibility in carving a democratic setup and revering democratic values, the opposition likewise cannot be indifferent to its role of improving the quality of democratic governance. Elections not only accord legitimacy to the government, they also provide the opposition the legal sanction to challenge executive caprice by scrutinising its operations (Richards 1978, p.59). Acknowledging each other's functional role is therefore a key element in the behavioural dimension of democratic consolidation.

In essence, in a consolidated democracy all are expected to follow the rules of the game, agreed upon by all concerned parties at the initial stage of the transition. The opposition, as the most potent political group, is not expected to unconstitutionally subvert a democratically-elected government or instigate political violence even when the nation is confronted with political and economic crises (Linz and Stepan 1996, p.15). In a similar token, the government, on its part, must not assume that once elected by the mass of citizens it has the divine right to rule without the opposition's exertion of any form of control over it. It must not dismiss at point blank opposition views and propositions about various facets of governance. Both must view conflict as a necessary collateral element of democracy and must be prepared to resolve them 'within the bounds of the specific laws, procedures, and institutions sanctioned by the new democratic process' which over time, with gradual consolidation the rules of the democratic game, 'becomes routinized and deeply internalized in social, institutional, and even psychological life' (Linz and Stepan 1996, pp.15–16).

The institutional elements of democratic consolidation have direct and profound implications for sound governance. The foundations of new political institutions may be laid soon after the transition has begun or simultaneously, the superstructures constructed more discreetly and over a period of time rather than in haste, lest they might give in to pressures of a political nature and deter the consolidation process. It may involve remapping of the state boundaries, reallocation of state functions along democratic lines, and the reform and revitalisation of existing institutions (Luckman and White 1996, p.7). Redesigning the system of governance, to configurate it with basic democratic values, and making it a potent tool in state-building and development then become imperative.

Sound governance links politics (policy) and government (administration) and is predicated upon exchange and institutional perspectives. Governance is the management of political exchange under certain conditions like a structure of rights and rules to enable coalition building and policy formation, and the distribution of preferences, resources and capabilities among political actors. The institutional perspective of governance 'recognizes the role of political institutions in managing exchange, in redistribution, in building a political culture, and in developing structures for the sustenance of civic virtue' (March and Olsen 1995, pp.11–12, 245). Strong party systems with internal democratic structures and linkages and transactions with a variety of social groups can facilitate the exchange and institutional processes of governance (Diamond 1997, p.33). Sound democratic governance also require a strong and autonomous legislature not only to perform law-making functions but also to enforce accountability among elective and appointive public officials.

Thus for democracy to become consolidated and sound governance to have any positive implications for state-building and development, five interrelated and mutually reinforcing structures, according to Linz and Stepan (1996), are necessary. These are, a robust civil society, an autonomous political society, rule of law, an efficient and responsive bureaucracy, and an economic society. We add three other dimensions – a public integrity system, a decentralised local governmental system and a free media.

10.3 THE STATE OF DEMOCRATIC CONSOLIDATION IN BANGLADESH

The events since 1991 demonstrate that Bangladesh has only been successful in becoming an *electoral democracy* rather than a *liberal democracy*. Two general elections, both free, were organised; one brought the principal adversary of the overthrown authoritarian regime into power, the other the incumbent major opposition party in parliament. Both elections were supervised by NCAs, headed by men of impeccably honest and honourable backgrounds. These electoral exercises acquired legitimacy because of the extent of political contestation they afforded within a multi-party framework, the clarity of party manifestos, the voters' spontaneity in exercising their franchise, the relative efficiency with which they were managed, the absence of large-scale rigging, and the low incidence of violence before, during and after the polls (Commonwealth Observer Group 1991; 1996; Timm 1996). The governments that resulted from these two elections were democratically-elected. Nobody questioned their right to form a government because of their majority in parliament and 'elect' their leaders as prime ministers. But as events have showed since the transition began, both the BNP and AL regimes have ridiculed constitutionalism and have adopted a kind of majoritarianism in practising statecraft. Obviously, the people who reposed their trust on them have been mystified by 'the fallacy of electoralism' and have become captives of the 'free-elections trap' (Mueller 1992 and Gelb 1991 quoted in Huntington 1997, p.7). They have consistently demonstrated a failure to commit themselves to 'self-binding' procedures of governance (Elster and Slagstad 1988, pp.1–18 quoted in Linz and Stepan 1996, p.19) by changing existing laws and making policies outside the purview of parliament and by ignoring the basic tenets of constitutionalism.

The AL in 1991 and the BNP in 1996 did not accept electoral defeats at the hands of their principal opponents and refused to accept the latters' legitimacy to rule the country for the specified term. For the major part of their term in opposition their dominant intents have been to obstruct the operations of government and to constantly threaten to bring it down, unconstitutionally, if necessary. The recurrent, and often continuous, boycott of parliamentary sessions by the opposition has had the effect of paralysing and destabilising constitutional politics (NED 1997). The few sessions attended by the opposition were enlivened not by animated debates on major policy and governance issues and serious consideration of proposed legislation but by plethoric disagreements on either procedural matters, personal attacks, and political mud-slinging (*The Economist,* 27 September 1997). Several key policy issues were unilaterally adopted by both the BNP and the AL governments without taking the parliament into confidence.[2] Indeed, both major parties in opposition had/has foresaken their responsibilities as representatives of their constituencies. The continued absence of the opposition reduced parliament to almost a political cipher; it has been used simply to endorse the legislative proposals of the government and to 'settle old scores' (NED 1997; *The Economist,* 23 November 1996). Unparliamentary behaviour of members, the speaker's partisan attitude in dealing with procedural matters, and inequitable allocation of parliamentary time among members led to the estrangement of the opposition from the house.

As a key component in governance, parliament, because of its in-built constraints and structural deficiencies, is ineffective in playing the role expected of it. The enthusiasm displayed by both treasury and opposition members in the initial sessions of the fifth parliament in moving various types of motions (N. U. Ahmed 1997) gradually evaporated and never reappeared in the seventh parliament. The committee system has been rendered unworkable, the government and the opposition failing to agree on the proportion of each other's representation on committees and the selection of chairs. The normal practice in parliamentary democracies of opposition members or treasury back-benchers presiding over committee work, especially in matters of finance and external affairs, has been unacceptable to either the BNP or the AL government. Furthermore, committees do not have any enforcing authority; nor do the public have access to committee findings. Investigative committees work behind schedules and by the time they complete their tasks their practical utility is lost (Menon 1997). Thus, in many respects, parliament lost its centrality in Bangladesh's political life when its *raison d'etre* and active operation were most relevant to democratic consolidation.

The extra-parliamentary strategy of the opposition to agitate against the government in the streets has made a mockery of constitutional politics. Regular confrontation between opposition activists and ruling party supporters with the aid of coercive forces, widespread violence, intolerant attitude towards each other, the opposition's non-acceptance of the legitimacy of the government, and the executive's arrogation of power *vis-a-vis* parliament exemplify the lack of seriousness among politicians to adhere to the norms of democratic politics (Rashiduzzman 1997). Both have shied away from the task entrusted upon them by the people to carve out a democratic polity and have adopted a rather undemocratic posture in approaching politics and governance. Both the government and the opposition have transcended constitutional boundaries in attempting to resolve their differences (S. Khan 1997).

The gap between rhetoric and action of the two democratically-elected governments has been critical in retarding the institutionalisation of democratic governance. Pre-election commitments and proposals to reform various sectors and institutions and initiate new programmes were either abandoned or carried out with half-hearted seriousness. This was especially evident in the local government, administrative, economic, social, legal and information sectors (Zafarullah 1996a; 1997; World Bank 1996a; Daily Star December 1997; Kochanek 1997; Z.R. Khan 1993; 1994). This dawdling attitude of the two post-authoritarian governments has endangered the consolidation process.

The continued discord between the two major parties has also arrested the development of certain dimensions of democratic governance. Policy formulation has become the monopoly of the government negating, as it does, the inputs from other sources. The ruling party has failed to form useful links and enter into transactions with either the civil society or other parts of the political society. This has warped the policy process. Agenda setting has by and large become a bureaucratic exercise, without the scope for negotiations, bargaining, trade-offs and compromises among those with stakes in certain policies. Even if such things occur, they are outside the bounds of normal political action and are extra-legitimate (Peters 1995, p.197). We find very little incentive for stake-holders in the process; the patterns of legitimate interaction between them and the government have not been permitted to find their way into the process. On the other hand, the political leadership's reliance on the bureaucracy alienated its own party from contributing to policy formation. Bureaucratic entrepreneurism has remained dominant over political entrepreneurism in the policy process in Bangladesh (N. U. Ahmed 1994).

The civil society in Bangladesh is still cystralising. It became active in the political arena during authoritarian rule and, since the democratic change-over, acquired an increasingly significant niche in several sectors. The non-governmental organisations supporting economic and social development are complemented by the universities, think tanks, professional groups, cultural, social and trade union movements which constitute the civil society. On their own, these organisations undertook, among other things, several programmes to educate voters on the eve of the 1996 elections, informing the people of their rights and civic responsibilities, and providing legal aid to the disadvantaged (Murshed and N. K. Chowdhury 1997, p.72). Some of these maintain close links with the two major parties and obtained benefits for their support during elections (Z.R. Khan 1997a). Some even went to the extent of openly campaigning for certain political parties (Farooq 1996, pp.60–61).

Nonetheless, in recent years, the gradual rise of the civil society has been one positive development in the process of democratic consolidation. The political advocacy and women's empowerment programmes of grassroots NGOs, the advancement of human rights and environmentalism by organised groups, the critical reviews of governmental policies and actions by learned societies, and the election monitoring activities of many voluntary agencies have the potential to promote democratic governance in the country. The most notable reflux has been in building and preserving constitutionalism and the rule of law.

Lack of consensus among the principal political actors on the fundamental elements of the constitution and how the country should go about resolving its perennial problems have had profound implications for political stability, sound governance, and social harmony. The often wayward misinterpretation of the constitution and erratic application of the law has made democratically-elected regimes undemocratic. The Special Powers Act (SPA)[3], enacted in 1974, has been indiscriminately applied by the BNP government and its successor AL in repressing the opposition and in suppressing anti-government actions of any kind. According to a report of the United States government, in 1996 alone about 1,400 arrests were made under the SPA during BNP rule (January-March) and 1,250 in the first three months of AL government. It has been argued that 'both the BNP and Awami League governments have used the SPA as a tool to harass and intimidate political opponents. While in opposition both parties despised this 'black law', yet when in power they used it to their advantage (USDS 1997). Its continued and unabashed use has undermined the significance of the rule of law and have deprecated the courts.

The judiciary is not totally independent of the executive. Judges of the Supreme and other lower courts are appointed by the government. The magistracy (criminal justice system) is still a part of the civil service and its members are accorded the same career privileges as their counterparts in other parts of the bureaucracy. The people have few opportunities and formal access points to challenge adverse administrative actions in courts and the administration of justice has been corrupted (TIB 1997).

An effective public integrity system synchronous with the machinery of government and the judiciary is yet to be fully designed in Bangladesh. Administrative law, a vital link between the government and the people, is conspicuous by its absence. The office of the ombudsman, enshrined in the original constitution, was never institutionalised and the possibility of its operationalisation in the forseeable future remains afar. This has permitted the bureaucracy to be largely nonchalant to societal needs, intransigent in its behaviour, maladroit in performing the functions of government, opaque in its actions, unethical in administrative practices and impervious to change. Corruption is deeply embedded in the social fabric and is prevalent in many agencies of the government as well as the judicial system (*Holiday* 14 and 27 October 1997; *Financial Express* 31 July 1997). Neither parties since the democratic transition has taken the initiative to build into the system of governance the norms of public integrity.

Years of pseudo-democratic and military/authoritarian rule preserved the bureaucratic nature of public sector management. Administrative reforms, attempted in the past, were piecemeal in nature, approximated a technical orientation, and only produced structural changes. None of the reform commissions considered behavioural and attitudinal change as a corollary to bureaucratic reform; neither were they able to provide any positive directions for changes in administrative operations (Zafarullah et al. 1997). The BNP government were under tremendous pressure from the international donor community to overhaul the administrative system. The World Bank's public sector reform proposals, the United Nations Development Programme's blueprint for comprehensive change, the Overseas Development Agency's financial restructuring plan were generally ignored by the government.[4] Administrative reform thus remained elusive. The World Bank's continued proposition for a paradigm shift in public management could create very little impact on the AL government. The BNP government's brainchild, the Administrative Reorganisation Committee, though very narrow and antiquated in its reform agenda, presented its reports to the AL government, which responded by appointing its own commission, almost entirely composed of bureaucrats, which it expects to design a new administrative system to work for a democratic government.

In the meantime, the AL government, like its predecessor, continues to use parts of the bureaucracy for fulfilling its parochial objectives. In the process, the bureaucracy has been politicised. Fragmentation within its ranks on party-lines has impacted upon its primary purpose of serving society. Field personnel have played a key role in working for either of the two major parties in both national and local elections (Zafarullah et al. 1997). The open support by a section of the bureaucracy for the AL in its crusade against a democratically-elected government prior to the 1996 elections points to a very dangerous trend (Rashiduzzaman 1997, pp.262–63). For an administrative system to serve as a responsible, responsive, accountable and efficient instrument of governance, such blatant political support by the servants of the people for any political party will not forebode well for either democratic consolidation or the bureaucracy itself. When the polity has sufficiently matured and when democratic institutions have been entrenched in the political fabric, will any kind of partisan attitude on the part of public servants have any positive effect. In the meantime, democratic consolidation demands functional neutrality of the public servants regardless of their individual political beliefs and their total commitment towards the policies and programmes of the government of the day, whatever may be its political complexion.

After assuming power, the BNP government pledged to move from a command economy to a mixed economy, which was slightly inclined towards a free-market ideology. Actually, such a trend was set by the preceding authoritarian regime but the BNP leadership, under pressure from the World Bank and the International Monetary Fund, adopted a more liberal approach towards structural adjustment by expanding its economic reforms to cover demand management and financial stabilisation. In line with the World Bank's scheme, economic liberalisation included several programmes creating investment opportunities, trade liberalisation, privatisation, improved government-business relations (World Bank 1994c). The AL, abandoned its earlier socialism stance and embraced the principles of market economy.

The espousing of economic liberalisation by the two parties has been one area in which they have displayed remarkable agreement. But for several reasons the implementation of economic reforms have been sluggish under both regimes. One reason is the continual political turbulence between the two parties resulting in frequent *hartals,* transportation blockades, and industrial violence have had a regressive effect on the economy (Kochanek 1997, p.41). The business community, reacting sharply to such phenomena, expressed consternation at the unconcern of both the government and the opposition and have demanded the latter to find alternative methods to articulate its grievances. It has warned that 'No way will be left for Bangladesh to survive in the global market if its socio-political environment remains hostile to investment and economic activities' (*Daily Star* 1 December 1997). The other reason is the bureaucracy which is not trained in the art of managing a liberal economy, given its long experience of working under authoritarian rule. The interface between the government and economy, in years before the advent of democracy, was based on the principles of strict state regulation of economic activities. The new liberalisation approach is being foiled 'by the thicket of 'administrative underbrush' and the coercive powers exercised by officials in government monopolies' (World Bank 1996a, p.77). A report further mentions, ' Efforts to achieve Bangladesh's microeconomic goals have been problematic. The privatisation of public sector industries has proceeded at a slow pace, due in part to worker unrest in affected industries. The government has also proven unable to resist demands for wage hikes in government-owned industries. Economic growth has been further slowed by an archaic banking system which has impeded access to capital – a serious problem in rural areas where many farmers have difficulty obtaining credit at reasonable rates' (USDS 1996). The search for a viable local government system continues. The decentralised scheme (Zafarullah 1996c), one of a few good achievements of the authoritarian regime, was discarded by the BNP government not because of its constraints, which could have been carefully rectified, but as a show of abomination against anything associated with that regime. The BNP's own scheme allowed for limited representation and that too only at the lowest tier, retained bureaucratic control over local affairs, and spurned both horizontal and vertical integration with other actors in local development (Zafarullah 1997). The AL's model is a rehash of previously tried experiments in local governance[5] and is geared to generate opportunities for central control and bureaucratisation (Z.R. Khan 1997a).

Finally, the media in Bangladesh is divided between one that is largely free but often constrained by censorship and the other which is monopolised by the government. The print media has the liberty to express the opinion of those they represents. There are several hundred newspapers and periodicals published from all over the country. Only a few of them project the independent conscience of the nation; most of them are affiliated to one political party or another and can be very partisan in the way they view and project events in the country (NED 1997). Some are sponsored by large business magnates and have the tendency to take very biased positions based on the business interests of their owners. The electronic media is state-controlled, lacking in autonomy in presenting news and views, which are entirely contrived to project the government's successes and the activities of the political executive and the ruling party. The opposition is completely ignored. Neither the BNP nor the AL has redeemed its pledge made after the fall of the authoritarian regime in 1990 of granting autonomy to state radio and television. The people, however, have alternative avenues to monitor news covering events in the country via satellite transmissions but this is not enough to keep them informed of the larger social, political and economic picture.

10.4   CONCLUDING COMMENTS

The road to democratic consolidation in Bangladesh has been hazardous. After a successful bid to lay the foundations of democratic rule in 1991 through the first ever free and fair elections after independence, continued political convulsion resulting from disagreement between the government and the opposition, the opportunity to institutionalise democratic governance received a serious jolt with the continued boycott and finally collective resignation of opposition members from parliament. A second chance came with another free election in 1996 under a constitutionally-mandated caretaker administration and the transfer of power from the erstwhile ruling party to the former opposition. This was a significant event in the country's political history. This opportunity is now being wasted. The two major parties are imitating each other. The country has passed the tests of an electoral democracy but it is yet quite far from meeting the conditions of a consolidated democracy. It can best be described as an illiberal democracy where the political executive defies parliament in setting the agenda of governance, where the ruling party transcends all norms of democratic behaviour to fulfil its political objectives, where the government takes recourse to laws beyond constitutional prerogatives to suppress dissent, where accountability is difficult to enforce due to systemic constraints, where the opposition behaves most irresponsibly and adopts extra-constitutional strategies to put pressure on the government to acquiesce to its demands, which often are based on fallacious grounds, where the bureaucracy is divided on political lines, is partisan in performing its functions and lacks competence in managing economic reforms, where the economy is the victim of political bickering, where local governance has remained under the baton of the ruling party, and where the people and those on the opposite side of politics have no access to articulate their view through the state-controlled media.

Bangladesh is not the only post-authoritarian polity which has been facing a host of problems in consolidating democracy. It can take lessons from other countries which have been successful, even if partly, in putting in place the fundamentals of democratic governance. While the politicians do have the vision, it is their lack of commitment, the absence of mutual trust, and an unwillingness to compromise which so far have stifled the process of democratic consolidation. Democratic consolidation has progressed only a small stride with the institutionalisation of the fair-election process but the extra-constitutional acts and unwarranted political performance of both the government and the opposition have retarded that progress significantly.

NOTES

1 Huntington refers to this wave as the 'third', the first occurring between the early 1800s and 1920, and the second taking place in aftermath of World War II. (Huntington 1997, p. 4).

2 For instance, the BNP's abolition of the decentralisation scheme, one of the very few achievements of the ousted authoritarian regime, was effected without elaborate discussion in parliament and at the face of stiff resistance. Likewise, the AL government's accords with India on the sharing of the Ganges water and with the tribal community in Eastern Bangladesh were not placed in parliament for discussion.

3 The Act provides for the detention by the government of any person without formal charge to prevent him/her from committing any prejudicial act.

4 For details, see Zafarullah (1996a).

5 The AL government has installed a four-tiered local government system based in the village, union, *thana* and *zila*.

11 Governance, Politics and Development Management in Bangladesh

Samiul Hasan

11.1 INTRODUCTION

In the recent past many governments in the developing countries have failed their peoples by not being able to undertake the desired measures, and the best possible governmental process to achieve the developmental goals. The World Bank attributed the failure of these governments in achieving the developmental objectives to the problems of governance (World Bank 1989). Governance can be seen as a form emphasizing on political plurality and economic liberalism, a process that is conscientious and transparent, the capacity of government in managing regulatory, service, and programme delivery activities through control and empowerment and the capacity to ensure accountability (Table 11.1; see also Hasan 1998b).

The principle of political plurality calls for responsible rule, and not for tyranny, of the majority. The facilitation of a majority rule requires an open and inclusive political system where the people can make free choice regarding the policy makers and the policy. Thus, a fair political system should also have a responsible political opposition. The role of the opposition is not to 'destruct' the government but 'construct' it through responsible criticism opinions. Parties in position as well as in opposition both have to play significant roles in achieving political plurality. Without the existence of political plurality other 'essentials' of governance mentioned in Table 11.1 cannot be achieved, and the 'tools' cannot perform.

In the more than twenty-six years of its existence, an effective and continuous political system has not been developed in Bangladesh to allow the political parties to play responsible roles in government. Recently, however, opportunities for that have been created, but the political parties have failed to act responsively. Two democratically elected governments have been formed since 1991, but the politicians are still negatively affecting aspects of good governance and development management. This chapter analyses the behaviour of the political parties, and show how these acts of the political parties and leaders have been procrastinating development.

11.2   POLITICAL PARTIES AND THE POLITICAL ENVIRONMENT

In the 1980s there were 160 political parties in Bangladesh (Hasan 1988a). Many new parties have been formed in the recent past, but some also have become inactive. Though an exact figure is not available, there is no reason to believe the number now will be much different. These political parties were not formed to establish any political ideologies or to achieve specific political agenda. Most political parties in Bangladesh are one-man with no supporters, and came into being mainly for five reasons:

- Frustration with the existing political system or parties;

- Struggle for power and benefits;

- Conflicts of opinion and personality among the party leadership;

- To enjoy (legal as well as illegal) benefits available to the political parties; and

- To help the military rulers gain a 'civil character' (Hasan 1988b).

General Zia, head of government between 1975 and 1981, with an intention of sorting out the problem of mushroom growth of political parties, attempted to limit the number of political parties. In 1976 General Zia introduced the Political Parties Regulation (PPR) to revive political activity in the country that had been under suspension following a military coup in August 1975. The PPR required the political parties to take fresh licenses, and prohibited any overseas-supported party, underground armed political activities, and propaganda advocating a personality cult. It required the political parties to get their programmes approved by the government. Sixty political parties applied for, but only twenty-one received licenses (Maniruzzaman 1977). The PPR also stated that any party that fails to win 10 per cent of the seats in an election would automatically cease to function as a political party.

This was obviously a constructive measure. Unfortunately, however, the Zia government failed to maintain the integrity of the regulation. In the following election thirty-four political parties participated, thirteen parties won any seat, but only two parties won more than 10 per cent of the seats (Table 11.2). Some small political parties, as a survival strategy or due to a 'carrot and stick' trick of the government supported programmes of General Zia and thus were allowed to continue as parliamentary parties and were saved from being subjected to the PPR regulation. The PPR regulation finally became inoperative and the problems of burgeoning political party continued. These political parties help the government in times of crises created by the unconstitutional activities of the ruling regimes. For example, General Ershad, the army general who came to power through an unconstitutional means, tried to use these one-man political parties to stay in power. All the major political parties in the country boycotted the parliamentary election held under General Ershad in 1988. The Ershad government, however, received support from seventy-six of these 'one-man' political parties grouped as Combined Opposition Parties (COP) (S. Rahman 1989, p.217). When the donors asked the government to arrange free and fair election, the government of General Ershad tried to convince the aid donors that it had the support from a 'huge' number of 'political parties'. This strategy did not work – the donors advised General Ershad to arrange for a free and fair election participated by all the major political parties (S. Rahman 1990).

Due to the ongoing political agitation in the country, General Ershad did not dare to arrange a fair election. A massive political upsurge in the country forced him to resign from the presidency in December 1990, paving the way for a fair election. The ineffectiveness of the support of these so-called political parties provided to the government of General Ershad became evident from the fact that none of the above mentioned seventy-six political parties won a parliamentary seat in the 1991 election held under a neutral caretaker government. In the same election BNP won the maximum number of seats and needed some support to form the government. Khaleda Zia, the chairperson, did avail the first opportunity to steer support from Jamat-e-Islami, the fanatic party blamed of supporting the occupation army during the War of Liberation in 1971. The major partner of the COP, JSD (Rab), won a seat in the parliament in 1996, and managed to 'earn' itself a cabinet position by supporting the government. The AL did not need this support to stay in power, but wanted to make the opposition weaker.

The inclusion of the JSD (Rab) in the present government proved again that the major political parties also are not sure when they will need these 'little brothers' supports. Thus, these parties do not wish to solve the problem. Only by undertaking some simple measures like the automatic abolition of political party that fail to secure a certain percentage of the cast votes, the problem of numbers and ill-motivated use of these parties by the 'big brothers' can easily be halted.

11.3 FAILURE OF THE POLITICAL PARTIES AND LEADERS

After independence the first government of Bangladesh was sworn in to power in January 1972 and the twentieth (present) government came to power in June 1996 through elections. In four more occasions the governments were changed through general elections (Table 11.3). All other changes in the government were in abnormal ways, including constitutional coup (January 1975), military coups (15 August and 3, 7 November 1975, and March 1982), and forced resignation of the President (1990). Within the first ten years of its independence (up to March 1982) Bangladesh experienced nine known attempts at *coup-d'état* (*Defence Journal* 1986) including five successful that resulted in changes in government.

In the last twenty-six years military generals have ruled the country for more than fifteen years. The generals captured power through unconstitutional means, and later legalized their rules with the help of some political leaders. The other political parties and leaders in the country thus have been under oppression, at times. Nevertheless, even under democratic government the performance of the government and the political parties are not very impressive and encouraging. As a result, the country has not achieved desired development. This section analyses the failure of the political system and the political parties in achieving the major objectives for people's development. The analysis also suggests that though it is true that the military leaders were obstacles to a democratic process, the activities of most political parties to-date are not at all democratic nor congenial to development.

11.3.1 Opportunist political parties and leaders

The fundamental characteristics of the constitution framed in 1972 have been severely damaged by the subsequent amendments made by the governments at different times (also see Chapter 9). The first major change in the constitution was initiated (known as the fourth amendment) by the Awami League, the party that framed the constitution while in government. The multiparty parliamentary system was changed to a one-party presidential form, with all the executive power vested in the presidency. All the governments and the leaders coming to power since August 1975, denounced the government of Sheikh Mujibur Rahman for amending the constitution and concentrating too much power on the presidency. Interestingly enough none of these governments deleted the authoritarian position of the president from the amended constitution, rather they all used the authority to further their interests. Through another major change in the constitution a parliamentary system of government has been reintroduced in the country, however, some 'black laws', e.g. The Special Powers Act, Press Censorship Act have been left untouched, because the government can reap the benefits of these laws without having to bear the blame for their enactment. One major opponent of the Special Powers Act, (that allows for the arrest and detention of anybody without trial) the BNP (as an opposition political party), revitalised the Act after forming the government through a democratic election. In 1992 there were 2,700 individuals in government detention without trial (Z. R. Khan 1997b).

The root of all the governments in the country between 1975 and 1990 was the armed forces. The army officers took over power as Martial Law Administrators and then left the army and formed 'civil' governments. All these governments used governmental institutions to further their parochial interests tricking other political parties and the general people. Some political 'elites were there to commit even abhorrent acts to further their political and material interests. This fact was proved twice during the civilianisation process of the military rules, once in the latter half of the 1970s and again in the early 1980s. General Ziaur Rahman planned to form a political party mainly with some retired military officers and a few political leaders who gathered around him for a give-and-take purpose (Rashiduzzaman 1977; 1979; Khan and Zafarullah 1979). In the end, the pro-Beijing radicals, like the National Awami Party (NAP, Mashiur) and on the other extreme, the Muslim League (along with other Islamic fanatics) gathered around him (Franda 1982, p.23). The leaders who had divergent beliefs and interests 'hastily assembled under this multi-dimensional umbrella party' (Haque 1980, p.224).

In the wake of the revival of political activities again in 1983, following the military coup in 1982, factionalism 'increased to an unprecedented degree and affected almost all the political parties'. Some leaders from various political parties deserted their previous parties in groups and gathered around General H. M. Ershad. The weaknesses of the political parties were manifested 'not only in their intense factionalism but also in their individual susceptibility to the government's 'carrot-and-stick' policy and their tenuous links with the 'grass-roots' (A. A. Rahman 1984, p.242). The scenario of 1977 was repeated in 1985, when the process reached a climax after two years of negotiation. A political front, the *Jatiyo* (National) Front, was formed with elements from many parties: the Awami League, BNP, and the Muslim League, and the radical leftist parties like the United People's Party (UPP), and the *Gono* (People's) Front. Some of these leaders while involved in the movement demanding the military to relinquish power negotiated their position in the military government and joined the military governments as cabinet ministers.

A unique example was set by an octogenarian politician, Ataur Rahman Khan, who also had joined the BAKSAL (the party formed by the government in 1975 to introduce a one-party system in the country). Mr Khan, an ex-premier of East Pakistan, accepted the prime ministership under General Ershad, within twenty-four hours after terming the government of General Ershad as a 'killer of democracy'. After he accepted the prime ministership the journalists asked him about his feelings of being the prime minister of the government of the 'killers of democracy', he answered delightfully 'let's now revive democracy'. It is not at all surprising that Mr Khan failed to revive democracy in the country during his nine-month tenure in office. When General Ershad came to power, some ministers of the previous BNP government were taken into custody on charges of corruption. Some of those people were freed and were even made ministers in the new government when they pledged to support General Ershad and to work to organize a political party for him.

The so-called political leaders thus shop-around for privileges and pay allegiance according to the benefit gained. People and the alleviation of their miseries through the undertaking of major and beneficial development programmes are secondary to them.

Not only some leaders, the major political parties are also skilful in making and then breaking promises, as these fit their interests. In the later part of the movement against the government of General Ershad the three opposition alliances signed a Charter of agreement. The Charter, among other things, stipulated that whoever wins the election after the fall of Ershad will form independent and autonomous bodies for mass media, including the radio and television, to make those function neutrally (Hakim 1993). BNP formed the government in 1991, but showed an utter disregard to the Charter agreed upon. Awami League, being voted into power in 1996, seems to have forgotten the Charter that could have eradicated the sources of some political problems in the country. In fact, the misuse of governmental resources including the media give the government additional power, so the governments do not want to destroy any 'tool' of yielding more power. The opportunist character of the political parties and the leaders never changes.

11.3.2   Poly-tricking in politics

The main characteristic of the political system in Bangladesh is the tendency of different government (or opposition) leaders (or parties) to 'trick people and other political parties to gain undue benefit for self or the party or the clique. After independence, Sheikh Mujibur Rahman, the leader of the Awami League (AL) and the Liberation War formed the government, and ignored the sacrifices and performances of other parties. AL registered all the credits for the War, and provided various privileges, to the members and the supporters of the party though the leadership of the Liberation War was actually in the hands of various factions of *Mukti Bahini* (Freedom Fighters or FF) and not solely on the Awami League. Sheikh Mujib did not pay any heed either to the demands of establishing a multiparty government and arranging a fresh election, demanded by the other political parties. Rather, he formed the Assembly to frame the Constitution of the Country with the members of the Pakistan National Assembly and East Pakistan Provincial Assembly elected in 1970.

To concentrate more power in his own hands, Sheikh Mujib in 1975, transformed the multiparty parliamentary form of government into a single-party presidential system. Sheikh Mujib claimed that the divisive activities of the opposition parties, and especially the leftist radical parties, compelled him to institute a single-party system and to suspend fundamental rights (Z.R. Khan 1983). The democratically elected government of Sheikh Mujib misread the people's mind and misused the mandate given to them in the general election held in 1973 and deceived the citizens to favour own party-men. The Awami League was ousted from the power in a military coup in August 1975.

Following the military coup in 1975, the political parties became briefly active between 1979 and March 1982, when another take over of the government by the armed forces occurred. The suppression by the military regime forced the political parties to come out in the street to call for the establishment of democracy. In 1986 the opposition groups' 15-party alliance led by the Awami League, a seven-party alliance led by the BNP, and some other opposition parties demanded the handing over of governmental power to a caretaker government. Until this condition was met, the political parties vowed not to take part in any election. The government issued an ultimatum to the political parties, to decide on participation in the election before midnight on the 21st of March 1986. As none of the opposition demands was met by the government, all the opposition parties took a unanimous decision, late that night, not to submit to the government's 'trick'. To the utter surprise of all the other opposition parties the Awami League, after a little while, unilaterally announced its decision to participate in the general election.

It appeared to some critics that the Awami League had already reached some understanding with the government (Islam 1987). Apart from that, however, the Awami League rightly understood that if it participated in the election without the BNP, Sheikh Hasina (daughter of Sheikh Mujib), President of the Awami League could become the leader of the opposition, and by that regain lost status for the Awami League. In fact, the Awami League and the

BNP sought each other's destruction as much as they sought the downfall of the Ershad regime (Islam 1987).

This decision of the Awami League was a blow to the joint efforts of the opposition parties that had been active since 1983. This move, in other words, benefited Ershad, who had been looking for ways of dividing and thus defeating the opposition movement. This act of the Awami League helped the government regain a second life that endured until 1990. The behaviour of the government leaders and these political parties and leaders prove that they can resort to any trick to further their interest, despite the loss caused to the people or the country.

The demand for the formation of a neutral caretaker government to hold the general election was raised again during the BNP rule. The BNP wanted to trick out the political opposition from the election so did not listen to the opposition demand and arranged a general election in February 1996 without the participation of the major political parties. The opposition and the people instituted a strong agitation against the government. Finally, the BNP government had to accept the demand and amend the constitution to include the provision that all general elections in the country be held under a neutral caretaker government. The BNP resisted the formation of a neutral caretaker government to conduct the parliamentary election, because possibly it understood that due to its misdeeds of 1991–96, it did not hold much chance of winning a fair election. In reality that is what happened when the election was held under a caretaker government.

11.3.3   Gaps between political party and the people

So far, parliamentary elections in the country have been held in Bangladesh in 1973, 1979, 1986, 1991 and June 1996 (the election held in 1988 was boycotted by all the major political parties so is not included; the parliament formed through the February 1996 election amended the Constitution to allow for a neutral caretaker government to arrange for the parliamentary election, but that election was not participated by the main opposition parties thus is not included in the discussion). Many political parties participate in these elections, but most do not have any contact with the people they wish to represent. This fact is proved from the results of the parliamentary elections. Seventy-six political parties participated in the parliamentary election held in 1996, but only six political parties won any seat in the Parliament. The ratio of success to the number of parties participating in the election was 1:14 in 1973, 1:11 in 1979, and 1:16 in 1991 (Table 11.2).

In all the fair parliamentary elections held in the recent past the party winning the government polled only a small number of the votes cast. The major problem occurred in the political scenes and in the development arena of the country when the party in power forgets that most of the voters voted against them. In the elections held in 1991, the BNP formed the government receiving only 31 per cent of the cast vote, and failed to reckon the fact that 69 per cent of the voters voted against them. The party took political and economic measures ignoring the opposition that collectively enjoyed more than double the support among the general voters enjoyed by the government. Thus the government antagonised the public and finally succumbed to their agitation. Eventually for its arrogance the BNP failed to come back to the office, because Khaleda as a prime minister was seen as 'haughty, proud, overbearing, vindictive and inept' (Kochanek 1997, p.221). In 1996 the Awami League with only 37 per cent of the cast votes formed the government. If the Awami League forgets the 'number' and ignores the opposition it might face the same consequences in the next election.

Another interesting factor stems from these election results. Many people participate in these elections, but only a few receive a reasonable endorsement from the electorates. In the elections held in 1991 and 1996, there were 1,786 (including 424 independent) and 1 827 (including 350 independent) contestants, respectively for three hundred parliamentary seats (Z.R. Khan 1997a). On an average there are around six candidates in every constituency, thus, the percentage of votes polled by the winning candidate remains very low. In some seats the winning candidate poll as low as 23 per cent of the cast votes (Hasan 1988b). Only in a few seats the winner polls more than 50 per cent of the cast vote. Since there are some constituencies where up to 12 candidates contest a seat, the percentage of votes polled against the successful candidates are often still much more than 50 per cent.

The recent election results, however, prove that the political parties in Bangladesh lack maturity, but the people, after a long political struggle under the authoritarian regimes, have achieved some maturity. The election results showed that on the face of the government's failure to limit the number of unwanted political parties, the people have made their choice and there is a trend that the parties without much popular base will be wiped out very soon. Table 11.2 depicts that in the election in 1991 twelve parties won any seats, in 1996 only six political parties managed to win any seats. Nevertheless, three major political parties won 294 seats, while three other parties won only five seats (one seat was won by an independent candidate). These candidates from the small political parties won the seats on party tickets, but their recorded popularity in the respective constituencies suggests that these are their personal achievements. They would have won the seats even if they had participated in the election as independents.

Another major feature of the recent elections is that only four parties in 1991 and three parties in 1996 polled more than 10 per cent of the cast votes. Had the Political Party Regulation of General Zia (discussed earlier) or any such measures been in place, all the other parties, including the three small ones winning seats, would automatically have been abolished by now, thus creating a three party political system in the country. This system would bring more opportunity in devoting and being involved in development activities rather than being involved in creating 'gains' for the party or 'destructing' other parties.

11.3.4 Absence of democracy within the political parties

In Bangladesh one main declared objective of all the political parties is to uphold and establish democracy in the country. It is very interesting that none of these political parties have ever practised democracies within their own organizations. The party offices are distributed by the leader, who happens to be the chief, of the party. The large political parties hold regular convention to 'choose' their leaders, but in practice the positions are distributed mainly among the 'yes-men' of the party by the chairperson. The convention is convened merely to endorse them formally. In some occasions the leader fails to nominate anybody in the key positions, because he or she has to satisfy all the contending interests within the party. For example, the Chairman of the BNP took almost six months after the convention was held in 1994 to fill in the position of the party secretary general.

Most times the 'leaders' lack required qualities to claim the positions they hold in the party. The party leaders, including the chairperson, are always afraid of losing their positions to more able individuals within the party, thus ascription, and not achievement, is practised and promoted in the parties. The leaders always try to suppress would-be challengers. The would-be leaders also do not want to ruin their prospects of becoming second, third or the fourth person in the party by becoming smarter and more sought about by the general members of the party.

Further, most political parties and their leaders are urban-based and do not have any organization at the grass-roots level. To win over the rural votes, most times they rely on the political touts functioning in the rural areas. They can win parliamentary or other elective offices, but they fail to win over, and remain alienated from, the general mass. The parties use the name of the general mass for their own benefits, yet they can never undertake programmes to benefit the general mass.

11.4   DISCUSSION AND CONCLUSION

Bangladesh was born in 1971, following a nine-month-long Liberation War, and incurring severe economic and infra-structural losses. The massive work of reconstruction and rebuilding required a strong and politically committed all-party government. It did not become real. The failure of the government in providing even the minimum necessities of life resulted in unrest among people within just a year of independence. The government took the shape of an authoritarian regime, and the military intervention in the political process followed.

The armed forces in Bangladesh intervened in the politics in 1975. For the next fifteen years military or quasi-military governments governed the country. Since 1991 in the wake of the world wide democratisation and redemocratisation process, Bangladesh again has seen a sign of permanent opportunity of reestablishing a democratic political system. However, due to above-mentioned factors the political process in the country is still in a very vulnerable position.

The problems of poverty and development are still there. The government made many promises but never tried to maintain integrity. The Constitution promised 'development' (see Chapter 12), the government created planning agencies that framed plans, but due to a lack of congenial atmosphere and economic institutions all failed (cf. Islam 1977). It is true that some developmental targets of the government are 'political', and sometimes the government lack a sincere intention. Yet apart from these, the activities of the political parties have been responsible for the failure in achieving development targets.

The opposition political parties are not cooperative in the democratically elected parliament. They also have been creating confusion and staging destruction on the streets. During the mass agitation against the BNP government between March 1994 and March 1996 the opposition political parties called nationwide dawn to dusk *hartals* on 92 days and continuous non-cooperation for twenty-two days (Kochanek 1997). During the *hartals* the country comes to a standstill, because it means stoppage of all the economy related activities including abstention from work at schools, colleges, and government administration. Even by a conservative estimate, a nationwide *hartal* can cost Bangladesh at least US$60 – 80 million a day (Kochanek 1997). The country also incurred losses from another sixty-one days of other political disturbances including local strikes staged during that period. The losses incurred by Bangladesh, a country with only US$240 per capita annual income, for these political problems are phenomenal.

As a result the annual GNP growth rate in the country during the early 1990s has been only 2.1 per cent (World Bank 1997b), against the annual growth rate of 4.3 per cent registered during 1981–86 (World Bank 1986). The rate of growth in 1995–96, however, increased to 4.7 per cent (Kochanek 1997). If the political parties can behave conscientiously, the country may achieve economic growth.

Until 1991 the problem in the country was the dominance of military or quasi-military governments and their oppression on the political parties retarding their participation in the political process. Now the problem is the failure of the parties in securing the hard earned democracy by poly-tricks, and political opportunism, leaders' ego, and jealousy. The country, however, cannot afford to bear any more of these. Good governance requires worthy support and constructive criticism from a responsible and competent opposition. The sooner the parties realise this, the better it is for the country, people, and the parties themselves. Otherwise, the smart voters will take their course by dumping irresponsible parties in political obscurity through general elections held under neutral caretaker governments. The trend is already there!

Table 11.1 Governance and development: essentials and tools

	Form			Process			Capacity	
	Essentials	*Tools*		*Essentials*	*Tools*		*Essentials*	*Tools*
Political Pluralism	Majority rule but not tyranny of majority; Political integrity and reciprocity; Preservation of minority rights; Micro-Level Institutions	Mutual respect and understanding among political groups; Political opposition; Political, Spatial, Functional, Structural Decentralisation	**Conscientiousness**	Predictable policy process; Equal opportunity; Social justice; Respect for human rights; Freedom of expression	Existence and involvement of civil society in decision making; Access to independent legal system; Free and responsible media; Adherence to law	**Enablement**	Impeccable policy environment; Minimal government; Creation, and use of effective institutions; Efficient use of Man, Money, Material to achieve maximum benefit for the maximum number	Effectual legislature; Government organisations only for regulation and control; Neutral, and people-focused administrative system; Participation
Economic Liberalism	Legal framework to encourage private sector in development; Enabling macro economic environment; Distributional justice	Free and responsible market economy; Savings and private investment; Private property rights	**Transparency**	Economic system ensuring efficiency; Corruption-free mechanism; Policy process to articulate interest through debate	Openness and inclusiveness; Free and open information exchange; Tolerance	**Accountability**	Political accountability; Administrative accountability; Monetary and Judgemental accountability	Honest, political influence-free, and accountable monitoring system; Economic journalism; Sanctioning process to reward or punish performance

Table 11.2 Bangladesh parliamentary election results

	1973	1979	1986	1988	1991	1996 June
No of parties participated	14	34	18	3+76**	63	76
No of candidates	1075	2125	1527	764	1786	1827
Vote cast (% of total)	55	48	60	52***	57	74
No of parties winning seats	4	11	11	4	12	6
No of parties polling 10%+ cast vote	1	3	2	1	4	3
Percentage of cast votes polled by different parties						
Awami league	73	25	26	Abstained	30	37
BNP	–	41	Abstained	Abstained	31	34
Jatiyo party	–	–	42	68	12	16
Jamate islami	–	10*	5	Abstained	12	9
Other (+ independents)	27	24	27	32	15	4
Number of seats won						
Awami league	291	40	76	Abstained	88	146
BNP	–	205	Abstained	Abstained	140	116
Jatiyo party	–	–	153	251	35	32
Jamat–e–islami	–	20*	10	Abstained	18	3
Other (+ independents)	8	35	61	49	19	3

Notes: *   Jamate Islami contested this election as Islamic Democratic League and jointly with Muslim League.
         **   JSD (Rab) gathered 75 other small parties to participate in the election as Combined Opposition Parties.
         ***   Main parties that did not participate claimed only 1% voters voted.

Sources: Z.R. Khan (1997a); Hasan (1988a).

Table 11.3   Chronological list and reasons for changes in government in
Bangladesh 1972–96

Nature of change	Date formed	Head of Government	Head of State
Independence	January 1972	Sheikh Mujib, PM	Justice A.S. Choudhury, President
General Election	March 1973	Sheikh Mujib, PM	Mohammadullah, President
Justice Choudhury resigns	December 1973	Sheikh Mujib, PM	Mohammadullah, President
Constitutional amendment	January 1975	Sheikh Mujib, President	Sheikh Mujib, President
Military coup	August 1975	K. Mushataque Ahmed, CMLA, President	K. Mushataque Ahmed, CMLA, President
Military coup	(3) November 1975	General Mosharraf, DCMLA	Justice A.M. Sayem, President
Military coup	(7) November 1975	General Zia, DCMLA	Justice A.M. Sayem, President
Internal arrangement	(30) November 1975	General Zia, CMLA	Justice A.M. Sayem, President
Justice A.M. Sayem removed	April 1977	General Zia, CMLA	General Zia, President
Presidential election	June 1978	General Zia, CMLA	General Zia, President
Parliamentary election	April 1979	General Zia, President	General Zia, President
Military coup	May 1981	Justice Sattar, Acting President	Justice Sattar, Acting President
Presidential election	November 1981	Justice Sattar, President	Justice Sattar, President
Military coup	March 1982	General Ershad, CMLA	Justice AFA, Choudhury President
Justice AFA Choudhury removed	December 1983	General Ershad, CMLA	General Ershad, President

Table 11.3 continued

Nature of change	Date formed	Head of Government	Head of State
Presidential election	October 1986	General Ershad, President	General Ershad, President
Caretaker government	December 1990	Justice Sahabuddin, Acting President	Justice Sahabuddin, Acting President
Parliamentary election	February 1991	Begum Khaleda Zia, PM	A.R. Biswas, President*
Caretaker government	March 1996	Justice H. Rahman	A.R. Biswas, President
Parliamentary election	June 1996	Sheikh Hasina, PM	Justice Shahabuddin, President **

Notes: *   A.R. Biswas actually became president in October 1991.
           **   Justice Sahabuddin became president in October 1996.

12 Dilemmas and Strategies for Development in Bangladesh

Ahmed Shafiqul Huque

12.1 INTRODUCTION

Development, in general usage, implies a high level of affluence, good public and social services, and a satisfactory quality of life. There are diverse views on the processes leading to development. Successive regimes that came to power after the independence of Bangladesh pledged to attain development, and each pursued this goal with vigour. At different stages, there have been claims from these regimes regarding the effectiveness of their strategies and the quick results they have produced. On objective evaluation, however, such claims are found to be baseless, and none of the desired outcomes of development appears to be present in Bangladesh.

Such a scenario leads to the need for serious rethinking on the process of development in Bangladesh. The desired results may not be obtained due to misunderstandings about the process and objectives of development and there are no indications that governments had a comprehensive understanding of the process of development. A number of dilemmas appear to have confronted the regimes in Bangladesh. There was confusion regarding the ideological basis for development and the strategies shifted from socialist to a mixed-economy orientation. It was not clear whether development merely required the construction of physical facilities or an emphasis on the human factor as well. It had to be resolved whether development should be financed by external resources or local resources. Will development still remain a desirable outcome if it shifts the balance of power in which the ruling group holds the upper hand?

This chapter seeks to address some of these issues by examining developmental efforts undertaken in Bangladesh. It will be useful to start with an effort to explain the concept of development as it is defined in the literature and relate those ideas to the realities in Bangladesh. The scenario of development in Bangladesh should be described with reference to the needs and objectives of the government as well as the citizens. The process of development will be briefly reviewed to identify the main strategies adopted for this purpose. This will shed light on the factors which influenced the adoption of particular strategies by different regimes in Bangladesh.

12.2   THE CONCEPT OF DEVELOPMENT

Development is an extremely vague and all-encompassing term which appeals to various groups who often view it in different ways, although related terms such as growth, modernisation and socio-economic progress are less difficult to understand. At the simplest level, development implies growth or maturation and advancement. The term came to prominence in the social science literature after the Second World War when major political and social changes were taking place across the globe. While the older political systems were acquiring maturity, new nations were emerging at a rapid rate, and 'development' became their chosen destiny. The term became particularly relevant for changes taking place in the Third World (a polite word to denote 'poor' countries), and development, in its broadest sense, refers to 'the process by which poor countries get richer, or try to do so, and also to the process by which rich countries get still richer' (Berger 1976, p.34). Similarly, 'it connotes a process of economic change brought about by industrialization' (Midgley 1995, p.2).

This is perhaps the best alternative to adopt as a framework of study in view of the more compartmentalised approach taken in the literature. Obviously, scholars in the field grappled with the task of defining development and ended up emphasizing specific sections of the process. Hence, there was a proliferation of studies on economic, political, social and even administrative development, and most of these concentrated on the growth, maturation and operation of specific institutions and their impact on the society. It has been found that although such studies are valuable as guides for understanding the pattern of 'development', they could not be seen as complementary parts of an overall framework for studying 'development' in a comprehensive manner. It was not possible to obtain guidance for determining the course to be followed by countries striving for development.

There are operational guidelines on specific aspects of development. For example, 'Economic development involves goal setting and the allocation of resources and authority via the political system' (Siffin 1966, p.6), while social development seeks to initiate efforts focused 'on communities and societies, emphasizes planned intervention, promotes a dynamic change-oriented approach which is inclusive and universalistic, and above all seeks to harmonize social interventions with economic development efforts' (Midgley 1995, p.8). Political development received more detailed treatment in the literature, and Diamant (1966, pp.26–27) proposed the following description:

- A political system is said to be developing when there is an increase in its ability to sustain successfully and continuously new types of social goals and the creation of new types of organization

- For political development to continue over time a differentiated and centralized polity must come into being which must be able to command resources from and power over more spheres and regions of the society

Another large group of studies focus on the process of development of rural areas since many developing countries are primarily agricultural in nature and governments view the strengthening of the rural institutions and the improvement of the quality of life in those areas as crucial for the modernisation of a country.

The focus of development may vary according to the need, perception or context in which it is considered. Therefore, in most post-colonial countries, developmental efforts revolve around the tasks of agricultural or industrial development. In countries with large numbers of rural population, rural development acquires immense importance. As the countries make some progress in these areas, economic development gains prominence, while political development occupies a place of importance at all stages. Administrative development appears to feature on the agenda along with economic and political developments since a competent arrangement of administrative framework facilitates the processes. At a later stage, social development receives attention as the citizens become more conscious of their rights and privileges and governments seek to enhance the level of development. Did the ruling regimes in Bangladesh seek to attain one aspect of development at a time?

In simple terms, development implies stable political systems, a sound economy, a general consensus of values among all participating groups, a responsive electorate, well developed political and civil institutions, and effective machineries for helping in formulating and implementing decisions (Heady 1996, Chapters 5 and 7). Depending on the stage of development a country is in, the emphasis may vary between agricultural, political, economic or social development, and a combination of these will indicate the level of development achieved. It will be useful to examine the strategies pursued by Bangladesh in attaining such a condition, and achieve the goal of development.

12.3   DEVELOPMENT EFFORTS IN BANGLADESH

None of the conditions described above can be said to exist at a satisfactory level in Bangladesh, although there have been encouraging signs on occasions. The process of development has been influenced to a great extent by the history, economy, politics and society in Bangladesh, and strategies adopted have been determined on the basis of perceptions of the ruling elite.

12.3.1   The early years

In the first step toward political development, a constitution was drawn up within a short period of achieving independence. The document reflected the mood of the nation at that juncture of history. The fundamental principles of democracy, nationalism, secularism and socialism were adopted unanimously, and were expected to be the general direction to be adopted by the new state. The constitution provided detailed plans on the new People's Republic of Bangladesh, its political structure, economic strategies, and the judiciary (GOB 1991b).

The spirit of development was reflected in the 'aim of the State to realise through the democratic process a socialist society, free from exploitation – a society in which the rule of law, fundamental human rights and freedom, equality and justice, political, economic and social, will be secured for all citizens' (GOB 1991b, Preamble). However, there was no specific commitment to development except for the resolution to 'adopt effective measures to bring about a radical transformation in the rural areas through the promotion of an agricultural revolution, the provision of rural electrification, the development of cottage and other industries, and the improvement of education, communications and public health, in those areas, so as progressively to remove the disparity in the standards of living between the urban and the rural areas' (GOB 1991b, Article 16). In other words, development was being treated synonymously with 'rural development' in the early days of the republic.

Befitting a socialist system, the first government of Bangladesh led by the Awami League (AL) sought to adopt a planned approach toward development. The constitution stipulated that the 'people shall own or control the instruments and means of production and distribution', although state, co-operative and private ownership were all recognised, (GOB 1991b, Article 13). Following the practice prevalent in many developing countries, Bangladesh chose to adopt the strategy of attaining development through five-year plans. However, the overcrowded agenda of the government resulted in the relegation of the goal of development to the background.

Although the issues of rural development as well as economic development often featured in the speeches of the leaders, the first few years of Bangladesh saw them preoccupied with more pressing matters. Efforts were made to streamline the political and electoral process, reconstruct the economy, reduce poverty, and achieve social justice. The First Five-Year Plan was launched in July 1973, and reflected the nature of development efforts undertaken by the first government of Bangladesh. The grandiose plan for development soon encountered problems, particularly due to the lack of adequate resources. 'The implementation of the Plan could not be fully undertaken due to shortfall in domestic and external resources, inadequate institutional support, lack of skilled manpower, unfavourable weather conditions and inflation and recession' (BPC 1980, p.I–2).

A number of rural development programmes were initiated before the independence of Bangladesh, and these were allowed to continue after independence since they appeared to be making progress, although in a limited way. Thus, in spite of some increase in productivity and scope for off-season employment for the rural poor, the gap between the wealthy and the rural poor continued to widen. Hence the goals of development remained unattained.

12.3.2   The Zia Regime

After a change of government in 1975, General Ziaur Rahman (Zia) pledged to restore stability and a return Bangladesh to a democratic system. He presented an ambitious nineteen-point programme that appeared to cover every aspect of life including development. Among other objectives, the programme sought to make Bangladesh self-reliant, ensure participation of the people at every level of administration and development programmes, accord top priority to agricultural development, and provide home, education and medical care to every citizen (See Appendix 2 in Zafarullah 1996c). The nineteen-points could be seen as an effort to provide a platform for the newly established Bangladesh Nationalist Party (BNP) which drew its support from a curious combination of political and military leaders. Aside from the shift in ideological base, the nature of developmental efforts remained much the same. Most ongoing programmes were allowed to continue, while the new government tried to sort out its priorities.

The first Five-Year Plan could hardly accomplish its objectives, and an effort was made by the new regime to put things in order. A two-year plan covering 1978–80 was prepared since 'the existence of a large number of unfinished schemes ... would have severely restrained the Plan's choices' (BPC 1980, p.I–6). This was intended to give breathing space for the government and sort out the chaotic systems of management in the governmental machinery. The Second-Five Year Plan (1980–85) did not differ to a great extent from its predecessor, and reflected similar patterns of thinking on the part of the two regimes.

Rural development appeared to dominate the agenda of the Zia regime. The vast rural electorate was identified as a potential support base for a leader who had no political organisation to back his claim to leadership. An extension of local government institutions to the lowest level of villages was considered beneficial to help develop a support base, while allowing the localities an opportunity to participate in developmental activities. Eventually, village level local governments were established and the new entities started operating in 1980. Zia was assassinated in 1981 and Bangladesh entered yet another period of military rule under a different leader.

Development strategies did not undergo radical changes during the Zia regime. The government was preoccupied with the restoration of discipline and order in the armed services, organisation of a new political party, and setting up of a power base for the ruling elite. In the course of pursuing these objectives, the Zia regime sought to introduce major changes in the system of local government for promoting development at the grass-roots level, and his nineteen points programme of development was vigorously publicised. Such efforts did contribute to small progress in the field of rural development and agricultural productivity increased on some occasions.

An overview of the budgets and plans prepared during this regime reflects strategies similar to those of the earlier governments. The emphasis remained on efforts to improve the arrangements for providing education, health and other services as well as strengthening capabilities of industrial units in the urban areas, while agricultural development focused on increased productivity in the rural areas. As evidenced by the statistics published by the government at regular intervals, the results have not been remarkable.

12.3.3 The Ershad Regime

General Ershad came to power following the assassination of Zia. Ershad followed the routines of legitimising military rule and a new political party, Jatiya Party (JP), was born. The JP differed little from its predecessor, the BNP, on ideological inclinations, and soon the government started claiming great achievements in developmental efforts. This regime was able to continue for over eight years and did have scope to introduce new programmes for development. Ershad followed Zia's strategies, and promulgated an eighteen-point programme for development. While Zia's nineteen-points were broad and encompassed a wide range of goals, Ershad's eighteen-points sought to achieve rural development, increase agricultural and industrial production, ensure land reforms, expand activities of the Grameen Bank, develop cooperative societies, reduce disparities, create employment opportunities, ensure health care and eliminate corruption. He pledged to check population growth, establish Islamic values and ideals, and ensure rights and status of women (See Hakim 1993, Appendix II).

The Ershad regime faced acute political crises during its tenure, but managed to survive most of those. Development was defined in a vague manner following the previous regimes, and sporadic programmes were undertaken or continued. The number of NGOs involved in development activities increased mainly as a result of the apparently stable situation as well as the need for their assistance. While the NGOs made progress with their own programmes, governmental efforts at development remained similar to the previous regimes. The JP had nothing distinctive in its ideologies to guide its development programmes, and continued to pursue the same policies as before.

Due to the length of stay in power, the Ershad regime was in a better position to review and improve upon the previous programmes. A number of programmes aimed at specific groups were devised to accelerate the pace of development. A programme for creating 'cluster villages' to rehabilitate 'landless destitute families' was undertaken (GOB 1990a), and the Pathakali Trust was established in early 1990 to promote 'welfare of destitute and underprivileged children and to reduce child labour' (GOB 1990b). The establishment of a formal local government council at the thana/upazila level resulted in a flurry of developmental works.

However, development efforts of the Ershad regime were seriously affected by a high incidence of corruption, and none of the programmes could achieve its objectives. Ershad repeatedly announced his affinity to rural Bangladesh, but abolished the village level local councils established by the Zia regime. Instead, the upazilas were made the focus of developmental activities, and the bureaucracy was able to retain control over programmes in the rural areas as well (Huque 1986).

12.3.4 Post-Ershad Period

Ershad was forced to resign after a mass movement against his regime, and a brief period of rule by a caretaker government followed. The BNP returned to power after the fifth parliamentary elections in 1991 and the constitution was amended to restore a parliamentary form of government. The second BNP government repeatedly referred to the corruption and irregularities of the previous regime, and was hardly able to settle down when the opposition political parties launched a movement to unseat the government. Continuous programmes of strikes and unrest kept the government almost paralysed for a period of time and the sixth parliamentary elections returned the AL to power after 21 years.

The AL took time to appreciate the realities of the nineties and was slow at the beginning of their second term in office to rejuvenate development programmes. The party decided to pursue a strategy of 'mixed-economy' and depart from the socialist principles. Although the AL's concept of a mixed economy is not clear, a programme of privatisation has been initiated. There has been a tendency among the successive regimes to reverse policies introduced by the previous regime, and this has contributed to a constant lack of stability in the process of development in Bangladesh. It should be noted that the current AL government has moved away from its earlier preference for a socialist system of government, and the second BNP government abandoned the 19-point programme which provided the platform for the party in its first tenure in office. Such changes indicate the absence of a clear view and strategy for development.

12.4   STRATEGIES AND DILEMMA

There have been minor alterations in the development strategies pursued by successive regimes in Bangladesh. Ideologically, the first AL government had a clear inclination toward socialist programmes, but the regime did not have adequate time to pursue them vigorously. Moreover, the strategy may not have succeeded in view of the socioeconomic conditions prevailing in Bangladesh at the time. Subsequently, the country was ruled by three regimes: AL (1972–75 and 1996–present), BNP (starting with Zia's rise to power in 1975–81 and during 1991–96), and JP (starting with Ershad's assumption of power in 1982–90). However, the choice of strategies has been influenced by a number of dilemmas faced by the successive governments. They appeared to be operating under similar constraints which led to the adoption of similar strategies for development. Although the more common explanations for the lack of development in Bangladesh revolve around the absence of political stability and the inadequacy of resources, a number of dilemmas stemming from the existing sociopolitical conditions have exerted strong influence on the choice of development strategies.

Development is usually guided by a strong ideological base which helps determine appropriate strategies consistent with the needs, capabilities, and objectives of a country. Governments in Bangladesh have frequently suffered from ideological confusion, and could never decide on a firm ideological anchor (see Huque 1997). While socialism appeared to be an attractive slogan in the early 1970s, it was not clear how a country like Bangladesh could make the transition without problems. Subsequent governments moved away from socialism, but were unable to provide an alternative ideology as the power base of these military governments was rooted in the armed forces while they continued to remain at a distance from a large section of the citizens. This dilemma has not been resolved and continues to affect the process of development in Bangladesh.

At the lowest level, there are visible signs of efforts aimed at agricultural development. A public corporation was set up to assist in the process and co-ordinate countrywide activities to facilitate agricultural development. Moreover, public officials are placed in the field offices to help farmers with input of required technology, advice and material. The activities undertaken by the government include assistance with irrigation and land improvement programmes, supply of seeds, fertilisers and manure, plant protection, storage of output, training, research, extension work, and agricultural marketing and pricing policy.

Industrial development lags behind for a number of reasons. It has not been developed much before the birth of Bangladesh and was badly affected by the liberation war. Moreover, the industrial sector suffered due to lack of skilled manpower as well as capable management and the various national problems confronting Bangladesh over the past three decades. Industrial development was viewed mainly as a set of efforts to ensure supply of essential consumer goods and key agricultural input as well as process agricultural outputs. In spite of various steps taken by the successive governments, it is now clear that industrial development could not be attained within the existing political and economic environment. The prospect of economic development has been similarly affected. Successive regimes have continuously appealed for investments, vitalisation of trade and commerce, and for boosting exports. On account of more private initiative than government efforts, the garment manufacturing industry has proved to be the largest foreign currency earner for the country, while other items of export have dwindled. Hossain found that only strong states can play a positive role in economic development, but a weak state like Bangladesh will not be able to do so (Hossain 1996c, p.45–46).

Development is an expensive process and Bangladesh does not possess the financial strength to finance it. There are reservations as well as limitations on the amount and extent of external assistance that should be utilised. Since external aid is contingent upon a variety of factors and carries the possibility of strings attached, it is felt that resources should be raised internally to finance development (see Blair ed. 1989). In spite of continuous efforts, it has not been possible to raise the level of internal resources. The dilemma of raising the resources before embarking on development projects remain as development is expected to enhance the capability of the community to contribute more to the public exchequer.

The concept of development has not been clarified by any of the successive regimes in Bangladesh, and the common approach to rural development has been to consider it as a process of establishing physical infrastructure. It has been felt by successive governments that the construction of more facilities such as buildings, embankments, silos for storing grains, and roads and highways are the main purposes of rural development. Transportation and communication facilities are certainly important, but subsequently the issue of enhancing capabilities of rural residents and the scope for their participation in public affairs are being recognised (See Huque 1995). Physical facilities are more visible and can serve as evidence of work by the ruling group, and thereby may help in gaining more electoral support. But such facilities may soon become useless due to non-utilisation or lack of maintenance if the people are not provided with the knowledge and capability of using them. Governments face this dilemma of choosing between electoral windfalls (short term) against the proper sequence of steps (long term). An alternate explanation may be the reluctance of successive regimes to genuinely empower the citizens.

There have been some variation of strategies pursued in achieving political development by the different regimes in Bangladesh. An amendment to the constitution to establish a single-party system was reversed within a short period. Subsequently, successive governments have concentrated on the performance of political rituals, such as the formation of political parties, holding of elections at regular intervals, and the continuation of parliamentary activities when the country was not under martial law. Due to the dominant presence of the military in the political system during 1975–1990, it was not possible to pursue specific strategies to achieve political development in Bangladesh. In fact, distorted political development took place during this period as efforts were made to 'create' political parties from scratch with no ideological base, concrete programmes, legitimate organisation or even a dedicated band of political workers. The apparent purpose was to civilianise military regimes.

These machinations led to the emergence of BNP which was described as 'anything but a cohesive, broad-based, and well-organised political party' (M. Khan and Zafarullah 1979, p.174). The JP was a product of similar circumstances, and both turned out to be groups of people with widely different ideologies and backgrounds who had banded together for pursuing their personal interests. The two parties were partially successful in enticing away some of the political workers from the more established AL, and these elements were rewarded in various ways.

Political development suffered as people gradually lost confidence in the efficacy of the system in which switching allegiance to the ruling group had become commonplace. However, there have been positive impacts of military rule in the sense that strong opposition to military dictatorship built up over the years and a commitment to democratic practices and principles could be noticed among the citizens. A combined front of opposition political parties, various professional groups in the society and student activists has contributed greatly to the re-establishment of a democratic system in Bangladesh, and development in this area can be considered as meaningful. Although the role of the opposition political parties in the system of governance since 1991 have frequently been open to question, it can be said that the foundations for sound political development have been laid.

The political angle gives rise to another dilemma in Bangladesh. Development involves the conscientisation and empowerment of disadvantaged groups in the society. As governments assume power based on support from the electorate, they face the task of choosing strategies for development. Such choice is difficult because the ruling group do not want to antagonise the electoral base that have voted them to power. Landless labourers and destitute farmers are in constant battle against rural large landowners, a group that provides crucial support to the government. Development programmes aimed at empowering and organising the rural poor can have unfavourable consequences for the existing powerholders in society. Governments have to resolve the dilemma of risking their position as opposed to achieving the objectives of development programmes.

Social development appears to have been relegated to the background in the early days of Bangladesh. Health and education received detailed treatment in the planning process and all the regimes pledged to modernise and expand the scope of these activities to provide benefit to a larger number of people. Other social issues were accorded less prominence and could be lumped with manpower and labour, women's affairs and youth development. The objective was to help disadvantaged groups become self-reliant through assistance to obtain training for employment, promote community development activities, education and care for children, and provide financial assistance to voluntary social service organisations (BPC 1980, p.XVIII–28). After a decade, the *Fourth Five Year Plan* continued to devote little attention to social welfare, although some changes could be noticed. The objectives have become more action-oriented and included creation of employment opportunities, rehabilitation of the elderly, formation of groups for participation in rural development programmes, programmes for self-reliance of destitute children, care and rehabilitation of juvenile delinquents and drug addicts, special education to handicapped children, subvention to voluntary organisations, and motivation of people to share responsibilities for socially disabled persons (BPC 1990c, p.XIII–2). But there is little indication of planned government involvement in large scale to promote dynamic change and enhance the quality of life for all groups in the society.

The non-partisan caretaker government which governed Bangladesh in the interim period before elections were held in 1991 set up a number of task forces to 'identify the development problems and policy options'. In the report the task force identified the alleviation of poverty, greater self-reliance, and a process of sustained growth as the objectives of development strategy (Task Forces 1991). It is clear that agricultural and economic growth were aimed at poverty alleviation and this stance reflected the general direction of developmental efforts in Bangladesh throughout its period of existence. However, the recommendations of the task force could not be vigorously pursued, and development efforts were relegated to the background as the BNP government struggled to hold on to office.

Finally, development as a rhetoric for gaining political advantage must be distinguished from the substance of such efforts. Development features in the speeches of every leader in Bangladesh, who pledge to attain this goal at any cost. Without going into a detailed analysis, it is possible to conduct an evaluation of development programmes by considering the available statistics. At a basic level, development should result in higher per capita income and gross domestic product, enhanced rate of literacy and employment, and lower infant mortality, and a favourable balance of trade. The performance of Bangladesh on all these counts is far from satisfactory. Marginal improvements have been accomplished in some areas and positive comments can only be made on the remarkable progress made in the area of garment manufacturing and export, and the extension of micro-credit facilities. It is obvious development is being used as a catchword for attracting the support of the citizens. If the substance of development could be pursued with the right intentions, the results would have been more positive. Therefore, the dilemma of the use of development as a rhetoric as opposed to a substantial programme must be resolved.

12.5 CONCLUDING OBSERVATIONS

Successive regimes, in spite of having different ideological inclinations and political platforms, have pursued similar strategies for development in Bangladesh. The objectives and targets for development were never specifically stated and it appears that they were never adequately understood. The process was aimed at a vague goal of development which was described as a process culminating in more wealth in the society, effective political and economic institutions and a good quality of life. There was hardly any discussion or debate in the parliament on the issue of development, and successive regimes took the liberty of defining development according to their convenience. As they sought support from the rural electorate to establish their claim to power, rural development received prominence, but there has never been a clear programme for effecting development on the basis of a concrete plan. Within the range of these programmes, agricultural development has featured prominently.

Success in the areas of economic and industrial development could have contributed to the groundwork toward the establishment of a more prosperous society. While sound agricultural development encompasses delivery of programmes/services as well as institution-building, the emphasis in Bangladesh has been mainly on the delivery of agricultural inputs. Due to sporadic efforts made in these directions, the results have not been successful and were further affected by the level and nature of political development in Bangladesh. The growth and sustenance of political institutions could not be achieved due to irregularities pursued in the electoral process and parliamentary proceedings, and democratisation and the development of a civil society remained unattainable.

The strategies for development have been determined on the basis of precedents and the needs of regimes in power. This has been done without clear and specific ideological guidelines and the result has been confused efforts. At the same time, a lack of understanding of the process has led to the adoption of inappropriate strategies, while there was no effort to learn from the inadequacies of the past. The process has been affected by dilemmas faced with reference to the ideological base and commitment for development (socialist, Islamic or mixed), the source of financial support (external or internal), human versus infrastructure development, the existing distribution of power in the society, and emphasis on the substance (and not rhetoric) of development.

Acknowledgements

The author is grateful to Professor Paul Wilding for reading an earlier draft of this chapter and providing invaluable suggestions for revision.

13 Health Centre Status and Accessibility in Rural Bangladesh: A Location-Allocation Model-Based Analysis

Shams-ur Rahman and David K. Smith

13.1 INTRODUCTION

There is a considerable body of evidence that geographical access to health facilities is very difficult for rural people in Bangladesh. In recent years, Bangladesh has given high priority to the development of primary health care in order to extend coverage of health services in rural areas and improve overall national health. This involves two approaches (Tanahashi 1978):

- deployment of more resources and technologies
- effective utilisation of available resources

While the government of Bangladesh has been gradually increasing funding for health over the years, these increased allocations are insignificant (Rahman 1991). This is due to limited availability of resources. Decision-makers and health planners must therefore make effective use of the available resources. In particular, decisions about the location of service facilities have frequently been taken locally by government officials concerned with a small region and/or elected leaders of the community concerned. In the absence of any formal analysis and generation of alternatives, the final decision is made on political or pragmatic considerations. As a result, decisions can often be far from optimal (Fisher and Rushton 1979; Hodgson and Valadares 1983; Rahman and Smith 1996).

However, there is evidence that when alternatives are generated after formal analysis and placed before the decision-makers, they are considered (Patel 1979; Datta and Bandyopadhyay 1993). The role of locational analysis in planning services for regional development is well recognised. It provides a framework for investigating service accessibility problems, measuring the efficiency of previous locational decisions and the current levels of settlement efficiency, and generating feasible alternatives for actions by planners. This chapter analyses the efficiency of past locational decisions regarding health facilities in rural Bangladesh. Locational efficiency is generally defined as the ratio of costs (access or distribution) associated with a given locational arrangement of a service to those costs associated with the best known alternative arrangement. Where costs are not the only measure of the benefits of a solution, other appropriate terms could be included. Similarly, locational inefficiency could be measured in terms of some accessibility characteristics, for instance, person-kilometre travelled, the average distance travelled, the percentage of population covered within a maximum allowable distance and the percentage of population in villages with facilities. There is no simple way of combining these characteristics, so they will be discussed in general terms.

13.2   HEALTH AND ECONOMIC DEVELOPMENT

Available data on health indicate that extremely high levels of preventable illness prevails in Bangladesh (UNICEF 1993). Communicable diseases are the main cause of mortality and so are serious health concerns. Diseases of concern are:

- infections such as cholera and diarrhoea, typhoid, tuberculosis, leprosy, tetanus, diphtheria, measles, whooping cough

- parasitic diseases like malaria, filariasis and worm infestations. It appears that diarrhoeal diseases (watery and dysentery), and lung and respiratory diseases (including pneumonia, asthma and tuberculosis) are responsible for about 34 per cent of total deaths. Among the causes of child mortality, diarrhoea is the most significant; it accounts for about 25.5 per cent of deaths among children under 5. Tetanus is the next most significant cause (UNICEF 1993).

It is important to note that most of the communicable diseases can be controlled through immunisation programmes, health education and better management of diarrhoeal diseases. These are the important components of primary health care (PHC). Since independence the Government's policy has been to provide comprehensive health care, particularly for the rural population. The Government recognized the inadequacies of health care facilities and their inequitable distribution, and so the First Five-Year Plan (1973–78) and the Two-Year Plan (1978–80) initiated a rural infrastructure for comprehensive health services with the objective of providing primary health care for everyone. The Second Five-Year Plan (1980–85) reflects the national objective of providing 'Minimum Care to All' in the short term and 'Health for All' by the year 2000. The Third Five-Year Plan (1985–90) reinforced the government's commitment of providing primary health care to everyone (BPC 1985).

Further improvement in health will largely depend on the capacity of health systems to deliver PHC services. This view has been widely accepted and well documented (UNDP 1997). The following objectives could be achieved by gradually extending the PHC services to the rural people of developing nations (Joseph and Russell 1980):

- to increase equity in the distribution of health benefits and reduce morbidity and mortality

- to reduce population growth rates in the longer run

- to stimulate economic growth through a healthier population

There is evidence to believe that the development of health is essential for economic development. For instance, a study in Malaysia demonstrated that reduction of malaria in a rubber estate caused output per worker to rise 17-fold (Barlow 1977). It is widely acknowledged that it is no longer tenable to draw a distinction between economic and health development. The development of health along with other social improvements is necessary to achieve economic goals. Correspondingly, economic development is necessary to achieve most of the social goals. The importance of health and its relation to development in developing countries can be observed in a statement of a President of the Institute of the US National Academy of Sciences. He said that 'Diseases in developing countries take such a terrible toll in human suffering and economic loss that they are at the heart of the whole problem of development.....The developing countries may become the never-to-be-developed countries unless the burden of illness can be greatly eased' (Knowles 1980). Evidently, development in health is a precondition for economic development of a nation. In a simple example of the economic benefits of health provision, Dinwiddy and Teal (1993, p.216) write: 'immunisation programmes for contagious diseases such as tuberculosis and measles benefit far more people than the number actually receiving the treatment.'

13.3   HEALTH DELIVERY SYSTEM

Research for locating health facilities in the context of the problems of developing countries has developed two categories of models. Some research has been directed towards the location of components of a health care system in which facilities are considered to be of one type (with respect to the level of service provided). Some examples are given by Patel (1979) and Berghmans et al. (1984). However, it is widely recognised that most health care systems in developing countries are organised as hierarchical systems. A patient in a typical developed country goes to see a doctor or nurse, relatively close to his or her home. If necessary, the patient attends a hospital which provides facilities which are not available from the doctor. Some patients will then progress to a third level of hierarchy, a specialist hospital. The same is true in developing countries. For example, the primary health care delivery system in Bangladesh consists of: Health Posts; Union Health & Family Welfare Centres (UHFWC); Thana Health Complexes (THC).

In this system Health Posts are considered to be the first point of contact between the rural people and the health system. A patient who is not cured at a Health Post may be referred to a UHFWC or THC, and a patient who goes to a THC may be referred to a UHFWC. The system consisting of these three distinct type of facilities may be termed a '3-hierarchical system'. Generalising this notion, it can be stated that a health care system that consists of f-(2) distinct types of facilities which collectively deliver services can be called a f-hierarchical system. For a detailed discussion on the hierarchical health care delivery systems interested readers may refer to Narula (1984) and Tien et al. (1983). Addressing the location problem on a regional level in the context of developing nations, some researchers have considered the problem as a hierarchical system (Banerji and Fisher 1974; Harvey et al. 1974).

13.4   LOCATION-ALLOCATION MODELS

A location-allocation model is a method for finding optimal sites for facility locations. The method involves simultaneously selecting a set of locations for facilities and assigning spatially distributed set of demands to these facilities to optimise some specified measurable criterion. The most important issue raised in the process of solving location problems is the selection of a suitable criterion or objective function. The formulation of an objective criterion depends greatly on the ownership of organisations. For instance, private sector facilities are often located to fulfil precisely stated objectives, such as to minimise cost or maximise profit. In contrast, the goals and objectives of public facility location are more difficult to capture (Rushton 1987). For example, if the problem is to locate emergency ambulance services, a possible criterion would be to minimise the average distance or time an ambulance must travel in order to reach a random incident or the patient must travel to reach the closest emergency medical service station. Another appropriate criterion could be to minimise the maximum distance that the ambulance must travel to reach an accident. Different interpretations of the goal of maximum public welfare lead to a number of possible location-allocation problems.

One of the popular models to public facility location problem is called the p-median problem (Hakimi 1964; ReVelle and Swain 1970). The problem can be defined in the following manner: given discrete demands locate a number (p or less) of facilities so that the total weighted travel distance or time between facilities and demand centres is minimised. Mathematically the problem can be stated as follows:

minimise $\Sigma\Sigma a_i d_{ij} x_{ij}$

subject to: $\Sigma x_{ij} = 1,$ $i = 1, 2, , n$ (1)

           $\Sigma x_{ij} = p$ $j = 1, 2, , n$ (2)

           $x_{ij} \le x_{jj}$ $\forall$ $i, j;$ where $i \le j$ (3)

           $x_{ij} \in \{0, 1\}$ (4)

where
x_{ij} =   1, if demand i assigned to a facility j
x_{ij} =   0, otherwise.
n   =   number of demand points
a_i =   population of demand i
d_{ij} =   shortest distance from demand i to facility j
p   =   number of facilities to be located.

Constraint (1) ensures that the demand from demand point i is met in full. Constraint (2) ensures that exactly p facilities are located while constraint (3) ensures that no demand is met from j if no facility exists there

The p-median problem is attractive, since the smaller the total weighted or average travel distance (time), the more convenient for one to get to the nearest facility. It is assumed that all users of the facility choose to travel to the closest one.

The locational problem in this study is considered as a p-median problem and modelled health facilities at union level. The health provision at union level is a UHFWC. UHFWCs are considered the nucleus of primary health care in Bangladesh. One UHFWC would be established in each union serving a population of about 25,000. There are 4,500 unions in the country and about 2,300 UHFWCs in operation now. The government of Bangladesh inherited a health delivery system under which health services at the union level used to be delivered through rural dispensaries (RD). Some of the RDs are still in operation. Recently, the government has decided to upgrade and convert RDs to UHWFCs.

13.5 EFFECT OF DISTANCE ON THE UTILISATION OF HEALTH FACILITIES

In rural areas of developing countries where most people travel on foot, distance significantly affects the utilisation of health care facilities. People living some distance from a health facility either tend to delay using its services or make no use at all. Some studies in this context have found that there is a strong negative relationship between distance from a health facility and the rate of utilisation of its services (Frederiksen 1964; King 1966; Stock 1983).

There is evidence to believe that in Bangladesh, distance influences the use of rural health facilities (Gish 1981; Shams-ur Rahman 1981; Ashraf et al. 1982). One major study in this context (M. M. Rahman et al. 1982), reports on the influence of distance on the utilisation of a diarrhoea clinic and the impact on diarrhoeal mortality in Teknaf, a thana, situated on the southern-most part of Bangladesh. The clinic was staffed by trained physicians, nurses and other staff. All necessary diagnostic instruments were made available to the clinic. Features of the clinic and its surrounding environment included:

- clinic providing free services to the people

- quality of services at the clinic being considered adequate and no other comparable treatment facilities were available in this area.

- there were no natural barriers which could impede people from attending the clinic.

- since there was no motorised transport available in the area, people would travel to the clinic on foot.

The effect of distance on the utilisation rate has been illustrated in Figure 13.1. The figure indicates that over 95 per cent of all reported diarrhoeal patients living within one mile of the clinic utilised the services. The attendance fell to nearly 63 per cent for patients located within two miles radius. About 10 per cent of patients utilised the services of the clinic if they were located within six miles. This figure also show that the annual mortality due to diarrhoea varied between 100 and 150 per 100 thousand persons for distances up to four miles and increased sharply to 270 for the population living six miles from the clinic. It indicates an inverse relationship between attendance by patients at the clinic and mortality. While other factors could have contributed to the utilisation of rural health facilities, this study suggests that distance between a health facility and a community is an important factor.

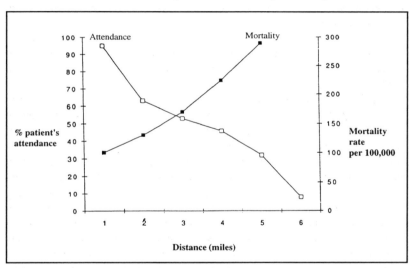

Figure 13.1   Relationship between distance and diarrhoeal mortality

13.6   STUDY AREA PROFILE

This study deals with the problems of locating health facilities in Tangail thana. It is one of eleven thanas in Tangail district, situated on the south western part of the district (Appendix 13.1). Tangail thana consists of 11 unions and one municipal area. A river flows through the thana which isolates three unions on the west (Kakua, Hugra and Katuli unions) during the monsoon season when most parts of the unions are inundated. Even in the dry seasons there is no road network between the villages. These three unions have been excluded from the study area. The municipal area is being well served by a number of private and public health facilities and therefore was also excluded from the study area. Hence, the study area consists of 8 unions comprising 161 villages. (Details of the study area are given in Appendix 13.2). The villages were identified on a 1:62500-scaled map produced by the Land Survey and Settlement Office of the Government of Bangladesh. The road network of the area was updated on the map with the help of the Head Surveyor at the office of Tangail thana. Metaled (Pucca), unmetaled (Kutcha) roads and footpaths were identified as networks connecting all the villages in the study area. Each link on the network was identified and measured and this data was used to compute a 161x161 distance matrix using a shortest path algorithm.

The study area has a total population of about 175 thousand persons and population density of 930 persons per sq. km compared with 605 for the nation. About 48.5 per cent of the population of the area are less than 15 years of age. Literacy rate is about 22.3 per cent and agriculture is the main economic activity.

At present, seven UHFWCs provide health care to the local people. To provide education, the Government has established one college, 18 high/junior high schools and 65 primary schools in the study area. There are also 17 madrashas which provide religious education to the local people, and 19 post offices and 2 telegraph offices. About 17 'hats' (village markets or bazaars) are located here which are generally open once a week. Out of 161 villages in the area, 93 villages have electricity. This means 58 per cent of the villages have so far been supplied with electricity.

13.7   LOCATION OF HEALTH FACILITIES AND LOCATIONAL
         EFFICIENCY

In this study an attempt has been made to find optimal locations of Union Health & Family Welfare Centres (UHFWC) in rural Bangladesh and compare with the existing locations of UHFWCs to evaluate the effectiveness of past locational decisions. UHFWCs are meant to organise immunisation activities, treat diarrhoeal diseases and fever cases, and work for the family planning programmes in the rural areas. Since these are outpatient facilities, no constraint has been imposed on their capacity. However, in this study, the variation in the demand for services among the facilities has been reduced by including a minimum population constraint for a village to be a potential centre. Any further variation of workload could be handled by allocating health personnel according to the demand at the facilities.

To locate the best sites for these, the Teitz and Bart (1968) method was used for facility location. Because the method is a heuristic, the algorithm was run 5 times and the best solution taken. According to government policy, 8 UHFWCs are to be opened to serve the 161 villages in the study area. However, seven are already operating in the area. In addition, there are three rural dispensaries (RD) in the area which, according to the government's plan, will be upgraded and converted to UHFWCs. This means that sites for 10 UHFWCs have already been decided and there remains no scope for finding one. Therefore, the study has concentrated on the following analysis:

- Compare the locational efficiency of seven existing UHFWCs with seven optimal UHFWCs

- Compare the locational efficiency of seven existing plus three proposed UHFWCs with seven existing plus three optimal UHFWCs

13.7.1. Analysis of the locational efficiency of seven existing and seven optimal UHFWCs

The results of the analysis are shown in Figure 13.2, Figure 13.3, and Appendix 13.3. Only one facility (Pakulla, in Silimpur Union) was found to be common between the existing set and optimal set of facilities obtained solving as p-median problem. The optimal locations of seven facilities found by the p-median method meant that the mean distance travelled fell from 3.1 to 1.9 km, an improvement of 38.7 per cent and the percentage of population covered within 4 km rose from 74.2 to 99.2 per cent , so that 96.9 per cent of the population which had been missed would be covered. It is noteworthy that in a system with 4 optimally located UHFWCs the number of person-kilometres travelled is approximately equal to the number of person-kilometres travelled in the existing system with seven facilities (Figure 13.2).

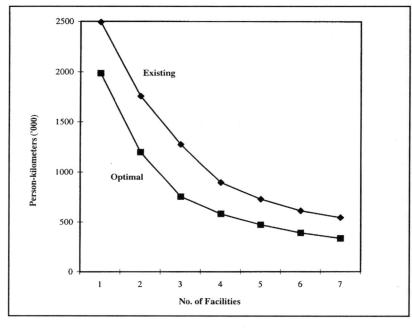

Figure 13.2   Locational efficiency of existing and optimal UHFWCs

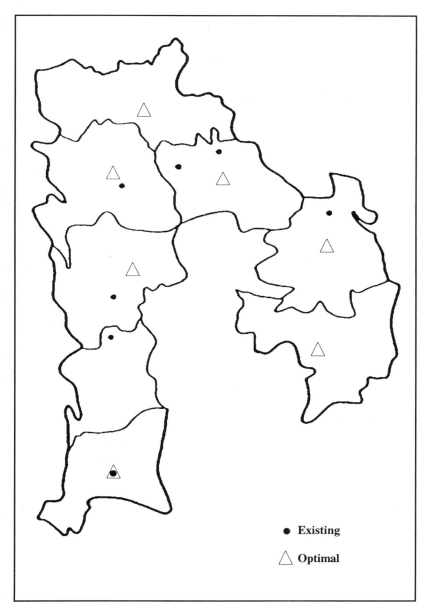

Figure 13.3   Location of existing and optimal UHFWCs found as p-
                median problem

13.7.2.   Analysis of the locational efficiency of seven existing plus three proposed UHFWCs and seven existing plus three optimal UHFWCs

These results are presented in Figures 13.4, and 13.5 and Appendix 13.4. No common facility was found between the proposed and optimal sites. The system with seven existing plus three proposed facilities produces a mean distance travelled of 2.3 km. In the system with seven existing plus three optimal facilities found by p-median method the mean distance fell to 1.7 km, an improvement of 26 per cent and the percentage of population covered rose from 87 to 100 per cent.

Fuller details of the calculations have been presented in Shams-ur Rahman (1991) and are not repeated here.

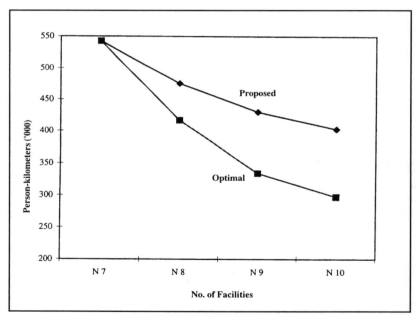

Figure 13.4   Locational efficiency of seven existing plus three proposed and seven existing plus three optimal UHFWCs

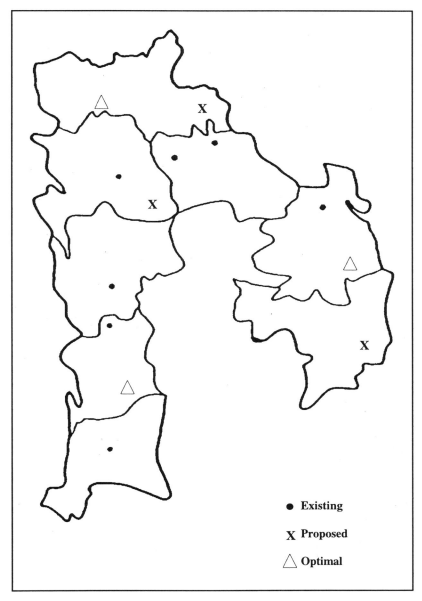

Figure 13.5 Location of seven existing plus three proposed and seven existing plus three optimal UHFWCs

13.8 CONCLUDING COMMENTS

The development potentials of any decision, according to Moos and Dear (1986), are to be evaluated by various groups in any society: politicians, influential individuals, bureaucrats and ordinary citizens. These groups form what they call 'the dialectic of control'. The amount of power commanded by these groups within the dialectic of control varies. In most developing countries, ordinary citizens possess no power in the decision making process. In the absence of any formal analysis and generation of alternatives by the bureaucrats/planners, final decisions concerning location of facilities are taken by the politicians and are generally far from optimal. Given these realities what useful role can this study play? By demonstrating that better solutions exist, the study provides community groups and bureaucrats with a stronger case against inefficient and inequitable proposals. The detailed spatial accounting system generated by a location-allocation model is information that could be used to prevent such interventions from politicians. As Rushton (1988, p.113) puts: 'So long as the ledger is blank, politicians have the opportunity to vie with one another to bring spoils back to their constituents, but with the accounts open and enough detail to count the costs and returns for alternative location, politicians have to pause before they intervene to counter the bureaucrat's recommendations.'

The results of applying location-allocation models in this study illustrate the potential usefulness of such models in health facility location planning and decision making. However, one must understand that by optimally locating facilities will not automatically lead to the improvement of rural health. To do that in addition to the equitable distribution of health facilities other necessary conditions have to be fulfilled such as willingness of trained and motivated medical personnel to work in rural areas, and availability of medicine and equipment.

Acknowledgements

The authors gratefully acknowledge the constructive comments and suggestions of an anonymous referee.

Appendix 13.1   A map of Tangail District

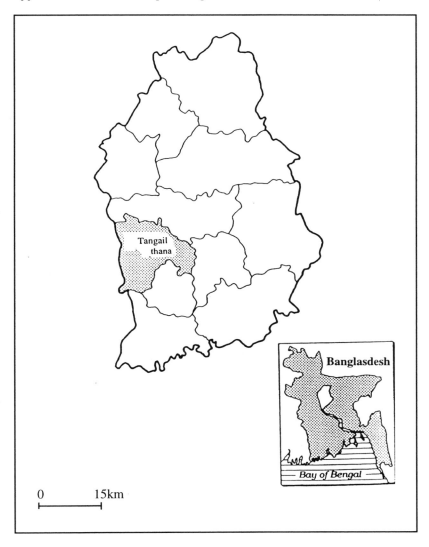

Appendix 13.2   Services and facilities in the study area

Union	UHFWC	RD	College	High School	Primary School	Madrasa	Hat/Bazar	Post Office	Water Supply	Electricity (no of villages)
Magra	–	1	–	4	12	4	4	2	15	8
Baghil	1	1	–	2	9	–	1	3	14	13
Gala	2	–	–	1	7	2	3	3	11	15
Danya	1	–	–	2	8	1	2	1	13	17
Gharinda	1	–	–	2	8	4	1	2	11	8
Kratia	–	1	1	3	10	5	2	4	13	23
Silimpur	1	–	–	3	7	–	3	3	6	4
Porabari	1	–	–	1	4	1	1	1	5	7
Total	7	3	1	18	65	17	17	19	88	93

Appendix 13.3 Locational efficiency of existing and optimal UHFWCs

Minpop	Accessibility characteristics	seven existing sites	seven optimal sites	% improvement of optimal over existing
		Value	Value	
1000	Average distance travelled (km)	3.1	1.9	38.7
	% of population covered within 4 km	74.2	99.2	96.9
	% of population in villages with facilities	10.2	11.8	16.8

Appendix 13.4 Locational efficiency of seven existing plus three proposed and seven existing plus three optimal UHFWCs

Minpop	Accessibility characteristics	seven existing sites	seven optimal sites	% improvement of optimal over existing
		Value	Value	
1000	Average distance travelled (km)	2.3	1.7	26
	% of population covered within 4 km	87	100	100
	% of population in villages with facilities	16.7	13.1	-7.7

14 Government and the Fourth Sector Partnership: Local Governance and Sustainable Development in Bangladesh

Samiul Hasan

14.1 INTRODUCTION

Since the World Bank (1989) attributed the dismal economic performance of the Sub-Saharan African countries to the problems of governance, the underlying assumption, has been that sustainable development cannot be achieved without good governance. The efforts of devising a process of sustainable development, that was intensified through the publication of *Our Common Future* (WCED 1987), now focus on: identifying measures in protecting the environment, and developing governmental capability to undertake the measures. The two most important aspects of governance are the process by which authority is exercised in the management of a country's economic and social development (World Bank 1992b; Crook and Manor 1995), and a government's capacity to discharge governmental functions by formulating and implementing policies (World Bank 1992b; Moore 1993). Governance is also the process of interaction between the public sector and the various actors or groups of actors in 'civil society'– the public life of individuals and institutions outside the control of the state (Harpham and Boateng 1997).

Non-government(al) organisations (NGOs) are the expressions of 'civil society's capacity for free organisation and of its vitality' (Frantz 1987, p.123), and existent in every society. NGOs are concerned with supporting social movements and/or initiatives of development that confront certain essential questions of life, e.g. common needs, common aspirations (Frantz 1987, p.123). NGOs also contribute to re-democratisation processes in their own societies and to creating, maintaining or expanding existing forms of democracy. NGOs are involved in self-help projects and thus, maintain democratic spaces, even under dictatorial regimes, within their projects by supporting and creating spaces for people's participation (Padron 1987). This chapter makes a distinction between NGOs which are community-based or local and the ones that are externally initiated and/or funded, and argues that it is the former type of NGOs or the 'fourth sector that shows greater potential in achieving sustainable development through an improved system of governance at local levels. The government can enhance and increase its capability by sharing responsibilities and authority with the fourth sector. The chapter recounts the factors responsible for the growth of voluntarism in Bangladesh and reviews potential advantages of local voluntary organisations in sustainable development. It argues that the 'fourth sector' NGOs, formed and based on indigenous knowledge, and operated by local volunteers, are important for sustainable development. These local voluntary organisations, having their close links with and bases in the local people, are in an advantageous position to deal with sustainable development. Thus the government in Bangladesh, in its quest for a partner in good governance and sustainable development planning, should consider the 'fourth sector as a viable institutional option for achieving its goals.

14.2   SUSTAINABLE DEVELOPMENT

Sustainability refers to the maintenance or enhancement of resource's productivity on a long term basis (Chambers 1988, p.1). Social conditions, however, influence the ecological sustainability of the people-nature interactions. Lele (1991) suggested that some ecological issues may have some social causes, because farming on marginal lands without adequate soil conservation measures may hamper ecological sustainability, but the phenomenon of marginalisation of peasants may have social roots, which would then be the social causes of ecological sustainability. The problems of sustainability in the developing world are thus derived mainly from poverty and related factors.

Poverty inhibits a sustainable 'long term' productive life, and so needs to be eradicated. The efforts aimed at the eradication of poverty need 'community knowledge and support' (WCED 1987, p.63). Frank (1996) emphasises the importance of community participation and beneficiary involvement in sustainable development programmes. Transforming human attitudes and practices, and empowering communities (IUCN et al. 1990) are also important for sustainable development. The above mentioned aspects of sustainable development can be achieved 'by decentralizing the management of resources upon which local communities depend, and giving these communities an effective say over the use of these resources' (WCED 1987, p.63)

Many local communities in the developing countries, and in Bangladesh, lost control of their own destiny during the colonial and neo-colonial period due to governmental inaction, inappropriate project interventions by the government, and through the influence of alien norms and values. Due to the West's increasing economic and cultural influences, Bangladesh, like other developing countries, is becoming a victim of a 'culture of maxima' (see M. Adil Khan 1996) or a culture of consumerism and materialism that is quite inimical to sustainable development. This has resulted in maldistribution of wealth and inequitable access to resources for development, and in environmental damages. The preservation of 'culture of minimal' may be realized effectively if local communities are involved in sustainable development programmes. For a developing and poor country like Bangladesh, the important principles that must be addressed for the success of sustainable development are thus: eradication of human poverty, empowerment through traditional institutions, and the introduction of locally-based planning with the participation of its beneficiaries (cf. Hasan 1991).

While governments role is important in devising suitable policy frameworks to address these issues, it may be argued that activities that involve closer human contact could be carried out better by institutions that maintain closer links with the community. It is in this context that this chapter suggests that the community-based organisations (the fourth sector) that emanate from and are operated by the community itself has a better chance of mobilising people in adopting a culture of sustainable development. The analysis looks at the performance of the 'fourth sector' in eradicating human poverty, and in empowering through traditional practices and local institutions in Bangladesh. Finally, the chapter suggests different measures required to achieve the goals of sustainable development with the participation of the community-based organisations and the beneficiaries.

14.3   VOLUNTARY OR COMMUNITY-BASED ORGANISATIONS: THE FOURTH SECTOR

Voluntarism, 'the offering of goods and services through ones own free will' (Miller and S. H. Khan 1986, p.139) consists of a set of values (volunteerism) and a set of structures (organisations) (Wilensky 1981, p.8), and is an outcome of values rather than of education. Voluntary organisations are the major vehicles for operationalising the volunteering aspect. The people involved in voluntary organisations provide financial support and offer required services through their free will.

Voluntary organisation, in this chapter means non-profit groups formed by the people of any community to accomplish some developmental goals. These local voluntary or community-based organisations or activities, which may also be called development agencies, or self-help organisations or programmes, in a body, are the 'fourth sector' after government, business, and national or international externally-funded non-government(al) organisations (NGO – the third sector). An NGO is established, organised, and financed by people outside the community where it functions, but a local or community-based organisation (CBO) is initiated and run by the people of the respective community. For the sake of simplicity, in this chapter, only one term, voluntary organisation (VO) is used.

14.3.1 Voluntarism in Bangladesh: Source and origin

Voluntarism is a part of cultural heritage in the Indian subcontinent and was sanctioned in ancient times. Voluntary and charitable organisations in the area received recognition, even in colonial days, as early as in 1860, through the Societies Registration Act (GOB 1985). In Bangladesh, the people were converted to Islam, before the Muslims became the ruler of the area, and so the new converts had to struggle against different social disadvantages. Thus, helping each other financially and emotionally became a social necessity among the people. This practice has continued, because Islam, the religion of 85 percent people of Bangladesh, provides much emphasis on charity. Apart from the *zakat* (annual compulsory charity), one of the five pillars of Islam, the Quoran suggests other forms and ways of charity (e.g. helping the neighbours, donating a percentage of agriculture produce to charity) that many Muslims in the country follow.

The organised form of voluntary organisation was first established in Bangladesh (Bengal) following the Bengal famine of 1943, which claimed the lives of three million people. Following the typhoon in 1970 that registered a death toll of 500,000 or one million (best guess) people in Bangladesh, the number of local VOs increased. The massive destruction of human lives, cattle, crops, and property followed by little or no actions of the government inspired the survivors and fellow citizens to organise themselves to tackle their own problems. Based on the principles of self-help and mutual cooperation, many voluntary organisations followed the earlier initiatives and started to operate at the local level.

The self-help movement in Bangladesh has intensified rapidly since independence in 1971. Almost 50 per cent of the voluntary organisations active in Bangladesh were created between 1975 and 1990 (Hasan 1991), when the country was under military or quasi-military rule following the military coups in 1975. The existence of military and authoritarian governments prompted local people in many parts of the world to organise themselves (Durning 1989). Actually, the failure of independent government in Bangladesh in meeting the 'needs' inspired the people to organise themselves to explore alternative methods for the fulfilment of their hopes and aspirations.

14.3.2   Local voluntary organisations and programmes in Bangladesh

Voluntary organisations in Bangladesh can mobilize and are mobilizing people for development. All the locally organised and funded voluntary organisations in Bangladesh (except one percent) are organised and run by volunteers (Hasan 1991). Thus, the major strength of the VOs is the volunteers.

Apart from voluntary labour and enterprise, the local voluntary organisations also have been able in the past to mobilise financial resources. Compared with the funds available to the lowest tier of local government (union council) in Bangladesh, the amount of money mobilised by the voluntary organisations from the internal sources is not negligible. More than 65 per cent of the VOs functioning at the local level have an annual budget more than the average annual budget (56,000 takas or 2,220 dollars in the 1980s) of the union council. These voluntary contributions include individual voluntary contributions as well.

In addition, many altruistic individuals committed to help others at the grassroots level have also been instrumental in developing voluntary development programmes in Bangladesh. The most significant contribution was made by Akhter Hamid Khan, a member of the (British) Indian Civil Service (1938–44), who left the lucrative job and became an apprentice locksmith (1944–46) to experience himself the hardship of poor people (Raper 1970). Khan is the pioneer of cooperative programme, known as 'Comilla Model' – a village-based cooperative programme for comprehensive rural development. He also established the East Pakistan Academy of Village Development (presently Bangladesh Academy for Rural Development, BARD) in Comilla. The BARD is now the major organisation in Bangladesh imparting rural development training to elected officials and to the members of public service.

Other development programmes organised by public servants (e.g. executive head of a district) are: *Palli Mongal Samities* (Village Welfare Societies) by T.I.M.N. Choudhury in the 1930s; promotion of development in Comilla (N.M.Khan) and in Pabna (H.S.M. Ishaque) both in the 1930s (Haq 1978). Rangunia Model co-operatives in the 1960s and the *Swanirvar* (self-reliance) programme in the 1970s were organised by Mahbub Alam Chashi (a district administrator) Ulashi-Jadunathpur (a major canal digging project for irrigation) in the 1970s was organised by Mohiuddin Khan Alamgir, also a district administrator (Stevens et al. 1976).

These initiatives were sporadically organised by some committed individuals, and thus made only a marginal impact and did not assume any institutional character. The programmes initiated by development administrators disintegrated or disappeared with the transfer of the administrator from the post, because of the lack of an institutional arrangement. Had there been a governmental programme to institutionalise the activities of the voluntary sector in the governmental development efforts, the result of these fragmented efforts might have been different and more enduring. Nevertheless, even with the present arrangements the local voluntary sector has gained some success in the aspects of development identified earlier.

14.4 VOLUNTARY ORGANISATIONS AND SUSTAINABLE DEVELOPMENT

The previous section showed that there have been altruistic individuals and voluntary enterprises and activities supporting and promoting development in Bangladesh. The local voluntary sector has gained some success in the eradication of human poverty and in the empowerment of communities through traditional practices and institutions. This section analyses the involvement and performance of the 'fourth sector' in these two essential aspects of sustainable development.

14.4.1 Eradication of human poverty

Poverty, 'the greatest polluter of all' (Indira Gandhi), is the result of a lack or misuse of resources to obtain the types of diets, participate in the activities and have the living conditions and amenities that are customary in the societies to which a person belongs (Townsend 1979). To deal with poverty, one needs to start with financial and other resources to provide 'customary' diets, health facilities, and education for the people concerned.

Dr. M. Yunus, a professor of economics, diagnosed the problem of poverty in Bangladesh as a problem of access to credit. The access to credit in Bangladesh shrinks further due to the non-availability of collaterals by the prospective poor borrowers. Professor Yunus created the *Grameen* Bank, a micro-credit organisation, to cater to the needs of poverty-stricken people with no collaterals. Two of the four objectives of the *Grameen* Bank are to:

- Organise the weak and landless poor people of rural areas, especially the women, so they can work together and use the loan from the Grameen Bank; and

- Introduce a new system of cooperatives that can reduce the defects of traditional cooperatives (Mahabub Hossain 1988).

The intended borrowers from *Grameen* Bank have to form groups of five men or five women having the same economic status, attitudes, and interests (Fuglesang and Chandler 1986).

One thousand and forty-two branches of *Grameen* Bank in 34,243 villages now have around two million literally landless borrowers (Shams 1995). The *Grameen* Bank success is derived from the fact that it has operated completely unlike other banks and that it derives its values, methodologies, and legitimacy from the same wellspring as the voluntary organisations (Smillie 1995). The field officers of the *Grameen* Bank are recruited from the respective community to help the interested and eligible people of the community to organise themselves for self-development.

Ganosastha Kendro (GK, People's Health Centre), another successful voluntary organisation started with traditional objective of a health centre-cure. Later the GK, after identifying the health problem as a linchpin in the 'vicious cycle of poverty', moved to a holistic approach of community development with the initiative of local people. The *Ganosastha Kendro* has been successful in providing complete health care, emphasizing 'prevention rather than 'cure', to 400,000 people living in a contiguous area. The objectives of the Ganosastha Kendro are to evolve a system by which the health care of the entire population of a particular area can be provided efficiently and effectively with minimum expenditure and maximum benefits, and with the employment of the minimum number of medical staff (Zaman 1984, p.158). Thus, the *Ganosastha* s community-based holistic approach for health and development is an efficient strategy for the eradication of poverty. Due to its success the approach became the 'blue-print for the government s rural health programme (Esterline 1990, p.140).

These and other VOs have achieved success in alleviating poverty situation in Bangladesh. A survey on the performance of voluntary organisations in rural areas in Bangladesh suggests that almost 83 percent of the people involved in voluntary organisation programmes saw a substantial improvement in their income in a very short period of time. In fact, 26 percent of these people have been able to more than double their income after they joined the

VOs (Hasan 1991). It is true a temporary increase in income may not be enough to make a sustained impact on the poverty situation of these people. Thus, as a major strategy of making a lasting impact on the peoples livelihoods, these VOs took initiatives in imparting skills development training to these people, and to raise their levels of consciousness and faith on themselves in their ability in transforming their own situation with only a little outside help. These voluntary organisations have been successful in skills development, consciousness raising, and thus poverty alleviation.

In Bangladesh, the local people themselves help to eradicate poverty, as well, through the mobilisation of resources in many ways. One of the major forms of resource mobilisation is *chanda* (voluntary contribution). Miller and S. H. Khan (1984) and Hasan (1993) provide good accounts of voluntarism through the contribution of *chanda*. Many different types of *chandas* are discussed in these two publications, but the most significant is the amount of money collected through *chanda* in Muslim congregations even in rural areas twice every year. The total monetary contribution collected in all the religious congregations held within a union council area, could be at least the size of the annual union council (the local government at the level) budget of the area (Hasan 1993). This money is then used to undertake some emergency projects within the area, such as, repair work on roads, schools, *madrasha* buildings, or expansion of the mosques or the community graveyard. These activities then help in the eradication of poverty through the improvement in the access to education and market.

14.4.2   Empowering communities through traditional practices and institutions

The traditional *panchayet* system that allowed the people scope to attain security and other basic human needs on a collective basis has survived in the region through all the reform efforts of the last few centuries. It still exists in Bangladesh as *samaj,* and is active in performing several important community functions, such as village defence, management and maintenance of religious institutions, organisation of festivals, cultural and recreational activities, and management of cemeteries (Hasan 1988a). The *samaj* is involved in the establishment, management, and maintenance of *madrasha* (educational institutions emphasising Islamic religious teachings) and *muqtubs* (primary religious teaching institutions providing some general education as well). Occasionally, *samaj* also construct and maintain rural roads, bridges, culverts, and dams by its own voluntary labour and financial support. A *samaj* can generate human and financial resources every year for repairing unpaved roads, extending paved roads, maintaining playgrounds, or even sinking tubewells (shallow water pumps).

Apart from the programmes sponsored by the *samaj,* many community-level groups, and individuals in Bangladesh organise many development programmes. Approximately 99 per cent of the total 4,200 *madrashas* in Bangladesh is established and run by community groups or individuals (BBS 1985). Some normal schools in rural areas in Bangladesh also enjoy voluntary labour and financial support from the respective communities. Many community groups are also involved in cattle and poultry care, agricultural cooperation, skills training, and adult education programmes. Local voluntary organisations also function as community organisations and have innovative ideas for development. They deal with non-traditional sectors of development, e.g. handicrafts using unheard-of materials, duck farming in fish ponds, lending money without collateral.

The VOs either have helped expanding these activities or have created scopes for other development activities through the participation of the beneficiaries. A major strength of these local voluntary organisations is their participatory approach. The local voluntary organisations do not dictate programmes, rather these organisations present ideas and invite the local people to form groups and come forward with their own programmes. These organisations encourage and respect the local people's traditional values and inspire them to participate in VO programmes. Another major reason for the success of the voluntary organisations is their interest and ability in having women participate in their programmes. Women are usually a very neglected group in Bangladesh and are almost absent from the governmental development programmes. The programmes of the voluntary organisations are open to women and most beneficiaries of development programmes are women. Often it is more than 50 per cent, and for *Grameen* Bank, it is as much as 90 per cent (Shams 1995).

The voluntary organisations have high levels of commitment and an eagerness to mobilize local people for development. These organisations also have a very high sense of solidarity. For these reasons VOs have been successful in undertaking people-centred development programmes. The direct participation of the local people in development efforts helps the organisers to identify the 'needs' and 'ways' to meet the needs with no or only a little outside assistance. This participation then becomes critical for sustainable development and an important aspect of local governance. Only a little support from the government can make a major difference in the community organisations efforts in achieving a permanent and appropriate solution to their identified 'needs'.

14.5   GOVERNMENT AND THE FOURTH SECTOR
PARTNERSHIP

The local voluntary organisations can handle some important sectors of sustainable development because such organisations are much closer to the poverty-stricken people of the locality than the government organisations, have the enthusiasm needed to mobilize local people for development purposes, are normally run by committed volunteers, and care about participatory planning. The local voluntary organisations do not perform the 'unpleasant' tasks of levying taxes, administrating the criminal justice system, or maintaining law and order so they can develop close links with the local people (Aremo 1983). Thus, the local VOs can provide an efficient and effective alternative to public sector in the delivery of programmes and projects for sustainable development (WCED 1987).

A major requirement for sustainable development is raising people's consciousness to ensure empowerment. Due to the trust the local VOs can muster in the local community, these organisations can undertake effective conscientisation (Friere 1972) programmes. The conscientisation programme aims to make people understand the importance of self-reliance, skill development, education, health, birth control, etc. These programmes make people realize their importance in the society and develop faith about themselves in undertaking development programmes. The existence and functioning of conscientisation programmes offered by the VOs are important for countries such as Bangladesh where due to lack of awareness the people are exploited in the society.

Governments can use VOs in this respect to eradicate exploitation in the society. No government in Bangladesh, however, so far has taken any initiative for a meaningful government and voluntary organisation partnership in this or any other regards. There are, however, some examples of government and voluntary organisation partnership in other developing countries. Some countries in the South, for example, Sudan and Kenya, are using voluntary organisations as integral parts of local government bodies (Abdelgabar 1987). Cooperative groups in some countries of Asia and Africa are doing some functions of local governments. For example, cooperatives in Egypt give farmers seeds, fertilizer and credit, and maintain markets to sell their produce. Similar functions have been the responsibilities of some cooperatives in Indonesia, Malaysia, the Philippines, and Sri Lanka (Hasan 1991).

In some countries, local voluntary agencies are sharing local government responsibilities. The Local Government Code in the Philippines, introduced in 1991, allows NGOs and the people's organisations 'to become part of the mainstream in local administrative bodies by making them formal members of such' (Brillantes 1994). The seventh Five Year Plan (1987–92) of India stated that '....various efforts will be made to involve voluntary agencies in serious development programmes, particularly in the planning and implementation of programmes of rural development' (cited in Shepherd 1986, p.3). In Bangladesh the Third Five Year (1985–90) Plan (TFYP) development strategies included strengthening and promoting voluntary organisations to provide social, health, and economic benefits to women in poverty (BPC 1989, p.286). During the TFYP the government s intention was to use voluntary organisations only for women's development, but the government ended up involving the voluntary organisations in different development programmes during the floods of 1988 and 1989, and beyond.

In fact, voluntarism in Bangladesh has been involved in governmental programmes in different forms for at least forty years now. In 1959, the local government system in the country (then East Pakistan) was restructured and given limited responsibilities for organising Rural Works Programme (RWP) and later the Food-for-Work Programme (FWP). This tradition has continued in independent Bangladesh. Apart from the local government efforts to mobilise voluntary contribution from the local sources, the government encourages voluntary participation in government-initiated programmes. According to government regulation, all Rural Works Programme (RWP) grants are to be matched by an equivalent amount of 'voluntary *taka*' to be mobilized at the local level (Miller and S. H. Khan 1984).

In addition, voluntarism has its roots and is existent in the programmes organised by the Bangladesh Rural Development Board (BRDB), a government organisation, as well. The projects under BRDB are implemented through voluntary cooperatives all over Bangladesh. The main features of this system are:

- Farmers are organised into agriculture cooperative associations, the KSS (local acronym for *Krishi Samabaya Samity*, Farmers' Cooperative Association)

- The KSS are then federated into thana (sub-district) level associations (TCCA) to perform both as a forum for coordination and training and as a channel for the distribution of inputs including credits, and capital items to and by the members; and

- The individual farmers receive storage, marketing, processing of product, and workshop facilities from the TCCA through the KSS (see Momin 1987).

Besides financial voluntarism, cooperative systems under the BRDB involve non-financial voluntarism, e.g. self-management of the members, recruitment of new members, organisation of regular meetings, and adoption of agricultural innovations (Miller and S. H. Khan 1984).

A large portion of government programmes of irrigation canal digging and rural road construction have also been supported by voluntary labour and funds from the community where the projects/programmes are situated. For example, in one self-reliance project, the Ulashi-Jadunathpur (UJ) project in Jessore, undertaken through voluntary labour, 5 million cubic meter canal digging work was done in 1977 to improve the irrigation facilities in the area (Q. K. Ahmad and Mahabub Hossain 1979). The funding structure of the UJ project involved three sources: one-third from the national government in cash or in kind; one-third from the lowest tier of local government-union council (either from regular tax sources or individual cash contribution); and one-third from the labour contributions or an equivalent amount of cash, both based on income, from the community (Miller and S. H. Khan 1984).

Thus it is seen from the above discussion that, local voluntary organisations in Bangladesh are involved in development, through their contribution of labour, cash, and other materials, but government and voluntary organisation relationships in development are not very encouraging. Many local voluntary organisations are involved in development activities in local areas, but in the local government structure, there is still no scope for the local voluntary organisations to participate in the formulation of any plans or development programmes of the local councils. At present, the voluntary organisations' involvement is limited in the implementation of canal digging and road construction programmes undertaken by the local government councils.

In some developing countries, many government officials see the involvement of VOs in development activities as the 'erosion of governmental sovereignty', because these organisations are increasingly being involved in executing state functions by people who are not answerable to them (Clark 1991). The public officials in Bangladesh see themselves responsible for development and are not ready to accept new ideas from the voluntary organisations. Further, some government officials also do not like the enthusiasm of the local people as to the perceived sincerity and trustworthiness of the voluntary organisations (Hasan et al. 1992). Thus, many public officials have a tendency to interfere with the functioning of the voluntary organisation programmes.

But the fact of the matter is, a democratic government is normally strengthened, not weakened, when it faces a vigorous civil society (Smillie 1995). The government in Bangladesh should be proud and consider fortunate that many organisations, community associations, and individuals are ready to share the burdens of the governmental responsibilities. Once the voluntary organisations are recognized as partners in governmental sustainable development initiatives, these organisations and their members will become a big asset for development. Thus the achievement of the overall goals of sustainable development will be easier.

14.6   CONCLUSION AND RECOMMENDATIONS

The people in Bangladesh have a tradition of involvement in voluntary activities in different forms. Local culture, the struggle for independence, natural disasters, and neo-colonial authoritarianism also have played important roles in the formation of voluntary organisations in Bangladesh. The major growth in the voluntary sector, however, primarily followed the failure of the government in meeting the needs of the people.

The governments in Bangladesh pledge to eradicate poverty, improve the quality of life, provide education and health to the people, but have failed to take necessary measures to achieve these goals. Many organisations and communities are involved voluntarily in activities to achieve the above objectives for the people, but the government have failed to share responsibilities with the voluntary sector. The government should undertake the following measures to encourage participation of the voluntary organisations in sustainable development:

- Recognise the existence of the voluntary organisations and the contribution that the voluntary organisations make in different aspects of sustainable development of the country

- Realise the fact that the voluntary organisations are much closer to the local people than the local bureaucrats, so the local VOs should be allowed to work with the people without any obstacle

- Review the rules and regulations and remove the obstacles in the proliferation and functioning of the voluntary organisations; and

- Devise some mechanisms to allow the local voluntary organisations take part in the development process at the local level.

Without the partnership between the government and the fourth sector within a country, these local voluntary organisations will face threats of becoming extinct. Unless the voluntary organisations become a part of the overall development process of the country concerned, the voluntary organisations will lose enthusiasm and ultimately may fade away, and a potential vehicle for undertaking local-based sustainable development may be destroyed. The local and national governments in Bangladesh should accept the fourth sector in a good spirit. The involvement of the local VOs in development process will also ensure good governance in the country. The VOs as a partner in the development process, on the one hand, and with a closer link with the local people, on the other, would serve as a tool for a transparent system – an important prerequisite of good governance. The closer involvement of VOs in development and their collaborative effort with local bureaucrats should also improve other aspects of good governance, e.g. better accountability of the system to its clients or the people they serve. The more the government creates 'space' for collaboration with the voluntary organisations the more vibrant civil society will be in creating a congenial atmosphere for good governance for sustainable development.

Acknowledgements

The author gratefully acknowledges the valuable suggestions provided by Professor Bruce Mitchell (University of Waterloo, Canada), Dr Adil Khan (UNDP, Myanmar), Mr M.T. Fagence (The University of Queensland) on an earlier draft of this work. The usual *caveats* apply.

15 New Approaches to Research, Development and Extension for Sustainable Agriculture and the Environment: Implications for South Asia

Shankariah Chamala

15.1 INTRODUCTION

Sustainable agriculture is challenged by several environmental and social issues such as soil degradation (soil erosion, salinity, alkalinity, soil contamination, etc.), water degradation, loss of biodiversity, increased population pressure and greater incidence of poverty (either absolute or relative poverty). To address these environmental issues there is a need for formulating appropriate policies and institutional changes.

This chapter briefly summarises traditional research and extension models practised in many developing countries followed by a brief review of some of the new approaches taken by developed and developing countries. The Dutch Agricultural Knowledge and Information System (AKIS), the US Cooperative Extension Interdependence Model, and the Australian Cooperative Research and Landcare Extension Approach are briefly summarised. Several developing countries have also initiated new approaches to attain agricultural and environmental sustainability. Brief summaries of the Indian and Bangladeshi approaches are given. India has initiated Joint Forest Management (JFM) programme while Bangladesh has been trying to change the Training and Visit (T&V) system of extension with its Agricultural Support Services Project (ASSP) and Farming System Research and Extension. These trends in research, development and extension indicate the presence of experimentation with new participatory approaches and the development of social innovations to bring various stakeholders together from the community level to national and international levels. These new approaches have some implications for South Asian countries, which could use some of the participatory philosophies and principles to bring about a paradigm shift in its approach to solving sustainable agricultural and environmental issues.

15.2   MAJOR CHALLENGES FOR SUSTAINABLE DEVELOPMENT

The World Commission on Environment and Development (WCED) Report (1987), *Our Common Future*, presented to the United Nations (UN) General Assembly in 1987, promoted the concept of sustainable development: the means of meeting the needs and aspirations of present generations without compromising the ability to meet those of future generations. It stimulated much debate all over the world on issues such as economic growth, the control and use of resources, the relationship between poverty and environmental degradation and the responsibilities of governments. While agricultural production has been increasing to meet the growing demands of the population of the world, problems related to sustainability in terms of social, economic and ecological factors are becoming major issues of development.

Table 15.1 summarises the major challenges for sustainable development faced by developing and developed countries alike. There could be several other challenges specific to each country or region but this broad-brush approach provides a useful pointer at the global level.

Concerns of developing and developed countries have given rise to the emergence of common concerns of sustainable development. Revolutionary developments in information technology have created global information super-highways; instant television, radio and newspaper transmission of world events; and made this planet into one world. No one country or community can live in isolation or is able to solve its problems on its own. While nations and states are politically and socio-economically different, ecological and environmental problems could have transboundary issues. What happens to forests in the Amazon, the construction of a dam in Tasmania and poverty in some countries is not only of concerns to the local inhabitants. People from all parts of the world share these concerns and would like to have a say and get involved in resolving these issues in order to help each other. As a result of these developments, major concerns that arise in one country have become a global concern. Both developed and developing countries have become dependent on each other for common survival and future development.

Table 15.1 Major challenges for sustainable development

Developing countries	Developed countries

■ Food security
 	
■ Poverty and increasing gaps between rich and poor
 	
■ Environmental degradation – deforestation, mass ignorance and poor educational services
 	
■ Population growth and poor health services
 	
■ Internal stability and increasing internal migration and social disruptions
	■ Environmental degradation of natural resources – soil, water, air, flora and fauna
	
	■ Surplus production – butter mountains, beef mountains, etc. Increased competition among developed countries
	
	■ Equitable distribution of wealth
	   – welfare to active involvement in health generation
	
	■ Declining relative living standards
	   – farm income vs urban income
	   – rural services to urban services

15.3 RESEARCH, DEVELOPMENT AND EXTENSION APPROACHES IN DEVELOPING AND DEVELOPED COUNTRIES

Multinational corporations (MNCs) have traditionally been among the primary agents of technology transfer. Affiliates of U.S. and MNCs in the mid-1980s accounted for 40 per cent of all exports of machinery and 20 per cent of chemical exports from Latin America. In Asia, the average equivalent share was lower, about 7 per cent on average, but was up to 20 per cent in specific industry sectors and countries. But recently concern for technology for development has been superseded by concern for technology for sustainable development (Schmidheiny 1992). Sustainable development calls for new technologies that are economically efficient, commercially attractive, environmentally sound and that bring social equity.

Within the context of the increasing complexity of current global concerns, many actors and/or agencies have emerged who are providing new green technologies, information, education and training, and finance and marketing services to individual farmers and groups to attain their goals in a sustainable way. Many new approaches are being developed to understand the complexities and changing roles of the actors involved and to find ways of working together to solve common concerns and utilise new opportunities for growth and development.

15.3.1   Traditional models of research, development and extension: Scenario in developing countries

Many developing countries still continue to practise traditional linear models of research and extension with government organisational structures. Figure 15.1 depicts linear model of research and extension which encompasses a clear division of labour, starting with basic research, followed by applied research, and then transfer of new technologies to the farming community. This model of research and extension uses a predominantly one-way process of communicating research outcomes to the farmers, and farmers are seen as a target for promoting and selling the new technologies. Farmers thus assume a very passive role with limited opportunity for bottom-up communication. This trickle down approach, based on the linear model of research and extension, has been the predominant approach practised in several developing countries. In this approach new technology is demonstrated by technology providers and resource-rich farmers are the first to adopt it. The technology then trickles down to other farmers over a period of time. People who adopt first are labelled 'innovators' those who do not adopt, or who adopt later, are labelled 'laggards'. However, research into the diffusion of technology has clearly demonstrated that there are no universal innovators or laggards. If the technologies are relevant to local resources and agro-climatic conditions, then the small farmers also respond. This realisation has led to the need to understand the conditions of these resource-poor farmers and to develop technologies appropriate to their needs and socio-economic conditions. This approach is popularly known as Farming Systems Research and Extension (FSRE). The major emphasis, however, is still on the linear model.

In many countries single government departments and/or agencies that are running parallel to serve the same client groups undertake the delivery of extension services. Figure 15.2 clearly depicts how extension services are delivered by government departments, non-government organisations (NGOs) and agribusiness industries to the same farming community. These parallel services are confusing to the client community and in many cases they fail to identify the right service provider for specific services. Only the better-informed, elite farmers can capture all the services available and combine this knowledge to their advantage. This service delivery mechanism has been proved to be extremely inefficient.

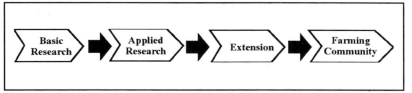

Figure 15.1 Linear model of research and extension

15.3.2 Training and visit (T&V) system of extension

The T&V extension system has been introduced in more than 40 countries as it was adopted, recommended and financed by the World Bank. The system has fast spread in major South Asian countries including Bangladesh and India due to its success especially in irrigated agriculture. Subsequently, many African countries joined the bandwagon of the T&V system where the effectiveness of the system was not always so impressive (van den Ban and Hawkins 1996). It should be noted that the T&V system has never been used in developed countries. The World Bank's 1994 review of extension projects summarised the strengths and weaknesses of the T&V system, as follows:

Strengths of T&V

- It provides a well-defined extension method with fortnightly visits to villages and disseminates impact points to Contact Farmers

- It improves the resource base of field extension staff through regular fortnightly training and provides technical backup in the field through Subject Matter Specialists (SMSs)

- It ensures that staff numbers are available at various levels to enable adequate coverage

- It improves linkages between research and extension to ensure the development of relevant technology

- It provides support facilities, like transport, to enable better farmer coverage

- It avoids service functions not associated with agricultural technology transfer

- It facilitates the feedback of farmers' concerns to extension and applied research

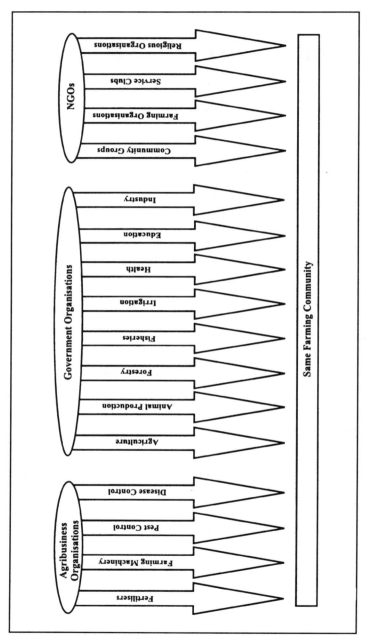

Figure 15.2   Parallel single extension services to the same client community

- It increases technology demonstration in large numbers of small plots in farmers' fields.

Weaknesses of T&V

- Most countries did not adapt T&V to suit their conditions
- The T&V system was implemented mechanistically
- Contact Farmers did not perform their roles and in some cases they did not know their roles
- There was an overemphasis on impact points based on research that may not be relevant to resource-poor farmers

Consequently, in many countries the T&V system has failed to attain rapid technological change at a desirable level. It is a less efficient extension model than initially perceived by rural extension experts in delivering appropriate technologies evolved through farming systems research to the end users especially resource-poor farmers. As a result, many countries have started to experiment with alternative models for efficiently delivering extension services.

15.3.3   The Dutch agricultural knowledge and information system (AKIS)

In the Netherlands a great number and variety of actors are supplying goods and services to the agricultural sector. According to the Ministry of Agriculture, Nature Management and Fisheries (1992) there are four categories of actors in AKIS and they adapt their roles constantly according to environmental policy. The roles of the AKIS actors and the environment in which they perform they operate are discussed elsewhere (see, for example, Chamala 1996).

Neils Röling and Paul Engles have pioneered the development of the concept of the Dutch AKIS which represents an attempt to break out of the fixed, linear and reductionist thinking supporting the Transfer of Technology (TOT) model into more holistic and systemic ways of thinking. AKIS proposes that research, extension and farmers potentially form systems – with emergent properties over and above the sum of their individual capacities – and that such synergy fosters innovation and enhances access to relevant information and technology among its stakeholders.

Röling (1992) describes the following attributes of a knowledge system:

- The actors constitute the system be they individual networks or institutions. These actors are differentiated and interdependent, two critical notions in the context of sustainability

- Integration occurs through communication between actors and also externally to other systems

- Coordination and contributions between actors are stimulated by outside forces (e.g. government policy, consumer demand or competition) and from within through management, social control, shared ideology and consensus

- Power is an essential ingredient influencing the feedback loops and the degree of centralisation and client and system articulation

- The constituent actors define the mission of the system

Röling (1992) further suggests that innovation, knowledge process and configuration are 'separate, yet mutually articulated and consistent building blocks' of the knowledge system models.

AKIS provides a diagnostic framework for analysing knowledge systems and deducing interventions to improve their performance. Rapid Appraisal of Agricultural Knowledge Systems (RAAKS) is an analytical toolbox for developing an understanding of the ways in which information and knowledge is created, shared and used among individuals and institutions involved in a common purpose or activity (Engel and Salomon 1993). The RAAKS approach is participatory and depends on teamwork, skill, the process of sharing learning experiences and seeing the system from the perspective of others, hopefully in a way that encourages an understanding of how the performance of the system as a whole can be improved (Engel and Salomon 1993). Some of the Dutch AKIS initiatives are collectively involved in multi-year crop protection plans and some have involved voluntary changes that have been initiated to develop sustainable farming methods.

15.3.4 United States: Cooperative extension interdependence model

Research, Development and Extension are undergoing major changes in the U.S. On the one hand agribusiness is investing heavily in developing high-tech (biotechnology, genetic engineering, new biodegradable chemicals, laser and geographic information satellite communications and information technology, etc.) precision agriculture through strategic alliances with universities and land grant universities. This technology is sold through commercial methods. On the other hand, sustainable agriculture is focusing on clean air, clean water and wild life corridors and set aside programmes focusing on sustainable use of natural resources. Clearly, there has been a change towards strategic alliances among agribusiness, government, environmentalists and community at large.

Two dominant types of conceptual models representing extension are in vogue in the U.S:

- The Research-Transfer Model

- Adult Education Model

The Research-Transfer Model first considers research agency and industry roles, processes and output and then considers extension roles, processes and output. The Adult Education Model first considers extension roles and processes, then considers research contributions to the subject matter content of extension programmes. Claude Bennette (1992a; 1992b) has proposed a new Interdependence Model in which he describes:

- the concurrent roles, actions and outputs of extension and related elements of the public and private sector, and

- the continuous, mutual interdependence of these elements in resolving public issues and clientele needs

The Interdependence Model identifies five elements in the public-private sector complex.

- Cooperative Extension System (Extension) is an information transfer and education agency that represents the State Land Grant Universities, county governments and the USDA. Extension may be viewed as one agency in a complex comprising several public and private sector agencies and users

- Research – public and private research agencies and organisations.

- Industry – private organisations that generate and market technologies commercially

- Intermediate users – public agencies, regulatory agencies, media, private consultants and special interest associations receive technologies and practices from research, extension and/or industry and then transfer them to end users

- End users (e.g. farmers, merchants, home-makers) use technologies and practices to address their needs and public needs. They receive inputs from all the above four elements in the complex

Fifteen generic roles in four stages of the complex have been identified in this new interdependence model. Bennette (1992a) has reviewed these cooperative roles in a generic way in order to understand the linkages between the different stakeholders. The five elements share 15 generic roles in the generation and adoption of technologies and practices (Bennette 1992a). Extension's distinctive performance of eight of them is crucial in the interdependent model. These are as follows:

Stage 1	Roles to plan and develop. Extension roles are: (1) network, and (2) develop
Stage 2	Roles to test and improve. Three roles: assess, adapt and systemise
Stage 3	Roles to extend and educate. Two major roles – transfer and educate – are identified for extension
Stage 4	Roles to use and plan. Use and evaluate are the two roles

According to Bennette (1992a) the interdependence model can help identify extension's distinctive capabilities and comparative advantages. Extension should place a high priority on the performance of roles for which it has, and will have, a comparative advantage. Extension roles are coordinated with the roles best performed by other elements of the public-private sector complex, so that the cost-effectiveness of the complex will be increased (Bennette 1992a).

15.3.5 Australian cooperative research and landcare extension approach

Australia has been initiating research, development and extension (R,D&E) programmes through various reviews over the last few years. Government policies are differentiating between public and private good. Wherever private good is involved, it encourages business investment and a user pay and cost recovery policy. When it comes to common good, the Government is investing in R,D&E programmes and the major approach is to provide service through group-based activities such as Landcare programmes. There are nineteen R&D Corporations which are coordinated through the Department of Primary Industries and Energy. Industry is also involved in research work and participates in commercialisation activities. There are also trends to involve various stakeholders in cooperative research programmes. Similarly, the Federal Government has initiated an innovative Landcare programme with strong stakeholder involvement at the community and catchment levels.

Cooperative research centres

A range of programmes has been initiated to establish closer links between research and industry. By 1990, the largest and most ambitious of these new initiatives was the Cooperative Research Centre (CRC) programme which involves universities, state departments, the Commonwealth Scientific and Industrial Research Organisation (CSIRO), R&D Corporations and industry. There are 16 CRCs focusing on agricultural and rural-based manufacturing and nineteen rural R&D Corporations, through the Department of Primary Industries and Energy, are encouraging greater industry involvement in research (Stirling 1996). These CRCs have been instrumental in forcing the development of formal linkages among public institutions and between public institutions and industry. Involvement by various stakeholders in CRCs is a major trend in Australian research and development and while CRCs are primarily research oriented, their programmes also have an extension component (Marsh and Pannel 1998).

Landcare in Australia: A grass roots participative approach

The initiative in tackling soil conservation problems has historically fallen to Government agencies, particularly State Governments in Australia. These have played a key role in providing technical assistance and have used both carrot (subsidies) and stick (legislation) approaches. Government agencies and voluntary groups have worked together and with district soil conservation works and programmes in their areas.

Landcare programmes in Australia in the 1990s resulted from (1) concern about land degradation among landholders and (2) recognition of the benefits of working cooperatively at local, district and catchment levels thus all relevant stakeholders working together forms the basis for landcare in Australia. By early 1998 more than 2500 Landcare groups were established nationwide. By 1992 more than 900 schools and many landcare groups were involved in water quality monitoring. Landcare programme is state supported but community stakeholders are involved at landcare group level and catchment management level. It is beyond the scope of this chapter to review the landcare programme in Australia but it is important to understand how the stakeholders have participated in this programme.

A generic Participative Action Management (PAM) model (Chamala 1990a, 1990b, 1995) provides an analytical and action framework for developing landcare groups where all the relevant stakeholders work together to achieve sustainable production on their farms as well as at group and catchment levels.

15.4   PARTICIPATIVE ACTION MANAGEMENT (PAM) MODEL: A GENERIC MODEL FOR R,D&E.

Based on several years of teaching 'group dynamics', 'community development' and 'extension organisation and management' and empirical studies conducted on soil and water conservation, this author developed a generic model called 'The Participative Action Management (PAM) Model' for the National Soil Conservation programme in 1990 and 1991. This model can be adapted to other extension projects to encourage participation of relevant stakeholders within the total systems perspective.

The PAM Model is not just an extension education or communication method, but an organisational system, a convergent action model that provides a framework for using several techniques to manage the extension system (Figure 15.3). It offers true partnership to all stakeholders. The PAM Model suggests that stakeholders from industry, government and the community be organised into converging and energising group(s) (or teams or councils). The energy conveyed by the PAM 'lens' can then be diverged or redirected for participative action. A skilled facilitator may assist this process but empowered and enabled groups can manage it themselves with the assistance of participating agencies and/or individual people.

In the PAM model, the participation action team:

- is representative of all agencies, groups and individuals who have a legitimate interest in the primary industry

- has a philosophy and structure that enables it to draw on opinions, aspirations, plans, information and resources from all sections of the community and then develop, implement and evaluate the results of the team action plan. In other words, it is a convergent action model.

The PAM Model aims at the empowerment of community people and government agencies (Chamala 1995).

■ Showing them triggers the imagination
■ Involving them gives them understanding
■ Empowering them leads to commitment and action
■ Telling adults provokes reaction

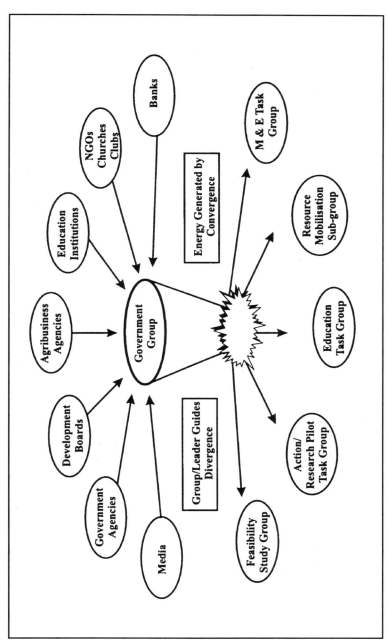

Figure 15.3   The P.A.M. Model (Source: Chamala 1990b)

15.4.1   How does the PAM model operate?

PAM operates through:

- shared vision and management
- participative problem and/or opportunity identification
- participative planning for research and development
- participative implementation and monitoring
- developing participative structures by establishing groups and joint project teams and/or projects at various levels within the total perspective; and
- developing personal and/or group capacities through training, support, allocation of responsibilities and opportunities for learning by doing.

The PAM Model provides clear guidelines on how to establish the groups and what to do in the four phases, namely, (1) emergence, (2) establishment, (3) action and (4) expansion/extinction/re-emergence. Figure 15.4 depicts the planning cycle used in the PAM model and shows that Landcare groups are fully empowered. It involves the community and other stakeholders in planning, implementation, review and reflection processes. Mortiss and Chamala (1991) have also discussed several other participative planning methods, how to increase group members' capacity to manage these groups, and how to achieve sustainable development.

15.4.2   Development of management platforms with ecosystem focus at various levels

Empowered community groups may focus only on local issues whereas governmental agencies may develop strategic plans at national or State level. Unless there is a mechanism to connect the top-down and the bottom-up processes, the complimentary planning processes can not be integrated into a coherent programme. Hence there is a need to develop management structures which act as a ladder for the free flow of information. While some authors call these management structures 'platforms' this author calls them 'empowering structures,' because the term platform does not capture the idea of empowerment.

In Australia, an attempt has been made to develop management platforms with an ecosystem focus where stakeholders at each level can work together

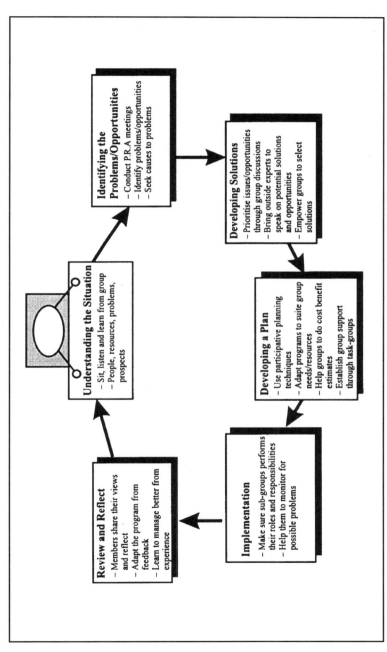

Figure 15.4   P.A.M. Planning Cycle (Source: Chamala 1995)

to resolve ecological, production, social and economic issues. These management innovations are essential mechanisms for developing shared common vision, for planning and implementing, and for monitoring programmes at each level. Figure 15.5 provides the framework for developing a ladder of coalition platforms with ecosystem focus at various levels.

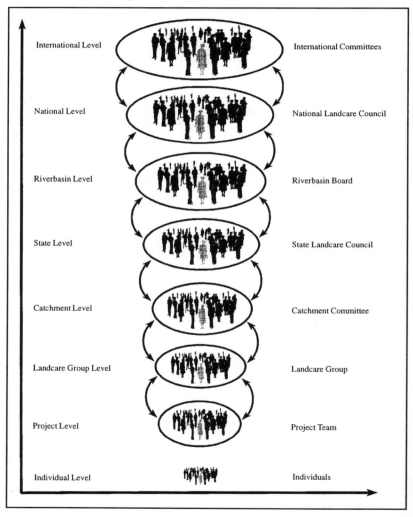

Figure 15.5   Framework for developing ladder of coalition platforms with ecosystem focus at various levels

The relevant stakeholders are government agencies, non-government organisations, and industry, educational, banking and farming sectors. These management platforms are not hierarchical in the sense of power and authority, but cooperative structures. Mechanisms should be developed that foster both top-down and bottom-up information flows. Scientific data on land, water, flora and fauna together with socioeconomic and social information could have a geographic focus so that the different perspective of each stakeholder could be developed into a shared vision based on factual information and socioeconomic reality. Geographic Information System (GIS) data and satellite pictures combined with socioeconomic data can provide information for ecosystem planning and development. These structures and processes will help achieve shared community-based natural resource management on a sustainable basis. Two-way information flow will help link top-down and bottom-up planning and implementation processes. This framework will also help to link local, regional and state programmes to national policy development.

These platforms are not formed through government directives but need to evolve as logical empowering structures for linking actions at various levels. Funding of these mechanisms together with building the human capacity of the members of these platforms is essential for their successful functioning. Similar frameworks have been developed to manage government-owned forests in many developing countries.

15.4.3   Use of the PAM model

In Australia, the generic PAM model has been used in implementing the following three programmes with modifications made to suite each of the programme.

- The Land and Water Resources Research & Development Corporation has adopted the PAM model to implement five irrigation technology development and transfer programmes across Australia

- The Department of Primary Industries (DPI) in Queensland has adopted the PAM model to help involve all stakeholders in implementing the Community Water Watch programme. This is a joint initiative between Federal and State Governments involving various stakeholders

- DPI has developed an innovative programme called Do-Our-own-Research (DOOR) and has used the PAM model to involve stakeholders in bringing about paradigm shift to a 'Transfer Of Technology (TOT)' model of research and extension. As a result of this Nurserymen are being trained to conduct research in collaboration with consultants. The DOOR programme is now being applied to the Wild Flower Industry in Western Australia and Queensland and is being funded by the Horticulture Research & Development Corporation. As a result of this a new model for Transferring the Technology Development Process (TTDP) has been developed.

These examples provide evidence of the generic PAM model's robustness and flexibility in helping programmes to involve stakeholders at various levels in R,D&E activities. It has provided a conceptual management framework, or platform, to facilitate the involvement of stakeholders and it may have some implications for other developed or developing countries.

15.5   PARTICIPATORY APPROACHES IN INDIA AND BANGLADESH

Participatory rural development (PRD) approaches initiated in main by the United Nations agencies in the 1970s have been instrumental to self-development and empowering rural poor in many developing countries. PRD strategies have resulted in many success stories in rural transformation and poverty alleviation in many developing countries (UN Interagency Committee on Integrated Rural Development for Asia and the Pacific 1990). PRD approaches entail less bureaucratic organisational structure and committed staff to expedite the development process in partnership with people. In that connection, NGOs are more prudent in implementing PRD strategies in developing countries. In India and Bangladesh a number of NGOs have successfully undertaken participatory development programmes with impressive outcomes. For example, in India People's Institute for Development and Training (PIDT) coordinates the activities of many NGOs who endeavours to address the problems of rural poor at grass root level employing PRD methodologies. In Bangladesh, NGOs like *Proshika*, Bangladesh Rural Advancement Committee (BRAC) and Rangpur Dinajpur Rural Service (RDRS) have been involved in various PRD programmes in different parts including remote areas of the country.

15.5.1 India's approach to joint forest management for sustainable development

Community development was pioneered in India during the early 1950s. Decentralised democracy was promoted to the village level, and government agencies worked with local communities. Agricultural development projects used several extension approaches with varying degrees of success. This section describes India's historic attempt to implement a Joint Forest Management (JFM) programme since 1990. The salient features of JFM are:

- Joint forest management should be implemented under an agreement with the village community, voluntary agencies and/or NGOs, and the State Forest Departments.

- No ownership or lease rights are to be given to the community.

- Beneficiaries should be entitled to a share in usufructs with agreements with State Forestry Departments.

- Access to forest and usufructory benefits should only be available to village-organised institutions.

- Beneficiaries should be given usufructs like grasses, lops and tops of branches and minor forest produce. If they successfully protect the forest they may be given a portion of the proceeds (25 per cent is the village community share in West Bengal).

- The selected site should be worked in accordance with a working scheme approved by state forests.

- Beneficiaries should be paid for the services of nursery raising, land preparation for planting and protecting trees after planting under the social forestry programme.

- Cutting of trees should not be permitted before they are ripe for harvesting.

By 1993, 14 states had issued JFM facilitating orders. There are several documented successful case studies where JFM is working well, and new forests are being established using social forestry extension with a JFM approach.

In addition, to overcome the weakness of state extension services, to increase its efficiency and to prepare it for the 21st century there is a greater need to introduce meaningful farmer participation in public sector extension management and planning in India (Macklin 1992). Government extension organisations need to work in close partnership with NGOs and the agribusiness agencies in implementing PRD programmes.

15.5.2 Bangladesh's approach to blending greater participation and sustainability with institutional strengthening

Chowdhury and Gilbert (1996) reviewed in detail the agricultural research and extension network in Bangladesh. The limited effectiveness of the Training and Visit (T&V) extension system has led to a greater need for participation of the private sector, non-government organisations and the farming community to address issues of sustainability.

The Agricultural Support Services Project (ASSP), supported by the World Bank, has helped to strengthen the institutional capabilities and has facilitated the development of a new extension strategy. The Department of Agricultural Extension has encouraged this new process. The major features of this new extension strategy are:

- Decentralisation of authority from the centre to the districts

- The use of groups rather than contact farmers in communications with farming communities

- Greater efforts to assess farmers' needs

- Strengthening linkages with public and private organisations

- A sharper focus on poor and disadvantaged groups, including women

While these new approaches attempt to reform agricultural research and extension in Bangladesh, the new approaches undertaken in developed and other developing countries (as described above) could be utilised to further reform and strengthen the research and extension strategies. Here, stakeholders work together to resolve the complex issues of alleviating poverty, increasing agricultural production and maintaining environmental sustainability. The new roles for Bangladesh agricultural extension for sustainable development could be as follows:

- a technology development role

- a technology transfer role

- a problem solving role

- an education role

■ a human development role
■ a community organising role

Chamala (1990a) after reviewing the megaforces, namely international agriculture centres, trade and bilateral aid agreements, provided a balanced critique on positive and negative impacts of modernisation in developing countries. He has suggested new approaches under two categories:

■ New approaches to agricultural technology development
■ New approaches to the management of delivery of services for modernisation and rural development

Among several new approaches, he suggested to link farm planning to family planning. This is essential if environmental and/or social disasters are to be avoided as population pressure is partly responsible for the use of marginal land and deforestation.

15.6   IMPLICATIONS FOR SOUTH ASIAN COUNTIES

The trends discussed above indicate that institutional, policy and programme changes have taken place in developed and developing countries. Several countries are experimenting with collaborative approaches and developing social innovations to bring the various stakeholders together from community to national and international levels. These new approaches have some implications for other developing counties. However, one cannot prescribe a 'blueprint approach' to solve the wide variety of problems of poverty and environmental degradation.

The philosophies and principles of new approaches undertaken in the Netherlands, the USA and Australia, and initiatives taken in India and Bangladesh provide some guidelines for formulating agenda for action for developing R,D&E programmes in South Asian and other developing countries. It is clear that the linear model is changing stakeholder participation in designing and developing appropriate technologies that help achieve sustainable agriculture.

■ The trickle down and T&V systems of extension are changing to a more convergent model of community participation. Agribusiness, agencies (both government and non-government) and the community need to come together in designing appropriate development policies and programmes including extension services. The PAM model could provide a basis for this reform in South Asian countries

- Use of information technology and decentralisation of services with empowering community groups can certainly lead to more-responsive structures to the problems of environmental degradation and social inequalities

- There is a need for training programmes for field extension agents and community leaders in this new philosophy of collaborative approaches to research and extension

- The extension strategy should also include reaching disadvantaged groups including women and creating new social innovations (social platforms) to promote active involvement leading to empowered actions. This training has to be different from the training phase of the T&V system – that is, a more action-learning approach with an emphasis on need-based learning to solve the environmental and social issues

The experiences, and the principles that emerged from these experiments, could be used in designing relevant approaches to improving agricultural research and extension in South Asian countries. Integrated development through stakeholder participation in R,D&E programmes should be the major approach in managing sustainable development. Hopefully, this participative approach with community empowerment will bring about a paradigm shift in the approach that developing countries take to solving sustainable agricultural, environmental and social issues.

16 Ecotourism Under Multiple-Use Management of the Sundarbans Mangrove Forest in Bangladesh: Issues and Options

M. Akhter Hamid and Bruce R. Frank

16.1 INTRODUCTION

The Sundarbans meaning 'beautiful forest' is situated in the southwest deltaic coastlands of Bangladesh and the southeastern part of West Bengal, India facing the Bay of Bengal. It is the largest single compact mangrove forest in the world covering an area of one million hectares. Approximately 62 per cent of the Sundarbans forest area (577 000 hectares) belongs to Bangladesh. About 67 per cent of Bangladesh Sundarbans area is land and the rest is occupied by open waters (Hussain and Karim 1994).

The diverse *flora* and *fauna*, which include some rare/endangered species in the vast pristine tract of the Sundarbans, have made it a leading ecotourist destination in Bangladesh. It has significantly high ecotourism value being the only natural habitat of the Royal Bengal Tiger, spotted deer and estuarine crocodile. It has almost been untouched in terms of 'resort tourism' based infrastructure development within the forest area. For ecotourists it offers a wide range of nature-based recreational activities without having any adverse impacts on the environment.

However, the ecotourism industry to date could not flourish significantly by exploiting its full potential. Indiscriminate clearing of the mangroves especially in the Chakaria-Sundarbans in southeast Bangladesh for agricultural, aquaculture and salt production has wiped out vast mangrove tracts in the country (S. S. Ali 1994a; Nuruzzaman 1994; Mazid 1995). Despite the government policies and Forest Department's policing, trees are being felled, animals are being illegally killed, forest resources, particularly non-wood products and aquatic resources, are being over-exploited. In sum, the Sundarbans mangroves suffer from improper resource management due to the absence of a single-outlet multi-disciplinary management system ensuring the participation of all concerned departments/agencies. All these factors have direct bearings on the ecological sustainability of mangrove resources, and growth and development of ecotourism in the Sundarbans.

Using direct observations and interviews of different stakeholders, this paper examines the status of ecotourism industry in the Sundarbans under the multi-use management system. It explores the predicaments of ecotourism industry as it relates to resource management and policy statements. It also suggests some remedies that would help overcome constraints being faced by ecotourism sector in the Sundarbans.

16.2   ECONOMIC BACKGROUND OF THE BANGLADESH SUNDARBANS

Mangroves are considered as one of the most productive natural habitats in the world (Nuruzzaman 1992). Mangroves offer economic returns in three different forms: forest resources, fisheries resources and ecotourism (FAO 1994b). Furthermore, mangroves play various crucial roles like protecting coastal areas from cyclone and storms, saving coastal lands from tidal surge and wind erosion, harbouring a wide range of *flora* and *fauna*, etc. (Vantomme 1995). Bangladesh's coastlines are very prone to recurrent natural disasters like floods, tidal bores and cyclones. To that end, mangroves along the coastline help protect the Sundarbans and thereby its ecotourism resources.

The Sundarbans has been under institutional management systems for more than one and a quarter centuries. It became a reserved forest in 1875–76. It constitutes nearly half of the country's forest reserve and is the single most important contributor to the forestry sector. The Forest Department has the sole authority to oversee all business in the forest including those relating to fisheries and tourism. Three wildlife sanctuaries were created within the Sundarbans reserved forest in 1977 (S. S. Ali 1994a). Its main sources of revenues from forest products are: silviculture operation and nypha leaves harvest. Being a multiple-use forest, it also earns revenues from ecotourism, fisheries and other resources within the reserve. Its fisheries resources are an important source of, *inter alia* the country's ever demanding shrimp fries.

Despite the resourcefulness of the Sundarbans, the surrounding region has high to very high food insecurity (GOB/WFP 1997). People living around the Sundarbans' fragile and vulnerable area heavily rely on the mangrove resources and mangrove-based goods and services including ecotourism for their livelihood. An estimate reveals that in the late 1970's around 45,000 people were engaged in some kind of activities in the forest on any given day during the peak harvesting season (Hussain and Karim 1994). About half a million people depend for livelihood on the Sundarbans They work as wood-cutters, nypha leaves collectors, fishermen, shrimp fry collectors and honey collectors (S. S. Ali 1994b). Furthermore, it is logical to assume that a significant additional number of people are employed in ancillary industries resulting from forward linkages of the Sundarbans forest industry and its tourism industry. Lack of reliable statistics makes it difficult to portray total number of people who directly or indirectly depend on the Sundarbans mangrove forest for their livelihoods.

16.3   WHY ECOTOURISM IN THE BANGLADESH SUNDARBANS?

The Bangladesh Sundarbans is one of the most remarkable natural systems in the world (Hartley 1996), and has better characteristic features than its Indian counterpart (Barua 1997). The resourceful, evergreen and virgin vegetation of the Sundarbans is set in a picturesque network of interconnecting rivers, canals and creeks. It is endowed with 330 plant species, about 400 fish species, 35 species of reptiles, more than 270 species of birds and 42 mammal species (Hussain and Karim 1994). All these species coexist in a unique fashion in their natural habitats.

As a rare exception amongst other mangroves in the world, the Sundarbans is not dominated by the population from *Rhizophoraceae* family. The tall woodland of the forest is dominated by 'sundari' (*Heritiera fomes*) and hence has been named as 'Sundarbans' because of the elegance of 'sundari' trees. Out of the 50 mangrove tree species of the world, 40 species are available in the Sundarbans (Barua 1997). It offers a magnificent floristic view of aesthetic beauty.

It is the only remaining natural habitats of the Royal Bengal Tiger (*Panthera tigris*) – Bangladesh's national heritage, spotted deer and estuarine crocodile. In addition, it has many species of mammals including macaque monkey, wild boar, jackal, fishing cat, common otter; reptile including python, common cobra, monitor lizard, turtle; and many bird species. The Royal Bengal Tiger, a source of national pride and immense fear, is critical to ecotourism, and a lead attraction for both local and international tourists alike. The forest is also a famous harbour for migratory birds.

The Sundarbans offers a wide range of recreational activities like beach relaxation, history interest, cultural interest, big game watching, bird watching, wildlife watching, botany, art touring, cruising, boating, walking, jungle trails, archaeology, herbal tour and educational tour (de Veer Moss 1994). All these activities, which can be enjoyed in harmony with the nature, have made it a popular destination for ecotourists.

16.4   ECOTOURISM IN THE SUNDARBANS: PROBLEMS AND PROSPECTS

The global ecotourism market is expanding at a fast rate. Ecotourism is an excellent source of economic returns that yields a host of social, political and environmental gains (FAO 1994b). Ecotourism in the Sundarbans mangroves has the potential to make substantial contribution to the socio-economic and environmental milieu of the mangrove belt. Figure 16.1 depicts the potential social, economic and environmental gains from Sundarbans' ecotourism industry. It is evident in the diagram that the social, economic and environmental factors are interlinked and complementary to each other in the impact of ecotourism in the Sundarbans.

Despite great potential for ecotourism or low-impact tourism in the Sundarbans, it is still at a preliminary stage. There are several constraints that limit the development of ecotourism in the Sundarbans:

- Acute shortage of safe drinking water inside the forest

- Lack of proper transportation facilities to and within the forest

- Lack of accommodation inside and nearby the forest

- Absence of power, telecommunications and health care facilities

These factors directly affect the tourist intake in the Sundarbans. In addition, there are some human interventions that affect the ecological sustainability of the forest and consequently lead to the deterioration of the ecotourism value of the forest.

First of all, poachers are felling trees and killing animals in an attempt to make easy living out of the mangrove resources. These threaten the bio-diversity and ecological sustainability of the forest. There is a tendency of locals, who enter into the forest for various activities like shrimp fry collection, fishing and nypha leaves extraction, to break tree twigs and cut trees to repair their vessels and make boat accessories. Firewood collectors do much damage to the forest reserve. Illegal timber merchants who are responsible for tree felling that does not follow the prescribed silviculture operation are exceptionally active in this region. In a bid for quick removals of the chopped

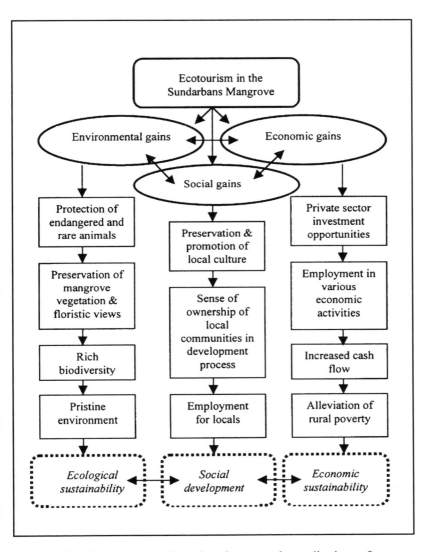

Figure 16.1   Social, economic and environmental contributions of
Sundarbans' ecotourism industry

timber trees, poachers drag them through the mangrove vegetation causing considerable damage to the forest cover. Illegal hunting of animals notably tiger and spotted deer has sharply reduced their population. Currently, there are only 360 Royal Bengal Tigers in the forest (Tamang 1994). In order to stop illegal felling and hunting, the Forest Department has blocked the mouth of some canals realising that poachers will not have easy access. Ironically, it has destroyed navigability of those waterbodies. The annual 'Dublar Char festival' severely damages the surrounding ecosystems by creating, among other damages, heavy noise and smoke pollutions. It is increasingly becoming a norm for the people who attend the festival to kill animals and grill them using firewood from the forest.

Secondly, construction of embankments and development of polders in the surrounding areas have shifted water flow. As a result, both the soil and water salinity of the forest has increased considerably which is believed to be one of causal factors of 'top dying' disease in the Sundarbans. Top dying disease has already caused considerable damage to the Sundarbans including its floristic beauty.

Thirdly, there are approximately 165 factories/industries in the surrounding cities/towns of the Sundarbans. All the factory waste/effluents are being released to the nearby waterbodies linked to the Sundarbans.

Fourthly, one of the largest seaports is situated near a pocket of the Sundarbans. Each year around 5,000 sea going vessels navigate through the Sundarbans (Barua 1997). These ships also aid in disturbed ecology of the forest. There has also been a reported case of oil spillage, which have been very damaging to the mangrove resources. All these have serious implications for the ecological sustainability of the Sundarbans mangrove resources, which again directly affects its ecotourism values.

The above factors while do not provide exhaustive lists of all the factors that hinder the growth of ecotourism in the Sundarbans are nevertheless critical to its development. These situations have been compounded by the resources management system that is in place. Under the government's Forest Act all activities inside the forest including issuing passes to enter into the forest are governed by the Forest Department (FD). Although, Bangladesh *Parjatan* (Tourism) Corporation (BPC) – National Tourism Board is the proper authority responsible for development, promotion and marketing of tourism, practically they do not have much to do with Sundarbans ecotourism. Ecotourism in the Sundarbans warrants effective inter-departmental coordination that is non-existent. Although, the FD, through the Forest Act 1855 has the sole power to administer all activities including drawing resource management plan and collecting revenues from the Sundarbans, they do not have any promotional or marketing activities. FD does not have any work unit solely assigned for tourism development in the Sundarbans. By the same token, BPC has no tourist promotion centre overseas for effective marketing of their goods and services. Despite sharp rise in number of ecotourists and high ecotourism value of the pristine ecosystems of the Sundarbans, BPC has taken very little or no initiatives to promote the ecotourism industry in potential market in home and abroad.

Private sector intervention is crucial in Bangladesh's tourism industry. At present only one private tour operator is doing business in the Sundarbans area. From discussion with concerned people it reveals that because of the absence of working relationship between BPC and FD, private entrepreneurs do not feel secured to invest in this sector.

By the same token, although the number of tourists entering into the Sundarbans is gradually increasing over the years, there are still ample scopes for overall development of the country's ecotourism industry particularly in the Sundarbans mangroves. *First of all* people's participation are needed to achieve nature and wildlife conservation. As de Veer Moss (1994, p.50) put it 'there can be no long-term future for wildlife or protected area management where local people are antagonised. Instead, they should benefit from the management of these resources and have vested interest in their conservation as sources of food and income'. The most obvious foundation for a successful ecotourism industry is to protect resources on which the tourism is based. When local people will become part of the whole industry and see tangible benefits of the industry for the local communities, they will themselves safeguard the resources.

Both public and private sectors should give more attention to improve infrastructural facilities like:

- provision of safe drinking waters by installing temporary water tanks in prime visitor spots/lookouts

- introducing transportation with modern facilities especially protected viewing deck

- local traditional boats can be modified for cruising in the canals and rivers inside the forest

- overnight self-contained accommodation (10, 20, 30 beds)

- existing accommodation capacity in two rest houses can be doubled without changing major structure

- only a few temporary mangrove bungalows can be developed

- introducing the provisions of accommodation, power, telecommunication and health care facilities in strategically close and feasible location and

- more signposts in various languages need to be installed

Release of industry waste to the nearby waterbodies, oil spillage, etc. should be banned by strict laws.

BPC should take aggressive multi-media marketing campaign in international ecotourism market. It would be helpful to enter with contractual arrangement with some international tour operators in major cities of the world to act as local promoters and sales points. It would be of added attraction to establish a Sundarbans Information and Study Centre in the gateway of the mangroves.

16.5   THE SUNDARBANS MANAGEMENT DILEMMA: NEED FOR A SINGLE-OUTLET SHARED APPROACH

In line with the management problems of the Sundarbans discussed above, a single-outlet multi-disciplinary management system needs to be introduced ensuring the participation of all concerned department/agencies. This will entail more relaxed attitudes of FD towards partner agencies. Under existing systems they might feel a bit insecure about the entry of other departments in any matters of the Sundarbans. The new management approach will accommodate all agencies in a 'mutually-benefiting' manner. Sundarbans Conservation and Tourism Council will be formed by drawing personnel from Divisional administration, FD, BPC, Department of Fisheries, Mongla Port Authority, Police department, representative from private tour operators, local government representatives and local leaders. This will be independent of any organisation. However, FD will be the commissioning body. The council will be headed by the Secretary of the Ministry of Civil Aviation and Tourism. Members of the multi-disciplinary teams will work towards the improvement and management of the forest by contributing their expert opinion in their respective field of specialisations. They will have regular quarterly council meeting to evaluate the ecotourism, and nature and wildlife conservation as well. The board will ensure that the tourist intake by no means exceeds the carrying capacity of the forest.

To conduct resource assessment they would adopt Participatory Appraisal of Sundarbans Mangroves (PASM) following some modifications of Rapid Appraisal of Coastal Environment (RACE) suggested by Pido and Chua

(1992). PASM is a multi-disciplinary process that includes both quantitative and qualitative analysis of resources. It is more detailed than Rapid Rural Appraisal (RRA). It is a combination of both formal and informal approaches (for details see Pido and Chua 1992). The suggested approach would result in effective interactions amongst ecotourists, locals and the mangrove ecology in a way that would be beneficial to all the stakeholders. This will preserve local cultural diversity, ecological sustainability of the Sundarbans and accelerate the growth and development of ecotourism in this mangrove forest.

16.6   CONCLUSIONS

The Sundarbans in southwest Bangladesh is the largest and one of the best mangrove vegetation in the world. It is an important source of renewable natural resources in Bangladesh. Endowed with diverse and rare *flora* and *fauna*, it is a natural sanctuary for the famous Royal Bengal Tiger, spotted deer and estuarine crocodile, and is one of the main attractions for local and international ecotourists. It is the forerunner of Bangladesh's ecotourism industry. Although the government has classified the Sundarbans as a reserved forest, mangroves are being destroyed and disturbed in many ways, and trees are being felled. Together with very complex management system, poor transportation, accommodation and other facilities, mangrove destruction has had an adverse impact both on the ecological sustainability and ecotourism industry.

Using direct observations and interviews of different stakeholders this study evaluates the status of ecotourism industry in the Sundarbans under multi-use management system. It studies the predicaments of ecotourism industry as it relates to resource management and policy statements. The analysis suggests a shared, holistic and rigorous evaluation approach that would help attain ecological sustainability in the Sundarbans and thereby maintain the Sundarbans as a lead ecotourist attraction in Bangladesh. This calls for a rationally coordinated system of policy measures that would protect the natural resources and promote ecotourism on a sustained basis.

17 Coastal Aquaculture in South Asia: Experiences and Lessons

Mohammad Alauddin and M. Akhter Hamid

17.1 INTRODUCTION

A formidable challenge that is likely to threaten sustainability in the agriculture sector in the developing world has been the growing dependence on agricultural lands and the consequent over-exploitation. This over-exploitation may vary from country to country in a global context or region to region within the same country. This challenge has seen the growth in the aquaculture sector–especially coastal aquaculture in many developing countries (Goldburg 1996; Lucien-Brun 1997). South Asian countries especially Bangladesh and India are no exception (ADB/NACA 1996; FAO/NACA 1995a; 1995b; FAO 1994a; 1995). This Chapter examines the spectacular growth in coastal aquaculture in South Asian countries. Experiences in many countries suggest that aquaculture exceeds the carrying capacity of the coastal waters resulting in lower production and often complete destruction of the yield. Thus the process of coastal aquaculture seems to have stressed the fragile environment to the limit and has resulted in significant changes in the overall socio-economic milieu. Furthermore, producers are primarily price takers. International market forces significantly determine their production trends and profitability. The aquaculture sectors in the exporting countries are required to comply with various requirements of international buyers. The buyers in many cases seem to behave like monopsonists.

This chapter investigates the process of coastal aquaculture in South Asia focusing on Bangladesh and explores environmental implications thereof. It also addresses the implications of international marketing mechanism on domestic production. Finally, it suggests value adding and product diversification as strategies for risk minimisation and reduction of market uncertainty.

17.2   COASTAL AQUACULTURE IN SOUTH ASIA: THE PROCESS

Recent years have witnessed a prolific growth in coastal aquaculture in South Asia. Over a period of a decade to the mid 1990s area under shrimp production in Bangladesh has more than doubled to over 130 000 hectares (Alauddin and Hamid 1996). This is against the background of shrimp area of almost next to nothing a decade earlier. Nearly 80 per cent of the area under shrimp farms are from the Khulna region comprising of the southwestern districts of Satkhira, Khulna and Bagerhat. The remainder of the shrimp farming area is located in the southeastern district of Cox's Bazaar (Alauddin and Tisdell 1998). Over the period of the last two decades Bangladesh's cultured shrimp production has increased from a very negligible base to nearly 30 000 tonnes. Bangladesh's annual shrimp yield is just over 200 kilogrammes per hectare. It is one of the lowest in the world. It is also very low even in comparison with her Asian neighbours with the exception of Vietnam.

In the southeastern coastal areas of Bangladesh (i.e. Cox's Bazaar region) shrimps are grown during the months of May to November. For the rest of the year the land is used for salt production (Alauddin and Hamid 1996; Mazid 1995). In some parts of the southeast tidal area, rice alternates with shrimp and fish production (ESCAP 1988). Alauddin and Tisdell (1998) report that in the Khulna region, during the wet season, the fields grow paddy. In the dry season once the rice is harvested and stubble removed they are flooded with brackish water containing shrimp *post-larvae* from nearby rivers and streams. Shrimp fields are then stocked, in most cases, with shrimp fry caught from the wild and occasionally with the hatchery-bred ones. These are raised extensively until they are ready for the market. The mature shrimps are harvested and the ponds are drained before the end of the dry season. The land is then able to be prepared for the rice crop grown for wet season. The cycle then repeats itself.

Shrimp represents a significant change in the structure of Bangladesh's export trade. In 1993–94, the export earnings from shrimps and frozen fish were US $197.67 million and US $12.85 million respectively. Foreign exchange earnings from the fisheries sub-sector of the country will therefore, mainly depend on shrimp production and export (Kashem 1996). As of the 1993–94 fiscal year shrimps contributed 57 per cent of exports in the primary goods category and (EPBB 1995) and has completely overtaken the once-dominant primary export commodity, namely raw jute. In 1994–95 frozen foods category, 85–90 per cent of which is comprised of shrimps, earned US $312 million, enjoying a growth of 49 per cent in export earning from the previous year. This elevated frozen foods to the second largest export earning group of commodities after ready-made garments (BFFEA 1995). Even though Bangladesh is a small player in terms of its share in international market, providing 4.2 per cent of the world production of farmed shrimp – it is the 7th largest cultured shrimp producer in the world. Bangladesh supplies world-class crops of farmed shrimps (Rosenberry 1995). Its shrimps are well recognised for their flavour, taste and texture since they are grown under 100 per cent natural environment (BFFEA 1995).

Shrimp culture, through a network of backward linkages, created a substantial volume of employment in shrimp farms as well as ancillary activities like trade/commerce, processing, marketing and exporting. It was estimated that in 1983, 4.1 million person days of on-farm employment was created for 51 thousand hectares of shrimp farms in the coastal areas of Bangladesh. Off-farm employment was 5.9 million person days (MPO 1986). Based on the projected expansion of shrimp farming areas, MPO estimation for both on- and off-farm labour requirements for 1990 were 22.6 million person days. The corresponding figure for 2005 is expected to be 59.4 million person days (MPO 1986).

India has experienced prolific growth in coastal aquaculture in the last decade or so. As of 1991–92 India had over 68 000 hectares of area under shrimp farming. However, as Alagaraswami (1995, p.158) reports more recently the area has increased to about 80 000 hectares. Of the ten states and territories along India's vast coastline four states West Bengal, Andhra Pradesh, Kerala and Orissa account for more than 90 per cent of both area under farming and production. Recently Tamil Nadu has experienced a phenomenal growth in shrimp production. There is also a significant variation in yield per hectare across states and territories. India's average yield is more than 2.5 times that of Bangladesh. Andhra Pradesh has an annual yield above 1200 kilogrammes per hectare per year.

Sri Lanka is a small producer but over the past few years there has been a rapid development in the shrimp farming industry in the North Western Province of Sri Lanka (Jayasinghe 1995, p.366). Shrimp contributes significantly to the total foreign exchange earnings from aquatic products ranging from just under 50 per cent in 1992 to over 70 per cent in 1986. After 1989 shrimp exports experienced a sharp reduction due to outbreaks of disease in shrimp farms (Jayasinghe 1995, p.366).

As mentioned earlier, farmed shrimp is a lead export item in Bangladesh. Shrimps are grown primarily for international market. Prior to Bangladesh's entry into international shrimp market, shrimp was much cheaper than fish in Bangladesh (Karim and Aftabuzzaman 1995). Now it is quite expensive and beyond the buying capacity of average people. It is also very popular in

Bangladesh (Cf. Karim and Aftabuzzaman 1995). Karim and Aftabuzzaman (1995) mention that shrimp was not an attractive food item in Bangladesh. It needs to be pointed out here that although shrimp was cheaper earlier, it was still expensive in terms of average people's affordability. Majority of the Bangladeshis could not afford to have shrimp even when it was less expensive. It does not mean it was a less attractive food item. However, local demands are now met mostly from open water shrimp catches that are not exclusively destined for overseas market. Shrimp is a popular food item all over the world because of its taste and boneless meat. It is also attractive to overseas consumers since they often find shelf-ready shrimps very handy for consumption. Since bulk of the production comes from extensive culture methods that involve none to very little of the modern technologies, it is logical to say that harvested crops are devoid of chemicals particularly artificial growth hormones.

In 1994–95, shrimps and frozen food category earned US $312 million enjoying a growth of 49 per cent in export earnings from the previous year (BFFEA 1995). Bangladesh's frozen foods (shrimps constitute 85 per cent-90 per cent of this category) are exported to about 40 countries of the world. USA, Japan and the European Union countries are the major importers of Bangladesh's shrimps (BFFEA 1995). As of 1993–94, European Union is the largest buyer of Bangladesh's shrimp accounting for 48 per cent of total export, followed by USA and Japan representing 34 per cent and 11 per cent respectively of total export (*Economics News* 1995; EPBB undated; BFFEA 1995). Although US and Japan are two of the largest buyers of Bangladesh shrimps, Bangladesh accounts for only less than two per cent of combined US and Japan shrimp market (ASCC 1995). In 1994–95, USA and Japan accounted for 30 per cent and 21 per cent of total exports respectively. As the single largest importers of Bangladesh shrimp US market has shown a downward trend in recent years (Alauddin and Hamid 1996).

As with Bangladesh shrimps from other South Asian countries find their destination primarily in the countries of the European Union, North America and Japan. In the world market South Asia has to compete with other major producers e.g. Thailand, Ecuador and China. The largest exporter in the world is Thailand accounting for nearly a quarter of the total world exports. By international standards South Asia is a small exporter accounting for less than 10 per cent of the total world exports in recent years.

17.3   COASTAL AQUACULTURE AND THE ENVIRONMENT

While the aforementioned recorded employment and export gains seem highly impressive, these have been achieved at considerable costs. In the context of Bangladesh, a case study by Alauddin and Tisdell (1998) indicates:

- lower paddy production due to declining yield per hectare

- destruction of trees and vegetation due to salinity

- decline in household incomes from non-farm sources, especially those of ecological reserves

- decline in the production of poultry and livestock

- various forms of social conflicts

- uneven gains between *her* (shrimp farm) owners and land owners especially the small land-owning households

- adverse environmental spillovers in the form of loss of green vegetation (e.g. vegetables, coconut trees, bamboo plantation) and also of other crops, loss of genetic diversity (loss or extinction of indigenous species of fish), declining rice yields

- increased employment opportunities off the shrimp fields – overall increase in employment.

In case of any ecological or environmental disasters resulting from shrimp farming, those who have the least to lose are the shrimp farm owners who often are not the owners of the land under shrimp culture. In the event of shrimp farmers being forced to quit shrimp farming leaving behind a legacy of environmental crisis, they can adjust easily in an economic sense. They represent a powerful class of people with accumulated surplus in other investable outlets primarily in urban locations.

In contrast, those with the most to lose from any possible irreversible damages to the environment are *primarily* the landowning and the landless households. For these two classes of people the land and water-based activity i.e. agriculture and related activity, subsistence fishing represent major occupations. According to a study (*Nijera Kori* 1996, p.13) at the beginning of the process the landless were the most adversely affected party. However, they were engaged in fry catching and other fringe jobs. Subsequently, the small landholders were the worst affected.

World Bank estimates (World Bank 1991b; Alauddin and Hamid 1996) indicate that over 10 million people are engaged in subsistence fishing in Bangladesh. To quote one important study 'A vital aspect of the subsistence fishing is its role in cushioning poverty. The significance of the small miscellaneous fish species as distinct from the principal commercial species – is that the 'miscellaneous species' constitute the main part of the catch in the subsistence fishery and as such are a key resource for the rural poor. They can be seen as poor people's fish and their economic and nutritional value for rural poor people must not be underrated, though they are of less commercial significance' (ODA 1990, quoted in M. Y. Ali 1991, p. 17).

Even though shrimp cultivation and ancillary activities have provided employment and income gains for these groups of households, they may have been achieved at the cost of the future. Thus it is at odds with the concept of sustainable development as defined in WCED (1987, p.43). This raises questions of intergenerational equity being undermined.

Shrimp farming has had a significant impact on the economy of Bangladesh in terms of its contribution to export earnings and employment generation on and off-farm through a series of backward and forward linkages. However, this process has entailed high environmental costs, including destruction of mangrove forests, reduction in crop production (especially paddy), water pollution and green vegetation. The process of shrimp cultivation therefore epitomises conflicting resource-use patterns. It has also set in motion socio-economic changes. All these may have serious implications for sustainability of shrimp farming itself, of rural livelihoods and of communities in the coastal belt of Bangladesh. The evidence from Bangladesh is supported by evidence from elsewhere in South Asia as well as other shrimp producing countries.

Coastal aquaculture in many developing countries of Asia and Latin America has led to the destruction of coastal mangrove forests to make room for the operations of large commercial farms. In Ecuador for example, about 20 per cent of the mangrove forests were converted to shrimp ponds between the late 1970s and early 1990s (Goldburg 1996). Shrimp production has taken a heavy toll on the mangrove forests in many Asian countries.

In Thailand cultured shrimp production has increased form about 11 thousand tonnes in 1981 to more than 225 thousand tonnes in 1993 (Menasveta 1997, p.37). According to Menasveta (1993, p.41) over a period of 32 years to 1993 more than 54 per cent of Thailand's mangrove forests have been destroyed to make way for shrimp farming.

In India 'vast areas of mangroves were destroyed for agriculture and aquaculture and other uses. In the more recent years, the mangroves have been protected by law. However, the satellite imagery pictures show destruction of mangroves in Krishna and Guntur Districts of Andhra Pradesh for construction of shrimp farms' (Alagaraswami 1995, p.154).

In Bangladesh mangrove has been reduced by *inter alia* expansion of shrimp farming in the coastal areas of Bangladesh (Mazid 1995; Mahmood 1986). While mangrove destruction has been a ubiquitous feature of shrimp farming in Bangladesh it is particularly severe in the southeastern Bangladesh. As Mazid (1995, p.77) reports 'Once the Chakaria Sundarban had a dense mangrove forest of 18 200 ha. With the expansion shrimp farming since the 1970s, over 50 per cent of the mangrove has been cleared for the establishment of shrimp farms and now only a small patch of forest remains in the interior. ... The conversion of mangrove forests would appear to be uneconomic if the potential yields are compared with the combined yields of the forests and traditional fisheries which are now both lost'.

As for Sri Lanka 'Removal of mangroves for construction of shrimp farms and for obtaining fence posts for shrimp farms has taken place in the North Western Province. ... Destruction of mangrove in the buffer zones between farms and open water resources has also been reported. With further expansion of the shrimp farming industry, mangrove areas on the north western coast of Sri Lanka are under threat' (Jayasinghe 1995, p.371).

The environmental issues stemming from the process of shrimp culture have serious consequences for the shrimp industry. The livelihoods of many could be unsustainable if the environmental issues are not addressed and remedial measures not undertaken. These issues, however, stem from *inter alia* externalities engendered by the process of shrimp culture but are *internal* to the shrimp-farming country. However, there are issues that are *external* to the country in which shrimp culture takes place. These are also the issues over which the producing country has very little control. Some of these are taken up for discussion in the next section.

17.4 SOME FURTHER CONSIDERATIONS

Shrimp producing countries of the developing world engage in shrimp farming primarily for export purposes. They export shrimps to the high-income countries of the Western Europe, North America and Japan. Other emerging markets are Singapore, Hong Kong and Malaysia. The exporting countries have to adhere to the rules and regulations of the importing countries. These include *inter alia* various non-tariff barriers including health and environmental standards, labour laws [1]. The consumers and hence importers are highly sensitive to quality of the products that they are importing. For example, green consumerism in the western world is a potent force that can hardly be ignored. Similarly, customers or lobby groups in developed countries can wage campaign to boycott products that use child labour[2]. This could be potential public relations setback for market access for the exporting country. Shrimp shipment from Bangladesh to USA is subject to automatic detention for examination imposed by USFDA (US Food and Drug Administration) because of previous export of unhygienic crop (*Market Asia* 1995). Recently the European Union (EU) has also expressed concerns for Bangladesh's shrimp crop. A EU team's visit to Bangladesh in February 1995 found that the hygiene level of the processing plants were not up to standard and the water used therein were not chlorine free (*Economics News* 1995). It is important to note here that BFFEA has immediately taken necessary measures to address these problems (*Economics News* 1995). Very recently the EU eventually cleared import of shrimp from Bangladesh and normal exports from Bangladesh have resumed.

Shrimp in Bangladesh's export trade is relatively more important than it is for other South Asian countries e.g. India. As can be seen from Chapter 7, Bangladesh's export trade lack diversification both in terms of range of products and market destinations. This poses risks for Bangladesh's export trade in general and for shrimp exports in particular. This is because shrimp constitute a food item, which is subject to stringent health and quarantine regulations in the importing countries. This calls for greater diversification of Bangladesh's export trade. These risks are interrelated and can be conceptualised in terms of the linkages portrayed in Figure 17.1.

Recent supply chain studies around the globe (see, for example, O'Sullivan 1998; Kinnucan and Wessels 1997) established that producers get a disproportionately low profit margin at the farm gate. From shrimp farms to the end consumers different players are involved. Processing industry/retailers are the major beneficiaries. Shrimp farmers can substantially increase their profitability by entering into value addition. Given the small scale of farming they could form large corporations that will contact international buyers directly to secure increased profit share. There is a global trend that primary producers become a part of giant supply chains by complying with their set protocol. This will ensure better marketing of their shrimp products.

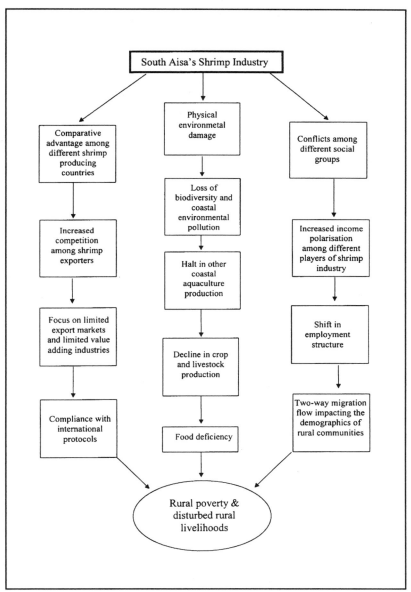

Figure 17.1   Risk exposure of South Asia's shrimp industry

17.5   CONCLUDING COMMENTS

Coastal aquaculture is at the crossroads. Sustainability of the industry is under serious question. Unless environmental externalities are addressed further deterioration will follow. As Lockwood (1997, p.53) points out that shrimp aquaculture entails 'conflicts between market economies, survival economies, and the nature's economy – the environment'. Those who pay the ultimate price are rarely those that pollute. As Lockwood (1997) argues that some low-cost shrimp farming operations impose considerable environmental and social costs without paying for these externalities. The market system fails to account for these external environmental and social costs that are real and from which the low-cost farmers benefit. This highlights the divergence between social and private costs and benefits resulting from shrimp aquaculture.

Value adding is an important challenge that must be taken seriously. This will create a greater volume of employment on a sustained basis. Quality sensitivity is much higher in high-income countries than in low-income countries. It is not just price that determines the competitive edge, product quality is of equal if not of greater importance. Health and quarantine regulations, labour laws, environmental standards in developed countries have important bearings on the demand for shrimp products in high-income countries. Recent restrictions by EU on shrimp imports from Bangladesh are a significant pointer that cannot be dismissed lightly. Enhancing the quality of the physical production environment would enhance international prospects for demand for shrimp and related products in a highly quality-sensitive marketing environment.

In conclusion 'The conflict resulting from the remarkable expansion of shrimp farming has aquaculture poised at the threshold of a historic moment in which aquaculture, as one of the world's newest yet basic industries, must be transformed to a higher level of environmental and social sustainability. ... Aquaculture sustainability requires full accommodation of market economics, people struggling in subsistence economies, and the nature's economy – the environment' (Lockwood 1997, p.52). These are some of the issues South Asia has to grapple with for a sustainable shrimp industry, environment and society.

NOTES

1 The mad cow disease adversely affected British beef exports. From time to time Australian beef exports or live sheep exports have suffered setbacks as result of alleged failures to meet health and quarantine requirements of the importing countries.

2 Some senators in the United States are particularly vocal against the use of child labour in the production of industrial goods, e.g. textiles, footwear and clothing. Recently a fact-finding team led by Iowa Senator Tom Harkins visited Bangladesh to verify the extent of child labour use in the ready-made garments industry which accounts for two thirds of Bangladesh's export earnings.

18 Women and the Environment with Special Reference to Rural Bangladesh

Nilufar Jahan and Mohammad Alauddin

18.1 INTRODUCTION

Studies addressing gender issues in socioeconomic development have proliferated in the last two decades (see for example, Roy et al. 1996). Declaration by the United Nations of 1975 as the International Women's Year and 1975–85 as the United Nations Decade for Women as well as international bodies and non-governmental organisations have been significant factors in generating heightened awareness of gender matters on development.

This belated recognition of the importance of gender issues in economic development is reminiscent of the neglect in orthodox development theory the distributional and environmental implications of the process of economic growth which has a narrower connotation than economic development as discussed in Chapter 1. This implies that there is a process of alienation which works to the disadvantage of many especially women and other vulnerable groups including children and people in lower strata of the society in many LDCs. According to Lele (1996, p.28) the striking feature of economic development in the last fifty years has been 'a single-minded pursuit of industrialization, either through centralized planning or through encouragement and assistance to capital in the pursuit of profits'. This has engendered major alterations in the lives and environments of common people. They, however, 'have been scrupulously excluded from an active involvement in determining the direction, intensity and consequences of these alterations'. This process of exclusion and alienation of 'most working people, women and men from decision-making has meant that economic growth has both expanded the means and arenas of subjugation of their dreams, ideas and activities'.

A substantial body of evidence suggests that women have consistently lost out in the development process (Pearson 1992; Jahan and Alauddin 1996; Tisdell 1996). An examination of micro-level indicators considered *inter alia* by Agarwal (1986, 1989), Ahooja-Patel (1996), Pearson (1992) and Roy et al. (1996) clearly suggests gender makes a difference in their share of benefits from development process. These include lower earnings of females relative to men, disparities in female-male literacy rates, representation of women in parliament and gender divisions of use of time. In each of these respects women compare unfavourably with men. This seems to have resulted from a process of no clear recognition of the fact that 'development process or policy inevitably affects and is affected by the relation between genders in any society. All policies however technical or neutral may appear to be, will have gendered implications' (Pearson 1992, p.292). One needs to emphasise that in a broader context gender relations are social relations rather than biological or natural relations which are essentially based on a stereotyped image of gender relations. It must be remembered though that '...social and economic discrimination in terms of gender, race, or similar characteristics is mutually reinforcing. These aspects together create a social and economic trap for them to escape by means of their individual efforts...' (Roy et al. 1996, p.23).

Given the predetermined division of labour accompanied by unequal access to and control over resources within the household, changes in rural policies and agricultural technology have not enhanced the status of rural women in Bangladesh. Even though women are regarded as an inconsequential element, they are, as usual, subject to unequal gender relations deeply embedded in a culture of patriarchy and subjugation (Pearson 1992). However, as a response to the challenge of feminisation of poverty, rural women are responding to their marginalisation and acting significantly in grassroots initiatives for change. In particular, in a growing crisis of survival, rural poor women of Bangladesh have always played an important role in their subsistence. Rural women have always contributed their physical labour as well as ideas for a more innovative and responsive rural economy and the environment.

This chapter emphasises specifically the role of gendered patterns of sustainable resource use and control in rural households. Women's response to subsistence growth and their potential capacity in protecting the environment are also examined in general as well as from the standpoints of social justice and equity.

18.2 GENDER ISSUES ESPECIALLY IN RURAL BANGLADESH

Women in Bangladesh enjoy a lower socio-economic status than men. Socio-cultural norms, religious taboos and barriers militate against an enhanced status of women in Bangladesh like those in many LDCs. In a pioneering study on the female status in Bangladesh, Chaudhury and N. R. Ahmed (1980, p.155) catalogue some factors for this lopsidedness in gender relations and discrimination against women. These, while not exhaustive, are important factors:

- lower literacy rate among women compared to men

- in practice marriage age of women on average being 8–10 years lower than men

- greater liberty for men to divorce their wives even at simple pretexts with little or no opportunity for women to exercise that right

- inheritance law discriminating women *vis-a-vis* men

- a society dominated by *purdah* restricting women's mobility and contact with the world outside

- women lacking control over means of production

A recent study by Majumder and Zohir (1994) relating primarily to urban context found significant socioeconomic changes have occurred in women's living with the garment workers experiencing the greatest change. However, the beneficial effects of the socio-economic transformation brought about by the wage employment in the garment industry is considerably neutralised by some negative implication such as exploitation in terms of low wage, irregular wage employment, job insecurity, gender discrimination in earnings, etc. Poor occupational health and safety standards are also matters of grave concern.

Rural women are usually overworked. Jahan (1996) found that in rural Bangladesh women on average worked 10–20 per cent longer than men. This is consistent with the situation elsewhere in the developing world (see for example, Pearson 1992, pp.297–8). Despite women's involvement in household activity and in agricultural production, their contribution to the national economy is still not given due recognition. For instance, official statistics have no reference to their contribution. This is primarily due to socio-cultural values and attitudes according to which it is not socially acceptable for women to be involved in field agricultural works (Safilios-Rothschild and Mahmud 1989). In fact women make substantial contribution to agricultural production and rural household. Since they usually do not own any land very little attention has been given to women's need for increasing their contribution to agricultural production. Hamid (1994, p.1 and p.38) in assessing the contribution of non-market work in national income estimates that women contributed more than 41 per cent to GDP in 1989–90 while their contribution to agriculture was about 37 per cent.

The Agricultural Sector Review of 1989 on women's roles in agriculture (Safilios-Rothschild and Mahmud 1989) reports that women's participation in agriculture is by no means less than that of men. Economic participation of women includes income-earning (marketing of livestock or of homestead horticultural produces) or contributing to value added (home-based crop processing, grain storage, etc.) activity. Even though women perform duties like transplanting, weeding, harvesting, irrigation on their family farm social reluctance militate against their inclusion as productive, such work confronts social resistance to be considered productive.

Despite the advancement in agricultural technology, women's lives and their economic position still remain at a disadvantage. The agricultural modernisation in the 1960s has had a negative impact on the economic position of women in land and other institutional support (Mahabub Hossain 1988). Apart from unequal access to income-generating opportunities, women have hardly any control over either through ownership or rights over the means of production such as land, tools, animal, transport and other necessary resources for the production and distribution of agricultural products (Jahan and Alauddin 1996).

The emergence of structural and technological changes in many ways provides limited avenues for rural female employment. Higher peak labour needs and time constraint for operation like fertiliser application, weeding, harvesting and liberalisation in agricultural input markets, in fact increase the requirement of casual hired labour. Demand for casual labour has opened up the avenue for female workers (Khuda 1982; Safilios-Rothschild and Mahmud 1989). However, the rate and nature of participation of women in farm households varies with differential access to land. In female headed households, women owning cultivable land area between 0.1 and 0.4 hectare are most likely to engage in on-field agriculture. Women's involvement in field agriculture when added to their domestic work should pre-eminently qualify their contribution to crop agriculture.

In the rural labour markets, wages are usually paid in a combination of cash and kind. Many women receive a part of their wages in the form of meals at work. In 86 per cent of the days of all employment, women's wage included food, either as the only payment or in combination with other components (R. I. Rahman 1991). Wage rates of unskilled rural wage workers are low and women wage workers constitute the lowest paid group. In such a situation, a single bread winner can hardly maintain a family of two or three above the poverty level. Female wage rates range between 45 and 60 per cent of their male counterparts (Jahan and Alauddin 1996). A survey undertaken by Jahan in two Bangladesh villages also reported similar female-male wage relativities. It appeared that as women are hired for casual work, they lack bargaining power for higher wages. Furthermore, to continue in their work and earnings, women have to comply with any wages offered to them even though the wages they receive may not be commensurate with the rise in price level. This picture is no different from that in the non-agricultural sector (Majumder and Zohir 1994).

H.Z. Rahman and Mahabub Hossain (1992) report that females have a nutritional intake of only 88 per cent that of males and typically earn 46 per cent of the male wage. Recent surveys and available evidence from Bangladesh suggest that women have shared a disproportionately higher burden of poverty and suffered chronic deficits in food intake, both in absolute term and in relation to men (Jahan 1997; Pearson 1992). In Bangladesh around 50 per cent of the rural poor live below the poverty line (a daily intake of less than 1850 kilocalories). The incidence of poverty is higher for women compared to men. Employing farm-level evidence from two Bangladesh villages and various measures of poverty (headcount index, Foster-Greer-Thorbecke poverty gap and distributionally sensitive Measure) Jahan (1996, p.91 and p.105) reveals that the burden of poverty is disproportionately borne by women. On further interpretation of Jahan's finding (Jahan 1996, p.105) it was clear that by every measure of poverty the female-male relativities was higher than unity and ranged between 1.13 and 2.17. This finding is supported by those of Alauddin and Tisdell (1998) who reported a significant intra-household disparity between male and female members in rural Bangladesh. A similar evidence was found in some West Bengal villages (Roy and Tisdell 1993). This is also consistent with R.I. Rahman (1985) who, after an extensive survey of literature, found overwhelming evidence of unequal sharing of food within the family – with female members getting a much lower share than male members both in terms of food quality and quantity.

Furthermore, due to deforestation, a chronic shortage in fuel also affects women's cooking arrangements in the form of meals nutritional quality by using less fuel and are able to cook fewer items. Thus while in general their diets are *a priori* less varied, less nutritious and dreary (see also Alauddin and Tisdell 1991), given the intra-household inequality against women they are more likely to bear the brunt of this decline dietary quality (Jahan 1996). The survey undertaken in two rural areas of Bangladesh is supportive of the view that women bear a higher burden of nutritional disadvantage in intra-household food consumption.

18.3   ENVIRONMENTAL DEGRADATION AND RURAL WOMEN

The 'female marginalisation thesis' explains women's worsening position in terms of reduced access to and control over the means and rewards of productive activity in the developing world (Beneria 1981; Beneria and Sen 1982). Factors such as the introduction of intensive agriculture, mounting population pressure on land, greater urbanisation, penetration of market forces and lack of well-defined property rights have significant influence in degradation of the rural environmental resources (see, for example, Alauddin and Tisdell 1991; 1998). Deforestation, soil erosion, desertification, waterlogging and other interrelated activities are an integral part of soil degradation and are causes and symptoms of environmental degradation (Jahan 1997; Alauddin et al. 1995).

The present environmental degradation which has been significantly due to the process of growth and is appropriated in the nature of development raises concerns about the sustainability of a balanced life. Voicing this concern the Rio Declaration (UNCED 1992) strongly refuses to allow the concept of *sustainable development* to be simply turned into an *economic notion*, restricted to new technologies and subordinated to the latest market products because these perpetuate *structural poverty* and wealth that arise from the dominant discourse of development whose validity has been seriously called into question (see, for example, Lele 1996, p.28).

In general, large population and poor people are blamed for environmental destruction, such as overexploitation of land, deforestation, unplanned use of natural resources. Overpopulation, poverty, underdevelopment and environmental deterioration are cyclically interlinked with each other. The links between poverty and the environment still remains a subject of considerable controversy or at best much more complicated than a simplistic cause-effect portrayal of the link (see, for example, Alauddin and Tisdell 1998; Lele 1991; Bifani 1992). Thus one should exercise caution against such a simplistic generalisation. Poverty is viewed as a major cause and an effect of global environmental problems. It is therefore futile to attempt to deal with environmental problems without a broader perspective that encompasses the factors underlying world poverty and international equality (WCED 1987).

In rural Bangladesh environmental degradation is mainly referred to as the product of resource-use pattern. The relationship between poverty and unsustainable agricultural practices is also cited in many recent publications (see for example, Alauddin and Tisdell 1998). Imprudent use of agricultural resource base irreversibly reduces the capacity for generating sustainable production.

Environmental degradation in Bangladesh is treated as an externality of huge population and poverty. The externalities do not treat the environmental degradation as a living system that affects people's lives. As a result, for subsistence, the poor rural women exert more demand on the subsistence economy. The pressure by the increasingly marginalised poor rural population on common lands is identified as an important link between socioeconomic development and environmental degradation. It can be argued, however, that such a view ignores the dominant cause of the environmental crisis, namely industrial toxic wastes and over-consumption of the affluent people (Bifani 1992). Thus environmental degradation cannot be attributable to the poor rural women especially, when a very small per cent of farmers own around 80 per cent of land and other resources of the country (see, for example, Alauddin and Tisdell 1991). It is true that lack of conservation practices, inadequate technology and increasing intensive production practices have contributed to accelerated degradation and consequently increases rural poverty which in turn can act to the detriment of the environment. Against this background it is now widely recognised that women play a critical role in bringing about social, economic and environmental change and in turn can be affected by these changes. These linkages can be complex and can be captured somewhat in terms of the conceptual model set out in Figure 18.1.

It has been said that rural women's activities to some extent aggravate environmental destruction. Given the limited access to private property resources, rural women and children usually use country forests and other village commons resources to collect their daily use of essential items- such as food, fuel, fodder and fibre. The dependence of poor rural women on forest and land is high for fuel and fodder (Agarwal 1989). But destruction and exploitation of forest has not been acted upon by the rural female fuel collectors, because collecting firewood and fodder are not destructive of nature. Rural women usually collect firewood in the form of twigs, fallen branches, leaves of trees, shrubs, and weeds for their daily domestic use, which do not destroy trees or other plants. Again the traditional practice of obtaining tree fodder by careful lopping often enhances overall fodder. Deforestation is mainly caused by the commercial exploitation of forest, such as logging. However, forest/ tree has different significance to rural women, their choice never coincide with tree felling they prefer trees as a provider of fuel, fodder and daily requirements.

Rural women's activity always aims to nourish the nature, look after it and use it for growth and development. Their poverty sometime exploits the resources, but by nature they refrain from overexploitation. To avoid overexploitation, they prefer and adopt recycling method in their daily life. From this point of view, rural women, in Bangladesh (and elsewhere) can usually be termed as 'caretaker' of the environment and not its destroyer.

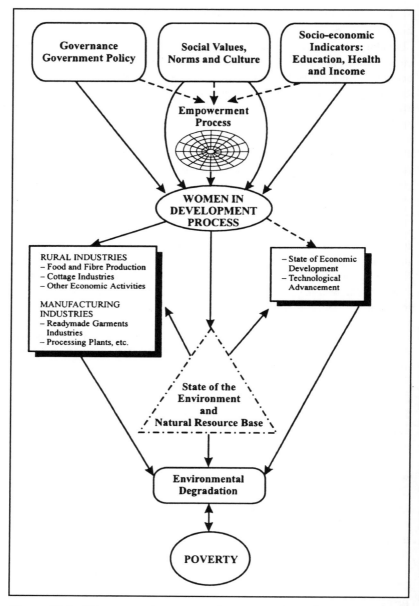

Figure 18.1   Women, environment and poverty: schematic representation

18.4   WOMEN AS GRASS-ROOTS ORGANISERS

In the process of development, rural women appear as passive victims. While the country's constitution is mandated to mainstream the role and activities of women in the production process in Bangladesh, the rural women, to some extent are deprived by the activity of technological improvements. Current women's movements in Bangladesh mainly highlight the problem of urban women. Very little importance has been given to rural women's problem, their access to, and control over resources. Historically rural women have played a very significant role in peasant movements against feudal and colonial control over land and produce, such as, in the *Tebhaga* movement of sharecroppers during the late 1940s and early 1950s, and in the liberation movement during the early 1970s.

With the agricultural liberalisation policy of Bangladesh as was initiated in different phases and as it spread to other sectors of the economy, it would raise the status of women, failed to deliver the expected result. The success of these types of policies usually depend on the specific policy measures and their implementation process. The impact of these policies on rural women is also guided by general patterns of resource use and control in rural households. The environmental justice in these context cannot be delinked from issues of equity and social justice (Figure 18.2).

In the last two decades, emancipation of rural women has given importance to several community initiatives. A variety of institutional initiatives have emerged in affirming the strength of unity in resisting gender oppression. For instance, the introduction of some simple income generating schemes have enhanced women's earning capabilities. Also, group approach rather than individual approach has been identified as a more appropriate initiative to enhance income generation and poverty alleviation initiatives. In Bangladesh, some organisations, such as the *Grameen Bank*, Bangladesh Rural Advancement Committee (BRAC), *Proshika* and some others have taken initiatives for social and environmental justice (Figure 18.3). These organisations emphasise the need of positive changes which involve the potential use of all the knowledge and skills available to the rural sector. Under these programmes, rural women are motivated for group action. Women organised into small groups are issued individual loans but with group liability in achieving individual project targets. Motivation to achieve specific policy option influence an individual with a wider range of external factors, while clear perception and strong incentive encourage an individual to use resources efficiently. Efficiency, then produces rational behaviour to achieve optimum use of resources, which in effect influence the behaviour towards

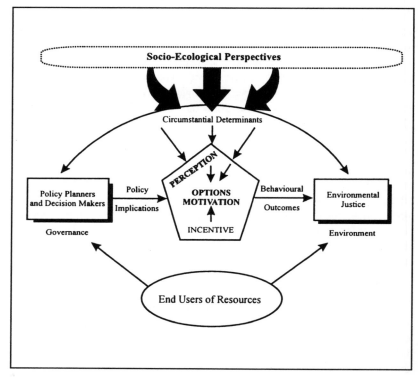

Figure 18.2   A conceptual framework portraying interrelationships between external factors (policy measures, governance, etc.) and their active interpretation for translation into action (incentives and motivation for behaviour). Adapted from Drijver and Zuiderwijk (1989, p.139).

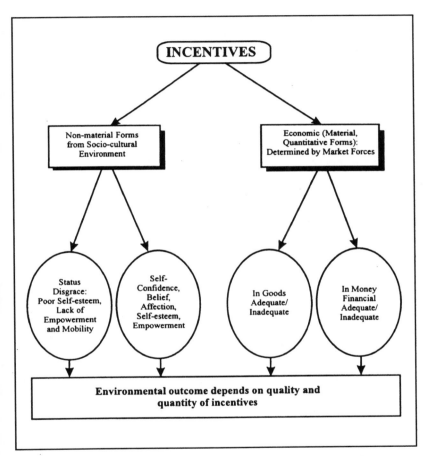

Figure 18.3 Material (cash or kind) and non-material (status, self-confidence, self-esteem empowerment) forms of incentives. Adapted from Drijver and Zuiderwijk (1989, p.139).

environmental justice. In the first instance, rural women ordinarily are motivated largely by economic considerations. The economic power as well as their behaviour are guided by socio-cultural considerations.

Rural women, historically have been good resource managers, although this aspect not received proper attention in environmental debate. The successful implementation of *Grameen Bank* projects clearly illustrate this phenomenon. Rural women poverty level in some of the *Grameen Bank's* area has improved by 11.5 per cent over an eight-year period (1987–94; see R. I. Rahman 1991; Jahan 1997). The collective control and management of productive assets (land, plantation, poultry, village forests) augment the bargaining power of women in groups and can lead to changes in the relation between local production and power relations. Grassroots initiatives at micro level clearly provide a potential for change in resource control.

Grameen Bank type operations at the local level have a significant impact on gender relations towards greater empowerment of women. However, the efforts and initiatives need to be continued and supported by macroeconomic policy framework. The social and ecological movements have strongly negated the models of development which deprived the local population of their bases of livelihood. The survival strategy the rural women are currently experiencing is not incompatible with practices of environmental conservation. In particular, initiatives at the micro-level indicate a strong likelihood for a change in environmental action. Rural women thus work as agents of change whose actions can reshape village life. The participatory process of rural female labour needs more encouragement and support from the national and international agencies, needs more attention to achieve the aimed goal of development. The bargaining power at the micro-level will enforce the rural women's emancipation strategy within a well-designed macro-policy framework. As Pearson (1992, p.312) rightly put it: 'The key to redressing the inequality of gender relations and the mismatch between women's contributions to society and their rewards goes much further than directing programmes to women. The importance of analysing gender applies at all levels of development policy – planning, implementation and evaluation'.

18.5   CONCLUDING COMMENTS

Despite earlier neglect gender is being increasingly acknowledged as a critical variable in analysis of development process. Rural women are a significant provider of family subsistence (Hamid and Alauddin 1998) as well as a significant but neglected agent of change. Given their unequal access to productive resources, control over social and political process and decision-making, employment and other income earning opportunities, and also rapid depletion due to over-exploitation of nature's resources, rural women continuously facing high socioeconomic inequality and have become more dependent on and vulnerable to the vagaries of nature. The process along-with the use of more advanced technology put women to more impoverished position, marginalise them, and make them the victim of discrimination, who are continually struggling to conserving nature's balance in order to preserve their means of survival. The experiences of organisations like the *Grameen Bank* initiatives for rural women provide useful insights on women's responses towards poverty and discrimination.

An improvement in the economic conditions of rural women also restores human dignity. The struggle of rural women is the struggle to carve out a place for an alternative existence that is based on equality and not dominance on one group by another. In the context of ecology movements, this is one that is based on co-operation with and not dominance over nature (Agarwal 1989).

The most important task is to transform the world of rural women in such a way so that development, redistribution and ecology can work in regenerative ways. For environmental justice, a greater empowerment of rural women is a prerequisite which demands an active collaboration of government, non-government organisation (NGO), local power bodies (political and social) as well as political parties. The Rio Declaration (1992) at the Earth Summit acknowledges women, as vital players in environmental management and conservation. The organisational intervention of different NGO's do provide a safe space to women but the voice of that intervention needs to be more organised to impact politically beyond the immediate local context. A critical factor in achieving sustainable development in Bangladesh is the empowerment of rural women through social justice and environmental justice.

To sum up, the poor relationship of women and the (biophysical) environment is the result of women's position in an inconducive sociopolitical environment which needs to undergo significant changes. Recent evidence suggests that women in Bangladesh have been somewhat successful in changing/influencing the socio-political environment through group-effort. Given this and their closer affinity to nature, women are likely to emerge as better environmental managers with appropriate opportunities and incentives. However, policy measures must be instituted both at the micro and macro-levels.

Acknowledgements

The authors wish to thank Professor Clem Tisdell, Dr. Apelu Tielu, Dr Samiul Hasan and an anonymous referee for useful comments. The usual *caveats* apply.

19 South Asia's Experiences, Challenges and Prospects in Global Context

Mohammad Alauddin

19.1 INTRODUCTION

Discussions in the preceding chapters of this volume conceptually and empirically established close and critical linkages embracing the three themes: development, governance and the environment. While the focus is primarily on Bangladesh, the other countries of South Asia are considered in order to obtain a comparative picture, draw parallels, identify areas where deficiencies exist and further improvements are needed.

This chapter proceeds first of all with a synthesis of the development-governance-environment nexus in the light of the experience of South Asia especially Bangladesh. Finally, transboundary and global aspects of South Asian issues are analysed in an environment of increasing globalisation.

19.2 DEVELOPMENT, GOVERNANCE AND THE ENVIRONMENT IN SOUTH ASIA: IN RETROSPECT

Significant changes have taken place in South Asia since the British left India more than fifty years ago. Since India's partition along religious lines (predominantly Hindu India and predominantly Muslim Pakistan), a new country Bangladesh emerged after nearly a quarter of a century of unhappy union with Pakistan.

Over the years significant structural changes have taken place in the respective economies of Bangladesh, India, Pakistan and Sri Lanka in terms of composition of GDP and occupational structure of labour force. There has been a gradual reduction of relative importance of the agricultural sector and increase in secondary and tertiary sectors in both GDP and labour force. One must exercise some caution in interpreting these structural shifts. All countries in the region except India have a disproportionately larger share of GDP and employment originating from the services sector. The manufacturing sectors of these countries are not a big source of employment or GDP. Still however, agriculture remains the main outlet for labour absorption. One should exercise some caution in this lopsidedness in the growth of the services sector. As Lewis (1966, p.181–82) points out '... it is important to get the right balance between commodities and services, since if the service sector is too large, the demand for commodities will exceed the supply, and inflation and a balance of payments deficit will result'.

In foreign trade significant structural changes have taken place due to a gradual shift from agricultural to non-agricultural exports for all countries. However, for Bangladesh this has resulted in little or no export diversification as her export trade is heavily concentrated on one item – ready-made garments (see, for example, Hossain et al. 1997; Alauddin 1997 and Chapter 7). Bangladesh has also moved away from its traditional export of jute and jute based exports in favour of shrimps. This has significant social, environmental and economic implications for Bangladesh (Alauddin and Tisdell 1998; Alauddin and Hamid 1996).

Until a decade or so ago South Asia (Sri Lanka excepted since 1977) adopted a policy of import substitution orientation or some times known as inward-looking policy paradigm. The policy paradigm of all the major countries at present hinge on export orientation or is outward looking. In other words, South Asia is now in reform mode: from predominantly regulated to a predominantly deregulated environment with greater reliance on market mechanism. As comprehensively analysed by Shand (Chapter 3) the performances of the South Asian economies following economic reforms have been mixed: the primary underlying factors being institutional and in-depth studies of governance issues in the performance of all sectors of the economy (see, for example, Sobhan 1998; Akash 1998).

South Asia remains predominantly rural despite growing urbanisation with this trend predicted to continue. As seen in Chapter 2, in 1995 Pakistan with 35 of its total population living in urban areas is the most urbanised of the South Asian countries followed by India (27 per cent) while Bangladesh (18 per cent) and Sri Lanka (22 per cent) do not differ much in respect of the degree of urbanisation. By international standards India has three mega-cities: Mumbai, Calcutta and Delhi with Bangladesh and Pakistan having one each respectively Dhaka and Karachi.

The South Asian region is one of the most densely populated regions inhabited by about 1.3 billion people. Sri Lanka the least populous country has been most successful in reducing population growth rate to 1.3 per cent in the 1990s. During the same period both Bangladesh and India have achieved considerable success in reducing their respective population growth rates to 1.6 and 1.8 per cent. Pakistan, however, has been a dismal failure in reducing its population growth rate that is still close to 3 per cent. In all countries of the region life expectancy at birth has increased quite significantly over the last several decades.

Political instability has plagued all countries of the region. Both Bangladesh and Pakistan have experienced military rules for more than half their existence as independent nations. In Pakistan generals still have their say in politics as recent events leading to the president being forced to resign suggest. Sri Lanka has been fighting a prolonged civil war for more than a decade. In the early 1970s it had to fight armed insurgency. Armed insurgencies with propensity for separatism or greater autonomy have been or are quite common in various parts of India. Until recently, for more than two decades Bangladesh had been fighting an armed insurgency in its northeastern part. India has had experienced minority governments at the centre since the 1990s but since 1996 successive unstable coalition governments. All these highlight problems of governance. On the positive side India always had democratically elected governments. In recent years all the countries in the Indian sub-continent have democratically elected governments in the 1990s.

As discussed elsewhere (Alauddin and Tisdell 1998; Hasan 1998a) high population growth, greater need for human settlement, urbanisation and extension of agricultural practices to marginal areas have taken a heavy toll on both the urban and the rural environments in South Asia. The green revolution has had a significant impact in increasing overall food production for millions of extra mouths to be fed. However, it rests on a narrow base and environmental problems have resulted from greater intensification of agriculture especially associated with the green revolution (Alauddin and Tisdell 1991; Mellor 1994). However, recent evidence seems to indicate that agricultural growth in South Asia may be tapering off (Shand and Alauddin 1997; Shand and Kalirajan 1997; Shand and Bhati 1997).

While the growth and changes in South Asia have been significant in supporting a growing population they have not resulted in a significant rise in the living standards of the mass of population. In South Asia significant manifestations of *inter alia* mass poverty, illiteracy, malnutrition, deprivation and poor sanitation still exist. According to *Human Development Report 1996* (UNDP 1996a, p.41): Safe drinking water is not available to a fifth of the population; about one third of the population are still illiterate, only half the entrants to grade 1 reach grade 5; half the world poor live in South Asia; nearly 85 million children under five are malnourished; between 1960 and 2000 the urban population is expected to nearly double as a share of the total population from 17 per cent to 30 per cent stretching the urban infrastructure to the limit.

These are sobering statistics indeed. Several measures of human development have recently been developed (see for example UNDP 1996a, pp.106–9). All these measures are primarily based on the conceptual underpinnings of the human development index (HDI) and complement or supplement one another. These are:

- **Human Development Index (HDI)** based on three indicators: longevity proxied by life expectancy at birth, educational attainment as messier by a combination of adult literacy and combined primary, secondary and tertiary enrolment rates, and standard of living measured by real GDP per capita (in terms of purchasing power parity dollars)

- **Gender-related Development Index (GDI)** based on the same indicators as HDI but adjusted by the average achievement of each country in life expectancy, educational attainment and income in accordance with the disparity in achievement between male and female

- **Gender Empowerment Measure (GEM)** based on indicators to measure the relative empowerment of men and women in political and economic spheres: parliamentary representation; managerial and administrative positions; professional and technical positions; shares of males and females in economically active population; incomes shares

- **Capability Poverty Measure (CPM)** composed of three indicators: living a healthy and well-nourished life; having the capability of safe and healthy reproduction; and being literate and knowledgeable. The CPM focuses on people's lack of capabilities rather than on average level of capabilities as measured by the HDI

While the technical merits of these measures and their comparability intertemporally or cross-sectionally will be matters of debate among professionals, policy makers and practitioners of development (see, for example, McGillvray 1991; Alauddin and Tisdell 1998; Sengupta 1998), these have, however, unequivocally established the primacy of human development as an objective of development policy. Sengupta (1998, p.1) rightly observes '... that human development reports have brought out the quintessential problem of development economics, the relationship between income growth and equity, where the concept of equity goes much beyond equality of incomes to equality of opportunities and capabilities. That is basically what is meant by human development through the removal of poverty, illiteracy and malnutrition and expanding education, health and social security'.

In each of the above measures the countries of the South Asian region perform poorly relative to East and Southeast Asian countries where demographic transition has taken roots several decades ago. South Asia is yet to come anywhere near that stage (S. Chakravarty 1990). This is despite the recent economic crises that have beset these countries.

In the light of the preceding discussion it seems clear that the South Asian economies have achieved mixed results in respect of economic development. Like rest of the developing world this region has not recognised the close complementarity even synergy involving development, governance and the environment. The development-governance-environment interactions and outcomes in the South Asian context are illustrated in Figure 19.1.

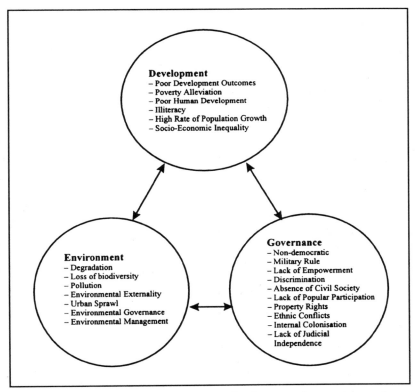

Figure 19.1　Development-Governance-Environment interactions and outcomes in the South Asian context

19.3   TRANSBOUNDARY/BILATERAL AND GLOBAL ASPECTS
OF SOUTH ASIAN ISSUES

The last decade or so has witnessed a growing openness and global interdependence from this change. Transboundary and global nature of political, economic and social changes are assuming increasing significance in South Asia but a number of issues that have been of importance for several decades.

19.3.1   Transboundary/bilateral issues of importance in South Asia

There are several aspects of transboundary issues in South Asia. These include resources, governance, economic and environmental matters and their interactions.

Shared water resources In particular, have been a bone of contention among various countries. For instance, a number of rivers are shared between more than one country: The Indus between India and Pakistan, the Ganges/Padma between India and Bangladesh, and the Brahmaputra among China, India and Bangladesh. Agreement through The Indus River Treaty was reached between India and Pakistan on sharing the water of the Indus in 1960. After decades of acrimony (see, for example, Crow et al. 1995; see also Bramer 1990b; Prins 1990). Bangladesh and India have reached agreement on sharing of the waters of the Ganges. The Brahmaputra does not appear to have been the source of international agreement, presumably because its waterflows are adequate to meet current needs. Nevertheless, deforestation in its headwaters appears to be increasing its sediment load and this has potential international environmental effects, for example, siltation and deforestation in its headwaters may be increasing the seasonal variability of the Brahmaputra's flow (see also Alauddin and Tisdell 1998, Chapter 3).[1] The Ganges is about 2,600 kilometres long while the length of the Brahmaputra is 2 800 kilometres. However, only 7.5 per cent of the total catchment area of the three major rivers – the Ganges, the Brahmaputra-Jamuna and the Meghna lies within Bangladesh and 90 per cent of Bangladesh's flood waters originate from India (Bramer 1990a, p.13; Ipe 1995). These are caused *inter alia* by: (1) excessive snow-melt due to rise in temperature in the Himalayas; (2) heavy rainfall over the Himalayas, India, Nepal and Bhutan (Bramer 1990a). Of the 2.4 billion tonnes of sediments that the Bangladesh rivers carry annually to the Bay of Bengal, the Ganges alone carries about sixty per cent or 1.5 billion tonnes (Brown and Wolf 1984, p.15). A large portion of this reaches the Bay of Bengal through Bangladesh.

The Treaty between India and Bangladesh (entered into in December 1996) on the sharing of the waters of the Ganges at Farakka, involves sharing on a 50–50 basis if the flow at Farakka of the Ganges is 70,000 cusec or less in a ten day period, 35,000 cusecs to Bangladesh if the flow is 70,000–75,000 cusecs with India's maximum off-take being 40 000 cusecs in a ten day period with excess water being available to Bangladesh. However, there has never been any attempt to augment the flow of the water during season (Crow et al. 1995). Nevertheless, the Treaty represents progress in the sharing of a transboundary natural resource. One might note that in the absence of any agreement Bangladesh received a much smaller volume of the Ganges water. For instance, in March 1993 flow in the Ganges at Hardinge Birdge was as low as 9,761 cusecs (Crow et al. 1995, p.219).

The Ganges Water Treaty however makes no provision for the quality of the water entering Bangladesh. The Ganges is seriously polluted as might be other rivers entering Bangladesh from India. Similar is the case with the Indus flowing from India into Pakistan. While agreement extends to sharing of the waterflows, there does not appear to be any agreement on the control of pollution emissions to these rivers. Consequently, the waters of the Indus, for example, are becoming increasingly polluted. Thus pollution seems to be a transboundary problem. Another example of this is the recent problem of arsenic pollution in the ground water in many parts of Bangladesh (MLG 1995; MOA 1994; Siddique 1995) and the Indian State of West Bengal (JU 1994) clearly exemplifies the transboundary nature of a serious environmental problem (D. Chakraborty 1995).[2]

The ongoing civil war in Sri Lanka for more than a decade has implications beyond its frontiers and remains a problem in the relation between India and Sri Lanka. The South Indian state of Tamil Nadu is sympathetic to the Tamil Tigers fighting for a separate homeland in the Jaffna Peninsula, just south of Tamil Nadu. India's apparent attempt in the late 1980s to get tough with the Tamil rebels did not succeed. As a revenge the former Indian Prime Minister Rajib Gandhi was assassinated in 1991.

The disputed region of Kashmir has been a point of disagreement between India and Pakistan since the end of the colonial era more than fifty years ago. The countries have been in a state of war over Kashmir ever since. A disproportionately high share of the budget is spent on defence. Both countries have tried (and continue to try) to outmanoeuvre one another with achieving superiority in military hardware. The latest manifestation of this is the series of nuclear testings in May 1998 by both countries.

The civil war in Chittagong Hill Tracts of Bangladesh had been going on for more than two decades until the recently signed peace Treaty between the Bangladesh Government and the *Parbattya Chattagram Jana Shanghati*

Samity (PCJSS, Chittagong Hill Tracts People's Solidarity Association). During this two decade-long civil war many tribals took sanctuary in the neighbouring Indian State of Tripura as well as other adjoining states of India and continued armed struggle against Bangladesh government from across the border. Over the years cross borders trafficking by armed insurgents of both sides have been fairly common.

The above issues apart there are some other transboundary/bilateral issues of importance in the region. These include *inter alia*: (1) repatriation of Pakistani nationals living in refugee camps in Bangladesh and settlement of Bangladesh's share in wealth and assets under Pakistani control since the former's independence from the latter; (2) Nepal-Bhutan refugee problems; (3) Indo-Nepal and Indo-Bhutan transit issues for port access in Bangladesh.

19.3.2 South Asian issues in global context: The mutual interdependence

On a global scale, South Asia is economically, environmentally and geopolitically significant. The region's economic growth and development, environment and political stability is important to the rest of the world. Conversely the rest of the world also has significant impacts on the South Asian region or potentially so (see also Alauddin and Tisdell 1998, especially Chapter 1 and Chapter 11). Some of these mutual interdependencies that can arise are as follows:

The sheer size of South Asia itself is globally important. Currently more than a fifth of the world population inhabit this region. With current population growth rate the relative importance of South Asia in world population will increase even further in the future (see for example Tisdell 1991; see also Chapter 2 of this volume). Its economic growth along with that of China is likely to have a significant effect on its as well the global environment. This is likely to result from a significant emission of greenhouse gases leading to changes in climatic conditions and rise in sea-level.

South Asia as a whole is a significant storehouse of bio-diversity and loss in bio-diversity in this region will be an international loss. These include the Royal Bengal Tiger, spotted deer and the world's largest mangrove forests in both the Indian and Bangladesh parts of the Sunderbans. As argued by Alauddin and Tisdell (1998, Chapter 2) substantial biodiversity loss has occurred in South Asia and the process is continuing in that every year 4 million hectares of land are deforested (UNDP 1996a, p.41; WRI-UNEP-UNDP 1994). However, India, in relation to other low income countries and especially relative to her neighbours, has a higher proportion of its land in protected areas while Bangladesh has the lowest percentage of land in protected areas (Alauddin and Tisdell 1998; WRI-UNEP-UNDP 1994). In so far as the international community values biodiversity, loss of biodiversity in South Asia has global consequences. The preservation of biodiversity can, however, impose high costs on low-income countries, although there can be circumstances where they themselves benefit economically from the conservation of natural environments. Each case must be assessed individually. Where a local community would be disadvantaged economically by engaging in nature conservation, but the international community's gain from conservation would exceed the loss of the locals, all could gain if the international community were to compensate locals adequately for any loss from engaging in nature conservation. However, it is sometimes difficult to devise suitable income transfer mechanisms. Furthermore, such transfers involve transaction costs that have to be offset against any benefits otherwise obtained.

It is now widely recognised that much of economic growth in the contemporary developing world has resulted from resource-depletion both in terms of quality and quantity (Repetto et al.. 1989; Thamapillai and Uhlin 1995). South Asia is not an exception. If this process continues and if as a result the future economic growth in South Asia cannot be sustained, the countries of the region may find it difficult or unable to meet the basic needs of their population. Such an economic melt-down is likely to pose a massive humanitarian problem for the rest of the world.

Environmental goods do not have a 'market' in the usual sense of the term. Therefore, environmental goods are underpriced or unpriced there is a high propensity to 'overuse' the environment (Pearce 1993). To what extent is the divergence between social costs and private costs, and social benefits and private benefits resulting from environmental externalities are being addressed in business decisions? Given that the overall concern with the environment is of recent origin and that the environmental issues are yet to be fully incorporated in policy decisions, the probability of that may not be very high. As Alauddin and Tisdell (1998, p.10) argue that a failure to internalise environmental costs in decision-making could result in South Asia being engaged in 'unfair and unjust' production for international trade. With South Asia in structural reform mode such policies may assume even greater global significance.

South Asian countries are increasing the use of fossil fuel over time. As a result the air pollution is on the increase. Bangladesh's capital, Dhaka has one of the highest lead content in its air in the world. High level of air pollution may be present in other South Asian cities. In the period between 1980 and 1994 commercial energy use in South Asian countries increased at rates faster than for those by low income countries as a whole. The magnitudes of increases in use of commercial energy in South Asia are: Bangladesh and Sri Lanka 2.5-fold, Nepal more than 3-fold, India more than 2-fold, Pakistan approximately 3-fold (World Bank 1997b, p.228). Based on the *World Development Report 1997* (World Bank 1997b, p.229), India's carbon dioxide emissions from its use of commercial energy amounted to 769 million tonnes. While it is less than 30 per cent of China's level (2668 million tonnes), they exceeded those of many high income countries, e.g. United Kingdom (566 million tonnes). But the emissions of the United Sates at 4881 metric tonnes were more than six times as high and Japan's emissions at 1093 million tonnes were 40 per cent higher than India's. For Germany the carbondioxide emissions actually fell from 1068 million tonnes in 1980 to 878 million tonnes in 1992. A similar trend could be observed for the United Kingdom during the period under consideration. Between 1980 and 1992 carbondioxide emissions for South Asia as a whole more than doubled compared to a 1.4-fold increase for all high income countries taken together. In per capita terms, however, low income countries including those in South Asia while differing widely among themselves emit only a fraction of those by the high income countries.

At the same time as South Asia is becoming an increasingly important source of greenhouse gas emissions, it is likely to be seriously affected by a rise in the sea level with serious consequences for the region. According to Buchdal (1996), for example, a rise in the sea level of 1.5 metres would flood one-fifth of all farmland of Bangladesh, equivalent to a 21.3 per cent loss in agricultural production. Consequences similar to that or of lesser intensity for vast coastline of India or other countries in the region may not be completely ruled out.

Issues of global warming, El Niño effects, sea level rises, green house gas emissions outside South Asia is likely are impact on the region. International conventions, such as the Convention on Biodiversity, Nuclear Non-Proliferation Treaty, Conference on Global Warming, UN Conference on Environment and Development (Agenda 21, UNCED 1992) would have implications for South Asia.

Strings attached to and conditions imposed on various forms of foreign aid and loans at bilateral and multilateral levels can set the tone of the domestic policy agenda as some of the countries e.g. Bangladesh is heavily dependent on foreign economic assistance. Furthermore, external pressures to economic reforms e.g. adopt structural adjustment policies may have environmental implications. Influence from the rest of the world on international trade where, for example, this trade is restricted by non-tariff barriers such environmental prerequisites, child labour free production environment, human rights issues, international sanctions. The transboundary and global aspects of South Asian issues are illustrated in Figure 19.2 and Figure 19.3.

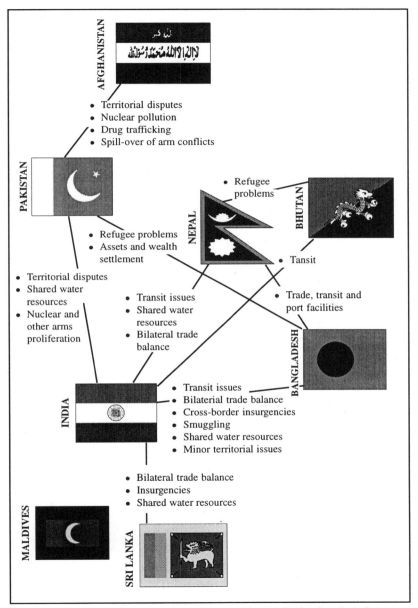

Figure 19.2   Major transboundary/bilateral issues in the South Asian context

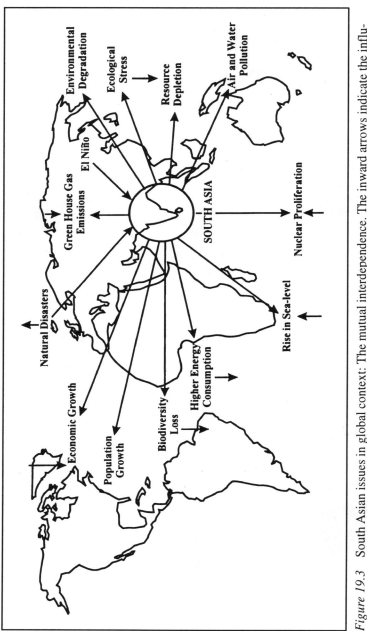

Figure 19.3   South Asian issues in global context: The mutual interdependence. The inward arrows indicate the influence on South Asia of the events and factors external to the region. The outward arrows indicate the implications of changes in South Asia for the rest of the world.

19.4   CHALLENGES AND PROSPECTS

In the light of the earlier discussion in this chapter and the analysis embodied in various contributions to this volume there is no denying the fact despite significant progress the problems of extreme poverty, hunger, disease, malnutrition and a deteriorating physical environment remain in South Asia. Nowhere on earth is there anything like such an enormous mass of population living in poverty. Just as great or even greater incidence of poverty may perhaps exist in other parts of the world, for instance, Afghanistan, or in parts of Sub-Saharan Africa

Historical experience of many contemporary high income countries supports the hypothesis that pollution and environmental degradation intensities at first rise with economic development, but eventually decline as income levels reach higher levels (see for example, Panayotou 1995). This is known as the environmental Kuznets curve reminiscent of the inverted U-shaped relationship between income inequality and income per capita (Kuznets 1965; 1966). This, therefore, suggests that broadly speaking, economic growth is the eventual solution to increased economic welfare and improved environmental conditions. One might be tempted to indicate that South Asian countries might try to emulate the growth patterns and processes that were adopted by Western countries. These entail polluting now and cleaning up later as well as and converting the 'maximum' amount of natural resource capital into man-made capital.

However, as Alauddin and Tisdell (1998, pp.198–99) point out that there are a number of possible difficulties for this approach that involves very weak conditions for sustainable development. These include *inter alia*:

- Rapid accumulation of greenhouse gases with South Asia and China becoming major contributor to greenhouse gas emissions as these countries become more industrialised

- Rising total pollution despite falling pollution intensities, e.g. per capita or per unit of output

- Irreversibility of some environmental impacts

- Cross-country variation in the appropriate composition between natural and environmental resources on the one hand and man-made capital on the other. It could be to South Asia's advantage, for example, to retain a higher ratio of natural resources and environmental capital relative to other resources than in other parts of the world

The above problems apart, the world is more polluted now than when the contemporary developed countries embarked on industrialisation and experienced greater pollution intensity. Furthermore, the contemporary industrialised countries were colonial powers and in the process of converting natural and environmental capital to man-made capital they inflicted greater destruction to the natural environments of their colonies than to their own. In examining the relevance of historical experience of contemporary developed countries to the Third World, Todaro (1997, pp.121–2) concludes that 'due to very different initial conditions, the historical experience of Western economic growth is only of limited relevance to the contemporary Third World nations'.[3]

The challenges that South Asia currently faces in achieving economic development consistent with good governance and a sustainable environment are formidable. They are no less formidable than those they faced at birth as independent nations. However, there is a positive side as well. Several decades ago South Asia had very little experience in terms of skilled man power, competent bureaucracy, managerial skills, flexible political institutions to support massive and ambitious development programmes. That problem still remains but the lessons of experience seem clear.

This also underscores, as Todaro (1997, pp.121–2) points out, 'the critical importance of concomitant and complementary technological, social and institutional changes, which must take place if long term economic growth is to be realized'. However, 'unless there is some structural and, attitudinal and institutional reform in the world economy, one that accommodates the rising aspirations and rewards the outstanding performances of individual developing nations, internal economic and social transformation within the Third World may be insufficient' (Todaro 1997, p.122). While there is enough truth in the Schumpeterian view that every case in economic development is a historic individual, in a world of increasing global interdependence developing economies need to show capacity for assimilating reforms thrust upon them from outside to be in accord with their own progress so that they can exert a stimulating effect on the economies concerned.[4]

Externally induced reforms such as trade liberalisation and other structural reforms including privatisation, price deregulation and similar microeconomic reforms unleash forces with significant effects on the society and the economy. These may take the form of closure of inefficient industrial units unable to compete with cheaper imports from abroad and consequent job losses and their impact on the livelihoods of the consequentially unemployed and those who have been dependent on their financial support.

In case of Bangladesh according to a recent report (Islam 1998) 'trade liberalisation – removal of non-tariff barriers and reduction of import duties – has adversely affected some 7,000 businesses, mainly small and medium enterprises. ... An ailing textile industry .. the biggest employer after agriculture, has been laying off workers, and shutting down units...'. Against global competition the local enterprises could face mounting losses and go out of business retrenching tens thousands of employees. Businesses warn that unless government takes initiatives to improve infrastructure including power supply, transportation, port facilities, services like customs facilities, quick government clearance in relevant matters, the local industry will find it very difficult to compete in the face of influx of foreign goods. Corruption and smuggling compound the problem even further.

Unfettered market mechanism may not necessarily be the panacea for all economic ills. One has to be aware that markets do fail and the causes of market failure cannot be dismissed lightly. Furthermore, as pointed out in an earlier section and as Pearce et al. (1989, p.51) argue '... if we leave the allocation of resources to the unfettered market, it will tend to *overuse* the services of natural environments'.

The social consequences of the economic liberalisation cannot be ignored as the pace of changes can inject fear of insecurity and the disadvantaged may feel disenfranchised, dispossessed and a sense of alienation. The opposing forces can prey on these fears of the unknown and seemingly succeed in arresting the momentum of the reform process if not in derailing it.[5] For instance, the reformist government of Prime Minister Narasimha Rao in India was swept out of office in the 1996 general elections which brought in its place a shaky coalition of opposing ideologies putting the reform process itself in considerable doubt. Continuing instability within the coalition and its subsequent collapse led to the premature general election in less than two years. The latest election results presented yet another shaky coalition government led by a religious fundamentalist party. This government by far seems to be the most inward-looking in orientation and least visionary in the history of independent India.

No plan or programme however well formulated can be fully implemented or have the desired results unless there is a total commitment on the part of the people or if significant section of the community is alienated or effectively economically disenfranchised. Despite sporadic success the overall policy discourse in South Asia is epitomised by trickle-down or top-down approaches. Valuable resources have been wasted by resorting to macroeconomic populism or planning by exhortation without real leadership rather than building institutions of critical importance for sustained economic and social progress. Misallocation of resources of much greater magnitude has occurred in order to legitimise the inherently illegimate regimes usurping state power through extra-constitutional means. Planners, policy makers and above all political leadership must resist the temptation of populism at the expense of quality of policies and must generate popular enthusiasm. To quote Lewis (1951, p.128), 'Popular enthusiasm is both a lubricating oil of planning and the petrol of economic development – dynamic force that makes all things possible. Even the most backward country will progress rapidly if its government knows how to tap this dynamic force'.

Religion has been the most outstanding source of political rivalry among people in the Indian subcontinent (A.R. Khan 1972, p.3). Despite India's division along religious lines, religion was in the background for quite sometime especially in the 1970s when Bangladesh emerged as an independent country. However, in recent years there has been a resurgence of politics based on religion or religious sentiments. Furthermore, the rise of Taliban Movement in Afghanistan will have significant ramifications for the neighbouring countries of the South Asian region especially Pakistan and India. For the first few decades of their existence as independent nations India and Pakistan have been at loggerheads spilling into open warfare on more than one occasion and have been fighting an incessant war of attrition. In the process of this, they have wasted valuable resources on defence budgets to maintain an oversized army instead of investing in social infrastructure especially education leading to demographic transition. Herein lies the difference between East Asia and South Asia (Haq 1998) their present difficulties notwithstanding.

19.5   CONCLUDING COMMENTS

To sum up, a critical appraisal of South Asia's development during the last few decades epitomises poor development priorities: more money on defence (especially India and Pakistan) than on education, health and the social sectors, lack of popular participation in the development process, lack of empowerment of the mass of population especially women, discrimination on the basis of ethnicity, gender and religion, environmental degradation and poor governance. In essence, development process in South Asia has not been sufficiently *humanised* (Bernstein 1992; Haq 1998) and *environmentalised* (Alauddin and Tisdell 1998).

In the background of the sobering statistics presented earlier in this chapter, South Asia is walking a tightrope as it strives for development with a view to enhancing living standards of the masses of population embracing the linkage involving development, governance and the environment. While one should not be unduly pessimistic, there is cause for concern as the region tries to extricate itself from a low-level equilibrium growth trap.

Acknowledgements

With usual *caveats* the author wishes to thank Professor Clem Tisdell, Dr Samiul Hasan and an anonymous referee for useful comments and suggestions on earlier drafts.

Notes

1   The combined discharge of water of the major river system, originating in the Himalayas is second only to the Amazon river which carries more water than any other river in the world. There is a great seasonality in the discharge of the Bangladesh river system: about two hundred thousand cubic metres per second during the peak monsoon season and about eight thousand cubic metres during the dry season (Hasan 1996, pp.232–33).

2   A recent example of tansboundary nature of environmental problem is forest fire in Indonesia which caused considerable air pollution in neighbouring Malaysia and Singapore.

3   In the context of pattern of labour transfer from agricultural to non-agricultural sectors Alauddin and Tisdell (1998, p.79) express a similar view in respect of extrapolating the development experience of contemporary developed countries of East Asia or of the West.

4   See, for example, Allen (1962, pp.190–91) in the context of postwar Japan. In the context of technology transfer Solo (1966) underscores the need for the LDCs to acquire capacity to assimilate advanced technology.

5   For example, the One Nation Party in Australia despite its simplistic policies offering no real solution to people's problems owes its rise and electoral success in the Queensland elections in June 1998 to the successful preying on the sense of vulnerability, alienation, disenfranchisement, weariness and to some extent ignorance of a significant percentage of the population. Despite failing to win a seat in the lower house of the Australian Parliament, the One Nation Party has polled more than 10 per cent of the votes cast in the federal elections held in October 1998.

Bibliography

Abdelgabar, M. E. A. R. (1987) 'The Role of Non-Governmental Organisations in Regional Development in Sudan', *Planning and Administration*, **14**(1), pp.93–9.

ADB (1993) *Annual Report*, Manila: Asian Development Bank.

ADB (1995a) *Asian Development Bank Annual Report 1995,* Manila: Asian Development Bank.

ADB (1995b) *Industry Sector Policy Review, Sri Lanka.* Canberra: Centre for International Economics.

ADB (various years) *Asian Development Outlook*, Manila: Asian Development Bank.

ADB/NACA (1996) *Aquaculture Sustainability Action Plan, Regional Study and Workshop on Aquaculture Sustainability and the Environment (RETA 5534)*, Asian Development Bank and the Network of Aquaculture Centres in Asia-Pacific, Bangkok, Thailand: The Network of Aquaculture Centres in Asia-Pacific.

Agarwal, B. (1986) 'Women, and Poverty and Agricultural Growth in India', *Journal of Peasant Studies*, **13**(4), pp.165–220.

Agarwal, B. (1989) 'Rural Women, Poverty and Natural Resources: Sustenance, Sustainability and Struggle for Change', *Economic and Political Weekly*, **24**(3), pp.ws46–ws65.

Ahluwalia, I. J. and Little, I. M. D. (eds. 1998) *India's Economic Reforms and Development*, New Delhi: Oxford University Press.

Ahluwalia, M. S. (1998) 'Infrastructure Development in India's Reforms' in Ahluwalia and Little (eds.), pp.87–121.

Ahmad, M. (1987) *State and Development: Essays on Public Enterprise*, Dhaka: University Press Ltd.

Ahmad, Q. K. (1998) 'Economic Reforms, People's Participation and Development in Bangladesh', National Professor Atwar Hussain Memorial Lecture 1998, The Asiatic Society of Bangladesh, Dhaka: Bangladesh Unnayan Parishad.

Ahmad, Q. K. and Hossain, Mahabub (1979) 'Economic Development Through People's Participation on a Self-Help Basis: Lessons from Ulashi, Bangladesh' in Friedmann, J. and Weaver, C., *Territory and Function: The Evolution of Regional Planning*, Berkeley: University of California Press, pp. 217–25.

Ahmad, S., Haq, N., Hossain, S. M. and Razzaque, M. A. (1997) 'Quality of Public Investment in Bangladesh', in Sobhan (ed.), pp.495–506.

Ahmed, A. (1996) *The Macroeconomic Impact of Foreign Aid to Developing Countries*, Unpublished Ph.D thesis, Geelong, Victoria: Deakin University.

Ahmed, I. and Doeleman, J. A. (eds. 1995) *Beyond Rio: Environmental Crisis and Sustainable Livelihoods in the Third World*, London: Macmillan.

Ahmed, M. (1970) *Government and Politics in Pakistan*, Karachi: Space Publishers.

Ahmed, N. U. (1994) 'Politicians and Bureaucrats in Bangladesh's Policy-Making Process: A Re-Interpretation', *Philippine Journal of Public Administration*, **38**(3), pp.237–59.

Ahmed, N. U. (1997) 'Parliamentary Opposition in Bangladesh', *Party Politics*, **3**, pp.147–68.

Ahooja-Patel, K. (1996) 'Emerging Gender Inequalities within Asia', in Lele and Tettey (eds.) pp.124–50.

AIDAB (1994) *Australian Overseas Development Cooperation: Statistical Summary 1992–93*, Canberra: Australian International Development Assistance Bureau.

Akash, M. M (1998) 'Governance and Development' in Sobhan (ed.), pp.95–116.

Alagarswami, K. (1995) 'India', Country Paper, in FAO/NACA (1995b), pp.141–86.

Alam, S. (1991) 'State-Religion in Bangladesh: A Critique of the Eighth Amendment to the Constitution', *South Asia Journal*, **4**, pp.313–34.

Alamgir, M. (1980) *Famine in South Asia: Political Economy of Mass Starvation*, Cambridge, Massachusetts: Oelgeschlager, Gunn and Hain Publishers.

Alauddin, M. (1997) 'The Readymade Garment Industry of Bangladesh and Changing Structure of Foreign Trade', in Roy et al. (eds.), pp.99–113.

Alauddin, M. and Hamid, A. (1996) 'Economic, Social and Environmental Implications of Shrimp Farming in Bangladesh: An Overview of Issues and Agenda for Research' in Alauddin and Hasan (eds.), pp.278–99.

Alauddin, M. and Hasan, S. (eds. 1996) *Bangladesh: Economy, People, and the Environment*, Economics Conference Monograph Series 1, Brisbane, Queensland: Department of Economics, The University of Queensland.

Alauddin, M. and Tisdell, C. A. (1991) *The Green Revolution and Economic Development: The Process and Its Impact in Bangladesh*, London: Macmillan.

Alauddin, M. and Tisdell, C. A. (1998) *The Environment and Economic Development in South Asia: An Overview Concentrating on Bangladesh*, London: Macmillan.

Alauddin, M., Mujeri, M. K. and Tisdell, C. A. (1995) 'Technology-Environment-Employment Linkages and the Rural Poor of Bangladesh: Insights from Farm-Level Data', in Ahmed and Doeleman (eds.), pp.221–55.

Alesina, A. (1992) 'Political Models of Macroeconomic Policy and Fiscal Reform', Policy Research Working Paper, No. WPS 970, Washington, D. C.: World Bank.

Alesina, A. and Summers, L. (1993) 'Central Bank Independence and Macroeconomic Performance', *Journal of Money, Credit and Banking,* **25,** pp.151–62

Ali, M. Y. (1991) *Towards Sustainable Development: Fisheries Resources of Bangladesh,* Dhaka: Bangladesh Ministry of Environment and Forest and National Conservation Strategy Secretariat.

Ali, M. Yunus. (1995) *Performance of International Joint Ventures (IJVs) in Developing Countries: A Study of IJVs in Bangladesh,* Unpublished Ph.D Thesis, Wollongong, Australia: University of Wollongong.

Ali, M. Yunus. and Sim, A. B (1996) 'Psychic Distance and International Joint Venture Performance', *Proceedings of the Academy of International Business Southeast Asia Regional Conference,* University of Otago, Dunedin , New Zealand, June 17–20, pp.362–67.

Ali, S. S. (1994a) 'Conservation of Faunal Resources', in Hussain and Acharya. (eds.), pp.733–44.

Ali, S. S. (1994b) 'Sundarbans: Its Resources and Ecosystem', A paper presented at the national seminar on integrated management of Ganges flood plains and Sundarbans ecosystem, Khulna, 16–18 July.

Allen, G. C. (1962) *A Short Economic History of Modern Japan,* London: Allen and Unwin.

Aremo, J. A. (1983) 'Popular Participation in Rural Development', *Ceres* **16**(3), pp.17–20.

Areskoug, K. (1973) 'Foreign-Capital Utilization and economic Policies in Developing Countries', *Review of Economics and Statistics,* **55,** pp.182–89.

ASCC (1995) *Asian Shrimp News,* Third Quarter, Issue No. 23, Bangkok: Asian Shrimp Culture Council.

Ashraf, A., Chowdhury, S. and Streefland, P. (1982) 'Health, Disease and Health Care in Rural Bangladesh', *Social Science and Medicine,* **16,** pp.2041–54.

Athukorala, P. C. (1997) *Economic Profiles in South Asia: Sri Lanka,* Canberra: Australia South Asia Research Centre, The Australian National University.

Athukorala, P. C. and Rajapatirana, S. (1998) 'Economic Liberalization and Industrial Transformation in Sri Lanka: A Latecomer's Story', Canberra: Australia South Asia Research Centre, The Australian National University (mimeo).

Athukorala, P. C. and Shand, R. T. (1997) 'Cultivating the Pearl: Australia's Economic Relationships with Sri Lanka', Colombo: Institute of Policy Studies.

Aziz, S. (1997) Prime Minister's Economic Revival Programme Statement in the National Assembly, Minister for Finance. Islamabad.

Bakht, Z. (1997) 'Bangladesh's Industrial Performance in the 1990s: Review of Recent Empirical Evidence' in Sobhan (ed.), pp.287–302.

Banerji, S. and Fisher, H. B. (1974) 'Hierarchical Location Analysis for Integrated Area Planning in Rural India', Papers, *Regional Science Association*, **33**, pp.177–94.

Bardhan, P. (1988) 'Dominant Proprietary Classes and India's Democracy', in Kohli, A. (ed.) *India's Democracy*, Princeton, N. J.: Princeton University Press, pp.214–24.

Bardhan, P. (1993) 'Symposium on Democracy and Development', *Journal of Economic Perspectives*, **7**(3), pp.45–49.

Bardhan, P. (undated) 'The Nature of Institutional Impediments to Economic Development', Berkeley: University of California (mimeo).

Barlow, R. (1977) 'Health and Economic Development: A Theoretical and Empirical Review', Unpublished Monograph, University of Michigan, (taken from Groone, R. N. and Harkavy, O. The Role of Health in Development, *Social Science and Medicine*, **14C**, pp.165–69, (1980).

Barua, P. (1997) ' Environmental Degradation in the Sundarbans', *Weekly Bichitra*, **26**(11), pp.39–46 (*in Bangla*).

BB (various issues) *Economic Trends*, Dhaka: Bangladesh Bank.

BBS (1976–1993) *Statistical Year Book of Bangladesh*, Dhaka: Bangladesh Bureau of Statistics.

BBS (1985) *Statistical Pocket Book, 1984–85*, Dhaka: Bangladesh Bureau of Statistics.

BBS (1993) *Twenty Years of National Accounting of Bangladesh*, Dhaka: Bangladesh Bureau of Statistics.

Beneria, L. (1981) 'Conceptualising the Underestimation of Women's Economic Activities' *Journal of Development Studies*, **17**(3), pp.s10–s28.

Beneria, L. and Sen, G. (1982) 'Class and Gender Inequalities and Women's Role in Economic Development: Theoretical and Practical Implication', *Feminist Studies*, **8**(1), pp.157–76.

Bennette, C.F. (1992a) *Cooperative Extension Roles and Relationships for a New Era: Meeting Public and User Needs Through the Generation and Adoption of Practices and Technologies – An Interdependence Model and Implications,* Summary Document, Planning, Development and Evaluation, Extension Service, USDA, Washington, D. C.

Bennette, C.F. (1992b) 'A New Interdependence Model – Implications for Extension Education', *Interpaks Digest,* **1**, Urbana, Il: Interpaks.

BEPZA (1997) *Report of Bangladesh Export Processing Zone Authority,* Dhaka, Bangladesh.

Berger, P. L. (1976) *Pyramids of Sacrifice, Political Ethics and Social Change,* New York: Anchor Books.

Berghmans, L. Schoovaerts, P. and Teghem Jr., J. (1984) 'Implementation of Health facilities in a New City', *Journal of Operational Research Society,* **35**, pp.1047–54.

Bernstein, H. (1992) 'Poverty and the Poor', in Bernstein, H., Crow, B. and Johnson, H. (eds.) *Rural Livelihoods: Crises and Responses,* London: Oxford University Press, pp.13–26.

BFFEA (1995) *Leaflet,* Dhaka: Bangladesh Frozen Foods Exporters Association.

Bhagwati, J. (1993) *India in Transition: Freeing the Economy,* Oxford: Clarendon Press.

Bhagwati, J. (1994) *India in Transition: Freeing the Economy,* New Delhi: Oxford University Press.

Bhagwati, J. and Srinivasan, T.N. (1993) 'India's Economic Reforms', New Delhi: Ministry of Finance (mimeo).

Bhattacharya, D. (1997) 'Bangladesh's Manufacturing Sector in the 1990s: An Update' in Sobhan (ed.), pp.303–34.

Bifani, P. (1992) 'Environmental Degradation in Rural Areas', in Bhalla, A. S. (ed.) *Environment, Employment and Development,* Geneva: International Labour Office, pp.99–120.

Binh, T. N and McGillivray. M. (1993) 'Foreign Aid, Taxes and Public Investment: A Comment', *Journal of Development Economics,* **41**, pp.173–76.

Blair, H. W. (ed. 1989) *Can Rural Development be Financed from Below? Local Resource Mobilisation in Bangladesh,* Dhaka: University Press Limited.

BOI (1992) *List of Foreign Investment in the Private Sector,* Unpublished Internal Document, Dhaka, Bangladesh: Board of Investment.

BOI (1997a) *Investment in Bangladesh,* Dhaka, Bangladesh: Board of Investment.

BOI (1997b) *Foreign Investment in the Private Sector,* Unpublished Internal Document, Dhaka, Bangladesh: Board of Investment.

BOI (1997c) *BOI Investment Newsletter,* Issue 8, January–June 1997, Dhaka, Bangladesh: Board of Investment.

BPC (1980) *The Second Five Year Plan, 1980–85 (Draft),* Dhaka: Bangladesh Planning Commission.

BPC (1985) *Third Five–Year Plan 1985–90,* Dhaka: Bangladesh Planning Commission.

BPC (1989) *Mid-Term Review Report of Third Five Year Plan 1985–90,* Dhaka: Bangladesh Planning Commission.

BPC (1990) *The Fourth Five Year Plan, 1990–95, (Draft),* Dhaka: Bangladesh Planning Commission.

Bramer, H. (1990a) 'Floods in Bangladesh I: Geographical Background to the 1987 and 1988 Floods', *Geographical Journal,* **156**, pp.12–22.

Bramer, H. (1990b) 'Floods in Bangladesh II: Flood Mitigation and Environmental Aspects', *Geographical Journal,* **156**, pp.158–65.

Brillantes, A. B. Jr. (1994) 'Redemocratization and Decentralization in the Philippines: The Increasing Leadership Role of NGOs', *International Review of Administrative Sciences,* **60**(5), pp.575–86.

Brown, A. J. (1948) *Applied Economics: Aspects of the World Economy in War and Peace,* London: Allen and Unwin.

Brown, L. R. and Wolf, E. C. (1984) *Soil Erosion: Quiet Crisis in the World Economy,* World Watch Paper No. 60, Washington, D. C.: The World Watch Institute.

Buchdal, J. (1996) 'Global Change and its Impact on World Agriculture', Global Change Information Programme', http://www.doc.mmv.ac.uk/cric/agricul.html.

Cassen, R. and Joshi, J. (eds. 1996) *India: The Future of Economic Reform,* New Delhi: Oxford University Press.

Central Bank of the Philippines (1982–90) *Statistical Bulletin,* Manila: Government of the Philippines.

Chakraborty, D. (1995) 'Arsenic in Drinking Water in West Bengal *vis-a-vis* Bangladesh', a paper presented in a conference held in NIPSOM, Dhaka, August.

Chakravarty, S. (1990) 'Development Strategies for Growth with Equity: The South Asian Experience', *Asian Development Review,* **8**(1), pp.133–59.

Chamala, S. (1990a) 'Establishing a Group – A Participative Action Model.' in Chamala, S. and Mortiss, P. D. (eds.) *Working Together for Land Care: Group Management Skills and Strategies,* Brisbane: Australian Academic Press, pp.14–38.

Chamala, S. (1990b) 'Social and Environmental Impacts of Modernizaition of Agriculture in Developing Countries', *Environmental Impact Assessment Review*, **10**, pp.219–31.

Chamala, S. (1994) 'Working Together for Sustainable Development: Management Strategies for Agricultural Research, Extension and Rural Development.' Keynote address given to the 43rd International Course on Rural Extension held at the International Agricultural Centre, Wageningen, The Netherlands.

Chamala, S. (1995) 'Overview of Participative Approaches in Australian Land and Water Management' in Chamala, S. and Keith, K. (eds.), *Participative Approaches for Landcare: Perspectives, Policies and programmes*, Brisbane: Australian Academic Press, pp.5–42.

Chamala, S. (1996) 'New Approaches for Research and Extension for Sustainable Agriculture and Environment: Implications for Bangladesh', in Alauddin and Hasan (eds.), pp. 255–77a.

Chambers, R. (1988) 'Sustainable Rural Livelihoods: A Key Strategy for People, Environment, and Development' in Conroy, C. and Litvinoff, M. (eds.) *The Greening of Aid: Sustainable Likelihood in Practice*, London: Earthscan and IIED, pp. 1–17.

Chaudhari, S. K. (1995) *Cross-Border Trade between Bangladesh and India*, Working Paper 58, New Delhi: National Centre for Applied Economic Research

Chaudhry, M. G (1991) 'Agricultural Transformation in South Asia: Self-Sufficiency to Surplus', A paper presented at the conference on the Future of Asia-Pacific Economies, New Delhi, 11-13 March (organised by Asian and Pacific Development Centre, Malaysia).

Chaudhury, R. H. and Ahmed, N. R. (1980) *Female Status in Bangladesh*, Dhaka: Bangladesh Institute of Development Studies.

Chelliah, R. (1996) *Towards Sustainable Growth: Essays in Fiscal Sector Reforms in India*, New Delhi: Oxford University Press.

Chenery, H. B. and Eckstein, P. (1970) 'Development Alternatives for Latin America', *Journal of Political Economy*, **78**, pp.966–1006.

Chowdhury, M. K. and Gilbert, E. H. (1996) *Reforming Agricultural Extension in Bangladesh: Blending Greater Participation and Sustainability with Institutional Strengthening*, ODI Agricultural Research & Extension Network Paper No. 61.

Clark, J. (1991) *Democratizing Development: The Role of Voluntary Organizations*, London: Earthscan.

Common, M. (1995) *Sustainability and Policy: Limits to Economics*. Cambridge: Cambridge University Press.

Commonwealth Observer Group (1991) *The Parliamentary Elections in Bangladesh, 27 February 1991*, London: Commonwealth Secretariat.

Commonwealth Observer Group (1996) *The Parliamentary Elections in Bangladesh, 12 June 1996*. London: Commonwealth Secretariat.

Covey, S. R. (1990) *The 7 Habits of Highly Effective People*, Melbourne: The Business Library and Information.

Crook, R. C. and Manor, J. (1995) 'Democratic Decentralisation and Institutional Performance: Four Asian and African Experiences Compared', *Journal of Commonwealth and Comparative Politics*, **33**, pp.309–34.

Crow, B., Lindquist, A. and Wilson, D. (1995) *Sharing the Ganges: The Politics and Technology of River Development*, Dhaka: University Press Ltd.

Daily Star, 1 December 1997.

Datta, S. and Bandyopadhyay, R. (1993) 'An Application of OR in Micro-Level Planning in India', *Computers and Operations Research*, **20**, pp.121–32.

DCCI (not dated) 'Readymade Garments: Present and Future,' Dhaka: Dhaka Chamber of Commerce and Industry.

de Veer Moss, P. (1994) *Tourism and Recreation*, BGD/84/056 Project Field Document 1, Integrated Development of the Sundarbans Reserved Forest, Khulna: United Nations Development Porgramme and Food and Agriculture Organisation.

Defence Journal (1986), **12**(4), pp.44–5.

Descola, P. and Palsson, G. (eds. 1996) *Nature and Society: Anthropological Perspectives*, London: Routledge.

Diamant, A. (1966) 'Political Development: Approaches to Theory and Strategy', in Montgomery, J. and Siffin, W. (eds.) *Approaches to Development: Politics, Administration and Change*, New York: McGraw-Hill.

Diamond, L. (1997) 'Is the Third Wave Over?', *Journal of Democracy*, **7**, pp.20–37.

Dickey, D. A. and Fuller, W. A. (1981) 'Likelihood Ratio Statistics for Autoregrassive Time Series With a Unit Root', *Econometrica*, **49** (4), pp.1057–71.

Dinwiddy, C. and Teal, T. (1993) *Principles of Cost Benefit Analysis for Developing Countries*, Cambridge: Cambridge University Press.

Dornbusch, R. (1993) *Stabilisation, Debt, and Reform: Policy Analysis for Developing Countries*, New York: Harvester Wheatsheaf.

Dornbusch, R. and Edwards, S. (1991) *The Macroeconomics of Populism in Latin America*, Chicago: Chicago University Press.

Dornbusch, R. and Fischer, S. (1981) 'Budget Deficits and Inflation', in Flanders, J. and Razin, A. (eds.) *Development in an Inflationary World*, New York: Academic Press.

Drijver, C.A. and Zuiderwijk, A. B. (1991) 'Incentives for Conservation: The example of Kafue Flats, Zambia' in Erocal, D. (ed.) *Environmental Management in Developing Countries*, Paris: Development Centre, Organisation for Economic Co-operation and Development, pp.133–56.

Drysdale, P. and Garnaut, R. (1982) 'Trade Intensities and the Analysis of Bilateral Trade Flows in a Many-Country World: A Survey', *Hitotsubashi Journal of Economics*, **22**, pp.62–84.

Dubey, V. (1994) 'India: Economic Policies and Performance', in Grilli, E. and Salvatore, D. (eds.) *Economic Development*, London: Greenwood Press, pp.421–85.

Dunham, D. and Kelegama, S. (1998) 'The Second Wave of Liberalisation in Sri Lanka 1989–93: Reform and Governance', Shand (ed.), pp.70–93.

Dunning, J. H. (1988) *Multinationals, Technology and Competitiveness,* London: Unwin.

Durning, A. B. (1989) *Actions at the Grassroots: Fighting Poverty and Environmental Decline*, World Watch Paper 88, Washington DC: World Watch Institute.

Dutta, D. (1998) 'Fifty Years of Economic Development in India: Rhetoric and Reality', in Basu, P. K., Karunaratne, N. D. and Tisdell, C. A. (1998) *Fifty Years of Indian Development: India in Retrospect, Future Directions and Investment Outlook*, Economics Conference Monograph Series 5, Brisbane, Queensland: Department of Economics, The University of Queensland, pp.6–24.

Economic Survey, of India (1969–1993) New Delhi: Ministry of Planning, Government of India.

Economics News (1995) *Bangladesh Economics News*, April–July 1995.

Economist, The (British weekly) 23 November 1996, 27 September 1997.

EIU (1997) *Bangladesh: EIU Country Report,* Third Quarter 1997, London.

Elster, J. and Slagstad, R. (eds. 1988) *Constitutionalism and Democracy,* Cambridge: Cambridge University Press.

Engel, P. G. H. and Salomon, M. (1993) *Rapid Appraisal of Agricultural Knowledge Systems (RAAKS)*, version 4.0. Unpublished manual. Department of Communication and Innovation Studies, Agricultural University, Wageningen, The Netherlands.

Engle, R. F. and Granger, C. W. J. (1987) 'Cointegration and Error Correction: Representation, Estimation and Testing', *Econometrica*, **55**(2), pp.251–76.

EPBB (1995) *Exports from Bangladesh 1972–73 to 1993–94*, Dhaka: Export Promotion Bureau of Bangladesh.

EPBB (undated) *Annual Report 1993–94*, Dhaka: Export Promotion Bureau of Bangladesh.

ESCAP (1988) *Coastal Environmental Management Plan for Bangladesh*, Volume II: Final Report. Bangkok: United Nations Economic and Social Commission for Asia and the Pacific.

Esterline, M. H. (ed. 1990) *Faith in Rural Poor: Ten Paths of Rural Development*, Biographies of Raman Magsaysay Award Foundation Awardees, Lanham: University Press of America.

Expert Group on the Commercialisation of Infrastructure Projects (1996) *The India Infrastructure Report: Policy Imperatives for Growth and Welfare*, New Delhi: National Council of Applied Economic Research.

FAO (1983) Zinc and Sulphur Deficiency Project, Dhaka: United Nation Development Programme/Food and Agriculture Organisation of the United Nations.

FAO (1994a) *Aquaculture Production 1986–1992*, FAO Fisheries Circular No. 815, Rev.6, Rome: Food and Agriculture Organisation.

FAO (1994b) *Mangrove Forest Management Guidelines*, FAO Forestry Paper No. 117, Rome: Food and Agriculture Organisation.

FAO (1995) *Review of the State of World Fishery Resources: Aquaculture*, FAO Fisheries Circular No. 886, Rome: Food and Agriculture Organisation.

FAO/NACA (1995a) *Survey, and Analysis of Aquaculture Development Research Priorities and Capacities in Asia,* , FAO Fisheries Circular No. 930, Rome: Food and Agriculture Organisation.

FAO/NACA (1995b) Regional Study and Workshop on the Environmental Assessment and Management of Aquaculture Development (TCP/RAS/ 2253), *NACA Environment and Aquaculture Development Series*, No. 1 Bangkok, Thailand: Network of Aquaculture Centres in Asia–Pacific.

Farooq, G. (1996) *Election '96: NGO, the Bureaucracy, Black Money and Corruption.* Dhaka: Mimma Prokashan (*in Bangla*).

Feldman, H. (1975) *The End and the Beginning: Pakistan 1969-71*, Oxford: Oxford University Press.

Fernando, L. (1997) 'Development Planning in Sri Lanka', in Lakshman (ed.), pp.101–26.

Financial Express (Bangladesh English daily), 31 July 1997.

Fisher, H. B. and Rushton, G. (1979) 'Spatial Efficiency of Service Locations and the Regional Development Process', Papers, *Regional Science Association*, **42**, pp.83–97.

Franda, M. (1982) *Bangladesh: The First Decade*, New Delhi: South Asian Publishers Private Limited.

Frank, T. R. (1996) 'Managing Sustainable Development: Definitions, Paradigms, and Dimensions' *Sustainable Development*, **3**(1), pp. 53–60.

Frantz, T. R. (1987) 'The Role of NGOs in Strengthening of Civil Society', in.Drabek, A. G. (ed.) *Development Alternatives: The Challenge for NGOs*, New York: Pergamon Press, pp.145–60.

Frederiksen, H. (1964) *Maintenance of Malaria Eradication*, Geneva: World Health Organisation.

Freire, P. (1972) *Pedagogy of the Oppressed*, Harmondsworth: Penguin.

Fuglesang, A. and Chandler, D. (1986) *Participation As Process: What We Can Learn From Grameen Bank, Bangladesh*, Oslo: NORAD.

Gang, I. N. and Khan, H. (1990) 'Foreign Aid, Taxes, and Public Investment', *Journal of Development Economics*, **34**, pp.355–69.

Gelb, L. H. (1991) 'The Free Elections Trap', *New York Times*, 29 May, p. A23.

Ghafur, A. (1996) 'Financial Sector Reform' in Sobhan (ed.), pp.87–100.

Ghafur, A. and Chowdhury, O. H. (1988) *Financing Public Sector Development Expenditure in Selected Developing Countries: Bangladesh*, Manila: Asian Development Bank.

Gish, O. (1981) 'Health and Family Planning Services in Bangladesh: a Study of Inequality', *International Journal of Health Services*, **11**, pp.263–81.

Gledhill, A. (1959) 'Constitutional Developments in Pakistan', *Indian Yearbook of International Affairs*, **8**, pp.49–58.

GOB (1983) *Bangladesher Shadhinata Juddho* : *Dalilpatra*, Vol 3, Dhaka: Government of Bangladesh (*in Bangla*).

GOB (1985) *Bangladesher Sechhasebi Samajkalyan Protisthan Somuher Directory* V.1 Dhaka: Ministry of Social Welfare and Women's Affairs, (*in Bangla*).

GOB (1990a) *Operation Thikana, Cluster Village*, Department of Films & Publication, Dhaka: Government of Bangladesh.

GOB (1990b) *Pathakali Trust*, Department of Films, Dhaka: Government of Bangladesh.

GOB (1991a) *Industrial Policy 1991*, Ministry of Industries, Dhaka: Government of Bangladesh.

GOB (1991b) *The Constitution of the People's Republic of Bangladesh (as amended up to 10 October 1991)*, Dhaka: Government of Bangladesh.

GOB (1995) *Bangladesh: Economic Review June 1995*, Ministry of Finance, Dhaka: Government of Bangladesh.

GOB (1996) *Bangladesh: Economic Review June 1996*, Ministry of Finance, Dhaka: Government of Bangladesh.

GOB/WFP (1997) 'Government of Bangladesh/WFP Resource Allocation Map for Food Assisted Development', Dhaka: Government of Bangladesh/World Food Programme.

GOI (1996) *Economic Survey, 1995–96*, New Delhi: Ministry of Planning, Government of India

GOI (1997) *Economic Survey, 1996–97*, New Delhi: Ministry of Finance, Government of India.

GOI (1998) *Economic Survey, 1997–98*, New Delhi: Ministry of Finance, Government of India.

Goldburg, R. J. (1996) 'Benefits and Risks of a Growing Aquculture Industry', *http://www.edf.org/pubs/EDF-Letter/1996Jan/1_aquacult.html*

Goldin, I. and Mensbrugghe, V. D. (1995) 'The Uruguay Round: An Assessment of Economy-Wide Effects of Agricultural Reforms', a conference paper on the Uruguay Round and the Developing Economies, Washington D. C.: International Economics Department, World Bank.

Griffin, K. B. (1970) 'Foreign Capital, Domestic Savings and Economic Development', *Bulletin of the Oxford University Institute of Economics and Statistics*, **32**(2), pp.99–112.

Griffin, K. B. and Enos, J. L. (1970) 'Foreign Assistance: Objectives and Consequences', *Economic Development and Cultural Change*, **18**, pp.313–37.

Griffin, K. B. and Khan, A. R. (eds. 1972) *Growth and Inequality in Pakistan*, London: Macmillan.

Hakim, M. A. (1993) *Bangladesh Politics: The Shahabuddin Interregnum*, Dhaka: University Press Ltd.

Hakimi, S. L. (1964) 'Optimal Locations of Switching Centers and Absolute Centers and Medians of a Graph', *Operations Research*, **12**, pp.450–59.

Hamid, M. A. and Alauddin, M. (1996) 'The Shrimp Industry and Employment Generation in Bangladesh', in Alauddin and Hasan (eds.), pp.301–321.

Hamid, M. A. and Alauddin, M. (1998) 'Coming out of Their Homesteads? Employment for Rural Women in Shrimp Aquaculture in Coastal Bangladesh', *International Journal of Social Economics*, **25**(2–4), pp.314–37.

Hamid, S. (1994) 'Non-market Work and National Income: The Case of Bangladesh', *Bangladesh Development Studies*, **22**(2–3), pp.1–48.

Haq, M. (1976) *The Poverty Curtain: Choices for the Third World*, New York: Columbia University Press.

Haq, M. (1998) 'Can South Asia Ever get its Act Together?', *AMITECH, News from Bangladesh*, http://Bangladesh-web.com/news, 18 May.

Haq, M. N. (1978) *Pioneers of Rural Development in Bangladesh*, Bogra: Rural Development Academy.

Haque, A. (1980) 'Bangladesh in 1979: Cry for A Sovereign Parliament', *Asian Survey,* **20**, pp.217–30.

Harpham, T and Boateng, K. A. (1997) 'Urban Governance in Relation to the Operation of Urban Services in Developing Countries', *Habitat International*, **21** (1), pp. 65–77.

Hartley, A. (1996) 'The Nature and Importance of Mangrove Forests: They Must be Conserved', Coastal Greenbelt Project ADB TA 2304–BAN, Dhaka: ADB Technical Assistance Team.

Harvey, M. E., Hung, M. S. and Brown, J. R. (1974) 'The Application of a P-median Algorithm to the Identification of Nodal Hierarchies and Growth Centres', *Economic Geography*, **50**, pp.187–202.

Hasan, S. (1988a) 'Political Parties in Bangladesh: A Study of Alienation' Conference Paper, Fifth Bangladesh Political Science Association Conference, Rajshahi, Bangladesh, June (*in Bangla*).

Hasan, S. (1988b) 'Development Administration Through Local Government: Recommendations for Bangladesh', Masters Thesis, University of Waterloo, Canada.

Hasan, S. (1991) 'Development Administration in the Third World: Voluntaractive Planning for Sustainable Development in Bangladesh', Unpublished Doctoral Dissertation, University of Waterloo, Canada.

Hasan, S. (1993) 'Voluntarism and Rural Development in Bangladesh', *Asian Journal of Public Administration,* **15** (2), pp. 82–101.

Hasan, S. (1996) 'Environmental Governance in Bangladesh: Problems and Issues' in Alauddin and Hasan (eds.), pp.227–46.

Hasan, S. (1998a) 'Problems of Municipal Waste Management in Bangladesh: An Inquiry into Its Nature', *Habitat International*, **22**(2), pp.191–202.

Hasan, S. (1998b) 'Governance and Obducracy: Opposition and Planning for Development in Bangladesh', Paper presented at an international conference on 'The State in the Asia-Pacific Region', City University of Hong Kong, June.

Hasan, S. and Mulamoottil, G. and Kersell, J.E. (1992) 'Voluntary Organizations in Bangladesh: A Profile', *Environment and Urbanization*, **4**(2), pp. 196–206.

Hassan, M. K. (1997) 'The Review of Financial Sector Reform in Bangladesh', in Sobhan (ed.), pp.55–98.

Hayami, Y and Ruttan, V. W. (1985) *Agricultural Development: An International Perspective*, Baltimore, Md.: Johns Hopkins University Press.

Heady, F. (1996) *Public Administration: A Comparative Perspective*, New York: Marcel Dekker, Inc.

Heller, P. S. (1975) 'A Model of Public Fiscal Behavior in Developing Countries: Aid, Investment and Taxation', *American Economic Review*, **65**(3), pp.429–45.

Hodgson, M. J. and Valadares, C. (1983) 'The Spatial Efficiency of Health Centres in Salcette, Goa', *National Association of Geographers of India, Annals*, **3**, pp.49–58.

Holiday, October 14 and 27 1997.

Holzhausen W. (1986) *Vision Creates Hope, Reflections on Development Issues in Developing Countries and Bangladesh*, Dhaka: University Press Limited.

Hossain, A. (1995) *Inflation, Economic Growth and the Balance of Payments in Bangladesh: A Macroeconomic Study*, New Delhi: Oxford University Press.

Hossain, A. (1996a) 'Dynamics of Bangladesh's Politics', in Alauddin and Hasan (eds.), pp.163–79.

Hossain, A. (1996b) 'The State, Economic Growth and Poverty Alleviation in Bangladesh', *Politics, Administration and Change*, **26**, pp.32–51.

Hossain, A. (1996c) *Macroeconomic Issues and Policies: The Case of Bangladesh*, New Delhi: Sage Publications.

Hossain, A. (1997a) 'Institutions, Stability, and Economic Growth: The Case of Bangladesh', *Bangladesh: Democracy and Development Conference*, National Centre for South Asian Studies and RMIT, Melbourne, 22–23 March.

Hossain, A. (1997b) 'The Real Exchange Rate, Production Structure, and Trade Balance', Department of Economics, University of Newcastle, (mimeo).

Hossain, A. and Chowdhury, A. (1996) *Monetary and Financial Policies in Developing Countries: Growth and Stabilisation*, London and New York: Routledge.

Hossain, A. and Rashid, S. (1996) *In Quest of Development: The Political Economy of South Asia*, Dhaka: The University Press Limited.

Hossain, A. and Rashid, S. (1997) 'Financial Sector Reform', in Quibria, M. G. (ed.) *The Bangladesh Economy in Transition*, New Delhi: Oxford University Press, pp.221–74.

Hossain, A. and Rashid, S. (1998) 'The Political Economy of Bangladesh's Large and Growing Trade Deficits with India', Department of Economics, Newcastle: University of Newcastle, New South Wales (mimeo.).

Hossain, I., Rahman, M. A. and Rahman, M. (1997) 'Current External Sector Performance and Emerging Issues', in Sobhan (ed.), pp.161–220.

Hossain, Mahabub (1988) *Credit for Alleviation of Rural Poverty: The Grameen Bank in Bangladesh,* Washington, D. C.: International Food Policy Research Institute, Research Report No. 65.

Hughes, H. (1994) 'Development Policies and Development Performance', in Grilli, E. and Salvatore, D. (eds.) *Economic Development,* London: Greenwood Press, pp.583–615.

Huntington, S. P. (1996) 'Democracy for the Long Haul', *Journal of Democracy,* **7** (2), pp.3–13.

Huntington, S. P. (1997) 'After Twenty Years: The Future of the Third Wave', *Journal of Democracy,* **8**, pp.3–12.

Huque, A. S. (1986) 'The Illusion of Decentralisation: Local administration in Bangladesh', *International Review of Administrative Sciences,* **52**, pp.79–95.

Huque, A. S. (1995) 'Development Programmes in Bangladesh: Hardware versus Software', *Governance,* **8**, pp.281–92.

Huque, A. S. (1997) 'The Impact of Colonialism: Thoughts on Politics and Governance in Bangladesh', *Asian Affairs,* **28**, pp.15–27.

Hussain, S. (1993) *The Bangladesh Textile Complex: Focus on Readymade Garment Industry,* MBA Research Report Brisbane: University of Queensland.

Hussain, Z. and Acharya, G. (eds. 1994) *Mangroves of the Sundarbans. Volume two: Bangladesh,* Bangkok: International Union for the Conservation of Nature.

Hussain, Z. and Karim, A. (1994) 'Introduction', in Hussain and Acharya (eds.), pp.1–10.

IMF (various years) *IFS Yearbook,* Washington, D. C.: International Monetary Fund.

IMF (various issues), *Balance of Payments Yearbook,* Washington, D. C.: International Monetary Fund.

Indian Institute of Bio-Social Research and Development (1992) *Problems and Prospects of Participatory Community Development,* IBRAD Working Paper No. 15, Calcutta.

IPC (1992) *Eighth Five Year Plan, 1992–96,* Vols. I and II, New Delhi: Indian Planning Commission.

IPC (1998) *Draft Ninth Five Year Plan, 1997–2002.* Vols. I and II, New Delhi: Indian Planning Commission.

Ipe, C. V. (1995) 'Issues in the Management of the Environment and Natural Resources in Bangladesh', *Journal of Environmental Management*, **45**, pp.319–32.

Islam, N. (1977) *Development Planning in Bangladesh: A General Study of Political Economy*, New York: St. Martin's Press.

Islam, R. (1983) 'The Status of the Unilateral Declaration of Independence in International Law: The Case of Bangladesh,' *Indian Journal of International Law*, **23**, pp.1–16.

Islam, R. (1987a) *The Bangladesh Liberation Movement: International Legal Implications*, Dhaka: University Press Ltd.

Islam, R. (1987b) 'The Seventh Amendment to the Constitution of Bangladesh: A Constitutional Appraisal', *Political Quarterly*, **58**, pp.312–29.

Islam, R. (1987c) 'The Separation of Powers and the Checks and Balances Between the President and Parliament of Bangladesh', *Lawasia*, **6**, pp.177–89.

Islam, R. (1996) 'Free and Fair Elections in Bangladesh under The Thirteenth Amendment: A Politico-Legal Post-Mortem', *Politics, Administration and Change*, **26**, pp.18–31.

Islam, S. S. (1987) 'Bangladesh in 1986: Entering A New Phase', *Asian Survey*, **27**(2), pp.163–70.

Islam, T. (1998) 'Trade Liberalisation Kills Bangladeshi Small Businesses', *AMITECH, News from Bangladesh*, http://Bangladesh-web.com/news, 28 July.

Ittefaq (Internet edition), 8 January 1998.

IUCN-UNEP-WWF (1990) *Caring for the World: A Strategy for Sustainability*, Glands: Switzerland, International Union for the Conservation of Nature.

Jahan, N. and Alauddin, M. (1996) 'Have Women lost out in the Development Process? Some Evidence from Rural Bangladesh' *International Journal of Social Economics*, **23**(4–6), pp.370–90.

Jahan, R. (1972) *Pakistan: Failure in National Integration*, New York: Columbia University Press.

Jahan, N. (1996) 'Agrarian Change and Rural Poverty in Bangladesh: Gender Dimensions', in Alauddin and Hasan (eds.), pp.83–105.

Jahan, N. (1997) *Changing Agricultural Productivity in Bangladesh: Its Impact and Implications for Poverty, Women, Off-farm Employment and the Environment*, unpublished Ph.D Thesis, Brisbane: Department of Economics, The University of Queensland.

Jalan, B. (1996) *India's Economic Policy: Preparing for the Twenty-First Century*, New Delhi: Viking Penguin India.

Jayasinghe, J. M. P. K. (1995) 'Sri Lanka', Country Paper, in FAO/NACA (1995b), pp.357–76.

Joseph, S. C. and Russell, S. S. (1980) 'Is Primary Care Wave of the Future?', *Social Science and Medicine*, **14C**, pp.137–44.

Joshi, V. and Little, I. M. D. (1996) *India's Economic Reforms 1991–2001*, New Delhi: Oxford University Press.

JU (1994) 'Arsenic in Groundwater in Six Districts of West Bengal, India: The Biggest Arsenic Calamity in the World', Calcutta: Jadavpur University, School of Environmental Studies.

Kalirajan, K. (1983) 'South-South Cooperation: Trade Relation between Indonesia and South Asia', *Pakistan Development Review*, **22**(4), pp.261–82.

Kardar, S. (1998) 'Privatisation in Pakistan' in Shand (ed.), pp.366–79.

Karim, M. and Aftabuzzaman (1995) 'Brackish and Marine Water Aquaculture Development and Management', A Paper presented at a seminar on the occasion of Fish Fortnight 1995, Dhaka: August 29.

Karim, N. H. (1994) 'Achievements of BRRI on Gender Issues in Agriculture', in Ahmed, N. U. and Miah, M. A. M. (eds.) *Gender Issues in Agriculture*, Dhaka: Bangladesh Agricultural Research Council, pp.39–50.

Kashem, A. (1996) 'Chingri Chashe Biplabattak Utpadan ebong Raptani Aye', *The Daily Ittefaq,* 25 February *(in Bangla)*.

Kelegama, S. (1997) 'Privatisation: An Overview of the Process and Issues' in Lakshman (ed.), pp.456–96.

Kelegama, S. (1998) 'Privatization and the Public Exchequer: Some Observations from the Sri Lankan Experience', Paper prepared for the Seminar on 50 Years of Independent Sri Lanka: Economic Development 1948–1998 and Prospects. Tangerine Hotel, Kalutara, March (mimeo).

Khan, A. R. (1972) *The Economy of Bangladesh*, London: Macmillan.

Khan, H. A. and Hoshino, E. (1992) 'Impact of Foreign Aid on the Fiscal Behavior of LDC Governments', *World Development*, **20**(10), pp.1481–88.

Khan, M. Ashgar (1983) *Generals in Politics*, New Delhi: Vikas Publishers.

Khan, M. Adil (1996) 'Sustainable Development: The Key Concepts, Issues, and Implications' *Sustainable Development* **3**(1), pp. 63–9.

Khan, M. and Zafarullah, H. (1979) 'The 1979 Parliamentary Elections in Bangladesh', *Asian Survey*, **19**, pp.1023–36.

Khan, M. M. and Ahmad, A. K. M (1997) 'Dimensions of Governance' in Quibria (ed.), pp.302–26.

Khan, M. M. and Zafarullah, H. M. (1979) 'The 1979 Parliament Election in Bangladesh' *Asian Survey,* **19**(10), pp.1023–36.

Khan, S. (1997) 'Blind Power, Brewing Storm', *Holiday,* 27 October.

Khan, Z. R. (1983) *Leadership in the Least Developed Nation: Bangladesh,* New York: Maxwell School of Citizenship and Public Affairs, Syracuse University.

Khan, Z. R. (1993) 'Bangladesh in 1992: Dilemmas of Democratization', *Asian Survey,* **33**(2) pp.150–56.

Khan, Z. R. (1994) 'Bangladesh in 1993: Values, Identity and Development', *Asian Survey,* **34**(2), pp.160–67.

Khan, Z. R. (1997a) 'Bangladesh's Experiment With Parliamentary Democracy', *Asian Survey,* **37**(6), pp.575–89.

Khan, Z. R. (1997b) 'Repugnant Act', *Holiday,* 24 September.

Khilji, N. M. and Zampelli, E. M. (1991) 'The Fungibility of US Assistance to Developing Countries and the Impact on Recipient Expenditures: A Case Study of Pakistan', *World Development,* **19**(1) pp.1095–1105.

Khuda, B. (1982) *The Use of Time and Underemployment in Rural Bangladesh,* Dhaka: University of Dhaka.

King, M. (1966) *Medical Care in Developing Countries,* New York: Oxford University Press.

Kinnucan, H. W. and Wessels, C. R. (1997) 'Marketing Research Paradigms for Aquaculture', *Aquculture Economics and Management,* **1**(1), pp.73–86.

Knowles, J. H. (1980) 'Health, Population and Development', *Social Science and Medicine,* **14C**, pp.67–70.

Kochanek, S. A. (1997) 'Bangladesh in 1996: The 25th Year of Independence', *Asian Survey,* **37**, pp.136–42.

Kojima, K. (1964) 'The Pattern of International Trade among Advanced Countries', *Hitotsubashi Journal of Economics,* **5**, pp.16–36.

Koutsoyiannis, A. (1977) *Theory of Econometrics* London: Macmillan, (2nd Edition).

Krishna, R. (1988) 'Ideology and Economic Policy', *Indian Economic Review,* **23**(1), pp.1–25.

Kuznets, S. (1965) *Economic Growth and Structural Change,* New York: Norton.

Kuznets, S. (1966) *Modern Economic Growth,* New Haven, Conn.: Yale University Press.

Lakshman, W.D. (ed. 1998) *Dilemmas of Development: Fifty Years of Economic Change in Sri Lanka,* Colombo: Sri Lanka Association of Economists.

Lall, S. (1994) 'Industrial Policy: The Role of Government in Promoting Industrial Technological Development', UNCTAD Review, Geneva: United Nations.

Leibenstein, H. (1957) *Economic Backwardness and Economic Development: Studies in the Theory of Economic Development*, New York: Wiley.

Lele, J. (1996) 'Introduction: Searching for Development Alternatives: Class, Gender and Environment in Asian Economic Growth' in Lele and Tettey (eds.), pp.1–37.

Lele, J. and Tettey, W. (eds.1996) *Asia – Who Pays for Growth: Women, Environment and Popular Movement*, Aldershot, UK: Darmouth.

Lele, S. (1991) 'Sustainable Development: A Critical Review', *World Development* **19**(6), pp.607–21.

Levin, M. A. and Strauss, H. S. (eds. 1991) *Risk Assessment in Genetic Engineering. Environmental Release of Organisms*. New York: McGraw–Hill, Inc.

Lewis, W. A. (1951) *The Principles of Economic Planning*, London: Allen and Unwin.

Lewis, W. A. (1955) *The Theory of Economic Growth*, London: Allen and Unwin.

Lewis, W. A. (1966) *Development Planning: The Essentials of Economic Policy*, London: Allen and Unwin.

Lifschultz, L. (1974) 'Bangladesh: A Stage of Siege', *Far Eastern Economic Review* August 30, pp.47–51.

Linz, J. J. and Stepan, A. (1996) 'Toward Consolidated Democracies', *Journal of Democracy,* **7**(2), pp.14–33.

Lockwood, G. S. (1997) 'World Shrimp Production with Environmental and Social Accountability: A Perspective and a Proposal', *World Aquaculture*, **28**(3), pp.52–55.

Loshak, D. (1971) *Pakistan Crisis*, London: Heinemann.

Lowenthal, A. and Dominguez, J. (1996) 'Introduction: Constructing Democratic Governance' in Lowenthal, A. and Dominguez, J (eds.) *Constructing Democratic Governance,* Baltimore, Md.: John Hopkins University Press, pp.3–8.

Lucien-Brun, H. (1997) 'Evolution of World Shrimp Production: Fisheries and Aquaculture', *World Aquaculture*, **28**(4), pp.21–33.

Luckman, R. and White, G. (eds.1996) *Democratisation in the South: The Jagged Wave,* Manchester: Manchester University Press

Macklin, M. (1992) *Agricultural Extension in India*, World Bank Technical Paper 190. Washington, D. C.: World Bank.

Mahmood, N. (1986) *Effects of Shrimp Farming and Other Impacts on Mangrove of Bangladesh*, Bangkok: IPEC Workshop.

Majumder, P. P. and Zohir, S. C. (1994) 'Dynamics of Wage Employment: A Case of Employment in the Garment Industry', *Bangladesh Development Studies*, **22**(2–3), pp.179–216.

Maniruzzaman, T. (1977) 'Bangladesh in 1976: Struggle for Survival as an Independent State', *Asian Survey*, **17**(2),pp.217–25.

Maniruzzaman, T. (1980), *Bangladesh Revolution and Its Aftermath*, Dhaka: Bangladesh Books International.

Maniruzzaman, T. (1992) 'The Fall of the Military Dictator: 1991 Elections and the Prospect of Civilian Rule in Bangladesh', *Pacific Affairs*, **65**(2), pp.203–24.

March, J. G. and Olsen, J. P. (1995) *Democratic Governance,* New York: Free Press.

Market Asia (1995) 'U.S. Market for Frozen Shrimp Grows Rapidly', **2**(2), http://www.milcom.com/rap/v22/shrimp.html.

Marsh, S. P. and Pannell, D. J. (1998) 'Agricultural Extension Policy in Australia: The Good, the Bad and the Misguided', Paper presented at the 42nd Annual Conference of the Australian Agricultural and Resource Economics Society. University of New England, NSW, January 19–21.

Mazid, M. A. (1995) 'Bangladesh', Country Paper, in FAO/NACA (1995b), pp.61–82.

McGillivray, M. and Papadopoulos, T. (1992) 'Foreign Capital Inflows, Taxation and Public Expenditure: A Preliminary Analysis of the Case of Greece', Working Paper Series, Faculty of Commerce, Geelong, Victoria: Deakin University.

McGillvray, M. (1991) 'The Human Development Index: Yet Another Composite Development Indicator?', *World Development*, **19**(10), pp.1461–68.

McGuire, M. C. (1987) 'Foreign Assistance, Investment and Defense: A Methodological Study With an Application to Israel, 1960–1979', *Economic Development and Cultural Change*, **35**(4) pp.847–73.

McLennan, W. (1996) *Year Book of Australia 1996*, Canberra: Australian Bureau of Statistics.

Meier, G. M (1970) *Leading Issues in Economic Development*, New York: Oxford University Press.

Mellor, J. W. (1994) 'Review of *The 'Green Revolution' and Economic Development: The Process and Its Impact in Bangladesh*, London: Macmillan 1991 by Mohammad Alauddin and Clement Allan Tisdell' *Economic Development and Cultural Change*, **42**(3), pp.683–88.

Menasveta, P. (1997) 'Mangrove Destruction and Shrimp Culture Systems', *World Aquaculture*, **28**(4), pp.36–42.

Menon, R. K. (1997) 'Making Parliament Effective: Role of Government and Opposition', *Daily Star,* 4 November.

Messkoub, M. (1992) 'deprivation and Structural Adjustment: in Wyuts, M., Mackintosh, M. and Hewitt, T. (eds.) *Development Policy and Public Action*, London: Oxford University Press, pp.175–98.

Midgley, J. (1995) *Social Development, The Development Perspective in Social Welfare*, London: Sage.

Miller, B. D. and Khan, S. H. (1984)*Local Voluntarism and Local Government Finance in Rural Bangladesh: An Overview and Recommendations*, New York: The Maxwell School of Citizenship and Public Affairs, Syracuse University.

Miller, B. D. and Khan, S. H. (1986) 'Incorporating Voluntarism Into Rural Development in Bangladesh', *Third World Planning Review*, **8**(2), pp.139–52.

Ministry of Agriculture (1992)*An Introduction to the Flow of Information in Dutch Agriculture*, Nature Management and Fisheries (LNV), The Netherlands.

MLG (1995) 'Arsenic Contamination of Groundwater in Bangladesh', Ministry of Local Government and Co-operative (mimeo).

MOA (1994) 'Role of Arsenic (*As*) in Agriculture', Dhaka: Ministry of Agriculture (mimeo).

Momin, M. A. (1987) 'The Integrated Rural Development Programme in Bangladesh and Its Growth-Equity Contradiction', *Community Development Journal*, **22**(1), pp. 98–106.

Moore, M. (1993) 'Declining to Learn From the East? The World Bank on 'Governance and Development', *IDS Bulletin*, **24**, pp. 39–50.

Moos, A. I. and Dear, M. J. (1986) 'Structural Theory in Urban Analysis: 1 Theoretical Exegesis', *Environment and Planning A,* **18**, pp.231–52.

Morawetz, D. (1977) *Twenty-five Years of Economic Development: 1950–1975*, Baltimore, Md., Md.: Johns Hopkins University Press.

Mortiss, P. and Chamala, S. (1991)*Group Management Skills for Land Care: A Trainer's Guide*. Brisbane: Australian Academic Press.

Mosley, P. (1986) 'Aid Effectiveness: The Micro-Macro Paradox', *Institute of Development Studies Bulletin* (Sussex), **17**, pp.22–35.

Mosley, P. and Hudson, J. (1984) 'Aid, the Public Sector and the Market in less Developed Countries', *University of Bath Papers in Political Economy*, **23**, University of Bath.

MPO (1986) *Final Report (Vols. I–III)*, Dhaka: Master Plan Organisation

Mueller, J. (1992) 'Democracy and Ralph's Pretty Good Grocery: Elections, Equality, and the Minimal Human Being', *American Journal of Political Science,* **36**, pp.984-90.

Murshed, Y. and Chowdhury, N. K. (1997) 'Bangladesh's Second Chance', *Journal of Democracy,* **8**(1), pp.70–82.

Myrdal, G. (1971a) *Asian Drama: An Enquiry into the Poverty of Nations,* (Abridged in one volume by S. S. King), Harmondsworth, U.K.: Penguin.

Myrdal, G. (1971b) *The Challenge of World Poverty,* Harmondsworth, U.K.: Penguin

Narasimham, M. (1991) Committee Report on the Financial System 1991. New Delhi: Standard Book Co.

Narula, S. C. (1984) 'Hierarchical Location-Allocation Problems: A Classification Scheme', *European Journal of Operational Research,* **15**, pp.93–99.

National Statistical Coordination Board (1976–1989) *Philippine Statistical Year Book,* Manila: Government of the Philippines.

NED (1997) *Democracy in South Asia: Report.* Washington, D. C. National Endowment for Democracy.

Nijera Kori (1996) *Profit by Destruction,* International Workshop on *Ecology, Politics and Violence of Shrimp Cultivation,* Dhaka: *Nijera Kori.*

Nuruzzaman, A. K. M. (1992) 'The Socio-Economic Importance of Mangroves to Coastal Environments in Bangladesh', A paper presented at the workshop on coastal zone management in Bangladesh, Dhaka, 30 November – 4 December.

Nuruzzaman, A. K. M. (1994) *Environmental Issues on Aquaculture Development in Bangladesh,* Dhaka: Bangladesh Agricultural Research Council.

ODA (1990*) Report and Recommendations of The ODA Fisheries Project Identification Mission to Bangladesh Under Fisheries and Flood Action Plan,* March 3 – May 1, London: ODA.

O'Sullivan, M. (1998 ed.) *Queensland Value Chain Analysis Series,* Volumes 1–4, Brisbane: Queensland Department of Primary Industries.

Pack, H. and Pack, J. R. (1990) 'Is Foreign Aid Fungible? The Case of Indonesia', *Economic Journal,* **100**, pp.188–94.

Padron, M. (1987) 'Non–Governmental Development Organizations: From Development Aid to Development Cooperation',in Drabek, A. G. (ed.) *Development Alternatives: The Challenge for NGOs,* New York: Pergamon Press, pp.145–60.

Pakistan Economic Survey, (1973–93), Islamabad: Ministry of Finance.

Palawija News (1997), *The CGPRT Centre Newsletter,* **4**(3), pp.7–9.

Panayotou, T. (1995) 'Environmental degradation at Different Stages of Economic Development', in Ahmed and Deleman (eds.), pp. 13–36.

Parikh, J., Bhattacharya, K., Reddy, B.S. Parikh, K.S. (1997) 'Energy System: Need for New Momentum' in Parikh (ed.), pp.77–94.

Parikh, K.S (ed. 1997) *India Development Report*, New Delhi: Oxford University Press.

Patel, N. (1979) 'Locating Rural Social Service Centres in India', *Management Science*, **25**, pp.22–30.

Pearce, D. (1993) *Blueprint 3: Measuring Sustainable Development*, London: Earthscan.

Pearce, D., Markandya, A. and Barbier, E.B. (1989) *Blueprint for a Green Economy*, London: Earthscan.

Pearson, R. (1992) 'Gender Matters in Development' in Allen, T. and Thomas, A. (eds.) *Poverty and Development in the 1990s*, London: Oxford University Press, pp.291–312.

Peters, B. G. (1995) *The Politics of Bureaucracy,* New York: Longman.

Pido, M. and Chua, T. (1992) 'The Application of Rapid Rural Appraisal Techniques for Assessment of The Coastal Zone in The ASEAN'; A paper presented at the ASEAN-US CRMP regional workshop on integrated coastal zone planning and management in ASEAN: lessons learned, 26–30 April.

Pigato, M. Farah, C. and Others (1997) *South Asia's Integration into the World Economy*, Washington, D. C.: World Bank.

PPC (1970) *Report of the Panel of Economists on the Fourth Five Year Plan*, Islamabad: Pakistan Planning Commission.

Prins, G. (1990) 'Politics and the Environment', *International Affairs*, **66**, pp.711–30.

Quibria, M. G. (ed. 1997) *Bangladesh Economy in Transition*, New Delhi: Oxford University Press.

Quibria, M. G. and Srinivasan, T. N. (1994) 'Introduction', Quibria, M.G. (ed.) *Rural Poverty in Developing Asia (Volume I)*, Hong Kong: Oxford University Press, pp.1–72.

Rahman, A. A. (1984) 'Bangladesh in 1983: A Turning Point for the Military', *Asian Survey*, **24**(2), pp.239–45.

Rahman, H. Z. and Hossain, Mahabub (1992) *Re-thinking Rural Poverty: A Case for Bangladesh*, Research Report, Dhaka: The Bangladesh Institute of Development Studies.

Rahman, M. and Bakht, Z. (1997) 'Constriants to Industrial Development: Recent Reforms and Future Directions', in Quibria (ed.), pp.77–114.

Rahman, M. M., Aziz, K. M. S., Munshi, H .M., Patwari, Y. and Rahman, M. A. (1982) 'Diarrhoea Clinic in Rural Bangladesh: Influence of Distance, Age and Sex on Attendance and Diarrhoeal Mortality', *American Journal of Public Health*, **72**, pp.1124–28.

Rahman, R. I. (1985) 'Seasonality of Workload of Women in Rural Areas of Bangladesh' *Bangladesh Development Studies*, **15**(4), pp.123–30.

Rahman, R. I. (1991) *An Analysis of Employment and Earnings of Poor Women in Rural Bangladesh*, unpublished Ph.D. thesis, Canberra: Australian National University.

Rahman, S. (1981) 'Determinants of the Utilisation of Maternal Child Health Services', Dhaka: National Institute of Population Research and Training (NIPORT) (mimeo.).

Rahman, S. (1989) 'Bangladesh in 1988: Precarious Institution Building Amid Crisis Management', *Asian Survey*, **29**(2), pp.216–22.

Rahman, S. (1990) 'Bangladesh in 1989: Internationalisation of Economic and Political Issues', *Asian Survey*, **20**(2), pp.150–57.

Rahman, S. (1991) *Location-Allocation Modelling for Primary Health Care Provision in Bangladesh*, unpublished Ph.D Thesis, Exeter, U K.: University of Exeter.

Rahman, S. and Smith, D. K. (1996) 'Locating Health Facilities in Rural Bangladesh', in Rosenhead, J. and Tripathy, A. (eds.) *Operational Research for Development*, New Delhi: New Age Publication, pp.184–96.

Rahman, S. H. (1992) 'Structural Adjustment and Macroeconomic Performance in Bangladesh', *Bangladesh Development Studies*, **20**(2–3), pp.89–125.

Ramanathan, R. (1997) 'Transport: A Crucial Infrastructure' in Parikh (ed.), pp.219–38.

Rana, P. B. (1997) 'Reforms in Bangladesh: A Comparative Assessment in Relation to Other South Asian Countries', in Quibria, M.G. (ed.) *The Bangladesh Economy in Transition*, New Delhi: Oxford University Press, pp.7–27.

Rao, M. G. (1998) 'Role of Subnational Governments in the Process of Fiscal Reforms in India', in Shand (ed.), pp.229–55.

Rao, M. G., Kalirajan, K.P. and Shand, R.T (1998) *The Economics of Electricity Supply in India*, New Delhi: Macmillan.

Raper, A. F. (1970) *Rural Development in Action: The Comprehensive Experiment in Comilla, East Pakistan*, Ithaca: Cornell University Press.

Rashiduzzaman, M. (1977) 'Changing Political Patterns in Bangladesh: Internal Constrains and External Fairs' *Asian Survey*, **17**(9), pp.793–808.

Rashiduzzaman, M. (1979) Bangladesh in 1978: Search for A Political Party', *Asian Survey*, **19**(2), pp.191–97.

Rashiduzzaman, M. (1997) 'Political Unrest and Democracy in Bangladesh', *Asian Survey,* **37**(3), pp.254–68.

Repetto, R., Magrath, W., Wells, M., Beer, C. and Rossini, F. (1989) *Wasting Resources: Natural Resource in National Income Accounts*, Washington, D. C.: World Resources Institute.

Report of the Disinvestment Commission (1997) New Delhi: Government of India.

ReVelle, C. S. and Swain, R. W. (1970) 'Central Facilities Location', *Geographical Analysis*, **2**, pp.30–42.

Reza, S., Rashid, M. A. and Alam, A. H. M. M (1987) *Private Foreign Investment in Bangladesh,* Dhaka: University Press Ltd.

Richards, S. G. (1978) *Introduction to British Government,* London: Macmillan.

Robinson, M. (1996) 'Economic Reform and the Transition to Democracy' in Robin, L. R. and White, G. (eds.) *Democratisation in the South: The Jagged Wave,* Manchester: Manchester University Press, pp.69–81.

Röling, N. G. (1992) 'The Emergence of Knowledge Systems Thinking. A Changing Perception of Relationships Among Innovation, Knowledge Process and Configuration', *Knowledge and Policy: The International Journal of Knowledge Transfer and Utilisation*, **5**, pp.42–64.

Rosenberry, B. (1995) *World Shrimp Farming 1995: Annual Report*, San Diego: Shrimp News International.

Roy, K .C., Blomqvist, H. C. and Tisdell, C.A. (1996) 'Economic Development and Women: An Overview of Issues', in Roy et al. (eds.), pp.1–24.

Roy, K. C. and Tisdell, C. A. (1996) 'Women in South Asia with Particular Reference to India', in Roy et al. (eds.) pp.97–124.

Roy, K. C. and Tisdell, C. A. (1993) 'Poverty among Females in Rural India: Gender-based Deprivation and Technologyical Change', *Economic Studies*, **31**(4), pp.257–79.

Roy, K. C., Blomqvist, H. C. and Hossain, I. (eds. 1997) *Development That Lasts*, New Delhi: New Age International.

Roy, K. C., Tisdell, C. A. and Blomqvist, H. C. (eds. 1996) *Economic Development and Women in the World Community*, West Point, Conn.: Praeger.

Roy, K. C., Tisdell, C. A. and Sen, R. K. (eds. 1992) *Economic Development and Environment: A Case Study of India*, Calcutta: Oxford University Press.

Rushton, G. (1987) 'Selecting the Objective Function in Location-Allocation Analyses', in Ghosh, A. and Rushton, G. (eds.) *Spatial Analysis and Location-Allocation Models*, New York: Van Nostrand Reinhold Co. Inc.

Rushton, G. (1988) 'Location Theory, Location-allocation Models and Service Development Planning in the Third World', *Economic Geography*, **64**, pp.97–120.

SAARC (1992) *Meeting the Challenge: Report of the Independent South Asian Commission on Poverty Alleviation*, Kathmandu: South Asian Association of Regional Cooperation (SAARC) Secretariat.

Safilio-Rothschild, C. and Mahmud, S. (1989) *Women's Roles in Agriculture: Present Ends and Potential for Growth*, Monograph for Agriculture Sector Review, Dhaka: UNDP and UNIFEM.

Salik, S. (1977) *Witness to Surrender*, Karachi: Oxford University

Sarkar, J. and Agarwal, P. (1997) 'Banking: The Challenges of Deregulation', in Parikh (ed.), Chapter 11.

SBP (1997) *Annual Report 1996–97*, Karachi: State Bank of Pakistan.

Schmidheiny, S. (1992) *Changing Course: A Global Business Perspective on Development and the Environment*. Cambridge, Massachusetts: MIT Press.

Sengupta, A. (1998) 'Growth with Equity: Humanising Development Economics', *AMITECH, News from Bangladesh*, http://Bangladesh-web.com/news, 7 August.

Shah, A. (1997) 'Telecommunications: Monopoly vs Competition' in Parikh (ed.), pp.239–50.

Shams, K. M. (1995) 'Government Must Side With the Poor', *Public Administration and Development* **15**, pp. 303–10.

Shan, Y. and Linz, J. J. (eds. 1995) *Between States: Interim Governments and Democratic Transitions,* Cambridge: Cambridge University Press.

Shand, R. T. (1998) 'Performance and Prospects in South Asia' in Shand (ed.), pp.495–528.

Shand, R. T. (ed. 1998) *Economic Liberalisation in South Asia*, New Delhi: Macmillan.

Shand, R. T. and Alauddin, M. (1997) *Economic Profiles in South Asia: Bangladesh*, Canberra: Canberra: Australia South Asia Research Centre, The Australian National University.

Shand, R. T. and Bhati, U. N. (1997) *Economic Profiles in South Asia: Pakistan*, Canberra: Australia South Asia Research Centre, The Australian National University.

Shand, R. T. and Kalirajan, K. P. (1997) *From Crisis to Confidence: Economic Reforms in India*, Australia South Asia Research Centre, Canberra: The Australian National University.

Shand, R. T. (1996) 'Foreword' in Alauddin and Hasan (eds.)

Shepherd A. (1986) *Non-Governmental Organizations in India,* Papers in Administration of Development #25, Birmingham: University of Birmingham, Institute of Local Government.

Siddique, M. A. (1995) 'Arsenic Contamination of Groundwater', Dhaka: Department of Public Health and Engineering (mimeo).

Siffin, W. J. (1966) 'Introduction', in Montgomery, J. and Siffin, W. J. (eds.) *Approaches to Development: Politics, Administration and Change,* New York: McGraw-Hill.

Sim, A. B and Ali, M. Y. (1997) 'Characteristics and Performance of Joint Ventures of Asian Multinational and International Firms Operating in a Developing Country', *Proceedings of Pan-Pacific Conference XIV,* Kuala Lumpur, Malaysia, June 2–5, pp.205–7.

Smillie, I. (1995) *The Alms Bazaar: Altruism Under Fire – Non-Profit Organisations and International Development,* London: IT Publications.

Smith, B. C. (1996) *Understanding Third World Politics,* Bloomington: Indiana University Press.

Sobhan R. (1997) 'Overview' in Sobhan (ed.), pp.1–41.

Sobhan, R. (1993) *Bangladesh: Problems of Governance,* Dhaka: University Press Ltd.

Sobhan, R. (1996) 'Overview' in Sobhan (ed.), pp.21–64.

Sobhan, R. (1998) 'Overview', in Sobhan (ed.), pp.45–94.

Sobhan, R. (ed. 1996) *Experiences with Economic Reform: Bangladesh's Development in 1995,* Dhaka: University Press Ltd.

Sobhan, R. (ed. 1997) *Growth or Stagnation? A Review of Bangladesh's Development 1996,* Dhaka: University Press Ltd.

Sobhan, R., (ed. 1998) *Crisis in Governance: A Review of Bangladesh's Development 1997,* Dhaka: Centre for Policy Dialogue and University Press Ltd.

Solo, R. (1966) 'The Capacity to Assimilate an Advanced Technology', *American Economic Review,* **56,** Papers and Proceedings, pp. 91–97.

Stevens, R., Alavi, H. and Bertocci, P. (1976) *Rural Development in Bangladesh and Pakistan,* Honolulu: The University Press of Hawaii.

Stirling, P. (1996) *Australian Research and Development Directory.* Hampton, Victoria: Hallmark Editions.

Stock, R. (1983) 'Distance and Utilization of Health Facilities in Nigeria', *Social Science and Medicine,* **17,** pp.563–70.

Tamang, K. M. (1994) *Wildlife Management Plan for the Sundarbans Reserved Forest,* UNDP/FAO Project BGD/84/056, Field Document 3, Khulna: Integrated Development of the Sundarbans Reserved Forest Project.

Tanahashi, T. (1978) 'Health Service Coverage and its Evaluation', *Bulletin of the World Health Organisation*, **59**, pp.295–303.

Tanzi, V. (1982) 'Fiscal Disequilibrium in Developing Countries', *World Development* **10**, pp.1069–82.

Task Forces (1991) *Report of the Task Forces on Bangladesh Development Strategies for the 1990s, Politics for Development*, Volume One, Dhaka: University Press Limited.

Taslim, M. A. (1994) 'Public Corruption, External Interference and Policy Making in a Dependent Regime', in Zafarullah, H. M., Taslim, M. A. and Chowdhury, A. (eds.) *Policy Issues in Bangladesh*, New Delhi: South Asian Publishers, pp.291–407.

Tata (1995) *Statistical Outline of India 1995–96*, Bombay: Department of Economics and Statistics.

Teitz, M. B, and Bart, P. (1968) 'Heuristic Methods for Estimating the Vertex Median of a Weighted Graph', *Operations Research*, **16**, pp.955–61.

Thamapillai, D. J. and Uhlin, H-E (1995) 'Environmental Capital and Sustainable Income: Basic Concepts and Empirical Tests', *Cambridge Journal of Economics*, **21**, pp.379–94.

TIB (1997) *Report of Survey, on Corruption in Bangladesh*. Dhaka: Transparency International Bangladesh.

Tien, J. M., El-Tell, K. and Simons, G. R. (1983) 'Improved Formulations of the Hierarchical Health Facility Location-allocation Problem', *IEEE Transactions on Systems, Man and Cybernatics*, **SMC-13**, pp.1128–32.

Timm, R. W. (ed. 1996) *Bangladesh: Parliamentary Elections '96 Observation Report*. Dhaka: Coordination Council for Human Rights in Bangladesh.

Tisdell, C. A. (1991) 'Population Growth and Environmental Protection. The Situation of Developing Countries in Global Perspective' in Roy, K. C., Tisdell, C. A., Sen R. K. and Alauddin, M. (eds.) *Economic Development in Poor Countries: Experiences, Obstacles and Sustainability in Global Perspective*, Calcutta: World Press Private Ltd., pp.224–38.

Tisdell, C. A. (1993) *Economic Development in the Context of China*, London: Macmillan.

Tisdell, C. A. (1995) 'Asian Development and Environmental Dilemmas', *Contemporary Economic Policy*, **13**(1), pp.38–49.

Tisdell, C. A. (1996) 'Discrimination and Changes in the Status of Women with Economic Development: General Views and Theories', in Roy et al. (eds.), pp.25–36.

Todaro, M. P. (1997) *Economic Development*, New York: Longman.

Townsend, P. (1979) *Poverty in the UK: A Survey, of Household Resources and Standard of Living*, Harmondsworth: Penguin.

UNCED (1992) 'Global Action for Women Towards Sustainable and Equitable Development', UN Conference on Environment and Development, Agenda 21, Chapter 24, Rio: June.

UNDP (1990) *Human Development Report 1990*, New York: Oxford University Press.

UNDP (1991) *Human Development Report 1991*, New York: Oxford University Press.

UNDP (1993) *Human Development Report 1993*, New York: Oxford University Press.

UNDP (1994) *Human Development Report 1994*, New York: Oxford University Press.

UNDP (1995) *Human Development Report 1995*, New York: Oxford University Press.

UNDP (1996a) *Human Development Report 1996*, New York: Oxford University Press.

UNDP (1996b) *UNDP's 1996 Report on Human Development in Bangladesh: A Pro-poor Agenda*, Dhaka: United Nations Development Programme.

UNDP (1997) *Human Development Report 1997*, New York: Oxford University Press.

UNICEF (1993) *The State of the World's Children*, New York: Oxford University Press.

United Nations (1990) *Participatory Rural Development in Selected Countries*. Bangkok, United Nations Interagency Committee on Integrated Rural Development for Asia and the Pacific.

USDS (1996) *Background Notes: Bangladesh,* Washington, D. C.: Bureau of South Asian Affairs, United States Department of State

USDS (1997) *Bangladesh Country Report on Human Rights Practices for 1996*. Washington DC: United States Department of State.

van den Ban, A.W. and Hawkins, H.S. (1996) *Agricultural Extension*, London, Blackwell.

Vantomme, P. (1995) 'Mangrove Forest Management', http://www.ncfes.umn.edu:80/iufro/iufronet/d1/wu10700/unpub/vantom95.html.

Vernon, R. (1971) *Sovereignty at Bay: Multinational Spread of U.S. Enterprises,* New York: Basic Books.

Walker, K. J. (1994) *The Political Economy of Environmental Policy: An Australian Introduction*. Sydney: University of New South Wales Press.

Wanasinghe, S. (1994) *Activating the Administrative Reform Process in Sri Lanka. Research Studies*, Governance Series No. 1, Colombo: Institute of Policy Studies

WCED (1987) *Our Common Future*, World Commission on Environment and Development, Oxford: Oxford University Press.

Weisskopf, T. E. (1972a) 'An Econometric Test of Alternative Constraints on Economic Growth of Underdeveloped Countries', *Review of Economics and Statistics*, **54**, pp.67–78.

Weisskopf, T. E. (1972b) 'Impact of Foreign Capital Inflows on Domestic Savings in Underdeveloped Countries', *Journal of International Economics*, **2**, pp.25–38.

Wilensky, H. L. (1981) *Voluntary Agencies in the Welfare State*, Berkeley: University of California Press.

Williamson, O. E. (1975) *Markets and Hierarchies: Analysis and Antitrust Implications*, New York: Free Press.

Woodhouse, P. (1992) 'Environmental Degradation and Sustainability', in Allen, T. and Thomas, A. (eds.) *Poverty and Development in the 1990s*, Oxford, U.K.: Oxford University Press, pp.97–115.

World Bank (1986) *World Development Report* , Washington, D. C.: The World Bank.

World Bank (1989) *Sub-Saharan Africa: From Crisis to Sustainable Growth – A Long-Term Perspective Study*, Washington, D. C.: The World Bank.

World Bank (1990) *Bangladesh: Managing the Adjustment Process: An Appraisal*, Washington, D. C.: World Bank.

World Bank (1991a) *India: 1991 Country Economic Memorandum*, 2 Volumes. Washington, D. C.: World Bank

World Bank (1991b) *Bangladesh: Fisheries Sector Review*, Report # 8830-BD, Washington, D. C.: World Bank.

World Bank (1992a) *World Bank Report 1992: Development and the Environment*, New York: Oxford University Press.

World Bank (1992b) *Development and Governance*, New York: Oxford University Press.

World Bank (1993a) *The East Asian Miracle*, New York: Oxford University Press.

World Bank (1993b) *Bangladesh: Implementing Structural Reform*, Washington, D. C.: World Bank.

World Bank (1993c) *India: Progress and Challenges in Economic Transition*, Washington, D. C.: World Bank.

World Bank (1994a) *Governance: The World Bank's Experience*, Washington, D. C.: World Bank.

World Bank (1994b) *World Development Report 1994*, New York: Oxford University Press.

World Bank (1994c) *Nepal: Fiscal Restructuring and Public Resource Management in the Nineties*, Washington, D. C.: World Bank.

World Bank (1994d) *Social Indicators of Development 1994*, Baltimore, Md., Md.: John Hopkins University Press.

World Bank (1995a) *Global Economic Prospects and the Developing Countries 1995*, Washington, D. C.: World Bank.

World Bank (1995b) *World Development Report*, New York: Oxford University Press.

World Bank (1996a) *Bangladesh – Government that Works: Reforming the Public Sector*, Washington, D. C.: World Bank.

World Bank (1996b) *World Development Report 1996*, New York: Oxford University Press.

World Bank (1996c) *Bangladesh: Trade Policy Reform for Improving the Incentive Regime*, Washington, D. C.: World Bank.

World Bank (1997a) *Pakistan: Recent Developments, Policy Issues and Agenda for Change*, Washington, D. C.: World Bank.

World Bank (1997b) *World Development Report 1997: The State in a Changing World*, Washington, D. C.: World Bank.

World Resources 1996–97: A Guide to the Global Environment, http:// www.igc.apc.org.80/wri/wr-96-97wa_txt1.html

Wright, D. (1994) 'Australia and Bangladesh', in Vicziany, M. and McPherson, K. (eds.) *Australian and South Asia: A Blueprint for 2001?*, Melbourne: The National Centre for South Asian Studies, pp.115–24.

WRI-UNEP-UNDP (1994) *World Resources 1994–95*, New York: Oxford University Press.

Zafarullah, H. (1996a) *The Zia Episode in Bangladesh Politics*, New Delhi: South Asian Publishers.

Zafarullah, H. (1996b) 'Toward Good Governance in Bangladesh: External Intervention, Bureaucratic Inertia and Political Inaction' in Alauddin and Hasan (eds.), pp.145–62.

Zafarullah, H. (1996c) 'The Dilemmas of Local Level Planning in Bangladesh 1982–1990', *Contemporary South Asia*, 5(1), pp.47–65.

Zafarullah, H. (1997) 'Local Government Reform and Accountability in Bangladesh: The Continuing Search for Legitimacy and Performance', *Regional Development Dialogue*, 18(2), pp.37–56

Zafarullah, H., Khan, M. M. and Rahman, M. H. (1997) *Civil Service Systems: Bangladesh*, A paper prepared for the Comparative Civil Service Research Consortium. Bloomington, USA.

Zaman, W. A. (1984) *Public Participation in Development and Health Programs: Lessons From Rural Bangladesh*, Lanham: University Press of America.

Ziring, L. (1992) *Bangladesh – From Mujib to Ershad: An Interpretive Study*, Dhaka: University Press Ltd.

Index